The Myth of Medea
and the
Murder of Children

Recent Titles in
Contributions to the Study of World Literature

The Myth of Medea and the Murder of Children

Lillian Corti

Contributions to the Study of World Literature, Number 89

GREENWOOD PRESS
Westport, Connecticut • London

Library of Congress Cataloging-in-Publication Data

Corti, Lillian.
   The myth of Medea and the murder of children / Lillian Corti.
      p.   cm.—(Contributions to the study of world literature,
   ISSN 0738–9345 ; no. 89)
   Includes bibliographical references and index.
   ISBN 0–313–30536–6 (alk. paper)
   1. Medea (Greek mythology) in literature.   2. Infanticide in
literature.   3. Literature, Comparative—Themes, motives.
4. Literature, Comparative—History and literature.   I. Title.
II. Series.
PN57.M37C67   1998
809′.93353—dc21   97–26892

British Library Cataloguing in Publication Data is available.

Library of Congress Catalog Card Number: 97–26892
ISBN: 0–313–30536–6
ISSN: 0738–9345

First published in 1998

Greenwood Press, 88 Post Road West, Westport, CT 06881
An imprint of Greenwood Publishing Group, Inc.

Printed in the United States of America

The paper used in this book complies with the
Permanent Paper Standard issued by the National
Information Standards Organization (Z39.48–1984).

10 9 8 7 6 5 4 3 2

Copyright Acknowledgments

The author and publisher gratefully acknowledge permission for use of the following material:

Excerpts reprinted from *The Collected Poetry of Robinson Jeffers, Three Volumes*, edited by Tim Hunt, with the permission of the publishers, Stanford University Press, © 1995 by the Board of Trustees of the Leland Stanford Junior University.

Excerpts from *Medea, Freely Adapted from the Medea of Euripides* by Robinson Jeffers (1946) are reprinted by permission of Lee Jeffers, Jeffers Literary Properties.

Excerpts from "The Bloody Sire" from *Selected Poems* by Robinson Jeffers. Copyright © 1940 and renewed 1968 by Donna Jeffers and Garth Jeffers. Reprinted by permission of Random House, Inc. Excerpts from "Cassandra" from *Selected Poems* by Robinson Jeffers. Copyright © 1941 by Yardstick Press. Copyright © 1944 by Oscar Williams. Reprinted by permission of Random House, Inc.

Excerpts from "Medea, Tragödie nach Euripides" by Matthias Braun in Karl Kerényi "Vorwort" *to Medea: Euripides, Seneca, Corneille, Cherubini, Grillparzer, Jahnn, Anouilhe, Jeffers, Braun* (Munich: Theater der Jahrhunderte, 1963) are reprinted by permission of Cornelia Isler-Kerényi.

Excerpts from *Stücke* by Heiner Müller Herausgegeben und mit einem Essay von Joachim Fiebach (Berlin: Henschel Verlag Kunst und Gesellschaft, 1988) are reprinted by permission of Suhrkamp Verlag Frankfurt am Main, all rights reserved.

Contents

Acknowledgments

Research on the theme of child-murder is not for the faint-hearted, and I must confess that there have been times since I embarked on this project when I thought that if I kept on looking into my chosen topic, I would surely turn to stone. In short, this book could not have been written without the help of many people. For the genesis of the thesis, I am indebted to my teachers at the Graduate School of the City University of New York: Fred Nichols, the wise mentor and learned friend under whose tutelage I wrote my first essay on critical problems implicit in the myth of Medea, Lillian Feder, the inspiring scholar who directed the dissertation on "Medea and Infanticide" which was an early articulation of the ideas developed in the present work, and Daniel Gerould, who patiently read the thesis, providing noteworthy insight and encouragement. I thank Donald Reiman and Doucet Fisher for their scholarly advice and devoted collegiality through the years during which I worked on the book.

I am especially grateful to my erudite and generous colleague, Doris Ann Bartlett, who read the entire manuscript and encouraged me with the particular wisdom and sympathy that only she could provide. I thank Sandra Boatwright, who brings the special insight of a creative writer to the task of critical evaluation. Among the many people who have read and commented on all or part of various drafts, I thank Miriam Brender, Vibeke Petersen, Véronique Adam, Charles Ganelin, Patricia Klingenberg, Janis Lull, Joan Worley, Terri Whitney and Maureen Sullivan. For proof-reading the manuscript and offering insight above and beyond the mechanics of editing, I thank Marianne Strong, Sheryl Clough and Dafna Ezran. For crucial guidance and patient instruction in the mysteries of the computer, I am grateful to my colleagues and friends, Lisa Burt, Michael Schuldiner and Ken Severin. I thank my students, Lorie Allred, Kelly Duklet, Jennifer Brice, Shelly Norris, Sandy Gillespie, Todd Sformo, Ellen Moore and

Elizabeth McRitchie, whose enthusiasm and intelligence have helped me to clarify my own ideas. For generous support and cheerful assistance in various crises, technological, existential and cosmic, I am grateful to Sarah Hall, Malle Burggraf and all of my colleagues and friends in the English Department at the University of Alaska. For patiently steering me through the complexities of preparing the text for publication, I thank Marcia Goldstein and Gillian von Nieda Beebe and Rachel Jones. My cousin David Lewis Schaeffer deserves special tribute for his persistent confidence and strategic support in bringing this project to a suitable conclusion.

My deepest gratitude is reserved for my children, Anna, Miriam and Paul Corti, whose good humor and generous insight sustained me through all the hills and valleys of this essentially troubling project. Finally, I dedicate this book to the memory of my father, Samuel Gordon Somers, and my mother, Susie Mae Mote Somers.

Introduction

In the wake of the media sensation caused by the case of Susan Smith, a seemingly ordinary woman who was tried and convicted for the murder of her two small sons, it seems remarkable that the act of child murder should ever have been dismissed as an insignificant detail. Yet the literary treatment of such gruesome deeds presents peculiar difficulties for critical analysis. Denys Lionel Page, for example, in a venerable commentary on Euripides' *Medea,* asserted that "the murder of the children . . . is mere brutality: if it moves us at all, it does so towards incredulity and horror. Such an act is outside our experience, we—and the fifth-century Athenian—know nothing of it" (xiv). In denying the human relevance of the act of child murder, Page may seem to echo the indignation of Euripides' Jason, the distraught father who wails: "there is no Greek woman who would do this thing" (*Medea*, line 1339). Though recent references to Page's judgment express either respectful disagreement (McDermott 25) or frank astonishment (Simon 87), the fact remains that it was not until 1977 that P. E. Easterling actually argued, in an essay entitled "The Infanticide in Euripides' *Medea*," that the psychology of criminal and abusive parents might indeed have some bearing on the classic tragedy of child murder. There are, admittedly, various reasons that the blood-curdling central act of Euripides' *Medea* is more likely to be the focus of open debate today than it was in 1938, when Page articulated his remarkable position. Yet the retrospective affirmation of Jason's dubious claim remains noteworthy precisely because the *Medea* is full of references to myths about parents who kill their children, the stories of Ino and Erechtheus being only the most obvious examples (*Medea*, 1284, 824-25). Far from being persuasive, Jason's statement seems to function as the invocation of a taboo.

The idea of a taboo against infanticide is evident in Barbara Johnson's observation that "when a woman speaks about the death of children in any sense other than that of pure loss, a powerful taboo is being violated" (38), and the significance of the injunction is underscored by Germaine Greer's assertion that infanticide is the "dark, secret side of motherhood itself." The apparent contradiction between Johnson's insistence on the taboo against discussing the deaths of children and Greer's claim that "motherhood, like nature herself, is red in tooth and claw" (228) is resolved by Alice Miller, who comments that "the victimization of children is nowhere forbidden; what is forbidden is to write about it" (*Thou Shalt Not Be Aware* 190). Although, in fact, the evidence of infanticidal practices and customs is abundantly and minutely documented, Emily McDermott's description of Medea's crime as "literally unspeakable" (26) is justified by the feeling of horror that the very mention of the act of child-murder inspires in most people. Unspeakable in the precise degree to which it is unthinkable, the act of infanticide has been cast, in the words of Maria Piers, "into the twilight of semi-consciousness, both by those who fail to see it and by those who commit it, and by the rest of us who permit it" (16). This emphasis on the role of the unconscious in the perception of destructive violence against infants and children is disturbing precisely because it suggests the ambiguous relationship between prohibition and desire that Sigmund Freud posited as crucial to the concept of taboo, a term which he defined as "a primaeval prohibition forcibly imposed (by some authority) from outside, and directed against the most powerful longings to which human beings are subject" (*Standard Edition,* hereafter referred to as "*S.E.*" 13: 34-35). Though the horror of infanticide may seem unambiguously compatible with every conscious standard of decency and common sense, the possible existence of repressed desire to commit the forbidden act is arguably inherent in the very fact of prohibition. Forbidden desire is, moreover, the connecting link between the concept of taboo and the aesthetics of tragedy.

A great admirer of ancient drama, Freud argued that its power to move modern audiences inheres precisely in the capacity to show us all the fulfillment of our deepest wishes. His particular intuition about the nature of those wishes led him to assert that Sophocles' *Oedipus the King* dramatizes repressed incestuous and patricidal wishes that are virtually universal. Yet the selective nature of his enthusiasm for ancient myth is worth noting—the index to his collected works contains a long list of references to Oedipus and only one to Medea. This disparity is remarkable because Freud's fascination with tragedy was explicitly based on "the particular nature of the material," that is to say, on its content, and the thematic parallels between the myths of Oedipus and Medea are conspicuous. Both Sophocles and Euripides based their tragic masterpieces on tales in which parental violence reaches down through several generations with destructive tenacity and fatal results. In fact, Freud's famous tribute to Sophoclean drama contains a problematic reference to the figure of the destructive mother: "There must be something which makes a voice within us ready to recognize the compelling force of destiny in the Oedipus, while we can dismiss as merely arbitrary such dispositions as are laid down in [Grillparzer's] *Die Ahnfrau* or other modern tragedies of destiny" *(S.E.* 1: 262). The reference to *Die Ahnfrau (The Ancestress),* glossed for the benefit of English-speaking readers of *The Standard Edition,* would have been immediately recognizable for Freud's German readers, and especially for his fellow Austrians. Described by Hugo von Hofmannsthal as "Austria's truly national poet" (Thompson 127), Franz Grillparzer was "perhaps the greatest nineteenth-century Austrian writer" (Kann 175), and his *Medea,* frequently performed during the last century, has been praised by George Steiner as having a "tough-minded dignity which rivals Euripides" *(Death of Tragedy* 228-29). Freud's familiarity with this celebrated work may be inferred, not only from his casual reference to a less important work by the same author, but also from the nature of his only mention of Medea, an observation in *Dora, an Analysis of a Case of Hysteria* that Medea was "quite content that Creusa should make friends with her two children" *(S.E.* 7:61). This comment evidently refers to Grillparzer's version of the tragedy, in which Medea makes a doomed attempt at befriending her Corinthian rival, a character who never appears onstage in the Euripidean model of the drama. In any case, the very mention of *Die Ahnfrau,* a play about a destructive female ghost who haunts her family until all her descendants are dead, might suggest to some readers that the distinction between the thematic concerns of ancient tragedy and those of the "modern tragedy of destiny" is not as clear as the father of psychoanalysis assumes.

Freud's disparaging reference to Grillparzer's maternal virago is curiously consistent with the idealization of maternal love that is evident in his description of the bond between mothers and sons as "altogether the most perfect, the most free from ambivalence of all human relationships" *(S.E.* 22:133), and it also tends to corroborate Madelon Sprengnether's perception of a textual pattern wherein Freud "invokes the pre-oedipal mother only to banish her." The fact that the "spectral mother" described by Sprengnether as "haunting the house of Oedipus" (63) is discernible in Freud's earliest articulation of his controversial theory would seem to confirm the percpetion of various scholars who detect a defensive quality in Freud's remarks on maternal love (Krüll 117-19; Slater 32; Sprengnether 20-21). Yet the denial of maternal aggression, like the celebration of maternal benevolence, is quite compatible with the general tendency of popular culture to stress the positive and mutual quality of love between parents and children. This propensity is abundantly justified, moreover, by the astonishing reproductive success of the human race as a whole. If the human potential for supportive and sympathetic nurturing did not far exceed the human capacity for abusive and destructive parenting, the race might well have died out long ago. The phenomenon of hostility to children remains, however, a subject of considerable psychological conjecture. It is also an aspect of the human condition that is openly affirmed in occasional flashes of eccentric wit, such as B. B. King's blues classic, "Nobody loves me but my mother and she could be jivin' me too."

In retrospect, it seems reasonable to observe that in the absence of such a phrase as "the battered child syndrome," first articulated in 1962 (Kempe et al.), actual events that might be placed under the rubric of such a term would necessarily remain literally *unspeakable*. In *L'Enfant et la vie familiale sous l'ancien régime* (published in English as *Centuries of Childhood*), Philippe Ariès argued that the concept of childhood is, in itself, an essentially modern phenomenon. His work marks the beginning of a period in which various historians have generated an abundance of scholarship focusing on the experience of childhood in past ages. The comparatively new discipline of psychohistory emphasizes the way in which the psychological and intellectual perspectives of any age are intimately connected with traditional and contemporary structures for nurturing children. A particularly sobering contribution to our understanding of the precarious nature of infancy and childhood, especially for girls, comes from anthropological and demographic evidence that female infanticide is related to a range of behaviors classified under the antiseptic title, "excess female mortality." Such practices have functioned and still do function as population-controlling mechanisms (Scrimshaw; Johansson; Harris and Ross 155-83). The question of whether and how such concepts may be relevant to the interpretation of literary texts is complicated by the fact that the evidence of actual cases of infanticide in particular cultural contexts tends to be controversial. The debate over the significance of the practice in antiquity is instructive.

Demographic evidence has been used in arguments for and against the belief that female infanticide was routinely practiced as a means of limiting the size of the ancient family. Donald Engels argued, in "The Problem of Female Infanticide in the Greco-Roman World" (1980) and "The Use of Historical Demography in Ancient History" (1984), that a high rate of female infanticide was unlikely to have been a factor in the ancient economy. Operating on the assumption that ancient populations, like modern preindustrial populations, had normally high birth and death rates, he calculated that the routine practice of infanticide in such a society would necessarily have destroyed the approximate equilibrium between the birth rate and the death rate, thus causing an unacceptably high rate of depopulation. Mark Golden criticized this argument in 1981, pointing out that the low rate of increase in ancient populations which Engels stresses in the premise of his argument is "at least partly a result of conscious efforts in population control, including infanticide" (320).

Golden's assessment of the evidence leads him to conclude that the rate at which unwanted female infants were "exposed" may have been as high as 10 percent (330). Sarah Pomeroy's analysis of demographic information obtained by studying Milesian inscriptions from the third century B.C.E. leads her to conclude that discrepancies in the junior age/sex ratios of the community under observation can only be explained by assuming the routine exposure of female infants. The position defended by Golden and Pomeroy has been criticized, however, by Cynthia Patterson, who objects that "not all social phenomena lend themselves to quantification," and the "psychic cost" involved in such customs as infanticide and slavery cannot be measured in "simple rates and percentages" (108). Patterson stresses the importance of linguistic and cultural nuances such as the difference between the practice of "exposure" at Athens and the actual murder of children, for which the Athenians had a separate term. She insists on differentiating between various categories of infants likely to be selected for exposure—the physically defective, the illegitimate, the female. Yet she stops short of speculating on the probable nature of the "psychic cost" of such "selections" on the survivors. Her concluding admonition that "exposure remains an individual act carried out by individual families in individual circumstances" (123) suggests a certain disinclination to consider the cultural importance of the custom.

When all is said and done, the pros and cons in this argument seem to bear a notable resemblance to their counterparts in the early decades of this century. Engels' insistence on the generally high level of ancient death rates as an argument against the hypothesis of widespread female infanticide recalls the contention by La Rue Van Hook, in 1921, that, in the absence of problems such as overpopulation, unemployment, and poverty in fifth century Athens, the citizens would not have resorted to such a brutal practice as infanticide. Though the argument presented in 1921 is not buttressed by the sophisticated statistical manipulations that Engels used in the 1980s, both Van Hook and Engels seem, in Golden's phrase, "to assume what they set out to prove" (320). Similarly, Patterson's cautionary advice against assuming "an unlikely demographic awareness on the part of the Athenian fathers" (108) goes against considerable evidence that the connections between individual acts and communal imperatives need not be conscious in order to be effective. Scrimshaw's reference to a process called "unconscious rationality" in the adaptation of individuals to social patterns (453) is, in fact, anticipated by nearly a century in William Graham Sumner's speculation, in 1906, on the possible operation of something equivalent to "population policy" among "uncivilized men":

All the folkways which go to make up a population policy seem to imply greater knowledge of the philosophy of population than can be ascribed to uncivilized men. The case is one, however, in which the knowledge is simple and the acts proceed from immediate interest, while the generalization is an unapprehended result. The mothers know the strain of child-bearing and child rearing. They refuse to undergo it, for purely egoistic reasons. The consequent adjustment of the population to the food supply comes of itself. (312)

Anticipating the objection that ancient patriarchal cultures would hardly have been likely to tolerate the degree of female initiative that this scenario seems to assume, Sumner hastens to add that "the women would not be allowed by the men to shirk motherhood if the group needed warriors, or if the men wanted daughters to sell" (312).

Though evidence tending to valorize Sumner's assertion that "the interests of parents and children are antagonistic" (308-09) is hardly scarce, it constitutes an interpretive challenge of the first order. The abandonment of infants in Rome from ancient times through the medieval period, and well into the early modern era prompts John Boswell to argue that such abandonment is not to be regarded as a euphemism for infanticide, but rather as part of a general system equivalent to "adoption" in modern times, the operative expectation being that the infants cast aside by some adults would be found and raised by others (398-99). In a similar vein, Shulamith Shahar questions the assumption that the notably high rate of mortality among infants and children in medieval times might indicate the existence of parental hostility toward children which regularly issued in criminal neglect or disguised murder (141-43). As if to defend the parents of ancient or medieval times against the implications that they were more irresponsible towards their progeny than we are today, Shahar insists that "we should endeavor to comprehend what we find unacceptable, or consider physically or emotionally harmful or even cruel, against the background or the character of the society, its weaknesses, and its inner contradictions" (5). Granting the essential importance of Shahar's insistence on the cultural context of individual and communal patterns of abuse, her defensive stance vis-à-vis the medieval parent seems somewhat perplexing. As disturbing as the studies of apparent neglect and abuse in the medieval period are (see Trexler and Kellum), they cannot be construed as suggesting that parents in the middle ages were more culpable than those of earlier and later periods for which information is available (Scrimshaw 439-40). Indeed, the abandonment of children in the cities of the United States in the last decade of the twentieth century prompts David Levi-Strauss to describe our own public policy toward the younger generation as a kind of "progenicide" (752-54), and the connection between private and public patterns of abuse has been underscored by Gil (16), and Greven (3-10). The most essential point about the interest in historical and literary discussions of infanticide is, perhaps, the emotional intensity with which such debates tend to be invested.

In a study entitled *Anjea: Infanticide, Abortion and Contraception in Savage Society*, Herbert Aptekar observes that "the behavior we designate by the terms 'contraception,' 'abortion,' 'infanticide' and 'abstention from sexual intercourse' arises from multiple sources, but it does not seem inappropriate to describe certain emotional overtones accompanying it as a negative desire" (36), or, in other words, "a desire to avoid children" which is "common to all mankind" (50-51). Immediately worth noting in this passage is the author's assumption of a significant connection between the words "infanticide" and "abortion." It is an assumption which is typical of demographic and anthropological discussions, an interesting example of which is the argument by Harris and Ross that, in our own age, the failure to substitute "modern contraceptive and other prenatal forms of fertility control for the covert postnatal fertility controls which continue to be heavily relied upon by contemporary preindustrial systems of population" will inevitably result in augmented rates of "indirect infanticide and pedicide" in the modern world (182-83). In this passage, the words *covert* and *indirect* function as chilling reminders of Scrimshaw's principle of "unconscious rationality," and the references to prenatal and postnatal "fertility controls" suggest the concepts of abortion and infanticide. Though I have no wish to muddy the waters of my own argument by stressing the inherently problematic connection between infanticide and abortion, the already existing discursive nexus between the two terms suggests that the emotional intensities of academic discourse on infanticide derive precisely from the continuing contemporary relevance of the social issues implied by the terms of the debate. In any case, as a feminist who believes in a woman's right to choose the option of abortion, I freely concede that my scholarly interest in the myth of Medea has always been related to my involvement in the emotional dynamics of the Euripidean scenario, in which maternal generative power collides spectacularly with the communal representatives of paternal control. Yet I am quite aware of the risk involved in juxtaposing modern and ancient perspectives. Abortion is very different from infanticide, and for the purposes of this essay, I must insist that the current rhetoric about the "unborn" does not concern me. Having said as much, I wish, nevertheless, to underscore the importance of Aptekar's conception of infanticide as an expression of "negative desire" for children.

Echoing Freud's emphasis on the ambiguity of the emotions (*S.E.* 19: 43), Aptekar asserts that "every constellation of sentiment contains within itself its own opposite" (37). He also notes that a balanced treatment of the parent-child relationship would necessarily deal with both the negative and the positive aspects of the human desire for children. Considerations of balance notwithstanding, the concept of "negative desire" seems especially relevant to the myth of Medea. In fact, the tragedy of Medea is not a balanced treatment of anything at all, but rather a brilliant dramatization of the shadowy and terrifying underside of a relationship that is often cast in cheerful and glowing terms.

Infanticide is a worst-case scenario that functions as the dreadful fulfillment of a human potential implicit in the negative desire Aptekar describes as "common to all mankind." In the terrible yet familiar emotions that drive the plot of *Medea,* Euripides evokes a nightmare that is as threatening to the individual psyche as it is to the communal matrix. Thus, the tragedy of *Medea* is disturbing and controversial precisely because it articulates and portrays disquieting and subversive passions that tend to be denied in the official discourse of any society. I will argue that the act of child murder in dramatic texts implies a concomitant theme of hostility toward children. Both the act and the theme are emblematic of negative desire for children that is nonetheless distressing because it generally occurs in a context replete with indications of positive desire for children. If the *Medea* by Euripides is the most important example of the literary conjunction between infanticidal themes and tragic form, it is also, as the oldest extant version of a myth which has haunted the Western imagination for over two thousand years, the first in a long tradition of masterpieces.

Beginning with a discussion of salient developments in the extra-literary discourse on the topic of infanticide, and proceeding to a demonstration of the way in which the concepts of denial, projection and unconscious rationality are related to the literary use of infanticidal themes, I articulate my general position on the dynamics of abuse in my first chapter.

In my second chapter, I examine the Euripidean text that is the model for all succeeding versions of the myth. In doing so, I focus on the textual connection between negative desire for children and the operation of commonly revered ideals.

Next, I deal with the *Medea* by the ancient Roman philosopher and poet, Seneca, whose drama stresses the connection between filicidal passions and the public excesses of sadistic tyrants endowed with absolute power.

In the fourth chapter, I discuss the seventeenth-century French *Médée* by Pierre Corneille, a baroque tragedy that articulates class and gender issues in terms of generational dynamics, emphasizing the occult power of the "bad" mother so as to suggest an imaginative connection between the mythical figure of the ancient witch and notorious witchcraft trials conducted in the author's day.

The subject of the fifth chapter is Franz Grillparzer's *Medea,* a text that demonstrates the interconnections between child abuse, sexual abuse, and communal persecutions. Anticipating the twentieth-century fascination with themes of remembering and forgetting, this stunning tragedy articulates the disruptive potential of repressed memory and illuminates the connection between individual misery and collective pathology.

In the concluding chapter, I discuss dramatic representations of Medea in our own century, including plays by T. Sturge Moore, Hans Henny Jahnn, Henri-René Lenormand, Countee Cullen, Maxwell Anderson, Robinson Jeffers, Jean Anouilh, Matthias Braun, Robert Duncan, Francine Ringold, Rudi Gray, Charles Ludlam, and Heiner Müller. I also refer to nondramatic texts such as Pier Paolo Pasolini's film, *Medea,* and Toni Morrison's novel, *Beloved.* The sheer number of modern works based on the ancient myth suggests, ultimately, that the figure of Medea somehow embodies those aspects of the human condition that confront us most urgently in the final years of the twentieth century.

In preparing this volume, I have consulted many texts, but my references to primary texts are keyed to particular editions. Citations from the *Medea* by Euripides are from the text edited by Alan Elliott (1979), and quotations from Seneca's *Medea* are from the one prepared by C. D. N. Costa (1973). In referring to other texts by these authors, I have used the Loeb Library editions. My discussion of Corneille's *Médée* refers to the text edited by André de Leyssac (1978). Based on the edition printed in 1639, before the standardization of French spelling, this text contains a number of archaic forms (*fruict* for *fruit, maistresse* for *maîtresse, aage* for *âge).* Trusting that any difficulty posed by such irregularities will be abundantly compensated by the advantage of examining the language which best conveys the author's original inspiration, I have endeavored to cite this edition as faithfully as possible. References to other works by Corneille are keyed to the *Oeuvres Complètes,* edited by André Stegman (1963). My analysis of Grillparzer's *Das goldene Vliess* refers to the text prepared by Peter Frank and Karl Pörnbacher (1969). Parenthetical references after quotations refer to lines of poetry. Translations are my own.

Performances and Productions

The Wingless Victory. By Maxwell Anderson. Dir. Guthrie McClintic. With Katherine Cornell (Oparre) and Walter Abel (Nathaniel). Empire Theater, New York 23 December 1936.

Medea. By Robinson Jeffers. Staged by John Gielgud. With Judith Anderson (Medea) and Florence Reed (the Nurse). National Theater, New York. 1947-48 season.

Medea in Africa. By Countee Cullen. Dir. Owen Doddson. Ira Aldridge Theater, Howard University Campus, Washington D.C. 25 April-3 May 1959.

Medea. Robinson Jeffers. Dir. Cyril Simon. With Gloria Foster (Medea) and Michael Higgins (Jason). Martinique Theater, New York. 28 November 1965.

Medea. Euripides. Adapted and directed by Minos Volanakis. With Irene Papas (Medea) and John P. Ryan (Jason). Uptown Circle in the Square, New York. 17 January 1973.

Medea. Ballet choreographed by John Butler. Music by Samuel Barber. With Mikhail Baryshnikov and Carla Fracci. Spoleto. 28 June 1975.

Medea. Opera by Luigi Cherubini. City Opera, New York. April 1982.

Medea. Robinson Jeffers. Dir. Robert Whitehead. With Zoe Caldwell (Medea), Mitchell Ryan (Jason), and Judith Anderson (the Nurse). Cort Theater, New York. 2 May 1982.

Cave of the Heart. Ballet choreographed by Martha Graham. City Center, New York. 22 June, 1982.

Medea Sacrament. Text and Performance by Conrad Bishop and Elizabeth Fuller. The Independent Eye, Lancaster Pennsylvania. CSC Repertory Theater, New York. June 1983.

Orgasmo Adulto Escapes from the Zoo. A program of one-act plays by Dario Fo and Franca Rame, including a Medea. With Estelle Parsons. Public Theater, New York. August 1983.

Medea and the Doll. By Rudi Gray. Performed in Harlem at the Frank Silvera Workshop early in 1984. Dir. Rany Frazier. With Maria Ellis (Nilda) and Juney Smith (Winston). Samuel Beckett Theater, New York. October 1984.

Medea. Opera by Robert Wilson. Music by Gavin Bryars. Opéra de Lyons, Lyons. November 1984.

Medea. Opera by Marc-Antoine Charpentier. 1693. Opéra de Lyons, Lyons. November 1984.

Médée. By Philippe Franchini and Junji Fuseya. Performed by Junji Fuseya. Théâtre du Temps, Paris. 29 June 1985.

Medea. Adapted from Euripides by Claire Bush and Alkis Papoutsis. Pan Asian Repertory Company. Susan Bloch Theatre, New York. 25 February-22 March 1986.

Medea. Euripides. Dir. Yukio Ninagawa. With Mikijiro Hira and Masare Tsukayama. The Toho Company, Delacorte Theater, New York. 3 September 1986.

Medea. By Charles Ludlam. With Everett Quinton and Black-Eyed Susan. Charles Ludlam Theater, New York. November 1987.

Medeamaterial. Heiner Müller. International Theater Festival, Madrid and Malaga. 15-23 July 1988.

Medea. Dance-theater solo by Ann Papoulis. Danspace series, St. Mark's Church, Manhattan. October 1990.

Médée. Marc-Antoine Charpentier. Dir. Jean-Marie Villégier. Brooklyn Academy of Music, Brooklyn. 22 May 1994.

Medea. Euripides. Trans. Alistair Elliot. Dir. Jonathan Kent. With Diana Rigg (Medea) and Tim Oliver Woodward (Jason). Longacre Theater, New York. 18 June 1994.

Medea the Musical. Written and Directed by John Fisher. Theater Too Cafe, San Francisco. Summer, 1995.

Cave of the Heart. Martha Graham Dance Company. Fairbanks, Alaska. 2 February 1997.

1

Murderous Desire, Psychological Defenses and Unconscious Rationality

Although Euripides' *Medea* is probably the most celebrated literary treatment of the theme of child-murder, it is by no means an isolated phenomenon. Aside from the ancient pagan tales of Tantalus, Procne, Thyestes, Erectheus, Agamemnon, and Ino, there are also biblical stories such as those of Jephthah and his daughter, Athaliah and her grandchildren, Abraham and Isaac, and the slaughter of the innocents by King Herod. Shakespeare dealt with the theme in *Titus Andronicus* and *The Winter's Tale*, as did Racine in *Athalie*, Corneille in *Rodogune*, and Goethe in *Faust*. The threat of child murder is central in many traditionally revered children's tales, such as "Hansel and Gretel," "Snow White," and "Jack and the Beanstalk." In fiction, the theme has inspired works by Gabriele D'Annunzio, Anton Chekhov, Bernard Malamud, Chinua Achebe, John Updike, Toni Morrison, Nadine Gordimer, Bessie Head, and Mariama Bâ. Films like *Ordinary People*, in which a mother wishes her child were dead, and *Mommie Dearest*, in which a mother tries to kill a child, present the same essential question as classical works dealing with the theme of infanticide: What is the particular appeal of the fantasy of child murder for readers and audiences?

The theme of infanticide in literature is a reflection of the actual human experience of violent hostility toward children. Although there has always been scattered evidence of child abuse and infanticide, the concept of destructive aggression by parents against children was never methodically documented before the articulation of the medical concept of the "battered child syndrome." In retrospect, the paucity of comment on this phenomenon, for which there has never been a scarcity of information, suggests the operation of a widespread tacit injunction against confronting the issue of parental aggression. The burgeoning of literature on all aspects of generational conflict during the past four decades suggests, moreover, that child abuse and infanticide may be merely the visible manifestations of a general problem. Though violence against children by adults is the focus of research in many disciplines, the most obvious link between the literary theme of infanticide and the broad category of observed infanticidal behavior lies in the field of psychology.

Child psychologist Dorothy Bloch describes children as being "universally predisposed to the fear of infanticide by both their physical and their psychological state of development" (3). Her study, *"So the Witch Won't Eat Me": Fantasy and the Child's Fear of Infanticide,* suggests that the fundamental appeal of infanticidal themes for both readers and audiences derives partly from the inevitable anxieties and fears of the dependent human child, who may well imagine that the adults who surround him or her are tyrannical giants, if only because of their enormous relative size and power. The terrors of childhood may be repressed in the process of growing up, but they remain all the more inexorable in the unconscious for having been denied. One source of the broad appeal of infanticidal themes, therefore, may be the capacity of the adult spectator to identify with the child-victim. There is considerable evidence, however, that the the irrational fears of children are not the only source of infanticidal fantasies.

Bloch documents cases in which children's fears of infanticide were exacerbated by the actual hostilities of parental figures. Whether aggression against the child is expressed physically or in more subtle ways, it takes its toll on the growing mind. Because children may experience any parental fulmination as a threat to life itself, they regularly retreat into fantasy to protect themselves from the painful awareness of such threats. In young children, projections of witches, ogres, and goblins may serve as defenses against perceptions of parental aggression; in adults, a variety of anti-social and self-destructive behavior patterns may be traced to defense mechanisms originating in juvenile reactions to parental hostility. This perspective on the roots of irrational conduct places Bloch in the same camp with writers who express impatience with Freud's theory of the Oedipus Complex, according to which the seeds of mental illness are inherent in the incestuous and patricidal fantasies to which all children are innately disposed. Underscoring the "phenomenal omission of the first part of the myth of Oedipus" in the formulation of Oedipal theory, she insists that if Freud had considered the myth of Oedipus in its entirety, "his theory would have established the link between cause and effect; the parents' wish to kill their child would then have been universalized as the inevitable first step in the Oedipus Complex and as the precipitating factor in the child's preoccupation with incest and murder" (9). This point, which has also been made by Marie Balmary, Jeffrey Masson, Alice Miller, Marianne Krüll and others, is important because of Freud's insistence on the concept of wish fulfillment: "King Oedipus, who slew his father Laius and married his mother Jocasta, merely shows us the fulfillment of our own childhood fantasies" (*S.E.* 4:262). Freud's conception of tragic form as an external representation of unconscious wish, when considered in the light of Bloch's documentation of murderous hostility toward children on the part of many parents, leads us to the sobering thought that audiences may derive vicarious satisfaction from the spectacle of violent excess on the part of the adult aggressor.

The question of whether generational conflict originates in the spontaneous fantasies of children or in the effects of parental hostility toward children is implicit in the psychoanalytic debate over Freud's "seduction theory." This controversial thesis, articulated by Freud in "The Aetiology of Hysteria" (1896), a lecture in which he argued that mental illnesses are caused by sexual traumas suffered in childhood (Masson 245-90), was eclipsed by the Oedipus Complex, as Freud began to have reservations regarding the testimony of patients who claimed to have been abused. His comment to Fliess written in 1897, that "it was hardly credible that perverted acts against children were so general" (*S.E.* 1:259), provides ammunition for critics such as Krüll, Balmary, Miller, and Masson, who argue that the transition from the "seduction theory" to the Oedipus Complex was accomplished by a process of repression and denial. Freud has been defended, however, by Charles Hanley and Leonard Shengold, who cite evidence that Freud never abandoned the seduction theory. Even energetic critics of his theory concede the difficulties inherent in Freud's position. Thus Alice Miller speculates on "the loneliness of the explorer" (*Thou Shalt Not* 107-18), and Leon Sheleff, in arguing that Freud's analysis of generational conflict was consistently biased against the young, hastens to add that his "errors are not a consequence of an extreme anti-child or anti-youth bias" but "an expression of the biases that adults often bring to bear in discussing generational contacts" (87). In short, the debate over the seduction theory is ultimately inseparable from the problems of subjectivity and perception that prompt Shengold to observe that the minds of human beings are "vast neglected historical museums" with many dark places between "the visible areas of display" (35).

The most convincing demonstration that knowledge of adult hostility toward children has regularly been stored in the "dark places" of the mind remains the medical discussion of the difficulties involved in the diagnosis of physical abuse in children. In commenting on what appears to be "the first case description in English of a battered child," Selwyn Smith reports that physicians at a meeting of the Medical Society of London in 1888 examined the mysterious "swellings" and "bruises" on the bodies of young children, and calmly speculated upon the possible discovery of a previously undocumented type of rickets. He notes that "none of the physicians present at that meeting suggested that maltreatment by the parents might be an alternative explanation" for the symptoms presented (21-22). So great was the reluctance of doctors to consider the possibility that parents might harm or kill their own children that the diagnosis of child abuse only became feasible when the refinement of roentgenological technique led to an improved understanding of the nature of traumatic injuries. Such studies, in turn, made it difficult to deny the physical evidence of maltreatment. The medical articulation of the "battered child syndrome" is essential to the literary discussion of the theme of infanticide precisely because, in the absence of such a term, the concept did not exist. In the absence of the concept, particular incidents of adult brutality to children were either not recognized as such, or they were rationalized in various ways. Individual incidents could be dismissed as either the deviations of isolated individuals or the aberrations of savage societies. Since the articulation of the clinical problem, however, an abundance of literature on child abuse and child murder has been published, and the perspective on destructive parenting that is possible today is radically different from what was possible a hundred years ago, or even thirty years ago. In hindsight, there may seem to be an analogy between the attitude of physicians and psychiatrists reluctant to recognize the effects of parental aggression against children and that of literary scholars disinclined to deal with infanticide as a significant theme. In each case, the paucity of serious discussion of a kind of behavior regarding which there was no scarcity of provocative evidence suggests the operation of a kind of censorship, as if infanticidal thoughts may be forbidden in the same way that Freud supposed incestuous and patricidal thoughts to be forbidden. Whereas the difficulty of conceptualizing problems such as child abuse and child murder has the quality of energetic resistance to a repressed subject, the medical discoveries of the early 1960s may seem to have broken down the collective psychic defenses against the banned topic, permitting a greatly expanded awareness of every aspect of the problem of adult hostility to youth.

The articulation of the battered child syndrome created a framework within which incidents formerly considered to be scattered and unrelated might be coherently discussed. Within the larger context of adult hostility toward youth, it is possible to regard infanticide as the extreme form of an antagonism toward children that transcends the boundaries of separate cultures and periods, while allowing that particular manifestations of the phenomenon may vary considerably from one social context to another. The literature documenting such behavior is interdisciplinary in character. In addition to the contributions by physicians, psychiatrists and psychologists, the work of historians such as William Langer, Richard Trexler, Barbara Kellum, Maurice Garden, David Hunt, Larry Wolff, Lloyd de Mause, and Philip Greven has explored and shed light on the subject. Marvin Kohl has edited an anthology of essays on the philosophical implications of infanticide, and Maria Piers uses historical perspectives on infanticide in an essay on contemporary child care. Glanville Williams has considered legal aspects of the problem, and David Gil and Richard Gelles have analyzed its sociological ramifications. It is especially interesting to note that biological and anthropological considerations of the the grim topic antedate the present "boom" by many years.

In *The Descent of Man*, Charles Darwin suggested that the practice of infanticide was, in all probability, the most important of those customs that Thomas Malthus described as checks upon the unlimited growth of population (429-30), and William Graham Sumner linked the practices of abortion and infanticide with the rise of population "policies" in very early societies. Aptekar's consideration of such matters led him to conclude that infanticide was probably a general practice at a certain stage of human social development: "infanticide . . . comes so near to being inherent in the primeval parent-child relationship that one is tempted to say of it: 'Here, if anywhere is a bit of behavior natural to primitive man' " (157). The title of Aptekar's study, focusing as it does on the incidence of infanticide in savage society, suggests an explanation for the curious fact that the anthropological evidence of infanticidal customs never had the impact on public consciousness which medical articulations of the battered child syndrome did. It is, after all, one thing for Australian bushmen or Eskimos or even the Chinese to practice the "savage" custom of infanticide. It is quite another matter for American doctors to assert that baby batterers represent "a random cross section of the general population" (Steele and Pollock 92), or for a psychologist to assert that "the aim of those who abuse a child is to kill the child; the reason for abusing the child is to be rid of him or her" (Bakan 55). Although earlier reports of infanticide and child abuse permitted a certain public complacency about "progress" and "civilization," the medical pronouncements of the sixties and seventies demonstrated that disturbing numbers of our own children are killed or given permanent physical injuries each year. When a respected medical practitioner asserts that "every parent is a potential 'baby-basher' " (Smith 61), it becomes difficult to dismiss the problem as a simple manifestation of deviant behavior.

The interpretation of evidence remains controversial in all disciplines dealing with the mistreatment of children. Whereas one historian complains about the "persistent refusal to disengage child-murder, child abuse, child labor and corporal punishment" that characterizes the discussion of these matters (Shorter 178-80), a psychiatric study that actually did distinguish between "physical attack on the child in an effort to make it behave" and "attack with intent to kill" concedes that "significant numbers of battered children do die because of repeated injuries" (Steele and Pollock 90), and the relevance of certain meticulous distinctions to the victims of such attacks would seem difficult to establish. Bakan, Smith, Radbill, and Piers, among others, describe child abuse and infanticide as different

6   The Myth of Medea and the Murder of Children

manifestations of the same problem, or as related phenomena having the common denominator of hostility to children. In any case, much of the relevant information is more remarkable for the statistical precision and general conviction with which it is stated than for its inherent originality.

In defense of an infanticidal character of his own creation, Pierre Corneille once observed that few women may have committed the crimes of Cleopatra, but many have in their nature a trace of that which led her to commit them (*Oeuvres Complètes*, hereafter referred to as "*O.C.*" 832). If this perception seems all the more acute from a distance of three centuries, it is also a good example of the way in which much of the material published on child abuse and filicide in recent years consists not so much of new discoveries as of the retrospective illumination of information that was previously available in scattered and neglected sources. The psychiatric community alone affords ample evidence of this phenomenon. Ferenczi, Rado, and Zilboorg wrote articles on the subject of adult hostility toward children in the 1920s and 1930s (Ferenczi 124-29; Rado 219-26; Zilboorg 32-43). Edward Stern articulated a theory called the "Medea Complex" to explain a "situation in which the mother harbors death wishes to her offspring, usually as a revenge against the father" (321-31). As early as the 1930s, several writers speculated on the effects of a "Laius Complex" (named after the father of Oedipus), describing the hostility of father toward son. Sheleff notes that these writers "had a minimal impact on the scientific community . . . and seemed themselves to be unaware of each other's work" (6). One difference between current research on generational hostility and earlier considerations of the topic is the degree to which contemporary scholars tend to be aware of the continuity between their own research and the work of colleagues in other disciplines. Thus, recent debates by classical scholars over the significance of infanticide in antiquity employ anthropological and demographical perspectives, and the psychoanalytic debate over Oedipal theory is ultimately inseparable from medical research on the nature of traumatic injuries. The most essential feature of recent work on the general question of adult violence against children is the sheer increase in volume of the material being presented. The way in which the accumulation of evidence has changed the nature of scholarly discourse on infanticide may be demonstrated with a single example.

In 1917, Oscar Helmuth Werner published a study called *The Unmarried Mother in German Literature with Special Reference to the Period 1770-1800*. The title of the work provides little indication of the fact that this book is an important source of information on the subject of child murder. Reprinted in 1966, the essay has been quoted by many researchers, including Smith, Bakan and Piers. Since Werner first directed his attention to this material, however, other scholars have also been drawn to it, and the titles of their essays describe the nature of their concern quite openly, as for example, *Kindesmord in der Literatur der Sturm und Drang Periode: Ein Beitrag zur Kultur und Literatur Geschichte des 18 Jahrhunderts (Child Murder in the Storm and Stress Period: a Contribution to the History of Nineteenth-Century Culture and History)* by Jan Ramekers, and *Die Kindsmörderin im deutschen Schriftum von 1770-1795 (The Female Child Murderer in German Letters from 1770-1795)* by Beat Weber. The very discretion of Werner's title seems, in retrospect, to be a concession to a general reserve with regard to the subject of infanticide in the early part of this century. Only after the validity and importance of the topic itself had been recognized did it become customary to declare the subject in the title as *infanticide* rather than the unmarried mother. Whereas the omission of the term *infanticide* from the title of a text focusing on that subject suggests the operation of collective denial, the most conspicuous of the defense mechanisms that occur in discussions of infanticide is *projection.*

Freud defined projection as a process wherein "internal excitations which produce too great an increase of unpleasure" may be treated "as though they were acting from the outside so that it may be possible to bring the shield against [external] stimuli into operation" (*S.E.* 18:29). The mechanism is implicit in the customary attribution of particular cases of child murder to the insanity of an individual or to the savagery of some tribe. In a narrowly clinical sense, the word has been used to describe the process by which seriously disturbed parents may "project their symptoms onto their children so that the child may become the hypochondriacal organ" and the parent, in killing the child, experiences actual relief from symptoms she believes she has destroyed in the child (Bender 46). With reference to entire communities, Piers uses the term to describe the process by which murderous rage toward children may be vented on designated victims such as witches, Jews and unmarried infanticidal mothers (122-23). The contexts in which the word has been used suggest that the repressed awareness of intense hostility toward the young may be a most painful "internal excitation" in adults. The above-noted reference to witches, Jews and unmarried infanticidal mothers is particularly interesting, moreover, not only because such figures occur with ominous regularity in the history of infanticide, but also because each one of these types is analogous to one of three essential aspects of the character Medea. For Medea, the "barbaric sorceress" and "folktale fiend" (Page xii, xxvii; Conacher 197-98) is a witch; Medea, the "oriental princess," the wanderer, the exile, the foreigner, resembles the figure of the Jew, and Medea, the woman who has been exploited and betrayed, is equivalent to the unmarried mother. Of all the ways in which Freudian projections have figured in the discussion of infanticide, the reference to witches is perhaps the most relevant to the story of Medea.

The witch has long been considered an imaginative projection of the unconscious reproach of the child toward the mother, and the title of Bloch's book, *"So the Witch Won't Eat Me": Fantasy and the Child's Fear of Infanticide.* reveals the infanticidal meaning of the projection. Bakan notes that the "association of witchcraft with infanticide is indicated by the fact that the German term 'Hexe' did not apply originally to human beings at all, but to child-devouring demons." The universality of the fantasy of infanticide is signaled by the variety of cultural manifestations of the witch. In Slavic folk literature, the ubiquitous Baba Yaga was supposed to cook children and eat them (Bakan 66). The Marquesans believe in a female phantom called the "vehini-hai" who brews poisons, lures men to their doom and continuously desires to eat the flesh of children (Deutsch 2:41). The vehini-hai is a good example of the relationship between imaginative projection and social context, because the people who entertain this grim fantasy have been noted for their harsh child-rearing practices. The anthropologist Abraham Kardiner observed that "these women are devoid of maternal instinct" (Deutsch 2:42). Deutsch comments on the parallel between the diabolic fantasy of the vehini-hai and the actual conditions of Marquesan society, as well as on the similarity between Western conceptions of child-devouring witches and the Marquesan vehini-hai. The continuing viability of the witch fantasy in our own culture is witnessed not only by the fact that such stories as "Hansel and Gretel" and "Snow White" are among our most popular children's tales, but also by the renewal of the theme in such novels as Ira Levin's *Rosemary's Baby*, Toni Morrison's *Sula*, and John Updike's *The Witches of Eastwick*.

The witch is as central in Western experience as the vehini-hai is in Marquesan culture. Bakan speculates that women designated as "witches" may regularly have served as instruments of infanticidal desires: "from the Volga to the Mississippi, from the Rhine to the Nile, the old witch has truly cackled 'Don't worry, Dearie, I will take good care of him' " (66-67). If many women actually did commit infanticide, it was a practice that never occurred on a large scale without the general complicity of society. During the Middle Ages, ecclesiastical courts routinely absolved married women of the "accidental" suffocation of infants, a common event which was known as "laying over." But thousands of unmarried women and so-called witches accused of infanticide were executed, and Trexler describes the prosecutions of witches and the Jewish ritual murder trials of the high and late Middle Ages as "translucent projections of infanticide appearing in judicial motifs" (99). William Langer outlines a grim picture of the European past in which, up to the nineteenth century, one form or another of infanticide was so widespread as to suggest the presence of a covert social sanction, the effects of which were tantamount to institutionalized infanticide *(Scientific American* 1972, 92-97). Piers underscores the fact that the murder of children by women often had the effect of benefitting men who either wished to avoid competing with their heirs for the attentions of very young wives, or who did not want the financial burden of supporting too many dependents (44-78). Infanticide was a practice that had salutary results for a society that could not well have sustained the increased pressure of unchecked population growth on its limited available resources.

Child-murder, however, was not a custom for which society was ready to assume responsibility. The dilemma of being unable to afford either the elimination or the approval of the practice gave rise to the need for scapegoats. Individual women accused of witchcraft were excellent candidates for the role. Often associated with actual incidents of infanticide that were officially deplored while unofficially encouraged, they were all too easily identified with the imaginary projection of the "bad mother." "Witches" were vulnerable because of their association with two groups of easily targeted "outsiders": the insane and the female. Although men were occasionally accused of and executed for witchcraft, the German Dominicans Jacobus Sprenger and Heinrich Kramer report many more female than male witches in their manual for the witch hunters of the Inquisition, the *Malleus Maleficarum*. They also make a point of noting that women are particularly susceptible to corruption and thus an enticement to evil (41-47). Lillian Feder suggests that the significance of confessions of child-murder by particular women "lies in their revelation of the individual transformation of unacceptable and conflicting desires, confusion and shame into the current mythology of witchcraft" (111). The peculiar phenomenon of the marginalized woman who accepts the role of the witch has been examined in a more recent context by M. J. Field, who found, among West African woman in the 1930s, that those suffering from depression—that is, from an overwhelming sense of failure and weakness in their actual lives—were disposed to accuse themselves of witchcraft, often including the murder of their children (Janeway 129).

The concept of self-inculpation through identification with communal myths suggests a comparison between the question of insanity in witches and the legal debate over the sanity of child-murderers. Glanville Williams refers to the "legal fiction" of a "lactation mania" that was sometimes invoked in the last century in order to avoid prosecution for murder in the case of a woman who had killed her own infant (126). Though reluctance to hold the perpetrators of such offenses responsible for their actions seems to have derived from a compassionate sense of judicial restraint, it might also indicate the need to dissociate the experience of the child-murderer from that of ordinary mortals by denying her full humanity. In fact, the hypothesis of a specific kind of mental disorder governing the behavior of those who commit such offenses is not supported by medical evidence. Steele and Pollock observe no one basic personality as being typical of their patients (121), and Flynn asserts that it was precisely the "extraordinary reliance on the ego-defense mechanisms of repression, denial and projection" that permitted certain patients to abuse their children (375-79). In other words, the difference between the abusive parent and all others is not so much the nature of his or her feelings or impulses, as it is a failure to control those feelings and impulses. Yet the association of madness with infanticide is a persistent one, and the question of the sanity of the murderer remains as critical for literature as for law. In the case of the plea of insanity, a kind of circular logic declares a person insane and, therefore, not responsible for his or her actions, precisely on the basis of the nature of those actions. In the case of the literary text, the expectation that a great work of literature should have something to do with generally recognizable human experience is difficult to reconcile with the assertion that the tragic character is out of her mind. Although Medea is not really one of the mad protagonists of literature, there is enough textual ambiguity concerning the question of her sanity to make it a crucial issue. The question of madness in the tragedy of Medea is thus a reflection of medical and legal judgments on the sanity or insanity of actual individuals accused of abusing or killing their children.

Certain psychological texts have the effect of dramatizing the association between misogyny, mental pathology, and malevolence toward children. In 1967, psychiatrist Joseph Rheingold posited the virtually universal existence, in women, of a "maternal filicidal impulse." Justly cited for his considerable, if problematic, contribution to our knowledge of adult hostility to children, Rheingold accumulated data from his own casework, compiled references to the literature of antagonistic parenting, and analyzed the writings of Freud and other investigators with notable acuity. However, his descriptions of the way in which he "gradually, and with a creeping sense of horror, became aware that there was a malignant, a 'necrophilous,' a lethal quality in the behavior of the mother," his denunciations of the "miasmal malignity" and "subtle sadism" of women, may rather fairly be described as oozing animosity toward women. His observation regarding the particularly disturbing type of female patient in question, that "such women have been described as 'witches'," is hardly redeemed by the pious reminder that "they are not satans, only the product of destructive mothers" (126, 132). Like the authors of the *Malleus Maleficarum*, Rheingold seems to attribute the witch-like character to some mysterious feminine predisposition toward corruption. The evil is transmitted from mother to daughter as if mothers and daughters existed in a vacuum devoid of other influences. Though Rheingold's theory of "maternal destructiveness" has been aptly described by Sheleff as a "non-sequitur to his impressive compilation of evidence of parental hostility by both sexes" (259), the designation of women as "witches" in a psychiatric text is important testimony to the difficulty involved in acknowledging the destructive effects on children of ordinary adult behavior. Perhaps it was precisely the mechanism of projecting the entire responsibility for such cruelty onto women that made it possible for Rheingold to explore this difficult area as extensively and as early as he did. The crucial point for the present discussion is that the role of the witch is not only a traditional aspect of the Medea motif, but also a curiously persistent component of discussions linking feminine psychology to the maltreatment of children.

In her study of child-murder in England in the Middle Ages, Barbara Kellum sheds light on the process of externalization by which fantasies may be projected onto designated "outsiders." First, she notes the "obvious, almost obsessional relish" that characterizes the descriptions of what the witches allegedly did to children, either sacrificing them to the Devil, eating their flesh raw, or roasting them and sucking their blood (375). She also observes that the children themselves were considered alien, parasitic creatures, "since mother's milk was thought to be whitened blood, and, therefore, with every feeding the infant was sucking away some of the mother's vital substance." Speculating that the high demand for wet-nurses among those who could afford them should hardly be considered surprising in the context of such beliefs, she cites, as evidence of the popular conviction that the feeding of children might be hazardous to one's health, the case of Sir Gomther, who as a child was said to have killed his wet-nurse. Kellum concludes that there was a "repulsive reciprocity" between the concept of the parasitic child and the popular fantasies of witches who "sucked babies' blood" and Jews who "drained childrens' bodies dry" (380). This analysis shares with certain other discussions of infanticide a tendency to span the ages with its implications, for the image of mother's milk as whitened blood is strangely reminiscent of the blood-reddened milk of Clytemnestra's dream in the *Agamemnon,* and, indeed, the "repulsive reciprocity" of Kellum's description recalls the brooding sense of balance between the sins of the fathers and the crimes of the children that pervades the entire *Oresteia.* Her text is equally suggestive of modern clinical references to child abuse, such as Smith's assertion that the basic anxieties of abusive parents "related to fears of annihilation which they handled by externalizing and attacking" (71). The irrational and offensive potential of "defensive" accusations is nowhere more apparent than in the blood-libels directed against the Jews, for whom it is forbidden even to taste the blood of animals.

The premise that charges of ritual murder directed against a group are actually projections of the accuser's own violent passions seems substantiated by the way in which accusations of ritual murder regularly function as an incitement to kill. Commenting on the way in which such a libel, published in *Der Stuermer*, led to the massacre of Jews in Paris on June 17, 1942, Stern observes that the "accusation [of ritual murder] is a projection of the accuser's desire for the death of his own offspring, and this death wish is later symbolically fulfilled by the murder of the victim's children" (329). The persistence of the irrational belief in Jewish blood rituals is reflected in the periodic renewal of the legend of the Jewish child-murderer in literature. Perhaps the most famous of such tales is the one about Hugh of Lincoln, first popularized by Matthew Paris (8:137-43), and retold by Chaucer in "The Prioress' Tale," which is the subject of a ballad used by James Joyce in the "Ithaca" episode of *Ulysses* (690-91). More recently, in *The Fixer,* Bernard Malamud presents a fictionalized account of the ordeal endured by a Jew accused of murdering two young boys for ritual purposes in Tsarist Russia at the turn of the century. The myth of the Jewish child-murderer is relevant to the Medea motif in two ways: first, because it implies the themes of wandering, exile, and persecution, and second, because of the aura of religious mystery.

The epithet "wandering" that is traditionally affixed to the name, Jew, describes the rootless life that Jason and Medea led from the time of their departure from Colchis until the scene of the grisly action in Corinth. Medea, in particular, is cut off and cast out from her homeland as punishment for her transgressions against her father, just as the Jews were exiled in fulfillment of the wrath of God. Though there would seem to be no inevitable link between the ancient themes of exile and child murder, clinical discussions of child abuse suggest that the connection may not be entirely coincidental. In fact, geographical mobility, flight, and isolation from the larger community have been noted as characteristic of abusive parents, and thus, the status of the "outsider" may seem to constitute a curious link between the traditional Jew and the contemporary child-batterer. The connection is admittedly tenuous. The plight of those who abuse their children because they are cut off from the supporting and restraining effects of human society ought not to be confused with the problem of those who, because of their exclusion from the dominant community, are accused of acting out forbidden desires. Jews may have been segregated and, therefore, easily singled out and forced into the role of scapegoat, but family and social ties within the traditional Jewish community were strong. On the other hand, the characteristics of mobility, flight, and isolation that are often associated with today's child-batterers indicate a breakdown of those supportive structures that help families with children to function and survive in traditional cultures. The analogous elements in the myth of Medea and the legend of the wandering Jew converge conspicuously in the *Medea* by Franz Grillparzer, whose protagonist bears a certain resemblance to a beleaguered Jew surrounded by abusive bigots. This aspect of the drama prompted the black actress Agnes Straub to revive the work in 1933 when she used it to make a statement about Nazi racist policies (Sarah Iles Johnson 4). In our own age, the thriving production of new versions of *Medea* seems related to the circumstance that exile is a nearly universal feature of modern life.

The second dimension of the symbol of the Jew that is essential to the meaning of the Medea myth is the idea of ritual sacrifice, a theme that extends far beyond its problematic association with Jews. Witches, like Jews, have been accused of practicing human sacrifice, and the infanticidal unmarried mother was often accused of witchcraft. In fact, ritual sacrifice is arguably more germane to the practice of infanticide than to the figure of the Jew with which it has often been connected. Though Frazer speculates that the myth of the Jewish child murderer is related to prehistoric customs of human sacrifice that were at some point abandoned or honored in rituals substituting animals for human victims (336-44), the symbolism of the "blood of the lamb" has been thoroughly Christianized. When George Bernard Shaw suggests that no self-respecting person would allow his own salvation to be purchased by the blood of an innocent victim, his barbs are evidently directed at Christianity (cxvi-cxvii). Even disregarding tenuous speculations and symbolic suggestions of ritual child murder, however, we are left with a large body of well-documented reports of the practice. Frazer describes fertility rituals in which child victims were sacrificed in many different cultures. In China, India, Mexico and Peru, children were cast into rivers as offerings to water gods to bring good harvests or other good fortune (Radbill 9) and there is archeological evidence suggesting that ancient reports of the sacrificial cremation of children at Carthage were probably well founded (Malcolm Browne). Of particular relevance to the myth of Medea are the legends of infant sacrifice associated with the cults of Hecate and Hera among the ancient Greeks; priestess and devotee of these goddesses, Medea is even reported by Diodorus Siculus to have been the daughter of Hecate. Farnell suggests that such myths as those of Iphigeneia and Medea are, themselves, survivals of prehistoric cults in which the "practice prevailed of paying posthumous worship to the human being that had been offered to the deity in sacrifice." Thus, the children of Medea "may represent the infants immolated in the prehistoric period in the worship of Hera Akraia at Corinth" (18). Medea, then, by virtue of her association with Hecate and Hera, is doubly implicated in traditions of sacrificial killing.

The symbolic overlapping of ancient pagan and Judeo-Christian traditions in myths of ritual sacrifice is particularly interesting in view of Freud's remarks on the "narcissism of minor differences," according to which the Christian preoccupation with symbolic purgation by blood and the Jewish horror of the "unclean" are but opposite sides of the same coin, the sacred and the unclean being but different aspects of the concept of "taboo" (S.E. 13:25; 11:14). The narcissism of minor differences is a principle which seems applicable to more than one type of infanticidal projection. Just as the disturbing reflection of himself that the Christian found in the Jew made the Jew an ideal object on which to project destructive fantasies, so the treatment of unmarried infanticidal mothers was all the more punitive in that married parents could see in them a reflection of their own dark wishes and deeds. Werner's study of the unmarried mother in German literature demonstrates a close correspondence between literary figures such as Goethe's Gretchen and actually documented cases of infanticidal individuals. Asserting that the unmarried woman who killed her newborn child was the most popular theme of the Storm and Stress epoch, Werner discusses a number of works that deal with it, the only one of which is still widely read today being Goethe's *Faust*. The infanticidal protagonists analyzed in his essay bear a noteworthy resemblance to the ancient Euripidean character. Described as being afraid of social disgrace, jealous of their rivals, angry at their seducers, and inclined to madness, many of them are, like their real-life models, associated with witchcraft (96). Pride, jealousy, anger, mental disequilibrium, and a reputation for skill in sorcery would seem to be typical attributes of the child-murderer, whether the type occurs in historical documents, in the literature of the Storm and Stress period, or in ancient myths.

Although, technically speaking, Medea actually was an "unmarried mother," Werner's terminology seems incongruous in the context of a discussion of tragic character because it suggests the stereotype of the passive female, "seduced and abandoned," which may have distinctly comic overtones for the modern reader. The Victorian flavor of Werner's language is related to the peculiar focus of his study. Dealing as he does with a particular culture during a specific period, he attributes the problem of the unmarried infanticidal mother to contemporary causes, such as the zeal of the Catholic Church for bolstering the institution of marriage, and the insistence of governments on maintaining large standing armies of soldiers who were not permitted to marry. It is worth noting, however, that the infanticidal mother is but one manifestation of a general category of human experience. The individual who, having been betrayed by a conspiracy of reproductive role and social convention, releases the full force of her violent despair on the child who is the fruit of a hapless union, need not be an unmarried female. John Updike's novel, *Rabbit, Run,* in which legally ordained marriage becomes a trap for both partners, and a young wife, abandoned by her restless husband, inadvertently kills one of their children, is a good example of the continuing relevance of the theme of infanticide as a reaction to betrayal.

The unmarried woman who kills her child, like the so-called witches who were frequently assumed to be possessed either by the devil or by madness, recalls Frederick Wertham's observation that the public would prefer to picture the murderer as possessed than be "reminded of how often his victims are the dispossessed" (260). The fact of being dispossessed is the distinguishing feature of the scapegoat; it also constitutes a common bond between the child-victim and those who, having been cast in the role of child-murderer, become the designated objects of communal wrath. The identification of the victim with the torturer or executioner is a feature of many ancient tragedies, including the *Medea,* the *Heracleidae,* the *Bacchae,* and both of the Iphigeneia plays. Such an identification is, indeed, inherent in the ancient origins of cults based on the posthumous worship of individuals formerly sacrificed as victims; among these, Dionysus, in whose honor tragedies were celebrated at Athens, is a salient example. The subject of ritual sacrifice is, in any case, a connecting link between the practice of ancient cults and the execution of witches, Jews, and unmarried mothers in later times, because such executions were often accompanied by ceremonies of a highly ritualized nature.

Werner describes the typical execution by "sacking" of an unmarried woman in harrowing terms. The victim "was stuffed into a black sack together with a dog, a cat, a rooster or a viper. The sack had to remain under water six hours and the choir boys sang 'Aus tiefer Noth schrei ich zu Dir.' Then the deceased was interred" (26). Commenting on this scenario, Piers notes that the obviously prescribed manner in which the execution took place, and the presence of a "quasi-professional group" intoning a "well rehearsed hymn" give the event every appearance of being the "ritual sacrifice of a human scapegoat" (70). She adds that such critics of contemporary mores as Frederick the Great charged civic authorities with inviting the very crimes that they punished so enthusiastically, so that the cruelly executed victims seemed to be "sacrificial beasts on whom governments could project their own guilt" (73). Whereas, in the ancient cults of Hecate and Hera Akraia, the infants themselves were sacrificial victims, and in later times, adults on whom the guilt for child murder was projected were preferred scapegoats, the practice of infanticide is essential to both traditions. The phenomenon of collective and individual violence toward children persists in our own age, as does the continuing importance of scapegoats in protecting society from a painful communal awareness of unpleasant matters. David Gil argues that sensational reporting of individual cases of child abuse and intense public interest in such incidents may serve to divert attention from the more damaging effects of institutionalized abuses such as poverty, discrimination, and deprivation in the lives of millions of children. Observing the communal scorn that is still reserved for child abusers, he asks the question: "Are abusive parents perhaps seized upon as convenient scapegoats to expiate society's collective guilt for abusing countless numbers of its young?" (16). The suggestion that the issue of child abuse is obscured by the media treatment of individual incidents brings the analysis of infanticidal projections back to the questions of selective perception and censored material with which it began. In fact, censorship was linked to generational problems long before the advent of modern technology. When, in Plato's *Republic,* Socrates argues that only certain stories should be told to the young, he singles out for special censure the stories of Uranus, who banished his children and was mutilated by his son, Cronos, and of Cronos himself, who ate his children and was, in turn, vanquished by his son, Zeus. Calling the latter a "foul story," and objecting to it on the ground that it would corrupt the morals of the young, Socrates asserts: "We shall not tell a child that, if he commits the foulest crimes or goes to any length in punishing his father's misdeeds, he will be doing nothing out of the way but only what the first and greatest of the gods have done before him" (70). Although the stories of both Uranus and Cronos begin with the destructive acts of a ferocious father, neither Socrates nor Plato is as much concerned with the example of abusive parenting as he is with the spectacle of filial retaliation. Thus Plato sees the problem posed by the violent behavior of the children but not the one posed by the initial aggression of the parents, just as Freud stresses the problem of incestuous and patricidal desires in children but not the filicidal provocations of the parents. The repeated denial of violence against children, whether committed by institutions, individuals, or primordial progenitors, tends to reaffirm the supposition that there is a subtle and profound injunction against "telling on parents," which is often unnoticed precisely because it is so pervasive.

The peculiar emphasis of some tradonal views on the theme of generational hostility seems all the more remarkable in view of the regularity with which parents kill their own children in creation myths such as the stories of Uranus and Cronos. The occurrence of such acts in myths of such fundamental importance is one of the surest indications that tales of infanticide are not mere reflections of individual pathology, but rather are representations of essential communal concerns. That the concepts of repression, denial, and projection that function as structuring elements of the *Medea* pertain not only to the irrational excesses of particular characters but to the "unconscious rationality" of the collectivity follows from the fact that the theme of human generativity at the core of all creation myths is also the central concern of ancient drama. Medea herself was associated with the powers of generativity by her role as priestess of Hecate, and was believed capable of bringing about "rebirth and regeneration by killing and cutting in pieces," the sort of thing that Dionysus is supposed to have undergone at the hands of the Titans (Kerényi, *The Heroes of the Greeks* 263-71). Along with Demeter, Harmonia, Eos, Thetis, Aphrodite, Circe, and Calypso, Medea is listed by Hesiod as one of those "immortal goddesses who lay with mortal men and bore them children who were like gods" (*Theogony* 151-55). In that the marriage of Medea and Jason, like the sacred marriages of Peleus and Thetis, Aeneas and Dido, and Uranus and Gaia, is celebrated in a cave, it is emblematic of the "cosmic hierogamy," or marriage of Heaven and Earth, that Eliade describes as a myth of the widest distribution (*The Myth of the Eternal Return* 21-25).

The marriage of Heaven (Uranus) and Earth (Gaia) is essential, not only as the prototype of the cosmic hierogamy, but also because the child-devouring Cronos who issued from that union exemplifies the infanticidal character of many such myths. In Navajo epic, Begochiddy, a god who is the son of the Sunlight and the Day, dismembers his sons, the Twin Warriors, in order to form the vital substances, male and female, into which he then breathes life (Freund 119). With reference to the biblical story of Adam and Eve, J. K. Newberry speculates that the fruit in the Garden of Eden might actually have been another kind of fruit whose name has been changed in translation: the peach, the grape, or the pomegranate. The symbolism of these fruits suggests the kinship of the Eden myth with the myths of such fertility gods as Dionysus and Attis, in which "plucking and eating the pomegranate was the same as slaying and eating the god to assimilate his virtues" (Freund 127-28). Summarizing the implications of Newberry's argument, Freund observes that Adam's sin in eating the fruit may be symbolic of his devouring the young fertility god, as the Titans, Zeus's foes, did with Dionysus. He concludes that "all these myths are linked, for the story of Adam and his original crime goes back to Persian and Vedic roots; as do Greek myths too" (127-28). The possibility of a connection between Eden and child murder is also the focus of anthropological speculation.

In an argument comparing the Paleolithic era to the mythical period before the Fall, Marvin Harris notes that the relatively agreeable lives of hunters and gatherers make it seem unlikely that people ever turned to agriculture as a result of "enlightenment" or "progress." Instead, he speculates that the depletion of big game resources probably made it impossible, at some point, to subsist without resorting to the back-breaking, time-consuming labor of tilling the soil. He therefore asserts that the need for maintaining low population densities in hunting societies probably led to the practice of infanticide even before the economic transition to agriculture, so that the waste of infant lives "lurks in the background of prehistory as an ugly blight in what might otherwise be mistaken for a Garden of Eden" (15-17). Infanticidal interpretations of the story of Eden are, perhaps, a poetic variation of the general suspicion that there may be an intimate connection between the practice of child-murder and the dawn of human society.

Insisting on the peculiarly human quality of infanticidal customs, Darwin noted that "our early semi-human progenitors would not have practiced infanticide . . . for the instincts of the lower animals are never so perverted as to lead them regularly to destroy their own offspring" (430). This view of human creatures was shared by

Aptekar, who described child murder as a function of peculiarly human problem-solving abilities: "Ever since man has been man, he has had enough intelligence for the adoption of infanticide" (179-80). In the same vein, Sumner noted that, at some point in the natural evolution of the family, "children came to be felt as a burden so that 'progress' caused abortion and infanticide" (312). Observations of animal behavior suggest, however, that man is by no means the only creature known to practice infanticide, and Piers cites Jane Goodall's documentation of infanticide among chimpanzees as invaluable in making us see the dangers of being too "high up on the evolutionary ladder." The evidence suggesting that the killing of offspring by parents precedes the earliest beginnings of human experience (Piers 34-36) does not necessarily invalidate Darwin's perception of the peculiar role of infanticide in the development of human culture, because the infanticidal motifs occurring in creation myths suggest that self-conscious realization of the dual possibilities of affirming and denying the powers of generativity was somehow a crucial turning point in the evolution of human culture.

Though it is easy to identify the connection between Medea and creation myths, or between Medea and the reverence for fertility, it is more difficult to argue that an understanding of the reproductive process entails a perception that the process may be controlled, or that such an awareness formed the heart of a work of ancient literature. The difficulty derives at least in part from extra-literary controversy over the social significance of infanticidal practices. Whereas Harris asserts that some form of infanticide was probably the most widely used method of birth control throughout much of human history (5), the economic emphasis of his argument is objectionable to Sheleff, who speculates that destructive hostility to children may transcend all rational considerations. In support of his argument, Sheleff refers to Charles Savage's finding, with respect to the ancient Athenians, that "children were sometimes exposed in order that parents might escape the trouble of rearing them" (Sheleff 195). This objection to the economic focus of Harris' argument seems problematic precisely because there is no easy distinction between "purely economic factors" and population pressure, any more than the "trouble of rearing" children is demonstrably separable from the relative abundance or scarcity of resources required for doing so. The suggestion, furthermore, that adults are inclined to be spontaneously hostile toward children seems quite as arbitrary as the theory that children are innately hostile toward adults. The truth of the matter must certainly lie somewhere between the two extremes, as Sheleff's own assessment of the two-way nature of generational conflict suggests. Parents and children may, by the very nature of things, be more than likely to come into competition for available resources, especially when, as is more often than not the case, those resources are limited. Arguments positing either the older or the younger generation as the source of the difficulty seem equally doubtful.

The question of whether generational hostility originates with parents or with children is related to the question of whether the urge to kill is innate in human beings as an inevitable concomitant of territorial instincts, as Robert Ardrey and Konrad Lorenz argue (Ardrey 315-18; Lorenz 228-65), or whether it is the result of learned reactions to common frustrations, as Marvin Harris and Ashley Montague insist (Harris 33-43; Montague 3-17). Regardless of whether aggression results from instinctive tendencies or from cultural adaptation, whether it is innate in the human infant or is the normal reaction to irritations imposed by adults on their helpless charges, the universally observable fact is that people do hate and fight and kill. Assuming, therefore, merely for the sake of argument, that all human beings are characterized by the presence of a certain capacity to experience murderous rage, there are reasons why social systems would tend to limit and regulate demonstrations of overt aggression beween individual adults and yet tolerate violence by adults against children. The use of force between adults presents a much greater threat to the survival of any community than does the use of force by a full-grown adult against a small child. David Gil argues that the "universal cultural taboos and legal sanctions against the use of physical force in interpersonal relations among adults seem to have evolved out of the recognition of man at the dawn of civilization that there exists an approximate balance of physical force between each adult and every other adult individual," so that the chances of hurting and being hurt are about even in antagonistic physical encounters between adults, and therefore, "forsaking the use of physical force in interaction between adult members of society would increase the chance of survival for all" (8). The death of a certain number of children, on the other hand, poses no threat whatsoever to the continuation of any group. In the context of the enormous human capacity for violence, the small size and inferior strength of children would, in themselves, inevitably contribute toward the abuse of children. Recognition of this circumstance, however, does not preclude the possibility that economic factors may contribute to the destructive violence of parents against children.

The economics of large-scale population pressures in any society are inextricably bound up with the most intimate experience of the smallest social units. Sumner's assertion that even in the absence of anything remotely resembling a population policy, women overburdened by the responsibility of child rearing might refuse to undergo it "for purely egoistic reasons" is not only interesting in that it posits a dynamic connection between the communal economy and the individual impulse, but because his use of the word "egoistic" takes us straight back to the problems of repression, denial, and projection that recur in discussions of the psychology of abuse. The importance of ego defense mechanisms in the emotional profiles of infanticidal adults is, like the general problem of "the labile nature of human parenting" (Piers 34), a result of the complicated and tenuous process by which human cultures nourish and mold the human ego. Even a casual glance at the literature of ego psychology suggests the complexity of the problems involved. Whereas Anna Freud emphasizes the importance of defense mechanisms, Erik Erikson stresses the decisive role of cultural determinants, the process by which "the style of integrity developed by his culture or civilization" becomes the "patrimony of the unique soul" (268). The crucial point for the discussion of infanticide, however, is the basic fact at the root of all the problems of ego psychology, which is that the more highly evolved a creature is, the longer is the period during which the young are dependent on their parents for care, protection and guidance.

The role of culture in the formation of a mature human being is relatively greater than the role of instinct, playing a much more important part than in the maturation of other young creatures. Whereas the cultural component of the human personality is the source of those accomplishments and qualities that most distinguish the human race from other groups of animals, it also constitutes a great margin for error in the developmental process. If we posit even a minimum of ego integrity as essential for the difficult task of raising children, the thought that preparation for such a task is entrusted to the vagaries of culture rather than to any "laws" of nature is, in itself, disquieting. Whereas the complexities of raising human children are relatively greater than the problems of nurturing nonhuman offspring, the procedure for doing so is relatively less dependable. In fact, the burden of rearing the young is so great for human parents that the task can only be done well by a person with a mature sense of self. However, the problems of making the transition from child to adult are such that there is an extremely high likelihood that individuals who are insufficiently mature will be subjected to the pressures of parenthood. The fact that young, unwed mothers are statistically more likely to commit infanticide than other parents (Daly and Wilson 496-97) is interesting but not essential in this connection, because psychological maturity is not necessarily a matter of chronological age.

It may be objected that talk of "ego immaturity" seems particularly out of place in the discussion of a protagonist who is sometimes described as representing the monstrous expansion of the self (Kott 237), rather than any weakness of the ego. In fact, the assumption of formidable strength in a character who kills her children because she is afraid people will laugh at her is a problem in Medea criticism. Bongie comments on Medea's agonizing compliance with a masculine code of honor (39-57), and Helene Foley regards the ancient child-murderer as an essentially reactive character, a "pathetically confused imitator of heroic masculinity." Foley's articulation of "Medea's entrapment in a female role" (74-83) recalls Janeway's perception that aggressive feminine types are only "negative caricatures" of the traditionally "compliant, pleasing woman," rather than personally defined roles. Arguing that the appearance of shrewishness among large numbers of women in a particular epoch is a "specific product of social breakdown" which results from the fact that, in times of stress and change, "it is easier to do the opposite of what was done before than to create something new," Janeway refers to the unwavering ideologues among the female cadres of the Chinese Communist Party, the shrew in Elizabethan England, and the vengeful *tricoteuses* of the French Revolution as illustrative examples (119-22). The suggestion that the ascendance of the witch-figure is a sign of social disruption seems particularly interesting with respect to Medea because dramatic versions of the myth have often been presented in times of great historical upheaval. More generally speaking, the very fact that sex roles are socially prescribed rather than individually defined seems to support Sumner's intuition of a link between seemingly arbitrary individual behavior and unarticulated social forces.

There are some indications that even when infanticide is absolutely forbidden by the moral code of a society, economic pressures on adults may result in a noticeably increased incidence of violence against children. It is a tendency that may be documented by such widely available sources as newspapers or with various erudite and scholarly publications. To begin with the former, we may note the assertion by Vincent Fontana, on the occasion of a grim instance of child-murder that took place during a period of economic stress in New York City: "People get frustrated and take it out on their kids" (Gooding, Johnson, and Egin). For those who prefer more scholarly evidence, there are statistics tracing the rise in the junior age/sex ratios during subsistence crises in Medieval England, and others documenting the atrocious abuses suffered by the children of the poor during periods of unprecedented population growth in Europe (Harris 171; Langer, "Checks" 91-100). I, personally, would prefer to spare the reader the superfluous documentation of the obvious and assert the connection between economic pressures and parental failure as a matter of common sense: if great pressure is brought to bear on large numbers of people, certain individuals, like the weakest links in a chain, will break. Although economic conditions are demonstrably related to the statistical incidence of violence against children, problems of individual psychology are nevertheless paramount in determining where the chain may break.

It is possible to argue that, whatever the causes of destructive aggression against children, the results are always effective in limiting the reproductive potential of the community. Bakan asserts that even where the death of the child does not ensue, child abuse checks the growth of populations by tending to limit the child's eventual procreative capacity: "At the very least, and in fulfillment of commonly held ideals, the judicious use of punishment makes them moral in the sense of inhibiting sexual expression. Thus, even the mildest forms of punishment are in this sense population-controlling" (115). The sensitivity of human sexuality to all manner of psychological disturbances, and the difficulty of raising the human young under even the best of circumstances, would seem to suggest that there is some truth in this assertion. The description by Steele and Pollock of a self-perpetuating culture of abuse in certain families (98), however, complicates the issue. Even if a considerable number of children from such families do die, and the ones who survive to adulthood become problem parents who are likely to abuse their own children, it is not possible to prove Bakan's thesis statistically, because families with histories of child abuse are hardly in danger of dying out. In the last analysis, it is much more certain that child abuse increases the sum total of suffering in the world than that it decreases the number of people.

It is interesting to consider the intuition of a hidden link between "commonly held ideals" and impersonal economic imperatives in the light of reported cases of child abuse by ministers and followers of fundamentalist religions. In the name of morality, children have been given electric shocks, beaten with rulers and ping-pong paddles, and "battered without mercy because they were 'witches, demons, whores, etc.' " (Disend 57-64, 182-87; Lachman 5). Greven recounts the case of a child who was literally "disciplined to death" (38-41), and his analysis of the cultural ramifications of the biblical maxim "spare the rod and spoil the child" stresses the continuity between repressive child rearing practices and authoritarian political agendas (198-204). His argument is consistent with Michael Disend's report on zealots professing that "the ideal system is totalitarian government with a righteous and a pure and godly leader." These bigoted crusaders described Jews as "followers of Satan" and asserted that the "obvious evils" of institutions that are "witch cults" should be "cleaned out." Presumably offended by the destruction of human life, they condemn abortion as murder, while conceding the necessity of capital punishment, and even advocating executions for such "offenses" as abortion and homosexuality (Disend 186). Their zeal for punishment is arguably a grim example of "unconscious rationality" in action. As if certain manifestations of enthusiastic bloodlust were in conformity with some essential hidden imperative, those who refuse to allow one form of population control regularly subscribe to other policies that could ultimately have a compensatory effect. The fact that corporal and capital punishment necessarily entail a much greater toll in human suffering than abortion or homosexuality might seem to be the very reason why they are preferred by some repressive and fanatic groups. To the degree that this is so, it is one more demonstration of the inseparability of individual psychology and social conditions. Although the evidence of unconscious connections between personal and communal purposes suggests that we need not insist on a great deal of demographic sophistication, either in the ancient parents who practiced infanticide or in the writers whose work reflects the world they lived in, I nevertheless believe that ancient authors were probably more aware of the population-controlling implications of certain themes than we often suppose.

With regard to the Tikopia, a people living on a small Polynesian island whose "principal means of population control were infanticide, celibacy, and suicidal sea voyages by young men," Laila Williamson observes that they themselves were quite aware "of the delicate balance between population and resources, and were concerned about the consequences of interference by Europeans." To the Tikopia, "the upsetting of an economic and social system, which would bring suffering and misery to many was more wrong than quietly disposing of superfluous infants" (67). The first point of interest in this report is that it would make sense to allow that citizens of Athens in the fifth century B.C.E. were capable of the same level of awareness concerning population dynamics as the inhabitants of an island-dwelling society in Polynesia, even if we did not know that the exposure of infants at Athens was common. Secondly, the mention of "suicidal voyages by young men" is especially interesting if we consider that the story of Jason and the Argonauts may reasonably be described as a ship-load of young men who were sent off on a sea voyage from which they were not expected to return.

On the subject of conceptual connections between the adventuring Argonauts and the theme of population pressure, consider the following passage:

Young scions were then pushed out from the parent-stock, and instructed to explore fresh regions, and to gain happier seats for themselves by their swords . . . . Restless from present distress, flushed with the hope of fairer prospects, and animated with the spirit of hardy enterprise, these daring adventurers were likely to become formidable adversaries to all who opposed them. . . . And when they fell in with any tribes like their own, the contest was a struggle for existence, and they fought with a desperate courage, inspired by the reflection that death was the punishment of defeat and life the prize of victory. (83-84)

The "young scions" and "daring adventurers" of this passage are not Jason and his Minyans; the "parent-stock" does not include Pelias; the "powerful motive" is not the quest for the Golden Fleece, nor is that fleece the "prize of victory." This passage is, in fact, a description by Thomas Malthus of the barbarous and abundant Scyths who overwhelmed their neighbors by force of numbers. That an excerpt from the famous *Essay on the Principle of Population* (47-48) reads like a comment on the epic background of the myth of Medea may serve to remind us that infanticide is only the most obvious of the commonly mentioned population-controlling practices that are analogous to thematic elements of the myth of Medea.

Considering the importance of the theme of witchcraft in all versions of the Medea story, it is worth noting that executions for witchcraft have been considered an important, if unintentional, means of limiting population in the many societies that have practiced such punishments (Aptekar 158). Large-scale executions of women are an effective means of diminishing the reproductive capacity of a group because the procreative potential of any community corresponds directly to the number of adult women in that group, a circumstance that prompts Harris to observe that most men are reproductively superfluous in any community (39). The connection between witch hunts and population pressure is to be inferred, however, not only from the "unapprehended result" of such policies, but also from the fact that separate acts of persecution may "proceed from the immediate interest" of particular individuals. Thus, in early modern Europe, many so-called witches were victims of an exclusively male medical profession for which female midwives and healers represented competition; the womens' accusers had a vested interest in discrediting and destroying them (Ehrenreich and English 17-19). Both the causes and the results of executions for witchcraft are associated with the same kind of economic factors that generally contribute to the oppression of minority groups. In the most notorious example of witch hunting in modern times, the mass murder of European Jews was prepared by the rhetoric of "Lebensraum" and the goal of "ending unemployment." To argue the importance of economic pressures is not to deny the operation of such ephemeral matters as the "spirit of the times," but merely to insist that belief and expediency may sometimes serve one another.

Even such ostensibly theological matters as religious rituals of human sacrifice are regularly articulated in economic metaphors that are highly suggestive of the supply-and-demand logic of population theory. Stern calls human sacrifice "a kind of life insurance for the survivors" (324), and Eliade refers to ritual sacrifice in certain societies as a means of ensuring "the circulation of the sacred energy between different regions of the Cosmos." In this vein, he presents a striking analysis of the spiritual economics of infant sacrifice in ancient times: "The blood of the child thus augmented the spent energy of the god, for the so-called fertility divinities expended their own substance in the efforts required to sustain the world and ensure its wealth; they were in need themselves, therefore, of being regenerated from time to time" (*Myths, Dreams and Mysteries* 142). The expression of the general dynamics of ritual sacrifice in terms of "augmenting spent energy," "expending substance" and "ensuring wealth" might be dismissed as a somewhat poetic analogy, were it not for the extensive evidence that economic factors may enter into the execution of religious policies as varied as the Crusades, the Inquisition, the Salem witchcraft trials, taboos on the eating of beef by Hindus and pork by Jews, and human sacrifice among the Aztecs. In a controversial study of the latter phenomenon, Sherbournc Cook observed that no purely religious urge, however powerful, "can maintain itself successfully for any material period of time counter to fundamental economic resistance" (Harris 107). Without discounting the importance of religious feelings and experience, we may affirm the part played by economic factors in defining the characteristic manifestation of devotion in a particular time and place.

Of all the population-controlling practices related to thematic elements of the myth of Medea, the most important is war, the classic "check" of Malthusian argument. Since the themes of war and infanticide are all but inseparable in the Euripidean prototype of the drama, it is important to note that war and female infanticide have been intimately connected in discussions of population dynamics. Harris describes war and infanticide as complementary customs deriving from the threat of starvation, asserting that "without reproductive pressure, neither warfare nor female infanticide would have become widespread and the conjunction of the two represents a savage but uniquely effective solution to the Malthusian dilemma" (41). In this instance, the apparent discrepancy between the anthropological emphasis on female infanticide and the dramatic focus on the murder of Jason's male progeny is easily resolved. Because the demographic pattern and the tragic structure are both consistent with the essential preference for males in warlike societies where the death of a male child is a greater loss than that of a female child, the killing of little boys is a particularly appropriate subject for tragedy. The act of child murder in *Medea* is, like the theme of ritual sacrifice in the *Oresteia* and *Iphigeneia in Aulis*, a symbol of the atrocious waste of war. Described by Eliade as "a decadent ritual in which a holocaust of innumerable victims is offered up to the gods of victory" (*Myths, Dreams and Mysteries* 200), and by Gaston Bouthoul as a kind of "deferred infanticide" (3-35), war is the stark field against which the figures of Jason and Medea emerge in the Euripidean scenario. The essential point for the present argument is that war, in this tragedy, is intertwined with a network of themes, all of which evoke the macabre spectacle of depopulation. Although it would be a mistake to posit an oversimplified interpretation of the themes of infanticide, witchcraft, ritual sacrifice, suicidal sea voyages, and war, it would be nonetheless an error to deny the individual writer a certain awareness of the larger implications of particular subthemes. Euripides, for instance, refers to war as the dismal remedy for earth's burden of mortality in several tragedies. In *Helen*, he says that Zeus "loaded war upon the Hellenic land and on/ the unhappy Phrygians, thus to drain our mother earth/ of the burden and the multitude of human kind" (lines 38-40). In *Orestes*, he describes the gods as having driven "Trojans and Greeks together in war/ and made them die that earth might be lightened/ of her heavy burden of mortality" (1640-42).

Population pressure is the hidden common denominator between the tribal migrations and wars that are as essential to an understanding of the historical, political, and social aspects of the tragedy of *Medea* as the concepts of the witch, the Jew, and the infanticidal mother are essential to the general delineation of character as projection of infanticidal wish. Although I have stressed the importance of economic factors in the discussion of cosmic issues, and psychological factors in the analysis of character, the crucial element of hostility to children is common to both the Malthusian and the Freudian visions. Malthus' description of the dynamic imperatives that prompt tribal migrations is, after all, quite similar to Freud's myth of the primal horde. The emphasis on sexual desire and the retaliatory murder of the patriarch by the frustrated sons may be absent from the Malthusian scenario, but the fundamental image of the generation of want by competition between fathers and sons is implicit in both conceptions of the remote past. In any case, the infanticidal themes of the tragedy of Medea are, without exception, related to political, social, and economic concerns of the first magnitude. Medea does not have a "Medea Complex" any more than Oedipus has an "Oedipus Complex." The importance of affairs of state in this play seem especially evident if the Euripidean tragedy is considered in the light of another famous fifth-century Athenian drama.

In denying Jason issue, Medea poses exactly the same threat to established order that Lysistrata presents in leading a sex strike. That we think of these two female protagonists as being poles apart is a measure, more than anything, of the formal difference between comedy and tragedy. We tend to consider *Medea* the tragedy of failed generativity, and *Lysistrata* the comedy of sexual frustration, forgetting that both infanticide and enforced celibacy have actually served to limit the reproductivity of various societies (Williamson 61-70; Langer, "Checks" 91-100). Furthermore, the extent to which generativity and sexuality are interconnected in the minds of the ancients is nowhere more apparent than in the fact that children are as essential to the comedy of *Lysistrata* as sex. *Lysistrata,* no less than *Medea,* is a play about a fight between male and female in which the stakes are children. *Lysistrata,* no less than *Medea,* is a play about the death of children. Lysistrata laments for the children of Athens, "Borne but to perish afar and in vain," and she states the problem in economic terms: "For I'm taxed too, and as a toll provide men for the nation." Finally when the young husband lures his wife out of the barricade of women in hopes of having sex with her, he does so by playing on her fear for the life of her child: "There now, don't you feel pity for the child?/ He's not been fed or washed now for six days" (Aristophanes 307, 310, 316). The contrast between the young father's abundantly visible readiness to engender new offspring and his cheerful indifference to the needs of the one he already has contributes much to the brilliance of an uproariously funny scene, yet the fact of the matter is that when you talk about not feeding and bathing a child for six days, you are talking about letting him die. Between letting a child die and killing him there exists the subtle distinction between sins of omission and sins of commission that occurs in clinical discussions of such phenomena as child-murder, child abuse, and harmful neglect. There is probably no surer indication that the appeal of infanticidal motifs depends on latent hostility to children than the fact that presentations of such material can provide comic as well as tragic pleasure.

It may be objected that the several points of comparison between *Lysistrata* and *Medea* are not so much remarkable textual similarities as corollaries of the fact that both plays were inspired by the same crisis of culture. But *Lysistrata* and *Medea* have both enjoyed popular revivals in modern times precisely because that crisis continues to be endemic in human culture. Although the official policy of ancient societies was concerned with the positive value of fertility rather than with the seemingly negative concept of birth control, the rituals out of which the ancient theater developed are all bound up with the creation myths implicit in the conceptual matrix from which the myth of Medea derives. It is in the nature of fertility rituals to enact the death of certain individuals in order to ensure the survival of others. Just as the question of who should be sacrificed has everything to do with the traditional characterization of the Medea persona, so the question of why some must die in order that others may live has everything to do with the social significance of the tragedy of Medea.

2

Euripides and the Tyranny of Honor

The question of moral responsibility for the disastrous denouement of the *Medea* has provoked a variety of answers, some of which stress the pathology of individual characters while others emphasize the predominance of particular mental functions. The mutually contradictory quality of certain positions is worth noting. Thus, Sale insists on Jason's "neurosis" (34), while Pucci deplores Medea's "abnormal psychology" (155); Mallinger's assertion that Medea kills her children "in obedience to a higher law of justice" (50) emphasizes the role of conscience, and Kott's observation that, in Euripides, "the id revolting against the superego is personified by woman" (224) suggests the operation of uncontrolled passion. On the other hand, interpretations focusing on the problematic quality of familial and social relationships tend to be consistent with each other. Analyses by Easterling and Simon linking literary structure with the psychology of abuse complement readings by Reckford, who underscores the "psychological consequences" of the "social mistreatment" of women (341), and Foley, who examines the abusive potential of sexist customs and discourse in the Euripidean text, arguing that "the heroic code itself oppresses women" (79). Simon's view of Euripidean art as dramatizing the process by which traumatized people move from a "passive position to the active one of traumatizing others" (81-82) emphasizes the interpersonal origin of Medea's dreadful revenge in a way that makes it difficult to avoid the human relevance of the act of child-murder. An examination of the degree to which the psychology of abuse pervades the world of this play would be justified if only for the purpose of reclaiming the humanity of a character whose criminal deeds are often dismissed as the work of a wicked witch or a perverse deity.

      Whereas an appreciation of the human significance of tragedy suggests the advisability of great caution in exploring the metaphorical implications of Medea's excesses, the temptation to attribute the act of child-murder to a witch-like character is persistent. Thus, Reckford insists on the process of "psychological deterioration" by which "the woman Medea is transformed . . . into the unequivocal witch of legend" (339, 342, 359), while Bongie and Foley seem to assume the essentially static nature of Medea's character, regarding the presentation of tragic action as a revelation of superhuman power rather than the disastrous development of an essentially human problem. Bongie's assessment of Medea as an indomitable dissembler who manipulates the image of "the passive and suffering woman, helplessly wasting away" (34), and Foley's reference to "the feminine mask" that "gradually slips to reveal first an archaic hero and then a near goddess" (77), tend to minimize the problem of Medea's actual suffering. Assuming the illusory nature of her vulnerability, they suggest that she has always been a superhuman force, and that her final ascent in the chariot of the gods is merely the unveiling of her omnipotence. Although the Nurse's early warning that Medea is not likely to yield before an attacker (44-45) may lend some support to this argument, it does not undo the general effect of Euripides' characterization of Medea as a human figure whose grief is entirely credible. Yet Easterling notes that "Euripides keeps close to observed patterns of human behavior," (188) and I will argue that Medea's "victory" is disturbing precisely because it dramatizes a psychological development that is all too recognizable.

Medea's transition from misery to triumph is analogous to the process whereby dependent children initially dominated by adult figures learn, through interaction with playmates and mentors, to exercise control over themselves, to negotiate on equal terms with peers, and eventually, to govern their own dependents. Since the action of the play takes place in a society where economics and politics are organized so as to exalt the exercise of power to the level of a moral absolute, the discourse of the characters reflects both the ethical standard of the group and the frustration of particular individuals with the uneven and hierarchical distribution of power. Having accepted a code exalting freedom and mastery, Medea chafes in the role of the trapped and dominated subject. The single most essential attribute of her character is a cruel conscience that mirrors the adamant imperatives implicit in her world and will not allow her to accept the inglorious role of homeless mother with dispossessed children. Her grief is emblematic of the fundamental contradictions in ancient Greek society, and the Chorus' sympathy for her suggests a community of interest between the defiant protagonist and the exploited groups on whose continued subjection Athenian "democracy" depended. In the *Medea*, Euripides presented in dramatic terms the likely result of a decision on the part of the underlings to act in accordance with the precepts of their masters. Thus, the act of child murder in this play is not simply the result of mental deterioration or the manifestation of divine power, but the dynamic culmination of an ordinary psychological process that regularly results in the death of children—sometimes metaphorically, sometimes literally.

The assumption of adult status in any authoritarian system entails a psychological transformation of the child-subject into an adult authority. The protagonist in this masterpiece of personal and political psychology makes the complete transition from afflicted child to persecutory parent, and the structure of the drama reflects her gradual acquisition of increasing power in her dealings with other characters. In the first episode, when she confronts Creon, she is clearly under his sway. Concerning this scene, it is not enough to say that the relationship between subject and sovereign is analogous to that between child and parent. When Creon addresses Medea as a fool and commands her to crawl away (333), almost as if she were a snake or a worm, his language suggests the dehumanizing potential of the master-slave relationship. The abject obedience he demands could only be expected of a child, a slave, a beast, or a woman. Since the situation requires it, Medea is fawning and conciliatory, but, after he leaves, her anger at herself for groveling at the foot of the tyrant erupts in the aggressively defiant question she hurls at the Chorus: "Do you think that I would ever have flattered this man if I had not been devising a plan or getting something out of it?" (368-69). In this passage, it is worth noting that the question of what the Corinthian women think of Medea is not entirely distinguishable from what she thinks of herself.

In the episode with Jason that follows the one with Creon, Medea confronts a figure who, although he is more or less her equal, presumes to exercise the power of a superior. The destructive potential of Jason's arrogance is evident in the negativity of his language, especially his rather conventional wish that children could be engendered without recourse to the "female race" (573-74). In this exchange, Jason demonstrates that power may depend on denial rather than affirmation, and Medea's parting words to him—"You marry in such a way as to deny yourself a marriage" (626)—suggest that she has learned her lesson well. Finally, in the scene with Aegeus, Medea confers with an august authority who promises her the support and approval she needs to defeat her enemies. Only through her alliance with the ironically well-meaning Aegeus does Medea emerge with the confidence of an established power to assert with terrible simplicity that she will kill her children (792). Thus, the first episode shows Medea as the passive recipient of abuse, the second presents her parrying insults with a peer, and the third casts her as the talented protégée of a powerful mentor. With the assumption of vindictive authority, her transition from persecuted child to tyrannical adult is complete, and the murder of Medea's own children, far from being a gratuitous incident, is a dynamic development which originates in the logic of victim and aggressor that is the bedrock of this tragedy.

Rationally speaking, of course, one might object that a person with access to a dragon chariot might dispense with the assistance of any mere mortal. According to this logic, Medea does not need to confer with Aegeus. For that matter, however, she does not really need to bicker with Creon or Jason, and least of all does she need to carry on about Jason's defection in the first place. But the truth of tragedy does not lie in the construction of rational argument; it lies in the presentation of emotional realities. In this connection, it is worth noting that of the three above-mentioned episodes, the one with Aegeus has, since the time of Aristotle, been especially troubling to critics. Whereas Schlesinger's speculation on the dramatic relevance of the episode (88) is affirmed by Easterling, who asserts that "the essential relevance of the scene must be its stress on the value and importance of children" (185), T.B.L. Webster objects that "the idea that Aegeus' childlessness suggested to Medea that she should make Jason childless is attractive, but Euripides would have told the audience if he had wanted them to think this. What he has told the audience is that Medea hates her children" (54). His observation is important in that it shifts the critical focus from details of logic and strategy to the fundamental emotional problem in this tragedy, but Webster does not go far enough. What is remarkable about this play is not the animosity of any particular individual toward the children, but the way in which all visible social structures and sanctions seem to conspire against the children. Before any of the principal players ever makes an entrance, we are told that Medea hates her children (36), that Jason does not love his children (88), that he treats his loved ones badly (84), and furthermore, that in this he is probably no worse than any man in the audience (85). That we are all implicated in the crimes of omission and commission perpetrated by Jason and Medea is precisely the message that such techniques as excessive emphasis on individual character or the isolation of discourse from historical context may serve to obscure. An interesting example is the case in which the text clearly states the desire that the children had never been born and the critic infers the wish that they had not been killed.

Speculating that the tragedy of Medea is contained, as if parenthetically, "between two desires that the action should not have happened" (36), Pucci cites, as the first of these desires, the opening lines of the Nurse, expressing the wish that the Argos had not sailed from Colchis through the Symplegades, that the timber to build the ship had not been cut down, and that the hands of the best men had never rowed out to sea in quest of the Golden Fleece (1-6). In wishing, however, that all the events leading up to the birth of the children had never happened, the Nurse may be regarded as opening the drama with a wish that the children had never been born in the first place. Just such a wish is blatantly stated by Jason at the end of the play when he refers to the dead bodies of the children he "ought never to have begotten to see them killed" by their mother (1413-14). Inseparable as this wish is from Jason's immediate sense of personal loss, the actual words he speaks express a desire that the children had never been born. Although the sentiment uttered is equivalent to that implied in the Nurse's opening speech, the claim that it negates the central action of the tragedy is doubtful. Pucci's reading of such "wishes" is, however, quite consistent with his observation that the Chorus' lengthy complaint about the trials and tribulations of raising children is "really not . . . so much against children as against our painful involvement in the misfortunes of people we love" (146). I believe, however, that in this tragedy culminating in the murder of children, the language that prepares the way for the central action regularly expresses antagonism toward children.

The tragedy of *Medea* may be read as a constant restatement of the wish that the children did not exist. Medea states the inconvenience of their existence bluntly enough: "If you were still childless, your wanting this marriage would be forgivable" (490-91). When the Tutor tells the Nurse of Creon's plans, he states first that the children are to be banished, and only afterwards adds that their mother will go with them: "I heard someone saying that Creon, the ruler of Corinth, is about to drive these children out of this land with their mother" (67-72). This articulation is a noteworthy reflection of the circumstance that the children themselves represent a threat to the royal succession in a way that Medea does not. The most spontaneous and gratuitous representation of hostility toward children in the entire play is, indeed, the reaction of Jason's new bride when his children show up: "But then she covered her eyes and turned her pale cheek away from the children, disgusted at their entrance" (1147-49). The choral song from lines 1081 to 1115 is, moreover, as direct a statement of the frustrations of parenthood as has ever been written. Most significantly, the Chorus says that "those who do not have children get further in fortune than those who do" (1090-93). Rather than being bracketed parenthetically within two wishes that negate its central action, this tragedy is replete with various statements of the problem posed by the presence of the children. If, indeed, the expressions of hostility to children contained within this play are regarded as separate instances of negation, then the Euripidean tragedy follows the logic of ancient Greek grammar, in which the effect of repeated negation is cumulative; the statements of negative desire by the Nurse and Jason are only the most conspicuously placed of many suggestions that the world presented by this play is one in which the lives of the children define the terms of the adult predicament and set the limits of adult possibility. If we consider that the existence of the children constitutes a factor in the scheme of the drama that negates the things that all of the adults would affirm with their lives, the precariousness of the children's situation stands out in stark relief. The best way to demonstrate the strength of this assertion is to examine the nature of the adult values and aspirations presented in the text.

Vellacott credits Euripides with putting the most perceptive judgments into the mouths of his least imposing characters (218), and it is, in fact, the Tutor who makes the most generally applicable statement concerning the dynamics of adult behavior in this play. When the Nurse denounces Jason as being unkind to his loved ones, the Tutor responds with a question: "But who of mortals is not?" (85). He proceeds to articulate the principle of egotistic self-interest as a universal condition: "Just now you notice this, that each and every man loves himself rather than his neighbor?" (85-86). Granting that a certain amount of generosity and selflessness are required for the nurturing of children, the vision of a world where adults are routinely selfish and competitive is hardly reassuring with respect to the survival of offspring. Although the Tutor admits that self-love may, in some cases, be justified, he does not seem inclined to make such an exception for Jason, suggesting, rather, that he is one who acts "for the sake of gain" and concluding that "their father does not love these children." Whereas the statement criticizing Jason is conditional—"if, for a new marriage, their father does not love these children" (87-88)—the condition under which it would be true is the apparent state of affairs, and so that Jason's not loving his sons is, from the very beginning of the play, given parity with Medea's hating them (36). While the basis of Jason's self-love is arguably less justified than Medea's, the effect of the dramatic action is to question every standard of justice articulated in the text. We may sympathize with Medea because her essentially defensive position compares favorably with Jason's enterprising offensive strategies, or because her actions conform to her ideals, in stark contrast with Jason's vain and capricious inconsistencies. Yet, Medea and Jason both justify their unjustifiable actions in terms of the same code of honor, the importance of which has been eloquently stressed by many scholars, including Knox, who describes Medea as heroic in the Sophoclean manner (297), Bongie, who observes that if "Medea is not acceptable to our own moral code, she is, in the code of the ancient heroic system, a veritable 'saint' " (55), and Foley, for whom Medea's "heroism" reflects both "the avenging archaic warrior Achilles and the clever and crafty Odysseus" (81).

Foley's analysis of conflict in *Medea* as a debate between masculine heroic and feminine nurturing forces is an essential articulation of the sexual politics inherent in the text. Describing Medea's ordeal as issuing in "the death and betrayal of her maternal self" and the Euripidean drama as a critical examination of "masculine heroism and masculine ethics" (82-83), she sheds considerable light on the subversive implications of the text. Her reading of the play is not, however, without its problematic aspects. The conclusion that

"Medea's inability to trust her maternal voice . . . destroys our hopes for a more enlightened form of human ethics, the authoritative female identity and integrity that could contest masculine ethics, whether archaic or contemporary" (83) seems inconsistent with Foley's own sensible observation that "for Euripides' audience a proper Greek wife had no fully autonomous self, no muse, no public voice" (77). In the absence of just such a "public voice," just what "hopes" may we reasonably nourish? Like Pucci's description of Medea as abandoning the morality of the slaves and espousing the morality of the masters (61-66), the conception of the character ignoring her own "maternal voice" suggests a parity between masculine and feminine ethical imperatives that seems rather anachronistic. As recently as 1933, Freud speculated that women are "weaker in their social instincts" and less capable of sublimation than men (*S.E.* 22:134), and it was only in 1982 that Carol Gilligan demonstrated the insufficiency of ethical paradigms derived from masculine experience for evaluating peculiarly feminine ethical perspectives. In fact, Gilligan's emphasis on "the silence of women" and "the difficulty of hearing what they say when they speak" (173) seems peculiarly relevant to the discussion of a text in which a community of women participates with the criminal protagonist in a conspiracy of silence, and the only person who anticipates disaster is a female servant to whom nobody pays much attention. Although the logic of coexisting moralities is appealing, Katha Pollitt's observation that "there is only one culture, and it shapes each sex in distinct but mutually dependent ways in order to reproduce itself" (806) is probably at least as relevant to the ancient Greeks as to ourselves. In any case, the consistency with which the "slaves" adhere to the "morality" of the masters contributes a good deal to the horror of this play, and the unequal distribution of power between male and female participants suggests that the antagonism between man and woman is complicated by the problem of reconciling the role of the compliant child with the integrity of a self-respecting adult.

Although it is something of a truism that patriarchal constraint tends to infantilize the traditional wife and mother, Gilligan's focus on the inconsistency between masculine ideals and feminine development is especially illuminating with respect to the moral dilemmas confronting individual women: "the conflict between self and other constitutes the central moral problem for women, posing a dilemma whose resolution requires a reconciliation between femininity and adulthood" (Gilligan 71). If Medea's crisis is regarded as a conflict between the claims of "femininity and adulthood" rather than a confrontation between the alternate claims of maternal and heroic ethics, the difficulty of her situation becomes all the more apparent, because she may only save her children by accepting a demeaning and tenuous status for herself. The precarious condition of the child in antiquity suggests, moreover, that the "demotion" Medea faces may entail, over and above the humiliating loss of dignity, an implied threat to life itself. In order to appreciate the terrifying potential for violence between adults and children in ancient Greece, we may consider the relationship between children and stepparents, which is an important element in the context of this play.

In an age when frequent divorce and remarriage make it expedient to discredit the myth of the wicked stepmother, we may with difficulty comprehend the traditional distrust of stepparents. The Euripidean interest in the dangers endured by stepchildren is apparent in the plots of many extant plays, such as the *Ion*, the *Electra,* and the *Alcestis,* as well as in plays of which only fragments remain, such as *Aegeus, Ino, Phrixus*, and *Kresphontes*. The problem is clearly stated in *Alcestis*, when the dying wife pleads with her husband not to remarry lest his new wife abuse the children of his first marriage. Though it would be difficult to imagine a more benign character than the woman who agrees to give up her own life in order to save her husband, Alcestis indicates, in her speech denouncing the cruelty and treachery of stepmothers, that she wants for her children exactly what Jason and Medea want for themselves—security and power (Euripides, *Alcestis* 304-10). The model of the good wife, Alcestis may die content as long as she has assured herself the triumph of her own reputation and the eventual exercise of power through her children. That these are things for which a woman might not only die but also kill is evidenced by the story of Ino, who, in marrying Athamas, was so eager to assure the inheritance of her own children that she tried to kill Phrixus and Helle, the children of Athamas' first marriage.

The importance of Ino for the *Medea* is emphasized by the choral reference to her immediately after Medea murders the children (1284). Referring to Ino's eventual murder of her own children, the Chorus reminds the audience of a mythical sequence of events which is linked to the story of Jason and Medea in several ways. According to legend, Jason was related to Athamas, both Athamas and Jason's grandfather Cretheus being sons of Aeolus (Apollonius Rhodius 3: 356-66); the quest for the Golden Fleece would never have been offered to Jason as a challenge if Phrixus and Helle had not fled from the wrath of their stepmother on the back of a talking ram with golden fleece that carried Phrixus to the land of Colchis. When the ram was killed, his fleece was enshrined in the sacred wood of Apollo, where it was protected by a serpent until Jason, with the help of Medea and her drugs, was able to retrieve it. The significance of this story is such that the very mention of Ino's name would probably suffice to make the Greek audience apprehensive regarding the probable fate of any children entrusted to the care of Jason's new wife, even if the Euripidean delineation of Creusa's spontaneous revulsion at the sight of Jason's sons were not so emphatically disturbing. In any case, it is unlikely that, with Ino's name echoing in their minds, the members of the audience would have missed the irony in Jason's indignant denial that a Greek woman would ever do such a thing as kill her own children (1339-40). The difficulty of leaving the children in their father's care is so obvious that few critics have questioned the validity of Medea's refusal to "leave them on hostile soil to be assaulted by enemies" (781-82, 1060-61, 1238-39).

The survival of the Greek child was so much a function of paternal responsibility that the infant was not even considered human until after a ceremony was performed in which the father signaled that the child was to be nurtured and not "exposed" (Sheleff 194-95). The degree to which the well-being of children depended on material provision by the father regularly gave rise to vicious competition between mothers of different children by the same man. That the obligation to provide for offspring represented a considerable burden for a married man is reflected in the ancient Greek language by the fact that marriage was called a "yoke" to be borne by the man. Medea says women are lucky if their husbands bear the yoke not by force, but willingly (242), and Aegeus lets Medea know that he is married by saying that he is not "unyoked of marriage" (673). Curiously enough, when Aegeus invites Medea to come to Athens, he does not mention the children, and she does not ask if she may bring them with her. This might be taken to mean that it goes without saying that the children would share in the bounties of Athenian hospitality as surely as their mother. Yet there may exist at least the hint of a question concerning the fate of the children when they get to Athens in the opening lines of the choral ode in celebration of Athens: "prosperous descendants of Erechtheus and children well-favored by the gods in ancient times" (824-25). The founding father thus revered is one who sacrificed his daughter, Otonia, in order to secure an Athenian victory. Thus, the allusion may be read as an ironic reminder that even the sanctuary of Athens was originally founded on the principle that some children must die in order that others might live.

This famous choral passage actually mentions a number of mythical figures whose names are not only associated with Athens, but also with the terrible tales of particular children. Along with the reference to Erechtheus, the one to "fair-haired Harmonia" (832) may be considered as having a vaguely dreadful resonance. Of Harmonia's four daughters, Agave and Ino killed their own children, while Semele bore the child, Dionysus, who was dismembered and devoured by the Titans; Autonoë, who joined her sister in the revels that were the undoing of her nephew, Pentheus, was the mother of Actaeon, who paid a heavy penalty for offending the goddess, Artemis. There is, moreover, at least a possibility that the allusions to Erechtheus and Harmonia may have been auxiliary to the generally ominous association between the dramatic spectacle of the homeless mother and child and the numbers of refugee women and children from the Attic countryside to which Athens opened its gates in the early spring of 431 B.C.E., in preparation for the Spartan invasion (Thucydides

2:14-17). Although the oration of Pericles abounds with optimism and confidence (Thucydides 2:60-64), the spectacle of so many vulnerable human beings crowded into spaces that were not prepared to accommodate them must surely have troubled some thoughtful observers. Such misgivings would prove well founded with the outbreak of plague in the following year. It is, therefore, altogether possible that the naive benignity of Aegeus' invitation to Medea contained an ironic suggestion, for the contemporary audience, of the infeasibility of extending the hospitality of the polis beyond its capacity to support its members. The Athenian audience would not have to be told that if Medea and her children were to find a secure future in Athens, they would have to depend, not only on the generosity of the city, but on the dubious enterprise of finding a male provider.

Even if she does remarry, Medea cannot thereby assure the safety of her children, the reputation of stepfathers for promoting the welfare of stepchildren being hardly better than that of stepmothers. In the recurring myth of the woman whose second marriage joins her to the man who killed her first husband in battle, the children of the first marriage are murdered in order to eliminate the possibility of eventual revenge. Such was the fate of Astyanax, son of Hector and Andromache, and also of Clytemnestra's son by a marriage prior to the one with Agamemnon (Euripides, *Iphigeneia in Aulis* 1150-52). Euripides dealt with mythical stepfathers in the *Electra* and also in the fragmentary *Kresphontes*. In these two stories, the infant son, who is hidden and saved from death, returns in early adulthood to challenge or murder his mother's new husband. Although Medea has not, like Andromache or Clytemnestra, been taken as a prize in battle, she must still contend with the reluctance of men to bear the "yoke" of marriage for other men's children, a problem that prompts Velacott to speculate, with respect to Alcestis, that the decision to die in her husband's place is less a matter of altruism than a realistic concession to the practical problem of providing for the children: "If Alcestis as a widow had married again, she would have bought her own prosperity at the cost of her children's; this she will not do" (105). If this is true of Alcestis, we may judge accordingly the despair of a woman for whom her children's safety cannot be bought at any price.

Of the options open to Medea, neither leaving her sons nor taking them with her will assure their well-being in the absence of a father's protection. The insolubility of her problem is acknowledged by the Chorus, which describes her predicament as a piece of divine mischief: ὡς εἰς ἄπορον σε κλύδωνα θεός,/ Μήδεια, κακῶν ἐπόρευσε (A god has guided you here, Medea, into an impassable flood of evils, 362-63). As significant as the qualifier "impassable" (ἄπορον) is the choral invocation of Medea as fruitless: μελέα τῶν σῶν ἀχέων (wretched of your own grief, 358). μελέα, meaning both "wretched" and "fruitless," is a word spoken by Medea herself in her first woeful lamentation, before she even enters on stage at the beginning of the play: ἰω,/ δύστανος ἐγὼ μελέα τε πόνων (Oh miserable and without fruit from my labors, 96). It is hard to see how the final act of child-murder could ever have been considered inconsistent or gratuitous in connection with a character who mourns the fruitlessness of her womb before ever coming out on stage.

That she has been deprived of the "fruit of her labor" is the essential fact of Medea's predicament, and it is also the basis of the common bond between her and the Corinthian women. The solitary lament that Medea first utters in isolation assumes the form of a communal complaint when she tells Creon that she has labored but not been given the fruits of her labor (334). In her use of the first person plural during the confrontation with the king, there is a suggestion that Medea is not voicing a purely personal grievance. Her position is equivalent to that of the women of the Chorus, who do not enjoy the status of citizens and yet are expected to display the same loyalty to invested authority as those who exercise full civic privileges. This is why she speaks for them, as they so often speak for her. Her complaint expresses the collective resentment of women required to supply the human fodder for military machines that may, at best, make token acknowledgment of their contribution. Though the subjects' identification with an idealized concept of authority may enable them to accept the objectives of the incumbent rulers, it will reconcile them to their own subservient position only with great difficulty. Hitler, for example, would probably not have been able to do quite as much damage as he did if many people listening to the rhetoric of the master race had ever imagined themselves as being slaves. The essential source of discord in this play is that Jason and Creon expect Medea to act like a slave while she insists, uncooperatively, on thinking of herself as one of the masters. There is every indication, moreover, that the Chorus of women takes vicarious pleasure in Medea's successful defiance of authority. The justice of her case is, curiously enough, no more disputed by her enemies than by her friends. Even Jason does not take issue with Medea's accusation that he has deprived her of the comfort and pleasure the children might bring her; he counters her indignation with a simple question that suggests that children are, for him, the means to a coveted end: "Why are children necessary for you, anyway?" (565). His own "use" for children is explained in his second meeting with Medea, when he cheerfully speculates on the prospect of having grown-up sons to help him out in his military campaigns (920-21). Since Medea is a woman and will not engage in battle, and since the essential utility of sons is to grow up and fight their father's enemies, she should have no use for the boys. His logic is unencumbered by any consideration that the survival of children is only assured to the degree that it may be regarded as an end in itself and not subservient to any ultimate "use" or purpose.

A skeptical examination of the world which this play presents might lead us to conclude that the children are doomed precisely because everybody around them regards them as a means to an end. Whereas Jason sees them as military reinforcements, Medea considers them her social security: "Really, wretched me, I had ever much hope in you, to take care of me in my old age, and dying in your hands to be clothed well, an enviable thing for men" (1332-35). Though there is more than a little selfishness in the attitude of both parents toward the children, a comparison of the two of them shows Medea in a better light than Jason. Jason is not only selfish but also belligerent and offensive, conceiving of the children as weapons against his enemies when the only foes in sight are allies whom he has attacked. Selfish as it may seem at certain moments, Medea's perception of the children is defensive rather than offensive. They would have been her bulwark against the natural calamity which must be the lot of every mortal creature. Although she finally accedes to the warlike logic that seems to be the human standard in her world, Medea nevertheless inspires more sympathy than Jason because she does not regard the children primarily as tactical auxiliaries.

In view of Piers' observations on the way in which infanticide may be promoted by "those who fail to see it" (16), the choral complaint that Jason harms his children by not seeing them is worth noting: "But you, wretch, ill wedded of princely alliances, since you do not see your children, you bring destruction on their lives" (991-93). Medea's great anguish, on the other hand, lies most evidently in the fact that she sees the children all too clearly: "Oh, oh! Why do you look at me with your eyes, children? Why are you laughing your last laugh of all? Oh, what will I do? For my heart is wiped out, women, when I see the bright eyes of my children. I might not have the strength" (1040-44). In this beautiful passage, the remarkable image of the mother and child fixed in each other's gaze is suggestive of the role played by eye contact in the process by which the nursing mother becomes bonded to her child, and also of the literary tradition of the accessibility of the soul through the eyes. Medea's reaction to the gazing eyes of her children underscores the positive nurturing quality of her role, dramatizing the strength of her maternal bond. Unfortunately, this passage also demonstrates that she regards her vulnerability to maternal emotion as weakness, as that which saps her strength and wipes her out (1042-44). That Medea feels threatened by her susceptibility to that part of her nature which others have defined as ignoble and worthless may be demonstrated by an analysis of the speech of various characters in the play.

It is characteristic of Jason that the first word we hear him utter is a negation and that the object of his denial is strong emotion: "Not now for the first time but many times have I seen what a useless evil is harsh emotion" (446-47). Negation is as typical of Jason as strong emotion is of Medea. It is tempting to regard this notorious couple in the light of Freud's judgment that "affirmation, as being a substitute for union, belongs to Eros, while negation, the derivative of expulsion, belongs to the instinct of destruction" (*S.E.* 19:239). In the *Medea*, we are told that the protagonist misses her homeland, that she hates her children, that she wants to die; all her passions, including the most noxious ones, are stated in affirmative constructions. One of the rare occasions when Medea expresses a negation is in the above-mentioned passage ("I might not have the strength"), where the object of denial is precisely the emotional capacity required for the act of killing the children. The negation of this "strength" thus emerges as an affirmation of the emotions that would deny the act: love, pity, fear. Jason, on the other hand, would expel passion from his life along with Medea, and he is consistently described in negative terms: he does not love his children, he does not see his children, he does not marry for the sake of love. His desire that children could be engendered without resorting to the "female race" denies the humanity of half the human race and also the wisdom of a cosmos in which women exist at all. Though negativity is the distinguishing feature of Jason's speech, his conviction that strong emotion is the source of human limitation is typical of the local ruling class.

No less a personage than King Creon is ashamed to feel pity and condemns the exercise of mercy as a weakness unworthy of a king: "At least my spirit was born worthy of a king, but many a thing have I ruined utterly in feeling pity" (348-49). At this point, Creon's misgivings are entirely justified, because, in banishing Medea, he has openly declared his hostility, and the first letter of Machiavellian law is that you do not show pity after having initiated aggression. There may be an ironic comment on hypocritic demagogues in the apparent inconsistency between Creon's desire to exercise inordinate power and his determination to present himself as a good fellow. If Jason and Creon sometimes talk like would-be crowd-pleasers, however, Medea has the dubious distinction of being a better general than either one of them. In denying mercy to her children, she conforms, ironically enough, to the adamant ideal that Creon rightly feels he is betraying, and the emptiness of her "victory" has more to do with the limitations of the military premise than with any defect in her logic. Jason himself may claim the unenviable distinction of having served as her master of strategy, because his insistence on crediting Eros for the fact that Medea saved his life (530-31) lets his nemesis know that sensuality and desire are her own worst enemies, that she has them to blame for her humiliation and defeat. Thanks to him, she is persuaded that her own life affirming impulses have caused her humiliation and defeat. Jason delivers his lecture with noteworthy inconsideration of what it might mean for his children if Medea should be as superior to the powers of Eros as he seems to be.

Euripides' special emphasis, in this text, on the continuity between erotic and maternal functions suggests that the denial of emotion is a particular threat to the survival of the children. Both sexual indulgence and bearing children are identified as sources of harsh, disfiguring pain for Medea. When Jason indignantly seeks her approval of the plan which would eliminate her from his life, he suggests that even Medea would cheerfully endorse his scheme "if desire did not grate at" her (568). The vividly concrete term κνίζοι, from κνίζειν, *to grate, to scrape,* or *to make itch,* stands out in this passage and underscores Jason's contempt for sexuality by the use of language immediately evocative of animal gestures and mechanical procedures. Medea uses a similarly suggestive term when she laments that she has been "shredded" by the labor of childbirth (1030-31). The word she uses, κατεξάνθην, is a derivative of the verb, ξαίνειν, *to card* or *to shred,* often used to describe the preparation of wool. Like κνίζειν, καταξαίνειν suggests the cruel action of an abrasive instrument against vulnerable living tissue. For one who has been "grated" by desire and "shredded" by childbirth, the pleasures of the flesh and the impulsion of the senses may well appear to be untrustworthy and inimical. Therefore, Medea is urged, not only by Jason but by her own disappointing experience, to repudiate the life of the body. This is in itself a disastrous development for her children, and not only because they are the ones who have "shredded" her.

The physical love that binds Medea to her sons seems, at certain moments, to stand as an obstacle between her and her determination to avenge herself. Her effusive and lyrical description of the children's bodies and the pleasures their closeness gives her (1071-75) suggests that she has great difficulty in tearing herself away from them. In this celebration of hands, mouths, bodies, faces, gentle touch, tender skin, and sweet breath of the children, Pucci sees an indication of the "justice of the mind" (137), and yet it seems that the mother's poignant lament is rather more remarkable for the love of the body than for the justice of the mind. When Medea says to the children that their father has taken away the sweet things of this life (1073-74), she means not only the fleshly pleasures of her children's presence, but all the earthly joys that have been her delight, all that Eros offers and Jason ridicules. It is really no wonder that Medea believes people will laugh at her if she does not control herself. The affirmation of physical pleasure which seems to be all that stands between the children and their doom has been identified by Jason as the source of Medea's suffering and disgrace. She has no "reason" not to believe him.

Reason, or at least the pseudo-rationality that passes as such in this play, presents a far greater threat to the survival of the children than anybody's "instincts." Creon and Creusa, indeed, have substantial "reason" for wishing the children out of the way; Jason uses "reason" as an excuse for abandoning them to a doubtful fate. The Chorus cheerfully expresses the logically unassailable point of view that people who don't have children are more likely to achieve a certain kind of worldly prosperity than people who do (1090-93). For Medea, the children are the tangible signs of her shame and bondage to her passions. We may object to certain unstated assumptions that seem to be the basis of human enterprise in this community. Though a mother's "instinct" is not enough to sustain anybody's children, reason alone would hardly require their deaths; what passes for reason in this play is not reason but the denial of Eros. Reason would question the very value of subjecting every human consideration to the ultimate goal of "getting ahead" or winning. In this play, however, only the servants are at liberty to question the priorities of "free" men and women. The Nurse says she would rather not pass the days of her old age in great estate (123-24), but the wisdom of accepting personal limits emerges as an isolated articulation in this text, whereas Medea's inability to embrace a subservient role for herself reflects the generally sanctioned lunacy. Pride may well cost Medea the lives of her children, but it hardly distinguishes her from her peers. In the end, she is persuaded, in the name of "reason," to squelch her most generous impulses, while everybody else depends complacently on the reflex action of maternal love as an escape hatch for evading personal responsibility.

Foley's argument that Medea's revenge is required by ethical imperatives rather than by emotional excess is not only persuasive in its own right but also eminently consistent with the psychological and anthropological evidence that the potential for parental violence against children is rather a failure of culture than of instinct. The hypothesis of the ruinous female instincts, moreover, can hardly account for the care with which Euripides depicts Medea's physical attachment to her children. To the degree that he deals with her maternal nature as such, he presents it in a positive light. Various characters may say that Medea hates her children, but Euripides demonstrates that she is the only one who loves them. Freud's remarks on the regularity with which love is accompanied by hatred may suggest, indeed, that there is no surer sign of Medea's love for her children than the very fact that she hates them (*S.E.* 19:43). If mothers killed their children merely because they hated them, few children would be safe. The text leaves little doubt, moreover, that if Medea could trust her "instincts" and the promptings of her senses that Foley identifies as a "maternal voice," she would not kill her children.

The critical difficulty posed by the internal debate in which Medea chafes against her own stubbornness (τῆς ἐμῆς αὐθαδίας 1028) and yet pleads with her passion for revenge (θυμός) as if it were somehow external to her (1056) is evident in the rivers of ink that have been consecrated to the explication of Medea's monologue. Foley's essay on this text is essential, not only because of her meticulous exposition of the scholarly bibliography, but because of the interpretive acuity of her argument. Particularly helpful is her evaluation of the word *thumos* as a "capacity located in Medea that directs her to act, a 'heart' that can (or at least pretends to itself that it can) choose to side either with the arguments of the revenger or the arguments of the mother (although it is predisposed to the former)" (70-71). Wisely rejecting traditional arguments that dismiss Medea's *thumos* as a relatively simple source of "irrational passion" or "rage," Foley insists on the complexity of the *thumos*, which "can impel Medea either to kill or to spare" the children, and "even comes close to representing what we might call a self." Regarding my own perspective on Medea's dilemma as an elaboration of Foley's, I would like to underscore her parenthetical observation that Medea's *thumos* is "predisposed to" endorse the arguments of the revenger.

Medea is predisposed to endorse the arguments of the avengers because every discernible personal ideal in this play, whether male or female, is a fierce parental figure. The spectacle of the protagonist pleading with a part of herself that is outside of herself recalls Freud's description of the superego as being the representative of our relation with our parents (*S.E.* 19:36), and suggests that the *thumos* that haunts Medea is a moral passion, the standard-bearer for past generations of angry parents, which she embraces with all the fervor of her own passionate nature. Thus, her *thumos* is ultimately inseparable from the many divine figures, identifiable as formidable parents or guardians of the young, whom Medea invokes in the course of the play. Paternal authorities with reputations for fiery tempers, such as Zeus, the father of all the gods and thrower of thunderbolts, and Helios, the father of Medea's own ruthless father, are complemented by maternal figures such as Themis, an earth-mother who upholds oaths, and Hecate and Artemis, guardians of the young associated with cults requiring the sacrifice of children. Medea's own superhuman "fury" is etymologically linked to the Aeschylean conception of revenge as the province of cranky maternal deities. In any case, the distinction between internal and external dimensions of the mind is largely irrelevant in the context of a culture that conceives of personal gods both in terms of anthropomorphic figures, such as Aphrodite, and the psychological manifestation of the passions that such deities symbolize. The intuition of a connection between Medea's predisposition to revenge and a heritage of abusive parental authority is reinforced, moreover, by the way in which Euripides juxtaposes statements of Medea's hatred for her children with reminders that she misses her father.

Immediately before her terrifying assertion that Medea "hates her children," the Nurse describes her mistress as one who is learning "that the land of one's father is not a thing lightly to be abandoned" (34-36); the servant thus formulates the conflicting claims on Medea's conscience in personal terms that illustrate the Freudian assertion that the ego "is a precipitate of abandoned object-cathexes and . . . contains the history of those object-choices" (*S.E.* 19:29). Later, Medea clarifies the connection between missing her father and hating her children by identifying the children as the living emblems of her mistake in betraying her father for Jason: "I was mistaken then when I left my father's household, persuaded by the words of a Greek who, with the help of a god, will render justice and not ever will he see his children, begotten of me, living out the rest of their lives" (800-04). In this passage, the imperative for revenge focuses on the children as if the act of killing them will not only hurt Jason but also undo the wrong she has committed against her father. Like the negative wish with which the Nurse begins her first speech, this statement of regret for the events that led up to the birth of the children constitutes a wish that the children did not exist. It is followed by a reference to the god on her side, which reinforces the sense of her spiritual obligation to her father. The conventional formula by which she anticipates her revenge—"he will render justice"—is not only an appropriation of the rhetoric by which all manner of abominations are regularly justified, but a revelation of the conviction that the death of the children is something Medea seems to feel she owes her father.

Medea's statement of her past error is comparable to Jason's claim that he was out of his mind when he led Medea out of her barbarian household into the land of Greece. Denouncing his former partner in crime as the "betrayer of father and sustaining homeland" (1332), he dismisses his own role in initiating the train of events that led to the birth of the children as attributable to temporary insanity but does not go so far as to say, like Medea, that he was mistaken. Just as he denies his children the support on which their lives depend and yet blames Medea for their deaths, so he benefits from her past misdeeds only to set himself up as her conscience, condemning her for betraying father and country. Ironically enough, Medea's constant sorrowful references to her father and fatherland suggest that she agrees with him. Lamenting that she has no reason to live since she has no fatherland (798-99), she seems to be haunted by the memory of her homeland (328). The recurring lament for homeland and paternal household (πατρίς, δόμους πατρῴους) contains the root of the word for father, and, like the constant invocations of the god who is her grandfather, takes its place in an intricate network of remorseful reminders of her absent parent.

The notion that Medea suffers as much from pangs of conscience as from uncontrolled passion suggests a connection between Euripides' depiction of tragic pathos and Freud's discussion of melancholia, especially the observation that a person who has to give up a sexual object often experiences "an alteration of his ego which can only be described as a setting up of the object inside the ego, as it occurs in melancholia" (*S.E.* 19:29). Medea's condition as described by the Nurse at the beginning of the play seems curiously similar to that of one suffering from melancholia: despondent and self-reproachful, she can neither eat nor sleep. Her transformation in the course of the drama from a mood of abject misery to one of exuberant triumph seems relevant, moreover, to Freud's account of the way in which the dejection of melancholia may change into the exaltation of mania. Although diagnostic terms such as *melancholia* and *mania* would seem to be at odds with the assumption of Medea's relative sanity on which my argument is based, they are, in any case, unnecessary. The character's distress at the beginning of the play may quite fairly be described as a state of mourning, which Freud described as a normal condition resembling the pathological affliction of melancholia (*S.E.* 24:253-55). As the action proceeds, the audience watches Medea assume control of herself by acquiescing to the parental authority within herself and deliberately adopting the standards of those against whom she has defiantly struggled. The briefest reflection seems likely to suggest that if Medea misses her father and seems to be in the process of setting him up as a role model, her children are already in trouble.

The ominous implications of Medea's mourning for lost objects are apparent in legends, associated with both her parents, which tend to recall Lloyd de Mause's view of the relationship between the ancient parent and child as being in "the infanticidal mode" (51). Although there is no mention of Medea's mother in most versions of the myth, an omission that suggests minimal emphasis on the nurturing and compliant qualities that were presumably within a woman's domain, Diodorus Siculus names as Medea's mother the witch Hecate, long associated with fertility cults, magic, and infanticide; he describes this particular goddess as being "known far and wide for her cruelty." The same author describes Medea's father, Aeëtes, and her paternal uncle, Perses, as "exceedingly cruel," Aeëtes especially being noted for his "natural cruelty" (4:45-46); Valerius Flaccus speaks of "the guile, the cunning of the faithless offspring of the Sun," commenting, moreover, that he "deserved to be abandoned and betrayed" (5:222-24). Having taken issue at an early age with the family custom of murdering all strangers who arrived on the shores of the kingdom, Medea was disciplined on suspicion of subversive activities even before the arrival of the Argonauts in Colchis (Diodorus 4:46). It is precisely because Medea abandoned family and homeland to save Jason and his friends from her father's cruelty that Jason's position seems so offensive: like her father, he is a deceiver of strangers. His identification with the callous parental tyrant in her past is in counterpoint with the textual suggestion of equivalency between Medea and her children.

In addressing the Chorus of Corinthian women, Medea says that "of all things which are alive and have judgment, we women are the most wretched creatures" (230-31), echoing the conventional Homeric expression that "there is not anywhere, of all such things that breathe and crawl upon the earth, anything that is more wretched than a man" *(Iliad* 17:445-47). Homer's language, however, distinguishes between men and inhuman things by the very use of the word for man (ανδρός), while the Euripidean formulation establishes the equation between woman and the creature as blatantly in Medea's speech as in Creon's command for the fool to slither off: ἔρπ ὦ ματαία (crawl away, you madwoman 333). Medea says that women are the most wretched things grown, equating a word for human beings (γυναῖκες) with the neuter noun for something grown (φυτόν). Denoting "a thing that has grown" and, by extension, a "plant," "creature," "descendant," or "child," the word φυτόν implies the equivalence of women and things, of children and things, and also, of women and children.

Like the German word *Kind*, the Greek word φυτόν and the more common τέκνον are neuter nouns that suggest the less than human status of the child within the social group. Even the word παῖς, which may be masculine or feminine, may, in certain contexts, mean "slave" or "servant," so that Finley cautions against the "warm overtones of the word 'child' " for modern readers, recalling that Aristophanes "once invented an etymology of *pais* from *paiein* 'to beat' "(96). A good indication of the unenviable lot of the child in any community is the fact that, even today, grown people may be insulted by being called "boy" or "girl." The vulnerability of the child to exploitation and abuse derives in great measure from the adult capacity to perceive of him or her as an alien creature. Thus, children may be victimized by the logic of pseudospeciation, according to which countries at war regularly encourage their citizens to regard the enemy as other-than-human (barbarians, Krauts, Gooks). Piers documents the way the "dehumanization of the doomed child" has served as a mechanism permitting parents to abuse, neglect, and murder children throughout history (17). The crucial importance of the other-than-human status of the child in the psychology of child abuse affords an interesting perspective on the linguistic phenomenon of the child as neuter thing.

The antagonism toward children of the "silent code of civilization" that adults hurl against the young in the form of criticism, restrictions, and injunctions of all kinds led Zilboorg to claim that "to the unconscious of the parents, the child plays the role of the Id" (39). The word *id*, literally meaning "it," has in common with φυτόν, τέκνον and *Kind* the fact that it is grammatically neuter. The significance of references to children as neuter objects is illuminated by Bettelheim's complaint that the translation of Freud's "das Es" as "the id" instead of the plain English "it" entails a problematic loss of emotional immediacy. He observes that all Germans, during their early years, "have the experience of being referred to by means of the neuter pronoun *Es*, and it reminds them of a time when their entire existence was dominated by the 'it' " (57). In describing the world of the instincts as "Es," Freud showed insight into the truth that certain languages reflect in the forms of familiar words: that the concept of "humanity" itself is somehow bound up with the idea of civilized control. The child, relatively lacking in such control, is not quite human. Therefore, if Medea sees the problem of transcending the state of child, animal, thing, woman, and slave as a matter of achieving personal integrity and human worth, we should not wonder. Her anguish resembles that of any human being in the difficult state of transition between the worlds of childhood and adulthood, and the resolution of her predicament is a grim illustration of Freud's maxim: "where id was, there ego shall be" (*S.E.* 22:80).

The textual identification of Medea as child is not only implied in the word φυτόν, but also in certain similarities between Medea's situation and that of her children. Medea, like her children, is hated. The Nurse tells us that Medea hates her children (36), and Medea uses the same word to describe herself when she speaks of her sons as "the cursed children of a hated mother" (112-13). Although Foley underscores the feminist implications of Medea's self-hatred, observing that "she has come to envision all that is female as despicable" (80), it is also worth noting that Medea hates in herself precisely that which may bother adults about children, that is, an unrestrained nature. Furthermore, both Medea and her children are presented as being trapped in an impassable situation that has been imposed on them by a powerful, threatening figure of authority. It is a god who has brought Medea into a flood of evils with no way out (362-63), and Medea's sons find themselves overpowered by her in the same way that she has been overpowered by the god. The child cries: "Oh, what will I do? How may I flee the hands of a mother?" (1271) and his question, τί δράσω; is a literal repetition of the dreadful question posed by Medea herself at the moment when she is confronted by the realization that she will kill the children (1042). The identity of the despairing exclamations of Medea and her children throws into somber relief the resemblance between the mother's desperate predicament and the helpless affliction of the children; both are at the mercy of a hostile, powerful figure who ought to be protecting instead of persecuting them.

The transition from persecuted victim to persecutory authority requires a process of rejecting one role and choosing another, and the "progress" from one to the other entails a kind of betrayal. Having been persuaded that the revolt against her father by which she sought to liberate herself from the status of persecuted child has failed because it was committed in the service of Eros, Medea laments her reckless youth. If, in regretting her betrayal of her father, she betrays the offended child she once was and affirms her father's hostile treatment of strangers and children, Medea has little alternative. The affirmation of her youthful rebellion would mean choosing the lot of the victim, and liberation from the status of the creature entails going from "obeying instincts to inhibiting them" (*S.E.* 19:48). In order to "grow up," Medea must embrace the cruelty and tyranny of the authorities with whom the law is identified in her mind, at least as her mind is represented in the language of this play. It is noteworthy that the obsession with punishment that is characteristic of Medea reveals the continuity of thought between child-victim and adult-aggressor.

The childishness of Medea's persistent concern with suffering, punishment, and vindication is evident immediately after the episode with Creon, when she tells herself, "You see the things you are suffering. You, being born of a good father and descended from Helios, must not bring laughter on yourself through marriage to Jason, relative of Sisyphus" (403-06). In the tone of an angry parent, Medea addresses herself as "you," literally standing apart from herself, as if in conformity with Freud's perception of the superego as "the capacity to stand apart from the ego and to master it" (*S.E.* 19:48). With the allusion to Sisyphus, she reminds herself and the audience of a legend of infanticide on Jason's side of the family. When Jason's great uncle Sisyphus, feuding with his brother, Salmoneus, seduced Salmoneus' daughter, Tyro, in order to harm her father, Tyro bore her uncle two children before discovering his scheme, at which point she killed the children (Tripp 533-34), presumably out of just such a combination of anger and filial loyalty as Medea seems to be enduring at present. In this passage, Medea's desire to avoid the laughter of enemies, described by Foley as "a logical extension of the shame-culture position" (60), seems inextricable from oppressive aspects of the bond between parent and child. When the character insists that she must not incur the laughter of Jason and relatives of Sisyphus because she is born of good family, the descendant of Helios, we are reminded, not only of the divine implications of her *agon*, but also of the painful evidence of her obligation to paternal authorities.

In the word ὀφλεῖν, from ὀφλισκάνειν, meaning *to owe* or *to incur*, which is used here and frequently elsewhere by Medea in the expression "to incur laughter," we find a curious sense of obligation and also the hint of a suggestion that laughter entails something more than humiliation. Occurring also in the phrase "to incur punishment" (580-81, 1226-27), the word ὀφλισκάνειν implies the passive suffering of an ordeal, so that "laughter," when it occurs as the grammatical complement of the verb "to incur," may register as a kind of punishment. Mocking laughter, like any humiliation, is endured helplessly, in much the same way as a child endures the aggression of a hostile adult or suffers from being the brunt of crude merry-making. The position of the child as outsider in an adult world actually has an intimate connection with the fate of the exile in the dynamics of this play because the terror of being excluded and ostracized by the group is not only a reflection of the plight of the ancient citizen banished from the protection of the city; the condition of outsider is, after all, the ordinary status of the child, and the peculiar vulnerability of children derives from their essential exclusion from the world of adults. To the degree that the members of any audience can identify with Medea's dread of humiliation, their sympathy derives from the fact that such anxiety is part of the virtually universal heritage of infancy. The adult horror of exile and the child's fear of infanticide are one.

It is precisely the infantile quality of much of the emotional interaction in this play that makes the representation of the passions so immediate and familiar. Jason and Medea are more like a couple of squabbling children than two mature adults with a grave mutual responsibility. When Medea feigns compliance with Jason in order to get the best of him, she admonishes him "not to counter childish things with childish things" (891). For these so-called grown-ups, daring and showing that you can take a dare are essential values, and yet, even this foolishness does not distinguish them from their peers. When Medea tells the Chorus of her plan to kill the children, the women tell her not to do it, but quickly ask, as if in fascination: "But will you dare to kill your children, woman?" (816). Their use of the word τολμήσεις from τολμᾶν, *to have the courage to do something* or *to dare* is significant, first of all, because the future indicative form of the verb suggests that the attempt to dissuade Medea from her brutal project may perhaps be less than whole-hearted. The response of these women to the proposed deed is notably ambiguous, suggesting a mixture of overt disapproval and covert admiration: "Miserable woman, so you really were of rock or iron who killed the crop of your children that you bore for your share with your own hand" (1279-81). Though the audience may be horrified by the begrudging tribute implicit in the phrase "made of rock or iron," there is no reason to doubt that the Chorus is on some level positively impressed by Medea's "heroic" daring. The irony of the passage resides in the disparity between the communal estimation of heroic values and Euripides' probable view of them.

In this play, the verb τολμᾶν is the textual antithesis of the verb ὀφλισκάνειν. Though τολμᾶν has the positive connotation of asserting oneself actively and ὀφλισκάνειν has the negative connotation of suffering passively, both words may have the English meaning *to endure*, the operative difference inhering evidently in that the former implies the act of enduring for the sake of honor, and the latter a state of being in which shame and disgrace are passively endured. Recurring with some regularity in Medea's speech, these verbs ultimately suggest that her determination to safeguard her honor is imperfectly distinguished from her fear of punishment. After sending the poisoned gifts to the princess, but before killing the children, she asks herself: "And so what am I enduring? Do I want to incur laughter, letting my enemies go unpunished? These things must be dared. But even the allowing soft words into my heart is from cowardice" (1049-52). Here, as in the earlier passage describing her situation as a contest of endurance (403-04), Medea's use of the verb πάσχειν, *to suffer*, is a reproach to herself for being too passive and thus inviting the fate of the victim. In this speech, however, the dread of incurring laughter is inseparable from the indignity of letting her enemies go unpunished, and the choice of words shows a certain change in orientation. As the one incurring laughter, she was herself the helpless sufferer; in suggesting that she might be the one to "punish" her enemies, she embraces the role of tormentor. When she says that these things must be dared (τολμητέον), she shows that, of the painful alternatives open to her, she chooses the one that is sanctioned by the code of honor. Her troubled impression that "even the allowing of soft words" into her heart "is from cowardice" serves as a reminder that if, in choosing to repress her "cowardliness" Medea seals the doom of her children, she also accedes to a certain internal conception of moral exaltation.

Medea speaks of necessity as a compulsion of the mind attributable partly to divine ordination and partly to her own contriving: "There is great necessity for me, old man; for the gods and I, thinking badly, have contrived these things" (1013-14). The evidence of the gods' involvement in her cause is conspicuous enough, Helios having provided the offensive weapons with which she destroys Creusa and Creon as well as her ultimate defense, the dragon chariot. The military description of the vehicle is noteworthy: "Helios, father of my father, is giving us such a chariot as a defense against an enemy hand" (1321-22). Not only significant is the warlike language of this declaration, but also the fact that the name of the god Helios is sandwiched between the nominative and the genitive forms of the word for father (πατρὸς Ἥλιος πατὴρ), as if to mock any possible attempt to dissociate Medea's crime from her paternal heritage. The fact that she rises above the station of ordinary mortals by exercising the ferocity of the warrior makes Medea all the more an embodiment of familiar and hallowed ideals. Even Achilles, who killed Polydorus, the youngest son of Priam, and refused mercy to Tros, the youthful son of Alastor (*Iliad* 20:407-18, 463-72), was not unacquainted with the act of child-murder. The fact that these murders take place on the battlefield instead of the inner quarters of a palace does not detract from their savagery, but merely demonstrates the circumstance under which such brutality might be assured of full social sanction.

The destructive potential of familiar ideals is underscored by Freud's observation that "even ordinary morality has a harshly restraining, cruelly prohibiting quality which gives rise to the conception of a higher being who deals out punishment inexorably" (*S.E.* 19:54), and the transition of such characters as Medea and Achilles from the role of badly treated subject to the office of merciless avenger demonstrates the process by which Freud's "poor creature," the self, may evolve into "a higher being who deals out punishment inexorably." Inasmuch as the fury of Medea and the wrath of Achilles are both reactions to the denial of desired objects by figures of authority, they suggest that there may be a fundamental link between the exercise of authority and the function of negation. It is a connection that transcends the boundaries of particular traditions. All but one of our Ten Commandments, for example, are negations, the single exception being the fifth command, to honor thy father and mother "that thy days may be long upon the land which the Lord, thy God, giveth thee" (Exodus 20:12). A passage in the history of pagan ethics that bears comparison to the biblical "Thou-shalt-nots" is the case of Socrates, who attributed his own moral authority to a voice that came to him from early childhood, always dissuading him from what he was proposing to do, and never urging him on (*Apology* 31 C-D). It was the very silence of this voice at his trial that persuaded him to accept the death penalty, as if the voice of the higher moral authority which responded with continual injunctions to the project of life, had finally consented to the project of death. The noteworthy correlation between this statement and Freud's observation "that the death instincts are by their nature mute and that the clamour of life proceeds for the most part from Eros" (*S.E.* 19:46) may suggest that the Socratic embrace of death was, no less than the crimes of Achilles and Medea, a simultaneous affirmation of honor and negation of life. The fact that the imperative of the superego may be experienced as a death wish is consistent, moreover, with the thesis that the voice of conscience is often conceived as a voice that says "no" to life. The prototype of traditional morality would seem to be a parent who says "no" to a child, and literally threatens death as the penalty for disobedience.

Although the concept of a death instinct is incompatible with the evidence that excessive aggression is a cultural rather than an instinctual problem, Freud's articulation of the death-wish seems peculiarly relevant to the discussion of a character who raises her voice to ask how she may die before she ever appears on stage (97), and who proceeds, in the course of the drama, to destroy everyone she loves and hates. Certain passages of Freud's in which he describes the inordinately strong superego as "raging against the ego with merciless violence," or where he speaks of a "pure culture of the death instinct" as "holding sway in the superego," seem to leap off the page and recommend themselves as impressionistic criticism of the *Medea*. The concept of the death instinct, like the paradoxical phrase "pure culture of . . . instinct," may, in any case, be a problem of translation, as Bettelheim's critique of the standard English edition suggests (104), and the phrase "eine Reinekultur des Todestriebes," when translated as "a pure culture of the death *impulse*," ceases to present appreciable difficulties. It is interesting to consider, moreover, that the effect of mistranslating the word "Trieb" (*drive*) as instinct is the same as that of attributing the violent action of a tragedy to an excess of instinct alone. In either case, the language is misused in such a way as to allow a certain distance between the speaker and the cultural implications of tragic pathos. With respect to the misuse of Freudian terminology, it is worth noting that such concepts as the id, the ego, and the superego were never intended to imply that the mind may be divided into neat compartments. Freud described every aspect of the mind as being continuous with every other part of it, positing the ego as a specially differentiated part of the id, and the superego as a part of the ego that is "always close to the id." His conception of the superego as being "farther from consciousness than the ego is" (*S.E.* 19:38, 52, 48-49) suggests that the question of whether "rage" or "reason" predominates in Medea's *thumos* is basically irrelevant. In fact, the assumption that conscience, the functional representative of parental dictates, is necessarily reasonable and opposed to demonstrations of spontaneous rage derives from the essentially abusive premise that all generational conflict entails confrontation between "good parents" and "bad children."

Whereas Foley's assertion that "there are rational as well as counterrational considerations on both sides of Medea's internal conflict concerning the children" (64) is an essential corrective to simplistic readings of the text, her emphasis on the gendered aspects of Medea's dilemma tends to obscure the implications of dynamic inequality in the opposing arguments. In fact, Medea's "maternal voice" offers little more than a childish whimper against the adamant insistence of the avenger. In the soliloquy following her feigned compliance with Jason's project, she twice rejects the plan to murder the children, pleading with her *thumos* to spare them in the name of the pleasure the living children would bring her (1058); she even articulates a new plan to lead them out of the country when she goes into exile (1045). When she finally rejects this plan, she does so precisely because of the necessity of repressing the desire for pleasure that she identifies with the cause of saving their lives. She literally disconnects her sensual attachment to the children by sending them out of her range of vision: "Go, go! I can no longer look at you, but I am overcome by bad things" (1076-77). Unable to look at the children because the sight of them disarms her vindictive resolve, she identifies the merciful impulses prompted by her sense of sight as an evil that overwhelms her, just as, in an earlier passage, she experienced the admission of "soft words" into her heart as cowardice (1051).

Having acquiesced in the general opinion that she is the fool of Eros, Medea may well feel threatened by her own affectionate feelings for the children, but the requirement of controlling her passionate longings can only be accomplished by the negation of the senses. She cannot look at the children and know what she must do. When she says she knows what a bad thing she is about to do (1078), she shows that even as she is besieged on all sides by opposing impulses, her basic perception of reality is exactly the same as our own. There is no more poetic suggestion of the weakness of the ego than Medea's inability to seize upon this slender shoot of good sense and declare it as her standard, in defiance of received opinion. She cannot deplore her tormentors in the manner, for example, of

Shakespeare's Emilia, who says: "Thou hast not half the power to do me harm/ As I have power to be hurt" (*Othello* 5.2.161-62), nor can she affirm her physical nature with the grandeur of Cleopatra, who calls herself "No more but e'en a woman, and commanded/ By such poor passion as the maid that milks/ And does the meanest chares" (*Antony & Cleopatra* 4.15.76-78). The only power Medea knows is the power of the victor; all she has learned of her own "poor passions" is that they have made her a loser. Knowing that it is the "cause of the greatest evil for mortals," she submits to the angry spirit inside her because it is stronger than her unalloyed desire to evade it. That this angry conscience should be strong enough to dominate her most vital longings is not so amazing if we consider the way in which parental commands may be enforced by subtle and not so subtle threats of murder. Medea's *thumos* has every appearance of harboring the angry phantoms of such threats.

The essence of Medea's confusion inheres in the fact that, of the raging impulses that seem to assail her from all sides, she does not know which ones to identify as "passions," that is, the treacherous promptings of Eros, and which ones are the honorable exigencies of conscience. Though she is able to perceive and evaluate the external world with clarity, her "self" seems too fragile to act on what she seems to know: that killing the children is bad, no matter what anybody says or thinks or does. It is this very uncertainty that underscores the moral quality of her dilemma. Whereas Freud called the id "totally non-moral," he described the ego as "striving to be moral" and said of the superego that "it can be super-moral, and then become as cruel as only the id can be" (*S.E.* 19:54). Medea's internal struggle is that of the "ego striving to be moral"; the outcome of her agony gives her every appearance of having chosen the super-morality of the fanatic. We need only reflect on the chaos wreaked by the moralistic refinements of Crusaders, Inquisitors, Puritans, Nazis, and various ethnic cleansers, to know whom Medea most resembles in her decision to kill her children. It is characteristic of crusaders, as of Medea in her triumphant ascent, that all vestiges of moral confusion have been banished from their minds, as if by higher decree, even if, to a nonbeliever, those who regard themselves as the "chosen few" or the members of the "master race" may seem hopelessly confused concerning questions of basic decency. Medea's determination to decide her course of action on the basis of "noble" and "moral" imperatives is, in itself, disastrous for her children.

That the *thumos* Medea experiences as external and, like the Freudian superego, able "to stand apart from the ego and to master it" may be conceived either as an "angry passion" or a "directing spirit" suggests that it encompasses not only the internalized negative dictates of an absent parent, but also the evolution in values from the physical concerns of the child to the sublimations of the adult. Although it is true, in any society, that self-mastery depends, to a great extent, on controlling the demands of the body, Medea's particular anxiety about being misled by the errors of the senses and duped by physical desires mark her as a true citizen of fifth-century Athens, and her final ascent in the dragon chariot is thoroughly consistent with the Socratic teaching that "true philosophers abstain from all bodily desires and withstand them and do not yield to them" (*Phaedo* 82C). Indeed, the textual identification of the children with their mother's carnal passions is especially disquieting because it occurs in the context of a culture where disembodied ideals are held in great esteem. Socrates observes that "every pleasure or pain has a sort of rivet with which it fastens the soul to the body and pins it down and makes it corporeal, accepting as true whatever the body certifies" (*Phaedo* 83D), and Medea's refusal to accept as true the argument, "certified by the body," in favor of sparing the children, constitutes a grim mockery of the Socratic ideal of the triumphant spirit. Shuffling off the constraining rivets of corporality by cutting her children away from herself along with the pleasures and pains of her humanity, she ascends to heaven in a literal liberation of the self from the weight of bodily matter. In this profoundly anti-Platonic document, Euripides seems to affirm the Socratic conviction that the soul's triumph over the body can only be achieved in death, but he strips the process of all glamour by presenting it in sensual terms. The images of Creusa's rotting flesh and the bleeding bodies of Medea's children have the effect of turning the rhetorical nicety of spiritual triumph into a loathsome spectacle.

It is tempting to speculate that the degree to which generations of scholars have been rather more inclined to celebrate the idealism of Plato than the sensual wisdom of Euripides may inhere in the circumstance that Plato flatters us precisely where Euripides offends us—in our narcissistic image of ourselves as exalted spiritual beings. Whatever the role of narcissism in the critical reception of Euripidean art, its relevance to the cultural context of his drama has been underscored by Slater, who describes life in fifth-century Athens as "an unremitting struggle for personal aggrandizement, for fame, honor, or for such goals as could lead to those (wealth, power and so forth)" (38). This observation seems relevant to the *Medea*, in which Jason's and Creon's concern for their children is presented as an extension of their love for themselves, and, conversely, Medea's rejection of her dispossessed and despised sons follows inexorably from their inability to nourish her own self-esteem. In fact, the murder of the the children has in common with the paternalistic arrogations that provoke it, the quality of aggrandizing and improving the image of the actor in her (or his) own regard. The Euripidean text also seems to illustrate Slater's perception of narcissistic disorders as being "emotionally contagious, particularly between parents and children" (51), because the girl Creusa, strutting admiringly before the image of herself in the mirror, seems emblematic of all the major characters in the play.

As royal princess and favored child of fortune, Creusa stands midway between the worlds of sovereign and slave, man and woman, adult and child. More of a caricature than a character, she gives dramatic emphasis to the narcissistic process by which the child assumes an adult identity. The expression of disgust (1149) with which she greets the entrance of Jason's children is not only a reflection of Jason's own attitude in rejecting family concerns for the sake of worldly goods, nor, in all probability, is it entirely attributable to the ruling family's interest in eliminating the threat to the royal succession. Rather, the spontaneous nature of her revulsion suggests that the daughter of Creon, like many an adolescent child, simply does not want to be around small children. Being not so far from childhood herself, she rankles at the very proximity of children, seemingly irritated by the reminder of an identity that is so much a part of her recent past as to be still too close for comfort. Yet Creusa, parading before the mirror in the golden wreath and variegated gown Medea has given her, is like a little girl dressing up in a grown woman's clothes.

Creusa is enchanted by her reflection in the glass, which Euripides' messenger eloquently calls "a lifeless thing, the laughing image of her body" (1162). Inasmuch as it is a "lifeless thing," this golden image that Creusa finds so much more entertaining than Jason's living children, is the textual equivalent of all the things the adults in Creusa's world value: gold, honor, victory, and good fame are all lifeless things, and yet they are generally held in greater esteem than the lives of these little boys. Even their father seems never really to notice them until after they are dead. Norman O. Brown's insistence on the Freudian maxim that gold, in the products of the unconscious, is equivalent to excrement, seems peculiarly relevant to the image of Creusa, and, indeed, to the entire project of interpreting a tragedy in which the lure of golden objects is essential. In Brown's reading of Freud, the adult preoccupation with gold, money, time, and such abstractions as honor, success, and glory, results from the denial of the child's body and the subsequent return of the repressed in dehumanized form (110-34). The articulation of repression as the denial of the polymorphously perverse infant body suggests that the rejection of corporality is equivalent to the hatred of the child, while the affirmation of spiritual values corresponds to love of the adult. Thus, Creusa's negative reaction to the children and her loving celebration of the golden phantom in the glass are emblematic of the process of repression by which the life of the body is inhibited in the routine transition of any individual from child to adult. As the child learns the standards of grace and beauty idealized by the adults in his or her world, he or she also learns that one is lovable and deserving of esteem to the degree that one conforms to those standards.

The narcissistic image of Creusa turning her back to the children and courting her own ornamented reflection in the mirror is the image of the entire tragedy cast in disarmingly familiar terms. The *Medea* presents the spectacle of a young soul in the process of forsaking the life-loving child within herself. For the protagonist, renunciation is required in order to be able to confront other adults on equal terms, and also, as Bongie observes, in order "to be true to her own self, to go on being someone she can respect" (52). The disastrous consequences of the acts by which Creusa and Medea deny the primary value of the body and embrace different conventional versions of human worth imply an ironic view of the adult world that Euripides saw before him in all its willingness to sacrifice the lives of countless young people for the abstract values of freedom, honor, and glory. The end of the play is tragic precisely because Medea succeeds so well in achieving the heroism and idealism that we tend to associate with ancient Greek civilization.

Medea's tragedy is that of fifth-century Greece, which wasted its land and children as a result of vain, pompous rhetoric, and the selfish interests of private individuals. Indeed, the degree to which the arguments of Medea and Jason correspond to certain contemporary debates reported by Thucydides is noteworthy. The complaint by an Athenian ambassador that the Peloponnesians feel more bitter over slight disparities "than they would if we, from the first, had set the law aside and had openly enriched ourselves at their expense" (1:77), suggests that the Athenians were not, any more than Jason, above accusing their subjects, rather arrogantly and in doubtful circumstances, of being ungrateful to their protectors. Telling somebody to be thankful that you do not take advantage of your superior strength to treat him worse than you do is like reminding a child that she should be grateful you did not kill her when she was born, and the irritating potential of such thrusts would seem to have been all the more problematic in a culture where every child owed his or her parents just such a debt of gratitude. In assuming the essentially parental role of persecutory protectors, the Athenians were evidently tempting the ferocious retaliation of their subjects.

Just as Jason's attitude is similar to that of certain Athenian ambassadors, so Medea's fears bear comparison with those expressed by Corinthian delegates to the Spartan assembly:

And let us be sure that defeat, terrible as it may sound, could mean nothing else but total slavery. To the Peloponnese, the very mention of such a possibility is shameful, or that so many cities should suffer the oppression of one. If that were to happen, people would say either that we deserved our sufferings or that we were putting up with them through cowardice and showing ourselves much inferior to our fathers. (Thucydides 1:122)

This speaker fears slavery, defeat, shame, and the effect of what people might say just as much as Medea does. He is just as anxious to suppress all visible signs of cowardice in himself as she is, and the bottom line for him, as for her, is proving himself worthy of a paternal ideal.

Though it would be absurd to consider any tragedy as an allegory of current events, the resemblance between the arguments of certain dramatic characters and the debates of various contemporary figures is surely an indication of the fact that both discourses are haunted by the ghosts of generational hostility. Among the wonders of Euripidean craft, no small place must be given to the way in which so many of his characters show the plight of the child so transparently through the veneer of adult posturing. Creusa dressed up in Medea's clothes plays at being grownup, while Jason is as much the spoiled little boy as the fatuous hero, and Medea is as much the frustrated little girl as she is the vindictive woman. Jason acts as if he were the growing child and Medea the suffocating mother, while Medea acts as if she were the mistreated child and Jason the tyrannical father. The poetical perception of the child within every adult contributes enormously to the timeless and universal quality of Euripides' characterizations.

Inasmuch as Medea's triumph is achieved by the sacrifice of the sensual child within herself, her tragedy is our own. And so, for all its horror, this drama has a certain exalting effect on the emotions of the spectator. What is exhilarating about the *Medea* is the spectacle of successful revolt against corrupt and abusive authority. The brutal parent who commands our attention seems to have the soul of a child desperate to thwart the hostile conspiracy of an adult world trying to destroy her. By daring to act, Medea throws off the bonds of an unbearable external domination and becomes the master of her own destiny, apparently heedless of the fact that nothing so much reveals her affiliation with her oppressors as the infanticidal nature of her rebellion. Whereas the psychological consistency of Euripidean characterization is an ironic indictment of the banal conventional rhetoric that serves the purposes of abusive power, the moral impact of his tragedy derives precisely from the dynamic ambiguity of our own fascinated revulsion with the act of child-murder.

3

Seneca and the Scourge of Anger

Writing in a tradition that emphasized the importance of *pietas,* an ancient concept roughly equivalent to the modern notion of "family values," Seneca focused unrelentingly on the murder of children. The centrality of child-murder in his dramas has been noted by Elisabeth and Denis Henry, who underscore the cosmic implications of the killing of children in *Medea, Thyestes,* and *Hercules Furens* (83-84), but these notorious tragedies are arguably only the most conspicuous examples in a recurring pattern. The slaughter of Iphigeneia is as essential to the *Agamemnon* as the killing of Polyxena and Astyanax are to the *Troades,* both the beginning and the end of the Trojan War having been marked by public executions that wasted the blood of children. The *Oedipus* and the fragmentary *Phoenissae* are dramatizations of different parts of a myth in which an entire family is wiped out by the destructive effects of parental antagonism toward progeny, and the fury of a vindictive stepmother proves the undoing of the protagonist in both the *Hippolytus* and *Hercules Furens.* Although the *Octavia* is no longer believed to have been written by Seneca, its thematic affiliation with the tragedies is evident in the ghost of Agrippina, who bears an uncanny resemblance to the malevolent Juno of the Hercules plays. The peculiar emphasis of these plays may hardly be dismissed as a reflection of their mythic models because Seneca's adaptations of Greek tragedy are notably selective, dealing neither with dramas of reconciliation, such as the *Eumenides, Philoctetes, Helen, Ion,* and *Alcestis,* nor with plays focusing on vengeful youths, such as the *Libation Bearers,* the *Orestes,* and the Electra plays. His treatment of the legendary trials of the House of Atreus emphasizes the sins of the fathers rather than the retribution of the children, passing over the material of the second and third plays in the Aeschylean trilogy and placing a distinctive mark on the *Agamemnon* by introducing the action with a soliloquy by the ghost of Thyestes. Even the generally discredited attribution to Seneca of the *Octavia,* with a cast of characters straight out of Suetonius and Tacitus, is a curious indication of the particularity and coherence of his poetic vision. Though the belief that Seneca might have written a play in which he himself appears as a doomed character may seem puzzling, generations of readers apparently preferred to assume the common authorship of these dramas rather than to consider that different authors responding to the same historical context might favor the same disturbing themes and the same spectacular conflicts.

If Seneca's Medea seems, at one and the same time, a more cruel parent and a more afflicted child than that of Euripides, she is all the more recognizably the imaginative projection of a citizen of Imperial Rome during the first century C.E. Operating in a dangerous political climate where dissent was punishable by ostracism, exile, or death, Seneca was prudently elusive and circuitous in the presentation of his basically subversive drama, employing various techniques to reassure the members of his audience that the malignant cruelty of his subject had nothing to do with them. Although the tactical importance of his strategies for avoiding censure is independent of such critical issues as whether the plays were performed publicly or recited in secret, Henry and Henry argue persuasively that the dramas were probably known to Seneca's contemporaries, including the Emperor Nero, whom they describe as having had a certain tolerance for "personal criticism, even caricatures." Speculating on the difficulty of supposing that Nero did not know his tutor and chief minister wrote tragedies, they conclude that the philosophical implications of the plays, rather than any sense of personal discredit, may ultimately have exhausted Nero's patience. Their view of Seneca's "insistence on the meaninglessness and the crumbling quality of the Imperial world, the sense that life may be intrinsically insupportable" (176), underscores the inseparability of tragic action, philosophical perspective, and historical context in Senecan drama.

Whereas the theme of murdered children is implicit in all the contemporary sources of Senecan thought, its recurrence in the historical record is perhaps most conspicuous. Suetonius observes that Nero regularly had the children of condemned men starved to death or poisoned, while Tiberius, instead, had them strangled (6.36.2, 3.61.5). In view of the role played by repressive archaic tradition in the Euripidean *Medea,* we may find a certain bleak resonance in Suetonius' comment on the pious regard for tradition that persisted in the midst of flagrant imperial abuses: "Because it was not permitted by ancient custom to strangle virgins, little girls were first violated by the executioner, then strangled" (3.61.5). This disconcerting report receives grim corroboration in Tacitus' moving description of the execution of the children of Sejanus (5.9). It is only one of many stories, moreover, which have the cumulative effect of impressing upon the reader a sense of the extreme danger of being born into a high-ranking family in the first century C.E. The vicious destructiveness of generational hostility in the imperial family itself is poignantly summarized by Suetonius' casual comment that Tiberius, who sentenced his grandchildren to extraordinarily cruel deaths, "used to call Priam happy because he had outlived all his kindred" (3.62.3). The historical texts are essential, not only with respect to the theme of child-murder, but also with reference to the stereotype of the wicked woman.

Seneca's *Medea* is the only extant Latin version of a motif for which the Romans had a good deal of enthusiasm, versions by Ennius, Accius, Ovid, Lucan and Curiatus Maternus having been partly or entirely lost (Duff 204, 223). The cultural importance of the myth is evident in the dazzling collection of female monsters presented by Tacitus. Not only does the historian record the "service" to imperial employers of such notorious professional poisoners as Plancina, Martina, and Locusta, he also presents, in such figures as Livia, Marcellina, Livilla, Silana, and Agrippina, a gallery of female bullies who are quite as jealous, treacherous, and vengeful as any Medea. Allusions to the "stepmotherly malevolence" of Livia (1.6) and the "stepmotherly hypocrisy" of Agrippina (12.26) recall the recurring figure of the *noverca* in the dramas. Judgments to the effect that Augusta was "a compliant wife but an overbearing mother" (5.1) and "a real catastrophe for the nation" (1.10), like the observation that the enemies of the tribal queen Cartimandua fought bravely because they were "goaded by fears of humiliating feminine rule" (12.40), suggest that the fear of female domination was not only a domestic problem but a national concern. Tacitus, indeed, seems not altogether without sympathy for the boy, Nero, whose mother's ruthless manipulations reduced him to the point of being "half dead with fear" (14.7). The personal demeanor of the odious matriarch was formidable enough to have inspired her enemies with fear that a "selected assassin might shrink from carrying out his dreadful orders" (14.3), and her untimely demise seems to have troubled nobody but Nero. It is indeed a matter of some interest that the emperor who murdered wives and children in confoundingly brutal ways owes his great notoriety to the fact that he collaborated in the successful group effort to assassinate the generally hated Agrippina.

There is little point in extending the catalogue of atrocities. In an age when absolute rulers honored by the ceremonial title, *pater patriae* (father of the fatherland), regularly inflicted orgies of blood-letting on their subjects, literary versions of the myth of *Medea* need not be construed as alluding to any particular tyrant or matron. The Roman Empire of the first century was still characterized by all the practices that prompted Lloyd de Mause to assert that "the image of Medea hovers over childhood in antiquity, for here myth only reflects reality" (51). The ancient customary law of *patria potestas* still gave fathers the power of life and death over children, regardless of age

(Sinniger and Boak 85), and the burden of rearing children made celibacy so appealing that Augustus enacted laws designed to reward married men, discourage childlessness, and give precedence to fathers in choosing candidates for public office (Sinniger and Boak 266). A reference by Tacitus to one of these laws, the Lex Papia Poppaea of 9 C.E., stresses the pragmatic aspect of imperial paternalism by describing the law as one under which "failure to earn the advantages of parenthood meant loss of property to the state as universal parent" (3.28). The ancient author notes that this measure "failed to popularize marriage and the raising of families—childlessness was too attractive" (3.25), and a modern scholar speculates that voluntary childlessness was a more probable cause of depopulation in the imperial age than tyranny itself (Duff 13).

The noxious implications of such a term as "voluntary childlessness" with reference to a period lacking reliable and safe birth control technology need hardly be stressed. Though Noonan argues that a certain variety of rude contraceptive and abortive methods were available to the ancient Romans, he readily concedes "the prevalence of more brutal forms of population control" (29). For the purposes of my argument, it is probably enough to know that the killing of an infant was not officially condemned until 374 C.E. In fact, the extent of the ancient Roman disinclination to regard children as human beings is nowhere more apparent than in the nature of certain arguments against mistreating them. In the *Controversiae* of Seneca the Elder (father of the playwright-philosopher), the following case is presented: "A man used to cripple children who had been exposed, forcing them to be beggars and demanding a fee from them. He is accused of harming the state" (10.4.1). This statement, introducing formal argument for and against the accused, takes for granted the exposure, maiming, and exploitation of children and only protests that such enterprise deprives the state of able-bodied citizens.

The *Declamations* (*Controversiae* and *Suasoriae*) that Seneca the Elder compiled "for the education and interest" of his three sons, as well as "for the preservation of past achievement" are an essential key to the world where his son's "mental and linguistic habits were formed" (Pratt 138). These formal exercises, rich in rhetorical flourishes and imaginative locutions, have been described by Norman Pratt as "essentially histrionic and theatrical," and also as a kind of "embryonic drama" (136-45). While the flamboyant language and polemical form of the *Declamations* are recognized as important elements in the development of Seneca's style, the content of the cases has been dismissed as repetitive and unexciting, Lucas' view of them as "fatuous imaginary cases" (55) finding virtual confirmation in Pratt's judgment that they are "essentially unreal situations" (149). A simple survey of the *Controversiae* suggests, however, that they are relevant to Seneca's drama in matters of both form and content.

The most usual type of argument in the *Controversiae* concerns the disinheritance of sons. For example: "A rich man disinherited his three sons. He asks a poor man for his only son to adopt. The poor man is ready to comply; when his son refuses to go he disinherits him" (2.1.1). In depicting sons at the mercy of unexplained or unprovoked parental attack, this case is not unique. There are also cases in which not only property is at stake but life itself: "A man lost his wife, by whom he had a son, married again and raised a daughter by his new wife. The youth died; the husband accused the stepmother of poisoning him. On conviction she was tortured and said her daughter was her accomplice. The girl is to be executed. Her father defends her" (9.6.1). Whereas this story of a bungling father, a trouble-making stepmother, and a poisoned son is curiously analogous to historical accounts of such imperial figures as Claudius, Agrippina, and Britannicus, other cases are vaguely suggestive of mythical plots. A youth is disinherited for refusing to kill his mother when his father, a disabled veteran, returns from war to find that his wife, like Clytemnestra, has been unfaithful in his absence (1.4.1). A mother brings charges of mistreatment against her husband when their two sons, like Eteocles and Polyneices, fight each other to the death. The boys had been told by their father that the loser of the contest of martial valor in which they were engaged would be disinherited (5.3.1). A young woman who refuses to leave her husband in the civil wars, although her father and her brother are fighting on the other side, finds herself in a situation comparable to that of Medea: "Her own side was defeated, and her husband killed; she came to her father; he would not admit her into his house. She said, 'How do you want me to make amends to you?' He replied, 'Die!' She hanged herself before his door. The father is accused of madness by his son" (10.3.1). The latter case is interesting, not only as an example of the theme of destructive parental hostility in the *Controversiae*, or as an illustration of the cultural context which inspires the horror of parental disapproval in ancient Medeas, but because of the ambiguous aspect of the young woman's death.

Doomed by her willingness to comply with a malevolent paternal command, the young widow demonstrates a response to extreme crisis that was sanctioned by Stoic teaching. Acts of suicide occur so frequently in the Annals of Tacitus that the author finally begs indulgence of his readers for the "slavish passivity" of his subjects, commenting that "this torrent of wasted bloodshed far from active service wearies, depresses and paralyzes the mind." The historian begs his readers to "forbear to censure" the "inglorious victims" because "the fault was not theirs," but rather "heaven's anger with Rome, and not an isolated burst of anger such as could be passed over with a single mention, as when armies are defeated or cities captured" (16.16). Thus, looking back on the afflictions of an earlier generation, the author expresses a wonderful mixture of impatience with their passivity and compassion for their suffering. There is, moreover, no small hint of Stoicism in his references to the destructive effects of anger and the inexorability of divine punishment.

The Stoic affirmation of suicide as the ultimate "defense" against persecution is a salient example of philosophical mediation between institutional abuse and individual misery. Thus Seneca's enthusiasm for "dying well" is rhetorically linked with an admonition to reconsider the value of human life: "Whoever does not know how to die well will live badly; therefore we must deflate the value of the commodity and count the breath of life as cheap goods" ("On Tranquility" 11.4). That the "commodity" of life should be devalued by the philosopher reflects the regularity with which the "breath of life" was literally counted as "cheap goods" in Imperial Rome. Understandably morose, Seneca railed at humankind: "Nothing is so deceptive as human life, nothing so treacherous" ("To Marcia" 22.3). Blanket condemnations of his fellows are as abundant in the *Moral Essays* as tales of sensational slaughter in the accounts of Suetonius and Tacitus. Warning his readers that "human nature produces treacherous souls, thankless souls, greedy souls, impious souls," he suggests that they put off judging the morals of individuals until they have considered "those of the general public" ("On Anger" 2.31.5). Although the history of the twentieth century may have the retroactive effect of valorizing Seneca's curmudgeonly perspective, his misanthropic conviction is nonetheless worth noting.

However justified by contemporary events, Seneca's negative view of humanity seems inseparable from a cultural context of abusive relational patterns. The element of self-chastisement that is implicit in the condemnation of his fellows is relevant, moreover, to both his philosophical and dramatic writing. Speculating on the Senecan hero's "loathing for his surroundings, and, by association, for himself," Thomas Rosenmeyer stresses the importance of such feelings in Senecan drama, asserting that the author's heroes and villains are textually identified with each other "through the agency of this loathing" (55). The conceptual relevance of self-contempt to the philosophical prose seems evident in the Stoic response to the problem of flagrant evil in a rationally ordered universe. Just as lack of self-esteem in battered children generally coexists with a tendency to exonerate, idealize, and exalt a brutal parent (Bloch 141-73), so Senecan Stoicism couples contempt for human nature with glowing tribute to a blameless deity. The impression of an analogy between the clinical paradigm and the philosophical perspective is rather strengthened by Seneca's way of articulating cosmic discrepancies in terms of generational metaphors.

For Seneca, God is a stern father and men are erring children in need of painful character-building. His description of the relationship between God and man approves both the suffering of the mortal child and the severity of the divine parent as essential components of the cosmic educational process:

A good man differs from God only in time, being his disciple and emulator and true progeny which that glorious parent, no mild exactor of virtues, like a strict father, educates harshly. Thus when you see that good men, acceptable to the gods, labor, sweat, climb up the hard way and that the wicked, moreover, run wild and are swept along by pleasure, consider that the modesty of our sons delights us, the license of our slaves; the former are restrained with more severe discipline, the latter are encouraged in audacity. So let it be clear to you concerning God. He does not maintain a good man in allurements but tests him, hardens him, prepares him for his own service. ("On Providence" 1.5-6)

In a telling assimilation of the relationships between God and man, parent and child, master and slave, this passage praises the wisdom of the "glorious parent" and "strict father" while extolling the benefit to the "true progeny" of "severe discipline." In terms analogous to Alice Miller's discussion of "poisonous pedagogy" (*For Your Own Good* 3-102), this passage justifies every sort of mischief as part of the divine instructional plan, reassuring the reader that if the wicked prosper while the virtuous languish in misery, it is because father knows best and suffering is for our own good. In fact, Senecan discourse illustrates both the principle of rational order and the effects of irrational excess with images of afflicted children.

    To the subject of anger, the philosopher devoted an extensive three-part essay that emphatically condemns the expression of irate emotion, asserting that "there is no quicker path to madness" than anger, and "no passion over which anger does not hold sway" ("On Anger" 2.36.4-6). Described as something like a disembodied scourge, anger presents a special threat to children: "With modesty trampled underfoot, it stains the hands with slaughter, scatters abroad the limbs of children, leaves no place empty of crime" (3.41.3). Nor is the "scattering abroad of children's limbs" an isolated image. Those who give in to the excess of anger are like Ajax in that they "call down death upon their children, poverty upon themselves, ruin upon their house" (2.36.5). Most interesting with respect to Seneca's *Medea* is his reference to anger as "a kind of bristly, hissing thing more foul than all the instruments by which it vents its rage" (3.3.6). In this concrete description of vicious rage inheres the essence of Seneca's own priestess of Hecate, Medea. Thus, the tragic character is only one embodiment of a general evil that the philosopher regularly describes as "calling down death upon children" and "scattering abroad the limbs of children."

    Whereas clinical evidence suggests that denial is an essential element in the psychology of abuse, Seneca's favored cure for the sickness is a vigilant self-restraint that looks suspiciously like denial. Locating the cause of anger in a sense of injury, he suggests an attack on the root of the problem: "the cause of anger is an impression of injury which must not readily be believed. Not even for open and obvious causes must we assent to such belief for even false ones bear the appearance of truth" ("On Anger" 2.22.2). To be sure, Seneca would have been all too familiar with situations tending to confirm the prudence of such advice. For example, Suetonius observes that, under Tiberius, "the testimony of no informer was rejected; every crime was received as a capital offense, even those of a few simple words" (3.61). But Seneca elevates the wisdom of moderate caution to the level of a philosophical injunction against the expression of anger in any circumstances, regardless of the provocation. He not only advises the wounded party to deny his suffering, but also to imagine that he has been benefited: "the mind should be called back from every external thing into itself . . . let it not feel losses and even interpret adversity kindly" ("On Tranquility" 14.2). Achieving beatitude against all odds is therefore merely a matter of retreating from the confrontation of hostile powers and trying to make the most of a dreary corner: "Nothing is so bleak that a patient soul may not find consolation in it" ("On Tranquility" 10.4). Apart from the problematic political implications of the suggestion that citizens should go sit in the dark as if they were naughty children, the statement that the mind should "not feel losses" amounts to a remarkable standard prescription of repression.

The imperial mission of controlling disruptive forces is implicit in Seneca's conception of rational mental order: "the lofty mind, always calm, at rest in a quiet place, crushing down all that engenders anger, is restrained, venerable and well ordered" ("On Anger" 3.6.1). The images of "calm" and a "quiet place," of a mind "restrained" and "well ordered" are perhaps wish-fulfilling reactions to all that was violent, lawless, threatening and disorderly in the philosopher's world. The vision of the mind that is "lofty," "venerable," and "crushing down all that engenders anger" suggests a psychological ideal based on the absolute empire of conscious intelligence over every impulse or sensation, as if reason were a benevolent father and the passions were unruly children. The imperialism of the intellect allows for the rationalization of even such offensive excesses as those of Caligula, regarding whom Seneca speculates that Nature brought him forth "in order to demonstrate what the highest vices combined with the highest fortune can do" ("To Helvia" 10.4). The degree to which the author himself identifies with divine authority is perhaps apparent in his insistence on the principle of refining morals by demonstrating the evil of the passions. Just as Nature created Caligula to show the wickedness of corruption to men, so Seneca writes his extended essay on anger because "the unbridled and frenzied madness of anger must be exposed" ("On Anger" 3.3.6). If all of Seneca's plays are dramatizations of evils to be avoided, they are presented in the pious conviction that "the mind is strong before things for which it is prepared" ("On Anger" 3.37.4), and a belief that "the knowledge of sin is the beginning of salvation" (Letter 28.9). Thus, the contemplation of atrocity is not a matter of prurient indulgence, but an essential part of the process by which the individual assumes intelligent control over life.

Although Seneca's insistence on rational control may seem somewhat problematic for a modern reader, the philosopher's general pessimism was abundantly justified by the course of events in his own life, and the survival value of a doctrine based on the repression of emotion and denial of injury is notably conspicuous in the experience of his contemporaries. Whereas it may once have been fashionable to debunk "the wooden inhumanity of genuine Stoics" (Lucas 71), a certain brand of philosophical detachment is not only expedient in its tendency to placate the powerful, but essential for the protection of the weak. Suetonius suggests, for example, that the boy Caligula was only able to outlive his youth at the court of Tiberius by affecting "an amazing indifference" to the murder of relatives and his own ill-treatment, behaving so obsequiously to his grandfather that it was said of him "that no one had ever been a better slave or a worse master" (4.10). Thus Caligula's "wooden inhumanity," though perplexing to modern observers, seems to have had some practical value for Caligula. The biographical allusion to the horrors endured by the notorious tyrant in his childhood seems all the more essential in view of Alice Miller's argument, with respect to Hitler, that the cultural implications of the Holocaust can only be understood in the context of the tortures endured by the child who would become der Führer (*For Your Own Good* 142-97). The textual suggestion of a troubled transition from the role of slave to that of master implies, moreover, that Caligula's problem, like Hitler's, was rather communal than personal in its dimensions.

The implication of virtual equality between children and slaves, inherent in the custom of referring to the master as *paterfamilias* and his slaves as *familia,* is especially sobering in view of Finley's observation that "the greatest difference between the slave and the free man is that the former 'is answerable with his body for all offenses' " (93). Finley's emphasis on the importance of physical punishment in ancient Roman culture (93-96) suggests that modern research on the psychic and social consequences of corporal punishment may have noteworthy relevance to ancient experience. Of particular interest with respect to Seneca, whose stylistic "disconnections" have inspired debate as to whether a single writer could have written both his dramas and his philosophy, is Philip Greven's focus on the mechanism of dissociation that enables traumatized individuals "to disconnect feelings from their contexts and to disconnect one's sense of self from the external world" (148). The critical importance of this typical reaction to "a history of suffering" is underscored by Henry and Henry, who observe that "the dissociations between form and content within the plays are like the dissociations in Seneca's own mind and in his actual life" (176). It is interesting to consider these dissociations in the light of Bloch's estimation that the fantasies of adults and children may serve similar purposes even when they seem very different in form. Whereas terrified children often maintain an idealized image of a threatening parent by projecting their anger and fear onto imaginary creatures such as witches, ghosts, monsters, ogres, and bogey-men (Bloch 12), adults may achieve the same result by means of denial. Denying their own worth and the primary hostility of a hateful parent, they entertain the fantasy that if they are good enough they will eventually win parental approval; they set great store on the importance of self-improvement and good works, sometimes instituting what amounts to a regime of perpetual self-punishment. The clinical observation that awareness of gratuitous and irremediable parental hostility may be more than most people can bear (Bloch 12-13, 41-43) is, indeed, comparable to the critical assertion, with respect to the theme of cosmic confusion in Senecan drama, that "human beings cannot bear such a universe as this" (Henry and Henry 90). In any case, the psychological defenses deriving from a culture of abuse are relevant to Seneca's writing in two ways: the habitual denial exhibited by adult survivors of abuse corresponds to crucial tenets of Senecan philosophy, while the projections of terrified children appear in Senecan drama as the witches, ogres, ghosts, and wicked stepmothers for which the author is famous.

It should go without saying that the emphasis on dissociative patterns in Seneca's work is not meant to call attention to the author's personal problems. Although the voluminous extant works of both the philosopher and his father provide us with rather more information about their lives than we have on many other ancient fathers and sons, their familial disagreements are neither particularly remarkable nor relevant to the present discussion. Lucas' suggestion that the antagonism between junior and senior members of this distinguished household is culturally representative, Seneca the Younger standing for the "new imperial generation" and his father for the last gasp of "an age that was dying," is interesting precisely because it focuses on the growing pains of Roman society at large rather than on the details of any specific quarrel. To the degree that his view of generational conflict as a reflection of cultural tension in a transitional period when "intellectually the children were against the fathers and the fathers against the sons" (25-26) emphasizes the rational aspects of a kind of struggle often conspicuous for its emotional intensities, the critic reflects the stoic orientation of his subject.

Although it would be easy enough to comb the *Moral Essays* for signs of insensitivity to children, there would be little point in doing so because the disparagement of children is as conventional as contempt for women in ancient culture, and Seneca's perspective is, for the most part, rather moderate by contemporary standards. Capable of complacently assuming the benevolent intentions of Spartan parents who allowed their children to be brutally scourged in publicly administered tests of character ("On Providence" 4.11), he also argues eloquently in favor of a progressive educational strategy that looks very much like positive reinforcement. Asserting that "the spirit grows with freedom" but "is diminished by servitude," that "it rises up if it is praised and encouraged in good hope for itself," Seneca displays conspicuous generosity of spirit. He is also adverse to cruelty, advising those entrusted with the care of a child to "let him suffer nothing mean, nothing servile, never requiring him to beg abjectly nor to reward him for begging, but rather to let things be granted for the sake of merit and for past accomplishments and good promise of them in the future" ("On Anger" 2.21.3-5). Even if our response to this sensible counsel is tempered by the thought that the expert in question has the dubious distinction of having been Nero's tutor, Seneca deserves credit for the wisdom of his pedagogical views, and our sense of his responsibility for the excesses of Agrippina's son must be limited by consideration of the way in which the tyrant's career complements the violence and vindictiveness of a punitive culture in an arrogant and ambitious age. In fact, the inconsistency of a body of writing that approves of legendary cruelty while advocating enlightened practice dramatizes the essential difficulty of making sense out of a heritage of abuse.

Whereas Euripides presents his protagonist in the process of dissociating her sensual experience from convictions of cultural obligation, Seneca's Medea seems conspicuously disengaged from familiar human experience by the time she makes her first entrance. Indeed, the salient differences between the Euripidean and the Senecan versions of this tragedy may be understood as the textual denial by Seneca of Euripidean elements tending to augment the sense of Medea's basic humanity. The bare fact that Seneca's play begins with Medea on stage alone, while she is preceded in the Euripidean drama by the Nurse, the Tutor, and the Chorus, all apparently sympathetic to her, means that Seneca's Medea is divested of the social context that makes her seem relatively understandable in the Euripidean text. Seneca's omissions of the address to the Corinthian women, the Aegeus episode, and the messenger's description of Creusa's death, all have the effect of disconnecting Medea from the world of her peers and negating sympathetic aspects of the Euripidean protagonist. The Roman poet also stresses Medea's inhumanity by focusing on mythical elements that Euripides minimizes, such as the importance of magic, Medea's role as sorceress, and the relative frequency with which his demonic character invokes the Furies. On the other hand, he makes Jason seem more human by rendering him vulnerable to the pain of indecision—a kind of suffering that is all Medea's province in Euripides' tragedy. Certain convictions expressed by individual speakers in the Euripidean model are sanctioned in the Senecan drama by the impersonal song of the Chorus, the Roman version of which condemns Medea, champions Jason's cause, and expresses a passionate preoccupation with the theme of punishment.

Rosenmeyer's observation that the terms of Senecan drama "deride the settled findings" of their "philosophical model" (78) is abundantly justified by the choral interludes of *Medea,* wherein conventional pieties are pronounced only to be undermined. Denouncing Medea as a disobedient daughter in the first interlude, and celebrating the glory of paternal ancestors in the second, the Chorus proceeds, in the third and fourth interludes, to complain passionately and indignantly about the harshness of paternal authority. That these subversive assertions are well camouflaged by the erudition of their symbolic allusions does not make them any less remarkable. Rather, it is tempting to speculate that the poet may have exploited the dissident potential of his Chorus all the more aggressively because he could assume that there would be some yawning and stretching during the interludes. A special example of the innovative wit and energy that Seneca brought to his recreations of Euripidean material, the choral songs demonstrate what Rosenmeyer calls a "knack of combining two or more strands of mythology into meaningful patterns" (170). This ability is particularly evident in Seneca's emphasis on the myth of Phaethon, a central element in the Roman *Medea* that does not appear in the Euripidean version.

The child in the runaway chariot was associated with themes of unbridled passion and ordained injustice in Roman literature. While Ovid's presentation of Phaethon's adventure, featuring an enthroned father (Phoebus) who is quite as unnerved by fear as his son (*Metamorphoses* 2.31-32, 64-66, 91-92, 169, 178-81), and a shrewish, nagging mother (2.272-300), is perhaps most interesting as an ironic view of divine domesticity, it also refers to Jove's thunderbolt as "unjustly hurled" (2.378), insisting on the theme of cosmic cruelty by describing Phoebus himself as chafing at Jove's harshness and going on strike to teach the king of the gods a lesson (2.392-93). Ovid's telling of the tale not only labels Jove as "unjust," going so far as to question the wisdom of capital punishment in cases of childish mischief, but exalts the child's disobedience to the level of tragic heroism in an admiring epitaph: "Here Phaethon lies, in Phoebus' car he fared,/ And though he greatly failed, more greatly dared" (2.327-28).

Though references to the disobedient child in the second century C.E. differ markedly in tone from the indulgent irony of the *Metamorphoses*, they still link the arrogant youth with the abuse of power. Suetonius says that Tiberius, noticing the innate cruelty of the young Caligula, remarked that he was raising a viper for the Roman people and "a Phaethon for the world" (4.11), and Tacitus' description of the orgy of bloodletting precipitated by the death of Livia contains a veiled reference to the unrestrained child: "While the Augusta lived, there was still a moderating influence, for Tiberius had retained a deep-rooted deference for his mother. Sejanus, too, had not ventured to outbid her parental authority. Now, however, the reins were thrown off and they pressed ahead" (5.3). Though subversive import seems to have attached itself quite regularly to the myth of Phaethon, the meaning of particular references varies considerably over a period of several centuries. Whereas Ovid's Phaethon appears to be the victim of established injustice, Suetonius and Tacitus use the same myth in referring to individual wielders of unbridled power. The question of the precise nature of Seneca's use of this myth is especially interesting because the locus of his play is a place very much like the Roman Empire.

When Seneca's Creon banishes Medea, she begs a favor that does not occur to the Euripidean protagonist, pleading with the king to grant her some refuge in his realm (250-51). The "realm" in question is clearly no "polis" but a vast geographical entity comparable to an empire in extent. Given the political implications of this expansive location, Jason's repeated protestations of fear evoke an ominous sense of impending disaster that is not allayed by Medea's disparaging responses. Her answer to his statement that he fears exalted scepters seems inappropriately flippant: "See that you don't lust after them" (529). When Jason pleads, in his own behalf, that he has persuaded Creon to change the sentence of death to banishment, he produces no mean argument in his own favor and seems not to deserve Medea's sarcastic reply: "I deemed it punishment but now I see that exile is a favor" (492). Seneca himself was, after all, not above accepting such favors.

But Medea's disdain for exile is not only unreasonable because of the grim alternative; her indignation over the prospect of banishment also makes little sense in the context of an imperial organization where exile is the common lot of most citizens, a point on which the Chorus insists. Celebrating the removal of boundaries and the building of walled cities in new lands, the singers observe that "nothing of the entirely passable world has been left where once it had its place: the Indian drinks the cold Araxes, Persians drink the Rhine and Elbe" (371-74). If every citizen of the realm drinks the water of a river far from his native land, empire has conferred the condition of exile on all subjects. Thus, the cutting edge of Medea's worst traditional complaint is blunted, just as the actual threat of death from on high tends to mitigate the sleaziness of Jason's conventional arguments. The simple fact of moving the action from a Greek city-state to a cosmopolitan imperial center thus changes the value of statements by individual characters, because the dependence of citizens on the protection of particular localities is diminished by the scope of empire, and the threat of ever-impending violence is increased by the implied concentration of power in the hands of an absolute ruler. A great deal of confusion regarding the source of the threatening disaster results from Seneca's deliberate suggestion that the real menace comes from the foreigner on the premises rather than from any local authority.

The uninterrupted monologue of a totally isolated woman that constitutes the first act of *Medea* is a concise and vivid presentation of those elements most essential to Seneca's characterization of the child-murderer. Not only does Seneca disconnect Medea from her peers by giving her a stark initial entrance unprepared by the prior discourse of any other character, he structures her speech so as to emphasize her identity as sorceress, foreigner, and madwoman. Her first words are no grieving exclamation of human pain, like the one with which the Euripidean protagonist first makes her voice heard, but a vindictive invocation of superhuman powers, including unnamed "gods of wedlock," Lucina, a Roman goddess of childbirth closely associated with Diana and Juno, Minerva, the goddess of war, Titan, the god of the sun, Hecate, Pluto, the god of the underworld, and Proserpina, his captured bride. Whereas many of the ancient Greek equivalents of these gods are invoked by Medea during the course of the Euripidean tragedy, they are not all called upon before the end of the first sentence. The tumbling crowd of sacred names that falls from Medea's lips before she ever stops to take her first breath establishes the strong initial impression that she is possessed. The irreverence of her dealings with the gods is underscored by the use of the epithet *impios* in referring to the "impious ghosts" of Pluto's realm: "noctis aeternae chaos./ aversa superis regna manesque impios/ dominumque regni tristis" (chaos of eternal night and impious ghosts in a realm remote from heaven and lord of the dark kingdom, 9-11). The references to "chaos of eternal night," to the "impious ghosts," and to the "dark kingdom" all conspire to suggest the ominous presence of an infernal figure. Medea's gruesome description of the Furies as "avenging goddesses of evil" who have "hair foul with writhing snakes" and "bloody hands grasping the smoking torch" (16-18) strengthens the diabolical impact of her speech. Her recollection of her marriage to Jason as an event over which the Furies presided suggests that her essential wickedness precedes her adventures in Corinth and is, like a law of the universe, not contingent on the deeds of others.

Lest any member of the audience nurture an inclination to sympathize with this speaker, Seneca hastens to suggest that she is not only a witch but a foreigner: "pelle femineos metus/ et inhospitalem Caucasum mente indue./ quodcumque vidit Pontus aut Phasis nefas,/ videbit Isthmos" (Drive away womanish fear and clothe your mind with inhospitable Caucasus; whatever abomination Phasis has seen, the Isthmus will see, 42-45). The apparent model for Lady Macbeth's famous invocation, "Come you spirits/ That tend on mortal thoughts, unsex me here/ And fill me from the crown to the toe top-full/ Of direst cruelty" (1.5.38-41), these lines pay passing tribute to the conventional assumption that feminine sensibility is inimical to the expression of "direst cruelty." Most notable is Seneca's insistence on the violence of the Caucasus, Pontus and Phasis, an emphasis underscoring Medea's remote origin as if to reassure the audience that the atrocious acts to be presented are committed by a savage barbarian and so have nothing to do with local affairs. The word *Isthmos*, which might refer to either Greece or Italy, is conveniently ambiguous. Finally, Medea alienates herself from the world of sympathetic humanity by announcing that she longs for madness: "accingere ira teque in exitium para/ furore toto" (Gird yourself with madness and prepare with wholehearted madness for destruction, 51-52). Since, in Stoic terms, the one who desires madness is, for all practical purposes, already mad, this damning passage serves to widen the conspicuous gulf between Seneca's Medea and her Greek prototype. Whereas the despair of Euripides' Medea is linked to her dread of insanity, Seneca's Medea embraces madness with a voluptuous enthusiasm.

The relegation of the child-murderer to the ranks of the demented, the exotic, and the occult may be a deliberate strategy reflecting the general danger of engaging in literary activity during the Imperial age. The nature of the difficulty is evident in Suetonius' casual reference to a writer of Attellan farces whom Caligula burned alive in the ampitheater on account of some ambiguous expression (4.27). Certainly, if the playwright had any idea at all of alluding to the bad temper of any powerful contemporaries when he presented his Medea, prudence alone would have dictated that his dramatic subject should be not Roman, not male, not sane, and not easily recognizable. For a writer focusing on the evil of child murder, whether literal or metaphorical, the wisdom of attributing repugnant cruelty and volatility to a foreign female lunatic whose crimes were, in any case, mythical and legendary, would be compelling. It is in the selectivity and emphasis of his allusions to the mythological tradition that Seneca's artistic concerns are most consistently visible. Whereas Juno, Titan, Diana, Hecate, Pluto, and the Furies are all either angry parental figures or demanding fertility goddesses whose Greek equivalents appear more or less prominently in the Euripidean version of the myth, Seneca's *Medea* emphasizes the importance of several mythical "children" who do not appear in the Greek version. These are Apollo's son Phaethon and Proserpina, the Roman equivalent of Persephone, beloved daughter of Demeter, goddess of bountiful harvests.

In her monologue, Medea calls upon Proserpina as "dominam fide/ meliore raptam" (mistress, captured in better faith, 11-12), inviting comparison of Medea's situation with that of Pluto's queen. Whereas both Proserpina and Medea were carried off by amorous men who made various commitments, Proserpina's mate honors his vows better than Jason, a fact no doubt related to the circumstance that Pluto's vows were made to Ceres (Demeter), the mother of his captured bride, as much as to the girl herself. A significant difference between the two brides is, indeed, the contrast between Proserpina's benevolent association with her provident mother, and Medea's image as the motherless daughter of a brutal father. Whereas the problems caused by the kidnapping of Proserpina are resolved by a compromise resulting in the harmonious alternation of seasons and the blessings of fertility, Medea's flight from her father ends in the destruction of a new generation. The reference to the "better faith" with which Pluto keeps his captured bride is ironic in that Medea is not generally depicted as an innocent girl torn away, like Proserpina, from the side of a loving mother, and the invitation to compare Medea with the divine maiden, probably entails some suggestion that Medea has brought her troubles on herself by being a bad girl. This impression is strengthened by the fact that the speech alluding to Proserpina also contains the first of many references to Medea's kinsman, Phaethon, whose wretched fate is recalled by Medea's prayer that her grandfather will let her ride through the air in his carriage, allowing her to "guide the fiery yoke with the blazing harness" (32-34). The child unable to control the huge steeds he has in harness is a symbol to which Seneca returns again and again in his characterization of Medea, and to the extent that the angry wife is conflated with the figure of the presumptuous child, she resembles the "impious ghosts" that she herself invokes. Thus, initially, Medea is depicted as an inverted image of the essential moral value, *pietas*.

With a primary meaning of "dutifulness" or "dutiful conduct," *pietas* may mean "piety" toward the gods, "patriotism" toward one's country, or "devotion" to relatives. After Medea introduces the suggestion of her own "undutifulness" with the invocation of "impious ghosts" and the allusion to Phaethon, the Chorus clarifies the nature of her "impiety" by stressing Medea's disobedience to her father. The epithalamium in honor of Jason and Creusa refers to Medea as an "unbridled wife" (103), not only underscoring the similarity between Medea and her unfortunate kinsman, but presenting Jason as escaping from the clutches of an undesirable barbarian to enter into a joyful union with the benefit of parental blessings: "felix Aeoliam corripe virginem/ nunc primum soceris sponse volentibus" (happily take up the Aeolian maid, now, for the first time engaged with the parent's will, 105-06). Medea's claim to Jason's loyalty is thus undermined by the choral assertion that Creusa is lovable while Medea is not, and the implication that Jason is turning from a frightful marriage to a happy one is the first of many details tending to suggest that Seneca's Jason is more complicated and less contemptible than that of Euripides. Yet there is little likelihood that the philosopher would have taken the theory of the individual's right to happiness very seriously, and the presentation of Jason's personal problems should therefore be taken with a grain of salt. The essential point of the choral song in honor of the hopeful couple is the affirmation of the principle of parental permission. The concept is stressed again at the end of the next stanza: "rara est in dominos iusta licentia" (rarely is license against our masters justified, 109). Medea is singled out as a particular example of the bad consequences of license when the Chorus concludes that she should "go quietly into the shadows since she married as a fugitive to a foreign husband" (114-15). This insistence on the justice of punishing the "unbridled wife" is a single element in an extended analogy between Medea and the *impius* child, Phaethon.

The subversive implications of Medea's affiliation with Phaethon are evident in her constant opposition to the gods. Banished by Creon with orders "to go bother the gods somewhere else" (271), she exuberantly embraces the role of troublemaker, declaring that she will "assail the gods and shake the universe" (424-25). Her propensity to "go against the gods and drag down the sky" (673-74) is noted by the Nurse. In the ingredients obtained from Phaethon that she uses in preparing the poisoned brew for Creusa (826-27), and even in her famous assertion of the self rising above adversity—"Medea superest"—she proclaims her kinship with her arrogant young relative. When, in the choral interlude preceding the final act, the Corinthian citizens sing of Medea's inability "to restrain her anger or her love" (866-67) and ask when "the Colchian" will return to "Pelasgian lands and free their kingdom and their kings from terror" (670-73), the unrestrained passions of the character recall, not only the mythical career of Phaethon, but the course of Roman history from republican restraint to imperial excess, inviting comparison with the notorious despotisms of the East. The political implications of this tragedy are noted by Henry and Henry (167), who also underscore the importance of the "heavenly chariot" with which Medea is associated "from her first speech to her last" (161). The subversive significance of the chariot is most evident in the prayer that the Chorus addresses to Phoebus, urging him to hurry his carriage along so that night may descend quickly: "nox condat alma lucem,/ mergat diem timendum/ dux noctis Hesperus" (may gentle night hide the light, let Hesperus, leader of the night overwhelm this dreadful day, 676-78). The choral prayer for darkness, though coupled with a cursory tribute to Hesperus, occurs in a text which regularly characterizes the sun as the supreme embodiment of authority, so that the wish for the sun's disappearance, coupled with the woeful allusion to "this dreadful day," suggests antipathy toward an established regime. Thus, ultimately, the insistence on Medea's unrestrained passions recalls the public dimensions of Seneca's condemnation of anger, the "unbridled frenzy" that is "the only passion that can at times possess a whole state" ("On Anger" 3.2.2). In any case, the textual distinction between the chief charioteer, Phoebus, and the doomed child at the reins is worth noting.

The identification of Medea as disobedient child suggests that the initially blatant characterization of the child-murderer as foreigner, witch, and madwoman may be deliberately misleading. Persistent invitations to conceive of a character in child-like terms, if only by means of symbolic analogies, tend to inspire sympathy for the character, and it seems unlikely that Seneca would have referred so continually to myths such as those of Proserpina and Phaethon if he wished to present Medea as a simple exemplum of noxious wrath. If, however, the portrait of the nightmarish apparition is only a mask, we must ask what it conceals. One possibility is that Seneca uses the exaggerated trappings of fantasy to veil the vivid realism of his characterization. For instance, at the beginning of Act Three, when the Nurse describes in great physical detail the frenzied ravings to which Medea is driven by anger, the effect of a mounting impetus toward disaster is achieved largely through the accumulation of descriptive phrases cataloguing the physical disturbances caused by anger: the face aflame, the deeply drawn breath, the shouting voice, the running about of restless feet, the strange simultaneity with which Medea's eyes pour forth tears while yet she beams with excitement (380-96). Both Pratt (90) and Costa (108) have commented on the great similarity between this monologue and Seneca's catalogue of the visible signs of pathological anger in "On Anger" (1.1.3-6). The Nurse's speech is, indeed, only one example of the way in which Seneca's portrait of the child-murderer draws on his clinical description of those possessed by anger. The curious insistence on spontaneously creaking joints in the essay ("articulorum se ipsos torquentium sonus"), resembles one of the dire afflictions that Medea wishes on her worst enemies: "vulnera et caedem et vagum/ funus per artus" (wounds and slaughter and vague creepiness through the joints, 47-48). In the bristling hair, standing up on end, that the philosopher observes in those possessed by anger ("horrent ac surriguntur capilli"), we find an essential feature of Seneca's wild-haired priestess of Hecate: "Tibi more gentis vinculo solvens comam" (For thee unbinding my hair from restraint according to the manner of my people, 752). It is entirely consistent with Seneca's method that a strange detail listed as a spontaneous symptom of ordinary anger in his prose work appears in the dramatic poetry as a sign of Medea's foreign birth.

The interest in the literary craft of realistic representation that Seneca shared with certain of his contemporaries has not always been admired. Duff praises Petronius for his creation of the realistic novel (150), but he seems equally exasperated by Lucan's "besetting passion for realism" (250) and the "unintentional comicalities" produced by Seneca's "dangerous realism" (209). A more positive view of Seneca's achievement is to be found in Carla Federici's discussion of the relationship between realism and drama in seventeenth-century France. Paying special tribute to Seneca, she begins with a forthright assertion that he was an early practitioner of artistic realism (1-15). Her claim on behalf of the ancient writer is no more extravagant than the attribution of realism to certain modern fictions. Rebecca West, for instance, argues that Kafka's stories are not fantasies, but "have a realistic basis," and "strain belief only because Kafka was looking at an institution about which he knew more than most people" (110). Similarly, Gabriel Garcia Márquez insists that his own fabulous fictions are merely reflections of an astonishing reality: "Poets and beggars, musicians and prophets, warriors and scoundrels, all creatures of that unbridled reality, we have had to ask but little of imagination, for our crucial problem has been a lack of conventional means to render our lives believable." Surely Seneca, as well as Kafka, may be considered to have written about institutions with which he was more familiar than we are, and the likelihood of there being some affinity between the "unbridled reality" of Márquez' vision and Seneca's Rome seems considerable. The arguments advancing the "realism" of Kafka and Marquez have interesting implications with respect to the interpretation of Senecan drama..

Rosenmeyer's description of Senecan art as a "dramaturgy of cosmic sickness" is eminently compatible with the fact that Seneca's Medea not only kills her children but also takes sadistic pleasure in doing so. After murdering her first son, she exults obscenely: "voluptas magna me invitam subit/ et ecce crescit" (a great joy comes over me against my will, and oh, it is growing!, 991-92). Though this is a remarkable refinement of horror, there is nothing unrealistic about it. The attribution of sadism to the child-murderer is, after all, only the inspired addition of psychological immediacy to the Euripidean portrait of the mercilessly driven fanatic. Indeed, Seneca's prose description of the spiritual infirmity of "habitual cruelty" is no less sophisticated for having preceded the Freudian conception of "sadism" by nearly two millennia: "tunc illi dirus animi morbus ad insaniam pervenit ultimam, cum crudelitas versa est in voluptatem et iam occidere hominem iuvat" (The grim sickness of that mind passes into the ultimate insanity when cruelty is changed into delight and rejoices in killing a man, "On Mercy" 1.25.2). The word *voluptas*, which is used here and also by Medea in the above exclamation, is especially revelatory with respect to the sensual delight the "sick soul" derives from cruelty. There is, moreover, no reason to assume that Seneca does not speak of observed abuses in this passage. For an explicit clue to the "realistic" connection between the Euripidean fanatic and the Senecan sadist, we need only consider Suetonius' description of the link between moral rigidity and sadistic cruelty in the Emperor Tiberius who "regularly did so many cruel and violent things, ostensibly out of austerity and in order to improve peoples' morals, but, in reality to gratify his own impulses" (3.59.1). In his *Medea*, Seneca presents a woman who, like Tiberius, argues the seriousness of the cause, and the need to punish the wrongdoer, but is really compelled by her own corrupt desire. The problem with Medea, then, is not that she is so "fantastic," but that she is so cruel. This circumstance may constitute something of an interpretive difficulty if we consider the textual affinity between Seneca's Medea and another of his characters who is presented in rather a more positive light than she—the beloved antagonist, Jason.

At first glance, the differences between Medea and Jason seem salient and pronounced. Whereas Medea makes her initial entrance with a certain flourish of demonic conviction, Jason's appearance is marked by a sense of confusion and persecution that recalls the suffering of Euripides' Medea. Deploring the cruelty of fate, he complains that "remedia quotiens invenit nobis deus/ periculis peiora" (God often invents remedies worse for us than our problems, 433-34). Aside from the notable irony in this lament, Jason's sense of himself as having gone from the frying pan into the fire is another trait he shares with the Euripidean Medea. Like her also, he is torn between opposing demands of conscience, complaining that if he wants to keep his faith as a husband he must put his head in the jaws of death, but if he doesn't want to die he must resign himself to a sorry state of faithlessness (434-37). Not only is his conscience troubled by a sense of abrogated loyalty, his very life is forfeit if he keeps his faith. Like Euripides' Medea, Seneca's Jason suffers from a sense of binding obligation to his loved ones: "non timor vicit fidem,/ sed trepida pietas; quippe sequeretur necem/ proles parentum" (Not fear has conquered faith but fearful piety; certainly the children would follow in the death of their parents, 437-39). In view of the contemporary practice of executing the children of the condemned, Jason's anguish seems well founded. The degree to which "piety" motivates his repudiation of his wife recalls the Euripidean protagonist, who resorts to crime out of a sense of what she owes her father. Piety is, indeed, the essential feature that distinguishes Seneca's Jason from his Medea. Whereas Medea is regularly associated with impieties ranging from the invocation of "impious ghosts" to the commission of "impious bloodshed" (134-35) and the machination of "impious crime" (260-61), Jason is insistently identified as *pius*.

Piety is not only a generally recurring concern in Jason's speech, it is his stated reason for refusing Medea's request that the children may accompany her into exile: "Parere precibus cupere me fateor tuis;/ pietas vietat" (I confess that I want to yield to your prayers, but duty prevents me, 544-45). Despite the tiresome self-righteousness in his constant claim to pious virtue, Jason's position is generally credible. We tend to accept his professions of paternal devotion, not only because of the human quality of his moral confusion and the passionate intensity of his insistence that the children are his reason for living (547), but because he seems not so much the free ally of Creon as a subject who fears for his life and is doing everything he can to make the best of a bad situation. His perception of Medea and Creon as opposing forces very likely to crush him is shared by Medea herself (515-17). In fact, the most convincing sign that Jason is operating under compulsion inheres in Medea's professed suspicion that he is shaking in his boots: "Timuit Creontem ac bella Thessalici ducis?/ amor timere neminem verus potest" (Did he fear Creon and the hostility of Thessaly's king? true love can fear no man, 415-16). This insistence on "true love" in the face of an implied threat of death distinguishes Medea's mad passion from Jason's determination to remain calm in the face of disaster. Yet the cool rationalism that sets Jason apart from Medea in both the Greek and the Roman versions of the tragedy has a more positive value in Seneca's play than in Euripides', because the quality of deliberate control that seems so negative and self-serving in the Euripidean manifests itself as an essential strategy of survival in Seneca's world. To the degree that Jason's stance in the face of ominous tyranny seems now and again vaguely analogous to that of Seneca himself, the character may even be endowed with a mild aura of heroism. The implication of heroism is, indeed, inherent in the textual emphasis on *pietas,* a quality that links Medea's antagonist to the Virgilian hero, *pius* Aeneas.

Jason and Aeneas are both heroes of the epic tradition, leaders of famous sea voyages, and protegés of powerful female deities, Aeneas being the child of Aphrodite and Jason the favorite of Hera. Both heroes are associated with golden emblems (Golden Bough and Golden Fleece); both make journeys to the underworld (Kerényi, *Heroes* 272), and each has three legendary liaisons with mortal women. Both heroes are seducers and calculators, Aeneas abandoning Dido just as Jason leaves Medea, for political reasons. Seneca's association of Jason and Aeneas by means of the epithet *pius* serves to improve Jason's stature relative to that of the Euripidean Jason, and also, in an ironic way, to tarnish the traditional concept of glowing heroism implied in the term *pietas.* A most interesting aspect of the textual references to "piety" and "impiety" in Seneca's *Medea* inheres, moreover, in the way the dramatist uses these very terms to nullify the distinction between Medea and Jason. It is, after all, Medea herself who is ultimately presented as enduring the most excruciating torment of clamoring *pietas*; in the frenzied crisis that culminates in the killing of the children, she laments that "ira pietatem fugat/ iramque pietas. cede pietati, dolor" (Anger routs duty and duty anger; make way for duty, sorrow, 943-44). The conspicuous role of "duty" in Medea's dilemma is evident in that, in this speech, forms of the word *pietas* appear three times in the space of two lines (*pietatem, pietati, pietas*). At this moment, no robes or masks of lunatic, witch, or foreigner can disguise the human suffering of the woman torn between the conflicting claims of anger (*ira, iramque*) and duty (*pietas*). Seneca's Medea is, in the end, just as much the victim as Euripides'. Her status as such is well prepared by means of various identifications.

After the confrontation between Jason and Medea in the Third Act, the Chorus sings of those who have, like Jason, enraged Neptune, the lord of the sea, by daring to travel in ships. A prayer to Neptune in favor of Jason is followed by a reference to the child who dared to usurp the heavenly province of another paternal deity (599-602), and it does not bode well for Jason that the plea for his welfare immediately precedes the allusion to Phaethon, the child who paid in full the penalty for heedlessly transgressing on divine territory. The essential point, however, is that the child, Phaethon, who has been identified exclusively with Medea until this point, becomes a general symbol of the victims of destroying wrath. The choral reference to the doomed child is embedded, moreover, in a catalogue of the disasters endured by Jason's fellow Argonauts as punishment for infringing on the domain of Neptune. In this remarkable compilation of victims, some of the stories are doubly and triply determined by the theme of child murder. The tale of Iphigeneia, for instance, is included not only because she was killed by her own father, but because Aulis, angry over the death of its king, the Argonaut Tiphys, has caused Agamemnon to kill Iphigeneia. Orpheus, Hercules, Nauplius, Meleager, Idmon, and Mopsus are all victims of Neptune's wrath even though many of them also suffer the pursuing fury of other parental figures: Orpheus is torn apart by maenads; Hercules is destroyed by his stepmother, Juno; Meleager is killed by his own mother to avenge the death of her brother. Jason himself is assimilated with the image of the child perishing for the sins of the father: "occidet proles, patrioque pendet crimine poenas" (The son shall perish and pay the penalty for the father's crime, 660-61). The Chorus pleads for mercy on the ground that enough victims have already paid the penalty for offending Neptune: "iam satis, divi, mare vindicastis; parcite iusso" (Now gods, you have avenged the sea enough; spare him who acted under orders, 668-69). With a strategy something like that of the lawyers for the defense at Nuremburg, the Chorus claims that Jason's culpability is mitigated by the fact that he was following the command of his paternal uncle when he set out to retrieve the Golden Fleece in the first place. The cumulative effect of all these allusions is to posit Jason unambiguously as a victim. The suggestion that he is being forced into the role of a scapegoat is not only a noteworthy departure from the Euripidean model, it also casts a doubtful shadow over the Stoic principle of rational order in the universe.

    Whereas certain essentially heretical passages in Senecan drama were once dismissed by speculation that "Seneca is dramatist enough to introduce non-Stoic views" into his texts (Duff 215), Rosenmeyer argues that Senecan drama is inherently irreverent: "The Senecan scene is the nexus of seemingly dominant operational causes belying faith in an orderly system" (78). Not only "belying faith in an orderly system," the plays present the gods as a "dramatic mechanism for evoking the interconnectedness of causes in a resistant cosmos" (Rosenmeyer 81-82). Critical emphasis on the "interconnectedness of causes" recalls clinical insistence on the interpersonal dynamics of abuse. Thus, Seneca's Chorus, arguing on behalf of Jason, stakes out a position similar to that of Alice Miller when she claims, with respect to a particularly harrowing case of child-murder, that "the accused never bears all the guilt by himself but is a victim of a tragic chain of circumstances" (*For Your Own Good* 199). The relevance of abusive paradigms to Senecan drama is underscored by Rosenmeyer's elegant reference to "the noxiousness of the unscrutable" (85), a phrase implying that ultimate power inheres in malevolent agents, as if the gods themselves were abusive parents. Whether or not the Chorus between Acts Three and Four, lamenting the fate of sons condemned for the sins of fathers, is unorthodox, it is certainly subversive in tone, as is the apparently conservative choral interlude between Acts Two and Three. The latter, glorifying the ancestors of the Empire, seems to be an innocuous reflection of Stoic doctrine, positing the nobility of the idealized forefathers and the corruption of the inadequate descendants (329-30), but it actually articulates a risky kind of nostalgia, since the technique of glorifying the "Romans of olden times" was a standard code for criticizing the incumbent regime (Duff 12, 153).

If Jason's identity with Phaethon implies that he is a scapegoat about to pay an inordinate price for essentially pardonable faults, the suggestion that Medea is a bad girl who deserves the punishment she gets is also undermined, because the resemblance of Medea and Jason to each other, established by their mutual association with the symbol of Phaethon, effectively destroys the distinctions between the "pious" and the "impious," between the "good child" and the "bad child." Since both "children" are being set up as victims, questions of innocence and guilt are irrelevant, and the crucial problem is the inexorability of the executioner. In keeping with the critical observation that "all Seneca's deliberate wrongdoers are monarchs" (Henry and Henry 68), the one genuine villain in this play is Creon. Characterized by Jason himself as "infestus Creo" (angry Creon, 490), the king enters and exits with threats of murder on his lips. Though his warning to Medea that she must die if she is not gone by morning (297-99) is an unremarkable reflection of the Euripidean model, Seneca's Creon couples the warning with a declaration to the effect that he would have killed Medea already if Jason had not dissuaded him from it: "abolere propere pessimam ferro luem/ equidem parabam; precibus evicit gener" (for my part, I was getting ready to destroy this worst of pests quickly by the sword; the prayers of my son-in-law prevailed, 183-84). Uneasy apprehension of the king is reinforced by the fact that Seneca portrays him as embodying some of the worst faults of Euripides' Jason. For instance, when Medea complains of injustice, Creon tells her to go and complain to the Colchians (197), with an arrogance which recalls that of the Euripidean Jason telling Medea she should be thankful to him for the privilege of suffering in Greece rather than in some barbarian backwoods. Creon resembles the Euripidean Jason in the persistent negativity of his language.

The king first speaks in order to ask a negative and hostile question: "Medea, Colchi noxium Aeetae genus/ nondum meis exportat e regnis pedem?" (Medea, noxious child of Colchian Aeetes, have you not yet taken yourself out of my kingdom?, 179-80). The matter-of-fact aggression and malice with which he introduces himself would render his claim to personal benignity questionable even if he did not insist on a conspicuous denial of hostility: "non esse me qui sceptra violentus geram/ nec qui superbo miserias calcem pede,/ testatus equidem videor haud clare parum" (That I am not one who wields the scepter with violence nor with arrogant foot tramples on miserable people is testified indeed not a little bit clearly, 252-54). Distinguished by the piling up of negatives and minimizers such as *non, nec, haud,* and *parum*, this speech advertises exactly those qualities of arrogance and bellicosity that the speaker seems eager to deny. As if to confirm Jason's presentation of himself as operating under compulsion, the king boasts that he has chosen a son-in-law stricken by affliction and terror: "generum exulem legendo et afflictum et gravit/ terrore pavidum, quippe quem poenae expetit/ letoque Acastus regna Thessalica optinens" (I am seen to choose for a son-in-law an exile both afflicted and stricken by heavy terror, indeed whom King Acastus demands for punishment by death, 255-57). The allusion to another king's desire for Jason's blood may remind anybody inclined to forget it that the threat of death is never far when an absolute tyrant is near, and on the whole, Seneca's Creon is presented so ominously that his declaration of fatherly regard for Medea's children is hardly reassuring: "Vade: hos paterno ut genitor excipiam sinu" (Go on; into my fatherly embrace as a father, I will receive them, 284). Fatherly indeed! The smug solicitude of this paternal demonstration only increases the sense of foreboding generated by the royal presence.

In the last analysis, the exaggerated quality of Medea's identity as outsider suggests that the mask of foreigner, witch, and madwoman that she wears is part of a diversionary tactic that Seneca employs in order to avoid calling attention to the real troublemaker on the scene. This is not to say that the author does not take Medea's atrocious cruelty seriously, or even that his Medea is ultimately no more of an unprovoked aggressor than that of Euripides. The point is simply that pragmatic considerations make it expedient for Seneca to deny the human familiarity of authorized madness and to displace it onto a notably exotic character. Thus, Creon is more of a menace than his relatively bland manner might suggest, while Jason and Medea, though they both bring their suffering upon themselves, are human beings more offended against than offending, and they do not deserve the treatment that they get. Whereas Medea reaps the whirlwind by calling forth passions she cannot control, Jason is a spineless braggart, as helpless in his love as in his hate, who actually invites Medea's vindictive assault by fatuously boasting of his paternal devotion. Both of them violate the Stoic teaching of imperviousness to the passions, thus proving themselves to be no better than the generally pessimistic Stoic view of human nature might lead us to expect them to be. There is little likelihood, however, that Seneca shares Creon's belief that people's heads should roll for such failings. No advocate of punitive cruelty, the author was rather inclined to argue that human shortcomings make mutual compassion a necessity: "Let us be more gentle with one another. We wicked live among the wicked. One thing only can make peace for us, an agreement of mutual indulgence" ("On Anger" 3.26.4). Though the myth of the child who forfeits his life as penalty for disobedience is the unifying symbol in this drama, it does not represent the author's idea of justice. Writing only a generation after Ovid depicted Phaethon as the victim of a thunderbolt "unjustly fired," Seneca expressed his own views on harsh punishment in straightforward terms, declaring that "it is the characteristic of a great soul to be tranquil and calm and look down from above on injuries and offenses" ("On Mercy" 1.5.5). He also moves from the recommendation of mercy to criticism of those who stubbornly refuse it: "And I think perhaps that nobody finds it more difficult to give pardon than he who often deserves to beg for it" (1.6.2). The skeptical view of abusive authority expressed in the prose works tends to confirm the suspicion of subversive import in the tragedies.

The essential rhetorical tension in the tragedy of *Medea* inheres in the opposition between the terms *pietas* and *ira*. The importance of *ira* as the epitome of noxious human passion has been noted, but a few words on the tragic implications of the term *pietas* are perhaps in order. Like the Greek word τιμή (*honor*), *pietas* suggests a sense of what the child owes the parent, thus recalling the problem of filial obligation in the Euripidean text. But the word *pietas* reflects a somewhat more complicated context of ethical expectations than is suggested by the word τιμή. Originally designating the quality of one who fulfills the rights and duties owed to a deity, *pietas*, like τιμή, implies a sense of what the subject (child, citizen, worshipper) owes the authority (parent, monarch, deity). Cyril Bailey suggests, however, that by the time of Virgil, *pietas* had come to signify, beyond the sense of what the subject owed the figure of authority, a certain sense of reciprocity, the idea "that there is something which the gods owe men in return for their piety" (85). The word *pietas,* therefore, connoting the mutual obligation of child to parent and parent to child, has no exact equivalent in ancient Greek. Bailey's assertion, based on analysis of the literary uses of the word *pietas,* is interesting because it suggests that there is more to the Roman view of self in relation to the world than what shows up in the overt statements of Stoic philosophy.

We may consider that, whether Seneca wrote his tragedies while in exile on the island of Corsica or during the years of his association with Nero, the conflict between the extremes of *pietas* and *ira* that animates the *Medea* was a matter of profound concern to him and not just a rhetorical nicety. The most forbearing of philosophies cannot have prevented the author from feeling somewhat perturbed over the apparently great disparity between what was expected of him by his lords and masters, and what he, in return, could expect from them. The essays deal with the problems of anger and duty, to be sure, but in intellectually sanctioned ways, conceding the existence of abuse but stepping gingerly around its human implications and, as a rule, dissociating experience from the feelings it may inspire. It is one thing to profess that anger must always be repressed, that the injury never justifies retribution, that there is a just rational order in the universe, that we have no choice but to submit to the gods and their earthly representatives at court. It is quite another thing to articulate the simmering core of all that is repressed and denied. To the question asked by Henry and Henry, "whether Seneca's tragedies were a means for him to express awareness of elements in life for which his consciously held beliefs could allow no place" (156), the answer must be an emphatic affirmation.

Conceived during a terrifying age, these tragedies haunted by the specter of child murder emerge as an extended cry of indignation and rage. The originality and energy of the poetry is in direct proportion to its concern with forbidden passions and subversive thoughts. Though the philosopher advises that anger should be denied in the self and ignored in the other, the dramatist creates a protagonist who exults in vitriolic excess; though the sage insists on the sanctity of the paternal ideal and the worthlessness of the corrupted progeny, the poet evokes the image of an erring child who is also a cruelly punished victim; though the Stoic asserts the existence of divine rational order, the playwright presents a Chorus denouncing the blood-lust of the gods, and characters who blaspheme with energetic acerbity:

Per alta vade spatia sublimi aetheris,
testare nullos esse, qua veheris, deos

(Go through the high spaces of lofty heaven; bear witness that where you go, there are no gods.) (1026-27)

Seneca expressed his cosmic certainty and human compassion in the *Moral Essays,* but found, in the drama, a form for his doubt and an arena for his rage. The brilliance of his dramatic writing inheres precisely in the degree to which the poetry is connected to the profoundest sources of his passion.

4

Corneille and the
Importance of Gratitude

The great age of French classicism, heralded in by Corneille's *Médée* (1634), and ushered out by Racine's *Athalie* (1691), begins and ends with tragic presentations of ferocious female child-murderers. The importance of progenicidal themes in seventeenth-century drama is underscored by Mitchell Greenberg, who notes that Racinian theater in particular is haunted by the "scenario of the child that must be killed" (141). Despite the apparent continuity between Cornelian and Racinian concerns, Greenberg insists on the differences between the treatments of similar themes by these two authors. While Corneille's Medea is "an all-powerful Phallic mother" (56) in a dramatic universe characterized by "sexual essentiality" (145), Racine's theater is notable for the "sexual indeterminacy of both victim and executioner" (153) and a "ritualized reenactment of the sacrifice of the other that inheres in us all" (172); the complexity of Racinian dramaturgy "inaugurates the reign of the modern, the impossible era of the divided self" (172). Considerable as the often-noted differences between Corneille and Racine may be, Greenberg's articulation of them seems problematic, if only because the suggestion that the self was somehow unified until Racine came along must come as a surprise to anybody familiar with the ancient antecedents of Corneille's *Médée*. Furthermore, the term *phallic mother,* evidently belying the claim of "sexual essentiality" in Cornelian theater, reveals the limits of a Freudian perspective positing "the descendants of Laius and Jocasta" as the "originary family of Classical subjectivity" (157) and the murder of the child as tragic largely because it is "a sign of the inability of Patriarchy to survive without castration—without that is, its self-mutilation" (172). It is precisely because the thematic concerns of myths such as Oedipus and Medea are not mutually exclusive that the insistently phallocentric emphasis of certain Freudian elaborations seems remarkable, especially with reference to a theater known for the representation of mythical matriarchs. With all due respect to King Oedipus, I suggest that the originary family of classical subjectivity is the one Corneille presents in his *Médée*.

Celebrating the dubious alliance between male and female figures of authority who ascend to glory while ignoring the good advice of skeptical friends and leaving a trail of dying children in their wake, Corneille's *Médée* is an overtly exuberant yet curiously ambiguous affirmation of political absolutism. Approved by public and critics alike during the author's lifetime, the play fell into obscurity during the following centuries, being performed not more than half a dozen times between the end of the seventeenth century and the middle of the twentieth (de Leyssac in Corneille, *Médée* 12-14), and dismissed as late as 1964 as evidence of youthful ineptitude on the part of its author (Wiley 138). Renewed interest in the text was sparked by André Stegman, who claimed, in 1962, that "in the evolution of Corneille's thought, *Medea* represents a more crucial moment than *The Cid*." Pointing out that after the success of this play, Corneille's real problem was to find subjects "less shocking to common morality than infanticide," Stegman asks whether it makes sense to insist that Medea's crimes proceed from a spirit distinguishable from that apparent in such later plays as *Horace, Pertharite,* and *Rodogune* ("La *Médée* de Corneille" 125-26). His references to *Horace,* in which an old man declares his willingness to kill his son with his bare hands, *Pertharite,* in which a woman offers her hand in marriage on condition that her son be sacrificed, and *Rodogune,* in which a monstrous queen kills her grown son in order to vouchsafe her own regime, suggest that Stegman's insistence on the importance of Corneille's *Médée* is linked to an intuition of the centrality of filicidal themes in the author's work. The social relevance of such themes is implicit in Marc Fumaroli's description of *Médée* as "one of those collective mirrors in which civil society may recognize itself and become aware of its inclination to pursue profane pleasures rather than religious salvation" (185).

In view of the recurring emphasis on child-murder in Corneille's dramatic poetry, it is interesting to note the tendency of his theoretical prose to describe the antagonists of his tragic heroes in parental terms. In his "Discours de la tragédie et des moyens de la traiter selon le vraisemblable ou le nécessaire" (Discourse on tragedy and the means of presenting it in accordance with verisimilitude and necessity), he invokes Aristotle's assertion that the threat of violence between close relations is a particularly appropriate subject for tragedy: "L'auditeur . . . se porte aisément à plaindre un malheureux opprimé ou poursuivi par une personne qui devrait s'intéresser à sa conservation" (The audience is easily moved to pity a poor soul oppressed or pursued by a person who ought to be engaged in protecting him, *O.C.* 833). In the "person who ought to be engaged in protecting" the tragic protagonist, we may easily recognize the persecutory parent of classical tragedy. That this figure is immediately discernible in a motif that Corneille borrows directly from Euripides and Seneca is only to be expected, and yet, Corneille drew his raw materials from a great variety of sources and altered them liberally to suit his purposes. The domineering parents and monarchs, the desperate sons, daughters and wards are as visible in his early comedies and late tragedies as in the celebrated plays of his middle years. His most famous comedy is about a young man who leaves home because of paternal abuse *(L'Illusion comique),* and the subversive thrust of his entire oeuvre is expressed in *Suréna,* when Euridice declares: "Mon père choisit mal" (My father is making the wrong choice, 82). There is no play which Corneille mentions more frequently in his "Discours" than *Médée;* by his own admission, there is no play for which he nursed a greater affection than *Rodogune.* The theme of child murder is ultimately inseparable in Cornelian drama from the ubiquitous conflict between exploitive, irresponsible elders and vulnerable, anguished youths; the filicidal plot of his first tragedy is no mere adaptation of an ancient theme but a genuine expression of his most characteristic convictions. The importance of the progenicidal paradigm is underscored by the author's apparent inclination to compensate for his "outrageously" compassionate presentations of erring young people by making critical apologies designed to mollify the hostile adult detractors of his work.

A good example of Corneille's tendency to bridge the gap between the subversive implications of his drama and the conservative perspective of his audience is evident in his remarks on *Théodore, vierge et martyre (Theodora, Virgin and Martyr)*, a play in which a young man and a young woman are destroyed by the collaboration of an ineffectual father and a vindictive stepmother. Neither the fact that the text in question is a well constructed drama that is genuinely tragic in effect, nor the piety of its religious source *(The Virgins* of St. Ambroise) could redeem the play from the damning fact that it deals with the theme of enforced prostitution. Therefore, in spite of a certain apparent affection for the work, Corneille finally sanctioned his hostile critics by judging the play to be "mal faite puisqu'elle a été mal suivie" (badly written because it was badly received, "Examen de 1660" 392). Similarly, in the wake of the notorious quarrel over *The Cid,* in which he was criticized for the impropriety of Chimène's behavior, Corneille regretted the noncompliance of his character with "la rigueur du devoir" (the rigors of duty, "Examen de 1660" 219). More remarkable than his own readiness to comply with the taste of his public is the tendency of modern critics to echo the complaints of contemporary grumblers. Samuel Solomon observes, for instance, that "in *Le Cid* our pity for the unexpected misfortune dealt the two lovers by a cruel fate is quite as great as our admiration for their adherence to the demands of parental honor" *(Pierre Corneille* xxx), as if the "unexpected misfortune" in question were entirely a matter of "cruel fate" and not at all the result of their fathers' foolishness. In *The Cid*, parental honor is the wheel on which young lives are racked, and young people grieve because a couple of squabbling old men cannot or will not restrain their egotistical ambitions. Corneille's concessions to the demands of his public are indicative of an internal split between creative impulse and critical capacity that corresponds to the typical antagonisms of his tragic scenarios. The abusive dynamics of the process by which external attack is transformed into self-criticism are implicit in Doubrovsky's description of Corneille's afterthoughts on his work as the "betrayal of the creator's primary intuition by the retroactive judgment of the pedant" (120). Although modern scholars are generally inclined to treasure the "creator's primary intuition" as opposed to the "retroactive judgment of the pedant," there is at least one notable exception.

Whereas, in his scholarly edition of Corneille's *Médée*, de Leyssac normally gives preference to the earliest versions of a text that Corneille revised repeatedly in his lifetime, the critic agrees with the author's decision to delete an allusion to an ancient myth of child-murder originally written into a speech for the Nurse, Nérine: "Celle qui de son fils saoula le Roy de Thrace/ Eut bien moins que Médée et de rage et d'audace" (She whose son sated the king of Thrace was neither as furious nor as audacious as Medea, 709-10). Apparently judged offensive, these lines were omitted from editions printed after 1660, and de Leyssac defends the deletion as an exception to the general rule that the poet's retrospective revisions usually weaken his original conception and eviscerate the psychological realism of his first inspiration (84). The wording of this observation makes it clear that the critical objection to the original lines derives from distaste for the peculiar brutality of the myth in question: "We may easily dispense with this terrible allusion which recalls all too vividly the atrocities of Seneca's *Thyestes*." Unless we are to believe that it is somehow less offensive to kill children than to eat them, the delicacy of this analysis seems perplexing. Dreadful as the allusion to the myth of Tereus, Procne, Itys, and Philomela may be, it is hardly irrelevant to the development of a play about the murder of children, especially when the writer openly acknowledges his enormous debt to the author of the *Thyestes*. In fact, Corneille's capacity to combine two or more myths into a meaningful pattern is comparable to that of his ancient Roman model.

The nurse's allusion to the woman who served the king a pie in which she cooked the body of his son is as essential to Corneille's *Médée* as references to the boy who was the victim of the gods are to Seneca's. Not only the themes of child murder and vengeance but also focus on the redeeming value of art forms a connecting link between the myths of Philomela and Medea. Just as Philomela weaves her story into a tapestry in order to let her sister know that Tereus, Procne's husband and the father of her child, raped Philomela and cut out her tongue, so Corneille's Medea is identified as a formidable opponent precisely because of her art (49, 62, 1120, 1239, 1262, 1591) and her *sçavoir* (knowledge, 338, 795, 1276, 1643). The suffering and revenge of Philomela/Procne and Medea are both precipitated by the sexual aggression of male seducers, and the philandering spouse or lover is an essential element in a text distinguished from its ancient antecedents by the fact that all the major characters seem to be in love—Medea and Creusa love Jason, Jason and Aegeus love Creusa and, assertions of "sexual essentiality" in Cornelian drama to the contrary, there is even some suggestion that Creon's affection for Jason also belongs on the list of Cupid's mischief. Corneille's skeptical view of love and marriage is perhaps most evident in the curious itinerary of the character Pollux, whose sudden disappearance from the scene is explained by the fact that he has to run off to attend the ill-omened wedding of his sister Helen to Menelaus (1340-45). In any case, mythical references to notorious marriages are not only a reflection of Corneille's increased emphasis on erotic intrigue, but an indication of the inseparability of child-murder from abuses that are sexual and familial in nature. In fact, the description of Medea as a "collective mirror" of "civil society" seems especially appropriate with respect to the question of contemporary marriage arrangements.

Bénichou's assertion that "medieval ways of thinking remained vigorous long after the decline of the social system that nourished them" (20) is an important indication of the relationship between the cultural context of Corneille's theater and a tragic text in which various children are destroyed by the willingness of adults to use them as pawns in dubious political maneuvers. Predicated on the principle of primogeniture, medieval marriage arrangements in France reflected the concern of established families not to disseminate their wealth and power among too many heirs. By designating oldest sons, married men, and heads of families as *seniores* and the younger brothers destined to remain unmarried and propertyless as *juvenes*, the system tended to institutionalize the disruptive force of sibling rivalry, fostering the growth of a restless class of bachelors who embodied a subversive potential built into the structure of society. The identification of these bachelors as "abductors by their very nature," who were "always tempted to take by force from another household the wife that would make them into elders" prompts Duby to speculate that the tendency of chivalric ideology "to extol the life of adventure" functioned as a kind of "mock compensation for the frustrations of 'youth' " (13). The historian's analysis is not only intriguing in its emphasis on the importance of age distinctions in medieval power arrangements, but also in the infanticidal logic implicit in the articulation of his argument: "each root stock sent forth only one stem. The adventitious branches were made to wither, so as not to sap the strength of the central trunk" (9-10). Whereas the preferred method of causing the "adventitious branches to wither" seems to have been the encouragement of military and ecclesiastical careers, the net effect was a broad exercise of parental discretion to choose which of the family's children would attain full adult status and which would be condemned to waste away in the perpetual no-man's land of "youth." Although the themes of youth's frustration and the legitimacy of possession that Duby stresses are inherent in the ancient myth of the Argonauts, Corneille emphasizes crucial aspects of his mythical material so as to illuminate and expose the internal contradictions in a system that was already being attacked in his day.

Observing that the privilege of the favored child that formed the basis of family structure from the end of the middle ages to the seventeenth century was weakened by the arguments of moralists and educational theorists during the second half of the seventeenth century, Ariès refers with some nostalgia to the world which was rapidly disappearing in Corneille's lifetime (*Centuries* 371). Although his admiration for the "gay indifference of the prolific fathers of the ancien régime" (406) is a disconcerting non sequitur to his abundant documentation of the precarious quality of childhood under the old order, his argument is essential to the explication of a play that is not only about the antagonism between age and youth but also about the murder of children. His famous assertion that the very idea of childhood did not exist in medieval society suggests, in the first place, that the absence of the child from the classical stage was no mere concession to *bienséance* but a meaningful reflection of the child's general exclusion from polite French society. Ariès' rather sanguine view of this exclusion is, in any case, rather controversial, having prompted David Hunt to observe that "indifference" to the real distinctions between children and adults is an indication of insensitivity rather than of tolerance. Insisting on a causal connection between parental indifference and the death of children, Hunt judges the argument of Ariès' *Centuries of Childhood* to be "biologically inconceivable" (49). Examining the same cultural material on which Ariès bases his thesis, Hunt finds "a telling indictment of the old régime" at the "core of its domestic life" (157). With reference to the particular phenomenon of the child's "absence," he suggests that if the child was not visible, it was probably because nobody enjoyed having him around. The very obligation of attending the physical needs of children was part of the stigma of indigence: "it was a sign of her poverty that the lower class mother had to take care of children while other more affluent women could hire a servant to perform this task" (82). Hunt concludes that the message conveyed to the privileged child of a powerful family by the employment of a nurse was that "his mother's breasts were forbidden to him and his father did not want him around" (108).

Corneille's *Médée* was presented in an age when infants were regularly consigned to the care of infanticidal wetnurses, when the "accidental" suffocation of babies by married women was routinely tolerated, when infanticidal unmarried girls were regularly executed, when the abandonment of infants was well on its way to reaching the epidemic proportions that would move St. Vincent de Paul to establish foundling homes for their care at the end of the century. Ariès himself concedes, in the "Préface" to the edition of *L'Enfant et la famille* published in 1973, that if he were to write the book again he would pay more attention to the phenomenon of "tolerated infanticide" than he did. The perspective of the history of childhood is particularly relevant to the discussion of the theme of child murder in seventeenth-century literature because the history of childhood is, in a very real sense, a peculiar outgrowth of seventeenth-century culture. Whether or not children were worse off in France during the *ancien régime* than at other times in other places is doubtful; what is certain is that more minutely detailed information on the lives and deaths of children was recorded during this period than is available for any earlier epoch. Both Ariès and Hunt refer extensively to the journals kept by the physician, Héroard, who was employed by Henri IV to supervise the care of the infant Louis XIII. In a biographical study of Louis XIII that depends heavily on Héroard's records, Elizabeth Marvick observes that "no other document in Western literature gives as complete a record of the development of an individual" as this physician's journals (xvii). Divergent as the interpretations drawn from such material by various historians of childhood may be, the cumulative effect of their work on the writing of more conventional scholars is clearly visible. In his study, *France in the Age of Louis XIII and Richelieu,* Victor Tapié makes short shrift of the question of children. "The seventeenth century," he observes, "had no love of children" (7).

With regard to the suggestion of a link between the psychology of abuse and the customs of the *ancien régime,* Ariès warns that the imposition of the "modern language of the abusive father and the spoiled child adds nothing to our understanding of either the world of today or that of the past" (*L'Enfant et la vie,* "Préface à la nouvelle édition" vi). On the other hand, there is nothing to be gained by suggesting that every practice was universally approved just because it existed. Whereas Ariès explains that "the family at that time was unable to nourish a profound existential attitude between parents and children," insisting nevertheless that "this did not mean that parents did not love their children but they cared about them less for themselves than for the contribution they could make to the common task" (368), Corneille overtly criticized the exploitive customs of his fellow citizens. Discreetly suggesting that contemporary parents could afford to be rather more considerate of the emotional needs of children and less concerned with "the contribution they could make to the common task," Corneille notes, in the "Examen" of *Théodore,* that the presentation of certain unsympathetic characters may serve the salutary purpose of correcting the excessive severity of those parents in the audience who stubbornly insist on enforcing marriage contracts and "refuse to waive their preconceived plans by mutual agreement between families when the children concerned, having attained marriageable age, do not wish to marry each other" (*O.C.* 392). This casual assertion shows that even in the absence of the "modern language of the abusive father and the spoiled child," it was possible for writers to suggest that marriages arranged without the consent of the parties concerned constituted a noxious imposition of parental power. The injunction against "anachronism" may therefore be tempered with some judicious care not to espouse an interpretive position more conservative than that of a sensitive citizen of the seventeenth century.

It follows from the transitional nature of Corneille's century that, in his day, many conventional practices were also controversial. For example, the changing attitude toward the time honored practice of burning "witches" at the stake deserves special mention in the discussion of a play in which magic and sorcery are emphatically stressed. Corneille's Medea, who not only stirs up noxious potions onstage but also brandishes a magic wand and casts spells of invisibility, made her theatrical debut while the famous exorcism of Ursuline sisters at the convent of Loudun was in progress. Persuaded that they were possessed by the devil, the nuns accused the priest Urbain Grandier of corrupting them, thus precipitating a notorious trial and series of exorcisms which lasted from 1632 to 1638. The importance of this case for the development of classical sensibility is underscored by Greenberg, who refers to it as the "'other stage' of Classicism, a darker, more brutally ambivalent stage upon which is played out in much more violent scenarios, the ritual sacrifice of desire to political necessity" (67). In fact, the opening of *Médée* during the winter of 1634-35 occurred within a year of Grandier's execution in August 1634, when the disturbing implications of the proceedings were fresh in the mind of the public. Noting the "blatant unfairness" with which Grandier was pursued, tortured and convicted "on the strength of his evil reputation, for acts which he had certainly not committed, yet in accordance with what was still the due process of law," Tapié asserts that "the horror which Grandier's trial and death aroused in public opinion even at the time shows that people already felt that there was no defense for justice such as this" (294). Whereas Tapié emphasizes the legalistic implications of the case, and Greenberg insists on the sexual dynamics of a spectacle he describes as an "erotogenic zone on the corpus of France" (69), the subtext of child abuse that pervades the historical record is worth noting.

A single incident in the great Witch Craze that haunted Europe from the fifteenth century until the middle of the eighteenth, the Loudun scandal took place during a period when small children were not immune to charges punishable by burning at the stake. The Prince

Bishop of Würtzburg reported in a letter to a friend in 1629 that "there have been 300 children of three and four who are said to have intercourse with the devil" and that he had "seen children of seven put to death" (Robbins 555). In the context of such horrors, it may seem trifling to note the potential for sexual abuse implicit in the ordinary customs of an age when "conjugal union was rendered indissoluble, regardless of age or mutual consent, by coitus" and "any female taken by a man in copulation belonged to him and his kindred" (Rush 32). Whether she was to be married off or put into a convent, a girl's fate was liable to be decided by the time she was six, and Rush cites G. G. Coulton to the effect that "it was not at all uncommon for a girl to be a bride at ten, or for one of tender years to be married to a septuagenarian" (31). Daughters for whom parents were unable or unwilling to provide dowries, or whose inheritances were coveted by relatives, were often sequestered in a convent by the age of nine, taking their vows by the age of thirteen, and the unwanted female children shut up in convent schools were easy prey for libertine priests who could seal their victims' mouths with threats of excommunication (37). For Florence Rush, the great irony of the Grandier case is that the priest who was no doubt guilty of molesting twelve- and thirteen-year-old girls was finally tortured and burned at the stake for imaginary crimes of which he was clearly innocent (42). The relevance of the context of institutionalized sexual predation to a text in which an old king tries to kidnap a young princess is underscored by Diane Marting's comment that Aegeus "should have met with a different fate, one more appropriate to a rapist" (124). The king's determination to acquire by force what he cannot obtain by persuasion is not an issue, however, for Joseph Marthan, who describes Aegeus as an "old man who, despite a hostile environment, embarks on the loving, patient quest of a young woman" (60). He also stresses the common bond between the old king and Medea, "la femme mûre délaissée pour un frais gibier" (the mature woman abandoned for fresh prey, 49). Aside from the puzzling quality of the reference to the rich old man oppressed by a "hostile environment," it is worth noting that Corneille never mentions Medea's age, and the frequency with which his contemporaries married their daughters off at puberty might suggest that there is no reason to regard this *femme mûre* as being more than twenty or twenty-five years old. The assumption of economic and sexual predation implicit in the word *gibier* is, nevertheless, an essential link between the tragic text and its troubled context.

The proceedings at Loudun, which may have held particular interest for Corneille, who was trained as a lawyer, haunt the text of *Médée,* not only in the juridical flavor of certain passages, or the figure of the reckless seducer, but in the special fate of Creusa and Creon, whose deaths by burning, albeit with invisible flames, occur on stage. The echo of the Inquisition is, indeed, discernible in certain critical comments on the text. Though Carlo François hastens to modify his description of Medea as "a despicable monster worthy of torture" by conceding that she is "not one of those ordinary possessed souls that a tribunal of judges or priests would quickly have chastised, burned at the stake or exorcised" (25-26), his language reflects the nightmare that hovers in the wings of Corneille's drama. The interpretive problem implicit in the abuses to which the text alludes is underscored by Greenberg's insistence on the difference between demonic possession and the disease that certain physicians would later call "hysteria." Whereas, in the nineteenth-century, Charcot argued that such phenomena as demonic possession, witchcraft, and religious ecstasy were actually cases of hysteria (Herman 15-16), Greenberg insists on distinguishing between the spectacles of Loudun and those of Charcot's Salpêtrière, situating the former in a "radically other place . . . where hysteria . . . is the site of a conflict that is about to create interiority as it moves towards the first revolutionary split . . . between the private and a public space" (70). Rush, on the contrary, stresses the similarity between symptoms of "possession" and those displayed by patients known to have been abused as children by various "spiritual fathers" (43-47). Her argument is supported by Judith Herman's testimony on the regularity with which the survivors of traumatic stress "describe themselves as outside the compact of ordinary human relations, as supernatural creatures or non-human life forms," regarding themselves as "witches, vampires, whores, dogs, rats or snakes" (105). In any case, the question of whether particular individuals, such as the nuns of Loudun, were "possessed," "hysterical," or simply coerced may be beside the point, because the dynamics of abuse are inherent in all accounts of the episode. The enterprising clergyman who preyed on his young parishioners became, in turn, the prey of ruthless opponents including the prosecutor whose daughter he was believed to have impregnated, and Cardinal Richelieu, who had his own reasons for wanting Grandier out of the way.

The history of the Loudun trials, illustrating the contradictions implicit in a period characterized by the worst abuses of medieval "justice," and also by an energetic inclination to question the old order, suggests that Corneille's presentation of the unchastened witch is no mere emanation of occult superstition or Baroque fashion, but the sign of a restless contemporary spirit that, if it was a long way from effective revolt, was perceptibly prerevolutionary in quality. The political and social instability of the age is implicit in Roland Mousnier's description of the seventeenth century as a period of "perpetual crisis" (17-25) and in Tapié's observation that from 1630 on, revolt was endemic in the land (218). With reference to the great mutinies and riots of school children that regularly occurred, Ariès notes that the "records of the time are full of references to pupils who had been punished and who took revenge by beating up their masters, who had to send for the police" (*Centuries* 317). Such accounts, like the convention of calling the civil wars of 1619 and 1620 between factions loyal to Louis XIII and Marie de' Medici the First and Second Wars between Mother and Son, are noteworthy in that they underscore the revolutionary potential of generational hostility. Yet these particular cases only serve to emphasize the general rule that every civil insurrection was, by definition, patricidal in nature.

Because the king was universally regarded as the father of his people, the theme of parental authority recurs constantly in the political theory of the age, and Hunt observes that "in justifications of monarchy, the fifth commandment did yeoman service" (150). In view of the filicidal threat implicit in the command to "honor thy father and thy mother that thy days may be long upon the land which the Lord thy God giveth thee," its frequent invocation by the theorists of the period is worth noting. That the anxieties evident in these references to the "patricidal" menace of revolt were not totally unfounded is apparent in the fact that, of the immediate royal predecessors of Louis XIII, both Henri III and Henri IV were assassinated (Skrine 10). The equation of king with father and people with children prompts Tapié to describe the objects of punitive royal policy as unfortunate children. For example, he refers to the execution of Montmorency for duelling as "the terrifying lesson taught to those unruly children, the nobility" (165), and to the Huguenots as "lost children--lost in a seething mass of Catholics" (290). He also notes that unruly nobles and outnumbered Protestants were not the only ones to suffer because of the consolidation of Absolutism. The increasing signs of poverty and deprivation among the French people during this period move him to comment that "the misery of the people was . . . accepted as the price to be paid for the glory of the state" (325). The observation suggests that the policies that provoked endemic civil strife were, by virtue of the familial analogy, filicidal in nature. Patricide was constantly feared because the sacrifice of the children was institutionalized.

The symbolic identification of the people as the "offspring" of the land is at least as old as the ancient tales of "earthborn men" that are an integral part of the story of Jason and Medea (Euripides, *Medea* 479; Apollonius Rhodius 418-20, 1047-49). The particular fascination which these myths exercised on Corneille and his public is evident in that numerous dramatic productions based on the adventures of Jason and Medea were presented under the old regime, versions by La Péruse (553), Jodelle (1558), Binet (1577), Quinault (1675), Thomas Corneille (1693), Longepierre (1694), J.-B. Rousseau (1696), Lafosse (1700), Pellegrin (1713), Clément (1779), Desriaux (1786), and Framery (1786) being noted by Mallinger (224-64). Corneille himself returned to the material of his first tragedy after a quarter of a century to create an extravagant and popular play entitled *La Conquête de la toison d'or (The Conquest of the Golden Fleece,* 1660) based on the Argonautica poems of Apollonius Rhodius and

Valerius Flaccus. A cursory reading of *La Conquête* demonstrates the peculiar emphasis of Corneille's poetic language. In the allegorical Prologue of the play, the author uses the term *entrailles*, meaning *entrails, insides, guts,* in a passage wherein France complains to Victory that all her sons are soldiers who presume to "gnaw her insides" for the sake of winning battles: "S'ils renversent des murs, s'ils gagnent des batailles/ Ils prennent droit par là de ronger mes entrailles" (If they knock down walls and win battles, they think they have the right to gnaw out my insides, 25-26). Similarly, in *Médée*, Nérine uses the word *entrailles* in pleading for the children: "Madame, espargnez vos entrailles/ N'avancez point par là vos propres funerailles" (Madam, spare your insides; do not in this way hasten your own funeral, 961-62). In Nérine's appeal, *entrailles* clearly means *children,* and the logic of Corneille's language, in which *entrailles* are to Medea what *entrailles* are to France, leads to the disturbing suggestion that Medea=France. Though we may choose not to insist on this implication, there is little doubt that the ancient identification of Medea as earth-mother and symbol of the land was part of the myth's appeal for writers of the old regime. The gulf that separates the ancient texts from Corneille's drama is most apparent in the fact that, in the latter, the curtain rises on a world from which the maternal presence is conspicuously absent.

Just as there is something peculiarly democratic about the Euripidean *Medea*, introduced by dialogue between a male and a female servant, and something bizarrely imperial about the Senecan text, dominated for the length of the entire first act by the eccentric ravings of an isolated individual, so the opening scene of Corneille's *Médée,* consisting of a polite exchange between two male peers, evokes the most essential quality of early seventeenth-century social life. If France under the old regime was no more of a "man's world" than the Athenian polis or the Roman Empire, Corneille's drama nevertheless suggests an awareness of the inequities of privilege that seems abruptly modern by comparison with any ancient text. The casual manner in which these gentlemen hold forth on the acquisition of wives and the disposition of children, as of so much property, is no less subversive than the speech by Euripides' *Medea* to the Corinthian women. In fact, it replaces the characteristic commiseration among slaves with an implicit confession of corruption by the masters, conceding the obvious inequities of gender and focusing instead on the relative values of youth and age. Thus Pollux recalls the magical procedure by which Medea succeeded in restoring the youth of Jason's aging father (49-50), and Jason reminisces about his wife's various achievements, including the rejuvenation of his father, the preparation of the elixir that changed an old ram into a young lamb (64-68) and the effects of Medea's fatal persuasion on the daughters of Pelias, who spilled "le vieux sang" (the old blood) of their father in the vain hope that Medea would also rejuvenate him. Though all the details of these magical feats are to be found in the ancient sources, their comparatively elaborate and prominent presentation in Corneille's drama is consistent with the augmented importance of the opposition between age and youth in this play. The theme of age is apparent even before Jason and Pollux begin to discuss Medea's powers of rejuvenation, because the exchange between these two figures corresponds to the conventional split in aristocratic society between the *seniores* and the *juvenes*.

Although Jason and Pollux may be assumed to be approximately the same age, having been youthful companions together on the expedition of the Argo, Jason is presented as a married man, a father and the head of a household, while Pollux is an unattached adventurer returning from his latest exploits in the East. Whereas Jason plays an arrogant and acquisitive *senior*, Pollux is a comparatively modest and unassuming *juvenis*. While the ambitious inclination toward self-aggrandizement is consistent with ancient conceptions of Jason's role, he tends in earlier versions to further his career largely at Medea's expense, and the egotism of Corneille's Jason seems all the more extravagant in that he demands tribute from a male friend. Boasting about the strategic utility of his erotic liaisons with Hypsipyle on the island of Lemnos and Medea in the land of Colchis, he wonders what his friends would ever have done without him: "Alors sans mon amour qu'estoit vostre vaillance?" (What would your courage have been worth without my love?, 33). A caricature of aristocratic narcissism, he flaunts the aspect of his conduct that was probably most offensive to the seventeenth-century audience, his faithlessness. Though Pollux is familiar enough with Jason's combined qualities as lady-killer and conquering hero, he is neither too heroic nor too devout to humor his old friend with a bit of flattery. Noting that Jason has never been one to waste himself on common mistresses and would consider it beneath his dignity to "wound other hearts" than those of kings' daughters, Pollux launches into a catalogue of Jason's romantic victories:

Hypsipyle à Lemnos, sur le Phase Medée
Et Creüse à Corinthe autant vaut possedée
Font bien voir qu'en tous lieux sans lancer d'autres dards
Les sceptres sont acquis à ses moindres regards

(Hypsipyle in Lemnos, Medea in Phasis and Creusa in Corinth, all possessions of equal worth, show that in all lands, without shooting any other arrows, he acquires scepters with his least imposing glances.) (21-24)

Though the contemporary audience familiar with the royal practice of consolidating alliances by marrying princesses off to reigning monarchs would no doubt have been amused by Pollux's description of Jason's amorous intrigues, the casual reference to his erotic "possessions" and the particular cast of characters listed by the speaker seem calculated to augment the ambiguity of Pollux's praise.

Recalling the epic scene of Apollonius' *Argonautica,* Pollux's tribute to Jason is notably ironic in tone, because the Apollonian account of Jason's adventures at Lemnos and Colchis is pervaded by an unstated understanding that the paths of glory will end in the Corinthian disaster articulated by Euripides. Corneille's own *Conquête de la toison d'or,* offered in celebration of the era of peace between France and Spain that the marriage of Louis XIV and Maria Theresa of Spain was supposed to initiate, shares the ironic quality of its source, and in *Médée* Pollux's glowing praise for Jason's "heroism" seems deliciously ambiguous. Although his talk of "wounding" *(blesser)* and "shooting arrows" *(lancer . . . dards)* refers to the convention of Cupid and his bow, the language is by its nature military, and the acquisitive character of Jason's campaigning is stressed by the participles *possedée* and *acquis.* The word *possedée* forms a verbal link between Jason and the ecclesiastical seducer, Grandier, whose fame and downfall both derived from his association with the scandalous "possession de Loudun." It is worth noting, however, that any irony implicit in Pollux's inflated praise is certainly lost on Jason, whose pompous response to his friend's speech is, despite its contemporary quality, entirely consistent with the traditional arrogance of the character. Unable to refrain from adding to the list of virtues enunciated by Pollux, he reminds his interlocutor that, unlike certain vulgar lovers, he always manages to adjust his amorous passions to his political goals (25-28). As remarkable as the cold-blooded calculations of his erotic policy is the complexity of the character who listens to his speech.

Corneille's insistence on the peripheral quality of characters like Pollux who "are only introduced in order to listen to the speech of the principals" (*O.C.* 174) may be one more example of the way in which the "retroactive judgment of the pedant betrays the penetrating intuitions of the creator." In fact, Pollux does a good deal more than listen to what other people say. His very first words, expressing astonishment at the news of Jason's impending marriage, distinguish him as a bastion of good sense in a world dominated by fools. Responding to Jason's announcement with disbelief, he asks a question that demonstrates a noteworthy appreciation of the difficulty of accomplishing the proposed maneuver if Medea is alive and behaving in character: "Quoy! Medée est donc morte à ce conte?" (What! Is Medea dead then? 7). Confronted with Jason's cheerful explanation that Medea is indeed alive but that her place in his bed is about to be occupied by another, Pollux poses another astute question: "Dieux! Et que fera-t-elle?" (Ye Gods! and what will she do? 9). Thus Corneille endows the speaker with a judicious sense of the human potential for action, presenting the entire tragedy as an answer to the question he asks in the opening lines of the play. Jason's friend is arguably not only the author's *porte parole*, but also an interesting and coherent character in his own right.

In a play notable for a generally skeptical view of marriage, Pollux is a bachelor who is always on the way to somebody else's wedding, being invited to Jason's nuptials in the opening lines of the play, and finally disappearing to attend his sister's marriage to Menelaus (1340-45). The fact that he is neither married nor expecting to marry is essential to his position as a relatively reliable observer, exempt from Corneille's own blanket condemnation of all the other characters: "Ici vous trouverez le crime en son char de triomphe et peu de personnages sur la scène dont les moeurs ne soient plus mauvaises que bonnes" (Here you will find crime seated in its chariot of triumph and few characters on the scene whose values are not rather more wicked than good, *O.C.* "Dédicace à Monsieur P.T.N.G." 173). Innocent of crime and committed to decency, Pollux often articulates essential psychological and moral insights, yet he is endowed with enough charm to engage in playful flattery, and has the courage to offer unwelcome advice to his powerful friends, beginning with Jason: "C'est toujours vers Medée un peu d'ingratitude,/ Ce qu'elle a fait pour vous est mal recompensé" (This still seems a bit ungrateful towards Medea, and ill rewards her for what she did for you, 142-43). Insisting on the feudal values of faith and loyalty, generally inclined to ask important questions and offer sensible counsel, Pollux demonstrates powers traditionally attributed to Medea in her capacity as wise counselor.

The quality of sage confidant who manages to endear himself to the mighty while criticizing their policies is especially evident in Pollux's dealings with Creon. When Creusa is rescued from her abductors, Pollux praises her rescuers in terms that border on sarcasm:

C'est vous seul et Jason dont les bras indomptés
Portoient avec effroy la mort de tous costés,
Pareils à deux lions dont l'ardante furie
Depeuple en un moment toute une bergerie

(With undefeated arms, you and Jason spread death and terror on all sides, like two lions whose burning rage depopulates a sheepfold in a moment.) (1079-82)

Though it is hard to see how any king would fail to be suspicious of tribute comparing him to a predatory beast depopulating a peaceful sheepfold, Creon is delighted: "Que prudemment les Dieux scavent tout ordonner" (How prudently the gods arrange all things, 1096). As unsuccessful with Creon as with Jason in piercing what amounts to a wall of smug self-satisfaction, Pollux nevertheless stands his ground, confronting the royal question—"Qu'avons nous plus à craindre?" (What more have we to fear?)—with blunt precision: "Medée/ qui par vous de son lit se voit depossedée" (Medea, who has been dispossessed of her bed by you, 1105-06). The acuity of the warning is diminished neither by the circumstance that nobody listens to it nor by the fact that the character who utters it is dismissed by the author as inconsequential.

The wit and integrity of the character who refers to his royal masters as "depopulators" of villages and appropriators of other people's possessions suggests that Corneille's eagerness to depreciate Pollux's importance is directly proportional to his sympathy for the wandering bachelor. If there is every reason to assume a special affinity between the dramatist, or any man of letters, with a congenial, detached fellow who understands the meaning of what will happen before it actually happens, and gets away with telling the truth because he is charming and amusing, the objects of Pollux' misgivings seem all the more antipathetic in that they rationalize their dubious plans in the name of paternal love. Like Seneca's Jason, Corneille's dashing heartbreaker displays his love for his children like a badge of distinction:

L'amour de mes enfans m'a fait l'ame legere,
Ma perte estoit la leur, et cet Hymen nouveau
Avec Medée et moy les tire du tombeau
Eux seuls m'ont fait resoudre, et la paix s'est concluë

(The love of my children has made my soul fickle. My loss would have been their own and this new marriage pulls them out of the tomb along with Medea and myself. They alone decided me and the terms of peace are settled.) (134-37)

This insistence on the twin claims of paternal love (l'amour de mes enfans) and civic responsibility (la paix s'est concluë) loses whatever credibility it may have in the Senecan model, first because Corneille's Creon is, on the whole, more foolish than frightening, and second, because Jason's sincerity has been discredited in advance by his own declaration of strategic interest: "Et que pouvois-je mieux que luy faire la Cour/ Et relever mon sort sur les aisles d'amour?" (And what better thing could I do than make love to her and raise my fortune up on the wings of love? 39-40). Though Jason would pardon his own fickle soul (ame legere) in the name of paternal love, the very qualification of his soul as *legere* underscores the flimsiness of his position. The dubious claim to have achieved peace by means of marital infidelity stresses the political and tactical nature of the entire network of allusions to paternal love in such a way as to accentuate the distance between the disinterested acuity of the lone bachelor knight and the expansive comportment of the paternalistic allies.

In public as well as personal affairs, impending disaster may be traced to the effects of a bungling form of paternal love. Threatened by Acastus, son of Pelias and king of Thessaly, who is determined to avenge the murder of his father, Creon is described as having no choice but to protect his person and his people against the threat of external invasion (117-18). Thus, the treachery that will soon cause the deaths of Creon, Jason, and all of their respective children is justified by the perceived threat of violence against patriarch and metaphorical children. The argument that the parricidal calamity inheres in the probability of external attack is undermined, however, by evidence that the threat of war results from unwise domestic policy, specifically from Creon's questionable agreement to grant Jason and his family a refuge from Acastus. Jason gratefully acknowledges the kindness with which Creon welcomes his family and himself, yet the very terms of his tribute to Creon suggest that the king has a vested interest in a policy of "kindness" (*benignité*) that transcends the proper bounds of civic authority and manifests itself as ordinary personal indulgence. Jason boasts that both the king and his daughter have succumbed to his notorious charm, so that Creon encourages Creusa to break off her previously negotiated engagement to Aegeus of Athens:

. . . . mon bonheur ordinaire
M'acquiert les volontes de la fille et du pere
Si bien que de tous deux esgalement chery,
L'un me veut pour gendre, et l'autre pour mary

(My habitual good luck acquires for me the good will of the daughter and of her father, so much so that I am equally cherished by both of them, the one desiring me as son-in-law, the other as husband.) (105-08)

The operative motive for Creon, as for Creusa, is desire; for each of them, Jason is the object of the verb "to want" (*veut,* from *vouloir*). The *bonheur ordinaire* of Jason's exposition is both the personal charm which he employs as the avowed weapon of his acquisitive campaign, and quite literally, the "ordinary happiness" which is, for Creon and Creusa, the most desirable and banal of objectives.

With respect to the claim of "sexual essentiality" in Cornelian drama, it is interesting to consider that Jason, Creon, and Creusa are situated in a triangular pattern that recalls Greenberg's analysis of the deployment of Orgon, Mariane, and Tartuffe in Molière's famous comedy, wherein the young girl "serves as the mediating object not only of Tartuffe's lust, but of Orgon's and even more perversely, of Orgon's lust for Tartuffe" (133). Whether or not Corneille hints at the operation of homosexual desire between Creon and Jason, or the presence of an incestuous component in Creon's regard for Creusa, is perhaps beside the point. The author is, in any case, very careful to discredit both the king and his favorite by demonstrating that, conspicuous claims of paternal benevolence to the contrary, the established seniors are acting out of motives rather more complex and less noble than the ones they publicly profess. Although Creon claims to have banished Medea in order to appease Acastus, the fact is that Acastus has offered peace only on condition that both Medea and Jason be turned over to him, and Creon has negotiated a deal whereby Medea is to be sacrificed in order to save Jason's skin (121-24). Thus, the machinations of policy provide a facade behind which Creon hides the egotistical indulgence of personal desire. For his part, Jason frankly admits that his claim of paternal obligation cohabits nicely with his erotic project:

J'ay regret à Medée, et j'adore Creüse
Je voy mon crime en l'une, en l'autre mon excuse
Et dessus mon regret mes desirs triomphants
Ont encor le secours du soin de mes enfans

(Regretting Medea, adoring Creusa, I see my crime in one, in the other my excuse, and my desires triumphing over my regret are yet bolstered by my concern for my children.) (165-68)

Thus, the tragedy that will end with "le crime en son char de triomphe" begins with a father's declaration that his paternal affection is a convenient auxiliary to the fulfillment of his *desirs triomphants*.

Although Corneille's elaboration of Jason's character is essentially faithful to the ancient models, it includes two remarkable innovations, the first being Jason's openly declared passion for Creusa, and the second, his statement of overt hostility toward the children. Both changes have the effect of undermining the character's conspicuous insistence on paternal love, and both increase the sympathy of the audience for Medea by discrediting her antagonist. In either case, the apparent novelty is less a radical departure from ancient precedent than a conflation of traditional conceptions of character with contemporary social concerns. After all, neither Euripides nor Corneille needed Freud to tell him that the desire for wealth and power may be invested with erotic passion. The rational discourse of the ancient Jason is, in its own way, just as much a cover for sexual impulses as the evident dissimulation of Corneille's Jason, and the inseparability of Creusa's charm from her economic and political utility is inherent in the myth. It is worth noting, however, that Corneille operates on the assumption that his audience is more likely to disapprove of lust than of greed or ambition. Whereas the ancients seem hardly to have considered the notion that a grown man might allow frivolous emotional impulses to interfere with such a serious transaction as marriage, and twentieth-century audiences might be inclined to feel that the experience of any genuinely affirmed sentiment would indicate an improvement in Jason's character, Corneille condemns Jason utterly by depicting him as a great nobleman repudiating his wife because he is infatuated with a pretty girl. Finally, the explicit filicidal intention articulated by Corneille's

Jason (1561-68) is arguably implicit in the Euripidean text, but it is never so insistently stated by Euripides as by Corneille because the ancient audience would not need to be told that a child whose mother was abandoned by his father was a child in mortal danger.

It is the essence of Corneille's originality that he reformulates traditional situations in unconventional ways. In the dialogue between Jason and Pollux, the poet presents the opposition between a conservative spokesman for the feudal value of loyalty and an enterprising devotee of personal aggrandizement through amorous campaigning. By positing the appropriator of other people's goods as a vain and false married man, and the dependable authority as an amiable and honest bachelor, the author reverses the pattern inherent in stories depicting unmarried adventurers as adulterers like Tristan and Lancelot, and fathers of families as steadfast fellows like Marc and Arthur. To be sure, the ideal of heroic adventure was rather the worse for wear by the time Corneille wrote his *Médée* and Pollux, as a virtuous knight errant in a sordid and corrupt world, may seem to be a chastened version of his illustrious literary precursor, Don Quixote. As such, he demonstrates the wisdom of Nadal's observation that Cornelian characterization tends to reflect and to attenuate the bizarre and fabulous conceptions that were fashionable in the period immediately preceding his own (149-50).

In any case, the shadow of potential antipathy between the smug plunderer and the dispossessed outsider that lies just below the surface of the polite exchange presented in the first scene of Corneille's *Médée* is perhaps the most essential feature of the tragedy. The significance of the relationship between Jason and Pollux is underscored by the circumstance that all of the characters in the play seem to fall into either one or the other of the camps represented by the two figures. Whereas Jason exemplifies certain traits of the rulers and old men like Creon and Aegeus, who are either abductors or appropriators, Pollux, in a political sense the only "young" man in the play, has more in common with the female underlings and outsiders than with the other male characters. He shares with the servant Nérine an inclination to criticize the reigning powers, with Medea herself the talent for giving shrewd advice, and with the Princess Creusa the symbolic state of youth.

Creusa is as important as Pollux for an understanding of what is peculiarly Cornelian in this play because she is, like Pollux, a character invented by the author. Whereas Creon's daughter never appears on stage in the plays by Euripides and Seneca, Corneille gives her a conspicuous speaking role, thus endowing the Euripidean sketch of an individual en route from childhood to adulthood with the details of a genuine portrait which is considerably more complex than certain critical judgments would suggest. Though M. J. Muratore dismisses her as "contemptible" and "hypocritic," Creusa is arguably a comparatively blameless figure. As luckless as the ancient models for her role, she resembles them in that she does little more to earn her fate than what is generally encouraged in the children of the privileged. Whereas the greed that is her specific fault does not distinguish her from the most honored elders in her world, her sharp wit and energetic spirit establish a close affinity between her and the other disenchanted "snipers" in the play. Corneille's sympathy for the character is evident in that he eliminates the single most offensive element in the Euripidean princess, her hostility toward Jason's children. While the Greek dramatist fixes the child-bride forever in our minds as one who responds with spontaneous revulsion at the very sight of the little boys, Corneille's princess promises Jason she will protect his sons, and she does so almost as soon as she makes her first appearance: "J'avois desja pitié de leur tendre innocence,/ Et vous y serviray de toute ma puissance" (I already pitied their tender innocence, and will serve you in this with all my power, 185-86). It is true that she proceeds to declare, with disconcerting candor, that she expects a favor in return for this service (191), but her gracious immediate gesture nevertheless suggests a certain softening of the ancient conception of the role. There seems to be little doubt that Creusa's ultimate failure to save the children is rather a function of her lack of power than a matter of genuine culpability.

In that the object of Creusa's greed is the fabulous dress that Medea brought with her from the East, her character is faithful to the Euripidean outline of the frivolous little girl who cannot wait to dress up in a grown woman's gown. Corneille explained in the "Examen" of 1660 that he preferred to have Medea give the dress to Creusa in compliance with a demand than as a voluntary offering because it did not seem likely that a gift would otherwise have been accepted from such an enemy (O.C. 174). It would be a mistake, however, to assume that the author's emphasis on the princess's greed indicates a lack of sympathy for her. Greed is, in the first place, implicit in the traditional delineation of the role, and furthermore, it is an essential component of contemporary assumptions about the nature of youth. That Creusa is identified as a very young person by a writer operating in a period when children were believed to be parasitic and greedy by nature (Hunt 119) suggests that her eagerness to acquire Medea's dress is only an incidental function of her relative immaturity, and on the whole, Corneille's insistence on her extreme youth tends rather to mitigate than to augment her fault.

As understandable as Creusa's caprice may be in a child, it has the unfortunate effect of making her a pawn in the dubious schemes of the adults who surround her. Regarding her as an avenue of access to her doting father, Jason begs the girl to intervene with the king on his behalf so that he may be granted custody of his sons when Medea goes into exile. Being courted with the deference reserved for royalty, Creusa responds quite frankly that the "price" of the children's salvation will be Medea's fabulous dress: "C'est ce qu'ont pretendu mes desseins relevez/ Pour le prix des enfans que je vous ay sauvez" (This is what I have in mind as a price for the children I have saved for you, 567-68). Far from being offended by the invitation to pay a "price" for his children, Jason seems delighted that his nearest and dearest may prove profitable to him. He also reveals a rather more astute appreciation of the sticky aspects of the proposed transaction than Creusa seems to have:

Que ce prix est leger pour un si bon office!
Il y faut toutefois employer l'artifice,
Ma jalouse en fureur n'est pas femme à souffrir
Qu'on la prenne en ses mains afin de vous l'offrir,
Des tresors dont son pere espuise la Scythie
C'est tout ce qu'elle a pris quand elle en est sortie

(What a low price for such a good office! But in any case, we will have to be crafty. My jealous, furious wife is not a woman to tolerate our taking it away from her in order to give it to you. Of the treasures for which her father exhausts Scythia, this is all she took with her when she left.) (569-74)

This speech is, in fact, remarkable for the way in which it confronts the princess's innocent greed with the speaker's intimate knowledge of worldly corruption.

In exulting that Medea's gown is a "low price for such a good office," Jason surely struck a responsive chord among spectators in an age when a wife's dowry was a husband's fortune and the sale of offices was not only a favorite means of raising public funds but a notorious abuse. His understanding of the mechanics of royal fundraising is evident in the reference to "the treasures for which her father exhausts Scythia," and his speech constitutes a generally cheerful admission that it will be necessary to lie (employer l'artifice) and to steal (qu'on la prenne) in order to fulfill Creusa's request. Variations of the word prendre (to take) occur three times in these six lines, le prix being equivalent to that which has been taken (qu'elle a pris) and that which may be taken (qu'on la prenne). As if to dispel any lingering doubt that these lines present a somewhat jaded view of royal fundraising procedures, Corneille counters Jason's allusion to the "treasures" of which Aeetes has milked Scythia with a speech by Creusa expressing her willingness to give all of her father's royal treasure in return for the wonderful dress:

Pour appaiser Medée et reparer sa perte
L'espargne de mon pere entierement ouverte
Luy met à l'abandon tous les tresors du Roy
Pourveu que cette robbe, et Jason soient à moy

(In order to appease Medea and repair her loss, the wide open coffers of my father set at her disposal all the treasures of the king, on condition that this dress, and Jason may be mine.) (585-88)

While Creusa's words reveal the prodigal frivolity of a young person used to getting everything she wants, her reference to the royal "treasures" is in one essential respect different from Jason's: she only knows that such wealth has always been at her disposal, Jason knows where it comes from. Furthermore, her plan of "appeasing Medea and repairing her loss" may be naive, but it is thoroughly consistent with the nature of one who is confident that she can make everybody happy while cultivating her own childish pleasures.

Though Creusa pays a terrible penalty for her avidity, Corneille's construction of the character suggests that her downfall entails something other than justice. In the first place, Creusa is rather more thoughtful and conciliatory than she is either encouraged or expected to be. In the second place, she has been set up. Having been betrothed before the action of the play begins to King Aegeus, she is assured by her father that the promise to Aegeus may be broken with impunity now that Jason presents himself as a preferable suitor. Though her own desires seem to be in accord with her father's, the fact is that Creusa is in a no-win situation, because any resistance to the king's desire would probably condemn her as an unnatural and ungrateful daughter, hardly an attractive alternative to the present case in which she will be reviled as a faithless and inconstant woman. Under the circumstances, her failings seem hardly in the same league with Creon's inexplicable recklessness. Since he has pledged his word, his inclination to indulge the desire he seems to share with his daughter is clearly irresponsible. To Creusa's credit, she seems somewhat apprehensive about rejecting Aegeus. When her father assures her that everything will turn out for the best (509), she expresses appropriate misgivings: "Je ne croy pas, Monsieur que ce vieux Roy d'Athenes/ Voyant aux mains d'autruy le fruit de tant de peines,/ Mesle tant de foiblesse à son ressentiment" (I do not believe, sir, that the old king of Athens, seeing the fruit of so much trouble in the hands of another, will temper his resentment with very much frailty, 517-20). Despite her evident concern for Aegeus' wounded feelings, Creusa's expectation of being indulged persuades her that she can appease the old king:

J'espere toutefois qu'avec un peu d'adresse
Je pourray le resoudre à perdre une maistresse,
Dont l'aage peu sortable, et l'inclination
Respondoient assez mal à son affection

(I hope, in any case, that with a bit of tact, I may persuade him to give up a mistress whose unsuitable age and lack of inclination can hardly correspond to his affection.) (521-24)

Though the hope of charming Aegeus into resigning himself to his loss is quite as naive as the plan to mollify Medea with cash payments, Creusa deserves some credit for being the only one in her immediate circle who even anticipates the possibility of trouble. Her persistence in a disastrous course despite her own serious misgivings is ultimately not as remarkable as the determination with which those who ought to know better continually nourish her dangerous sense of invulnerability, and Corneille's tendency to mitigate her responsibility by emphasizing her youth is clearly evident in various passages.

Creusa's youth is emphasized by comparison with Aegeus' age, which is apparent not only in the girl's reference to *ce vieux Roy d'Athenes*, but also in her father's observation that "Un vieillard amoureux merite qu'on en rie" (An old man in love deserves to be mocked, 534). Later on, in the stanzas he utters in the solitude of his captivity, Aegeus himself laments his advancing years in words that echo Creon's judgment: "Un vieillard amoureux merite plus de blasme/ Qu'un Monarch en prison n'est digne de pitié" (An old man in love deserves more blame than an imprisoned monarch merits pity, 1203-04). The condemnation of the "old man in love" by Creon and Aegeus corresponds to an opinion espoused by Corneille himself in his critical prose. In the "Discours de l'utilité et des parties du poème dramatique" (Discourse on the Utility and Structure of the Dramatic Poem, 1660), the author stresses the importance of depicting each character in accordance with the behavior appropriate to his type, asserting that extravagant love is a characteristic of youth and not age. He goes on to say that even though an old man may fall in love, he is a fool if he expects to be loved for his physical charm and not his property and position; he can only win his goal if he is dealing with a person sufficiently crass (*intéressée*) as to yield everything to considerations of wealth and rank *(O.C.* 826-27). According to this view, the king is out of line on two counts, because Creusa is both unsuitably young and evidently undisposed to worry about wealth and rank. By the terms of Corneille's own analysis, the theme of love tends to discredit the amorous old man and to excuse the young girl whose affections have been heedlessly pledged.

Creusa not only describes herself as being of an unsuitable age ("aage peu sortable") for Aegeus, but also as the fruit of his labor. The word fruit, regularly applied to Medea's children (178-80, 468, 1369), suggests the textual equivalence of Creusa and the children, thus underscoring the childlike quality of Creusa's character. Admittedly ancient, the equation of *child* with *fruit* derives from the same essentially agricultural view of the cosmos that generated the myths of the earth-born. Corneille's insistence on this particular metaphor is significant, however, because his designation of Creusa as fruit is no mere indication of the relationship between progeny and progenitor such as, for example, inheres in the greeting which Seneca's Creon extends to Medea, "the child of noxious Aeetes" (*Medea* 179). He does not apply the terms *enfant* and *fruit* to such adult figures as Creon and Aegeus, even though he might well have done so if he had intended the relatively banal significance of "offspring." Thus, the scarcity of specific terms designating the stages of biological development in children that prompts Ariès to insist on the "absence" of the concept of childhood in prerevolutionary France (25-29) does not prevent Corneille from suggesting that Creusa is a child in maturational terms as well as in a relational sense. The author's considerable sympathy for his youthful character is, moreover, revealed in his granting the girl a voice with which to commit the rather becoming offense of talking back to her elders.

Although Creusa's good sense is discernible in her skeptical reaction to her father's plan (2.3.517-20), it is not until her confrontation with Aegeus in Act Two, Scene 5, that she shows just how sharp she really is. In the course of this scene, Creusa makes an about-face in her tactics, beginning with a plea for indulgence (631-40), and concluding with a declaration of altruistic principles (669-70). What is remarkable about her role in this dialogue is that she seems to change, before our eyes, from a fawning child, frankly confessing weakness, to an assertive adult insisting on her strength. The abruptness of the transition suggests not only the confusion and malleability of an essentially unformed sense of self, but a certain inclination to imitate the adult models in her vicinity—in this case, the hypocritic Aegeus, who barely conceals his sexual motivation behind the facade of proprietary concern he presents to his betrothed. Initiated by the old king in response to the rumor of Creusa's impending wedding, the interview provides him with an opportunity to scold the girl for being careless of her reputation: "Madame, mon amour jaloux de vostre gloire/ Vient sçavoir s'il est vray que vous soyez d'accord/ Par ce honteux Hymen de l'arrest de ma mort" (Madam, my love, jealous of your honor, brings me here to find out if you have agreed to inflict the sentence of death on me through this shameful marriage, 610-12). Not content with this extravagant reproach, Aegeus also denounces his rival as a "murderer of kings" (615) and a "poisoner" (620), faults that are presumably less offensive to him in his friend, Medea, than in Jason. In response to this attack, Creusa defends Jason loyally, nevertheless deferring to Aegeus by beginning an essentially apologetic statement with a bit of flattery: "Non pas que je ne faille en cette preference,/ De vostre rang au sien je sçay la difference" (Not that I am faultless in my preference; I know the difference between your rank and his, 625-26). Having thus conceded the essential point, she appeals to the king in the name of love, reminding him that love is not inspired by pomp and grandeur but by personal attraction. She observes that her own crown is probably the least of what he likes about her: "en moy vous n'aymiez rien moins que ma Couronne" (In me you have liked nothing less than my crown, 630). The freshness and acuity of her insistence on the physical quality of love are all the more striking in the wake of Aegeus' windy remarks about Creusa's honor, the trembling of her people, and the murmuring of the court.

Proceeding energetically from her brilliant challenge to a series of allusions to classical tales of Love's power to enthrall gods and men, Creusa cites the affairs of Jupiter and Venus as precedents for her own predicament. She concludes on the same deferential note with which she began, apologizing for her foolishness in preferring Jason to the old king: "Je vous estimay plus, et l'aymay davantage" (I respected you more, and loved him better, 642). Predictably enough, this rhetorical feat carries little weight with Aegeus. For a king to proclaim that unrequited love will be the death of him is one thing; for this little snippet to evade his desire by means of a calculating confession of weakness is quite another. The irritated king parries Creusa's argument with an accusation of willful persistence in error: "Que me sert cet adveu d'une erreur volontaire?/ Si vous croyez faillir, qui vous force à le faire?" (What use to me is this admission of willful error? If you believe you are making a mistake, who is forcing you to do it?, 645-46). This logically unassailable attribution of *erreur volontaire* to Creusa is worth noting because "willful error" is the term that Medea herself applies to her plan of vengeance on Creusa: "Mon erreur volontaire ajustée à mes veux/ Arrestera sur elle un deluge de feux" (My willful error, adjusted to my desires, will inflict a deluge of flames upon her, 263-64). Indeed, it is ultimately true of all the principal players in this drama that they are adjusting their "willful errors" to their desires. Yet Creusa's piquant affirmation of irrational love, like Medea's exuberant declaration of criminal intent, is a conspicuous lapse in the hypocritical manner that is the normal modus operandi in the world of this play.

Though Creusa can hardly win her verbal sparring match with the august suitor who presumes to instruct her in ethics, she scores a few good points. Having been humiliated in the attempt to excuse her "faithlessness" on the grounds of involuntary passion, she expediently shifts to an obviously false, if resoundingly high-minded, assertion that she only prefers Jason to Aegeus out of concern for her patriotic and filial obligations: "Et vous recognoistrés que je ne vous prefere/ Que le bien de l'Estat mon pays, et mon pere" (You must realize that it is only the good of the state, my country, and my father, that comes before you in my regard, 669-70). This betrayal of her initial honesty with self-righteous double-talk shows a certain facility for adjusting her verbal moves to the measure of an interlocutor who preaches about dignity and honor while apparently suffering from erotic frustration. Creusa is, in fact, entirely vindicated in her suspicion that

Aegeus is more interested in her body than in her crown, because the king offers to give up his kingdom and become her slave if only she will accept his hand (679-80). Blatantly contradicting his own pious pronouncements on the importance of honor and glory, the king will soon act on this foolish offer by literally sacrificing the remaining shreds of his dignity in an ignominious attempt to kidnap the recalcitrant princess. The effect of the entire scene is to imply that hypocrisy is a social skill that children learn from adults. Like the initial dialogue between Jason and Pollux, the exchange between Aegeus and Creusa has the quality of seeming to confront the incisive intuition of youth with the foolish egotism of seniority.

Even such minor and conventional characters as the Nurse, Nérine, are ultimately assimilated into the opposition between *seniores* and *juvenes* that pervades this text. A faithful rendering of her ancient prototypes in that she speaks with humanity and good sense in a world overrun by power-hungry fools, Nérine also delivers the most emphatically subversive speech in the entire play. In her monologue at the beginning of Act Three, she expresses compassion for Creusa (701-02), for whom she predicts inevitable disaster (704), and she condemns the criminal project of a mistress whom she feels constrained to serve: "Moy, bien que mon devoir m'attache à son service,/ Je lui preste à regret un silence complice" (Although duty binds me in her service, I adhere with regret to a conspiratorial silence, 721-22). Less blindly devoted to Medea than her Greek and Roman prototypes, she confesses to fantasies of insubordination: "D'un louable desir mon coeur sollicité/ Luy feroit avec joye une infidelité" (Troubled by a praiseworthy desire, my heart would joyfully commit an infidelity, 723-24). Describing the imagined sabotage of Medea's revenge as *infidelité,* and the rebellious impulse (*desir*) as praiseworthy (*louable*), the speaker articulates thoughts tending to subvert the principle of duty (*devoir*) which binds her to her mistress. The reference to service as *silence complice a*nd the idea of joyful *infidelité* may be justified by the enormity of Medea's crimes, but they are also a radical departure from the unstinting loyalty of the ancient Nurse. Whereas the Euripidean Nurse mourns her lady's losses as if they were her own, Corneille's Nérine suggests that she is compelled to serve by fear of death: "Ma peur me fait fidelle et tasche d'avancer/ Les desseins que je veux et n'ose traverser" (My fear renders me faithful and tries to promote the plans which I wish to oppose but dare not, 731-32). Nérine's begrudging stance seems justified, moreover, by the augmented arrogance of her mistress.

Whereas the Euripidean Medea secures the servant's cooperation with an appeal couched in terms of common suffering and conferred trust—"but if you are a woman and well disposed to your mistress, say nothing of the things I have planned" (822-23)— Corneille's Medea commands absolute obedience: "Pour un si grand effet prends un coeur plus hardy/ Et sans me repliquer, fay ce que je te dy" (For such an important project, have more courage, and do what I say without answering back, 1067-68). This insistence on being quiet and following orders recalls the proverbial saying that "children should be seen and not heard." In fact, it is one of the truisms of seventeenth-century history that the roles of children and servants were, in a sense, equivalent to one another. Ariès notes that "the servant was a child, a big child, whether he was occupying his position for a limited period in order to share in the family's life, or whether he had no hope of ever becoming a master" (367). Although the identity of child and servant was related to the custom of apprenticeship, it transcended strict economic imperatives. Thus the young Louis XIII, when asked "Who are you?" would answer: "Papa's little valet" (Hunt 149), and Ariès makes the general observation that "the whole of childhood, that of all classes of society, was subjected to the degrading discipline imposed on the villeins" (262). The historical conflation of children's and servants' roles suggests that Corneille's Nurse may be an interesting character precisely because she demonstrates the capability of a shrewd adult while submitting to the humiliation of a helpless child. Not only exercising intelligent foresight and moral judgment, she dissembles very well in the cause of personal survival. Thus, after revealing an astute perception of impending disaster in her soliloquy, she immediately thereafter reassures Jason that Medea is calming down and will not hurt him (736-39). The dexterity with which she plays the role assigned to her accentuates the contradiction between her childlike status and her adult acuity. It also recalls Richelieu's observation that "dissimulation is the art of kings" (Skrine 38).

The character who hides "the art of kings" behind a mask of humble servility is not only an embodiment of the inequities of rank but a reflection of the flexibility inherent in seventeenth-century French class distinctions. Describing this period as one in which it was not uncommon for a single family to include "some members of the robe and others of the sword, some married into merchant families and others into jurists', some already ennobled, and others still commoners," Mousnier observes that "every new revolt spread all the more easily because there was no rigid separation of social classes" (20-21). Nérine's curmudgeonly grumbling about the oppression of *devoir* is consistent with Mousnier's description of a fundamentally destabilized social hierarchy, and her conspicuous aptitude for intrigue is also typical of the the paradoxical peculiarities of rank in this play. Pollux is a nobleman whose detached condition and expressed sympathies ally him with those excluded from his class; Jason and Creusa, both scions of royalty, seem representative of the noble class, the "spoiled children" of society. Distinctions between "royal" and "noble" characters, which do not exist in ancient tragedy, remain an anomaly even in Corneille's time, when the king was still technically the highest ranking member of an aristocratic class whose members were nevertheless his "peers." If *Médée,* written in the period immediately preceding the Fronde, when the nobility found itself increasingly at odds with the monarchy, is a text that stresses the problematic intricacies of rank, there is no character in the play who represents a more delicate balance of family and class dynamics than Medea herself.

The complexity of Corneille's protagonist is sometimes overlooked in critical discourse tending to emphasize the imposing and domineering quality of the character. Thus De Leyssac praises the poet for removing the element of "domestic squabbling" from the ancient plot and thereby elevating Medea to the level of the tragic (Corneille, *Médée* 44); Greenberg perceives in Corneille's filicidal mother a "barbarous other" who "refuses containment and triumphs over any semblance of (masculine) order, over any genealogy by and through the father" (50). If we consider, however, that Corneille's vision of a world divided by the rivalry of favored heirs and dispossessed grumblers embraces all of society in a familial model, and that, furthermore, Medea's final ascent to power is achieved in collaboration with a senior patriarch, such readings may seem to be interpretive simplifications that disregard much of what actually happens in Corneille's text. To be sure, the spectacle of Medea browbeating Nérine is consistent with the images of ascendance and triumph with which the Cornelian heroine is ordinarily associated, and the aristocratic quality of the character is abundantly evident in her exchange with Aegeus, when she refuses any reward other than sanctuary, haughtily asserting that she disdains to live by using her craft (1275-76). Her most celebrated lines occur in the striking declaration of absolute personal power that she presents to Nérine: "Ouy tu vois en moy seule, et le fer, et la flame,/ Et la terre, et la mer, et l'Enfer, et les Cieux,/ Et le sceptre des Rois, et le foudre des Dieux" (Yes, you see in me alone the sword, the flame, the earth and the sea, Heaven and Hell, the scepters of kings and the thunder of the gods, 318-20). Like much of the play, this speech reflects and pays tribute to the Senecan model. Whereas, with the language of domination, Corneille recalls his ancient master, he uses the contemporary identification of the child as servant, apprentice, and hostage to suggest Medea's desperate struggle to redeem herself from bondage.

Medea refers to the crimes of her youth as a "feeble apprenticeship" (250), and she rages at the thought that she might have to play a servile role such as that of Boccaccio's patient Griselda, whose noble husband ordered her to wait on the bride who was supposed to replace her. Responding indignantly to Nérine's counsel of moderation, she asks: "Ne dois-je point encor en tesmoigner de l'aise/ De ce Royal Hymen souhaiter l'heureux jour,/ Et m'offrir pour servante à son nouvel amour?" (Shouldn't I also pretend approval, wishing a happy day for this royal wedding and offering myself as servant to his new love?, 298-300). Medea also likens her present state to that of a hostage by alluding to the poisoned gown as a ransom:

"Tant d'invisibles feux enfermez dans ce don,/ Que d'un tiltre plus vray j'appelle ma rançon" (So many invisible flames enclosed in this gift, that with greater justice, I call my ransom, 1047-78). This reference to the gift as a "ransom" serves to identify the mother with her own children, who are called hostages by Creon: "Ses enfans si cheris qui nous servent d'ostages" (Her children, so dear, who serve as our hostages, 1149). In this articulation, the questionable implications of the word *ostages* seem to contradict the bland assurance of affection for the children implicit in the words *si cheris*. In keeping with Hunt's observation that even the most privileged child of the period had "the air of a hostage in an unfriendly land" (99), this casual mention of the children as hostages reinforces the network of words with which Corneille constantly evokes questions of moral legitimacy.

The word *ostage,* derived from *oster*, meaning *to take*, is used by Medea in debate with Jason, when she compares him to a marauding brigand who boasts of generosity when he only moderates his aggression: "Quand il n'esgorge point, il croit nous pardonner,/ Et ce qu'il n'oste pas, il pense le donner" (In refraining from slaughter, he thinks he pardons us, and what he does not take, he imagines that he gives to us, 851-52). Synonymous with *prendre,* the verb *oster* inserts itself into the family of words such as *pris, prix,* and *prenne* which occur conspicuously in Jason's speech (cf. 569-74). In this text, those who take, appropriate, rob, exploit, kidnap, drain and depopulate are kings and royal protegés, while the thing taken (*ostage, prix*), like the thing labored for (*fruit*) and the thing possessed (21-22), is regularly a human child. Indeed, it is the dehumanized logic of the child as captive and commodity that prepares the way for Medea's final taunt to Jason, in which she identifies the children as "wages" or "pledges" of love: "Ces gages de nos feux ne feront plus pour moy/ De reproches secrets à ton manque de foy" (These pledges of our love will no longer prod me with secret reproaches for your lack of faith, 1579-80). Yet the real originality of Corneille's Medea lies not so much in her triumphant mastery of proprietary imperatives as in the juridical defiance with which she challenges corrupt dominion.

Although a certain bellicosity is inherent in the ancient conceptions of Medea's character, the polemics of Corneille's Medea regularly go beyond the particular objects of her wrath to question the very basis of her antagonists' authority. In asking if the legitimate use of power permits that she be condemned for crimes that are profitable to her accusers (445-46), she rephrases a characteristic complaint in such a way as to suggest a possible reference to contemporary prosecutions that "yielded extensive booty for whatever local authority had jurisdiction" (Robbins 16). She is also capable of arguing the rights of the accused with the assertive energy of an eighteenth-century philosophe: "Quiconque sans l'ouyr condamne un criminel,/ Bien qu'il eust mille fois merité son supplice,/ D'un juste chastiment il fait une injustice" (Whoever condemns a criminal without hearing him, though he a thousand times deserved his torture, turns fair punishment into injustice, 396-98). This casual allusion to torture *(supplice)* underscores the relevance of the passage to controversial interrogations. It is only one of several subversive suggestions articulated by Medea. When Creon seeks to counter her righteous indignation by asking if the sorceress took the trouble to listen to Pelias before condemning him (399-400), Medea defends herself by taking the offensive, asking: "Escouta-t-il Jason quand sa haine couverte/ L'envoya sur nos bords se livrer à sa perte?" (Did he listen to Jason when his covert hatred sent him off to meet death on our shores? 401-02). Before Creon can defend himself against the accusation of "covert hatred," Medea clarifies it with an aggressive follow-up question: "Car comment voulez-vous que je nomme un dessein/ Au-dessus de sa force et du pouvoir humain?" (For what should I call a project beyond his ability, indeed, beyond all human power? 403-04). Effectively turning the implied charge of patricide into an accusation of attempted child-murder, this line of questioning confronts the patricidal order with the consequences of its filicidal policy. The peculiar contemporary resonance of the denunciation may best be appreciated in view of the fact that it was delivered while the Thirty Years' War was wasting large areas of central Europe, and while France was preparing to embark on a series of ruinous campaigns. These lines decrying a king who sends off a band of young men on an adventure likely to get them all killed are, at the very least, an irreverent restatement of epic events, and by no stretch of the imagination, a cynical description of all aggressive wars. As interesting as the implications of Medea's speech may be, the essential fact is that she speaks in defense of Jason. Her allusion to the "loss" her lover as a result of his uncle's plan may remind the audience that Medea's assistance to Jason when he was an underdog has availed her little. Her generosity having been turned against her, Corneille's protagonist resembles that of Euripides in that she can only reverse her own losses by allying herself with an enthroned monarch.

   The entente between Medea and Aegeus is a potential source of critical confusion. Marthan, for instance, comments on the troubling quality of an exchange in which "Aegeus, in an about-face which disconcerts the most attentive spectator, passes in the same breath from adoration of Creusa to a proposal of marriage to Medea" (63). In the first place, this statement assumes that Aegeus must be altruistic and Medea must be unattractive; secondly, there is no reason to suppose that Corneille would have been concerned with the modern view of marriage as a sanction for passionate love. The pact of mutual service which Medea and Aegeus contract in Act Four, Scene 5 is, for each of them, an affirmation of bonds of loyalty and obligation that were entirely compatible with traditional conceptions of marriage in the poet's day. To be sure, Medea and Aegeus are not the only ones to speak of duty in this play. Nobody has more to say about it than

Jason. But Jason honors the bonds of obligation mainly in the breach, while Aegeus and Medea not only pay their debts but engage in strategies of incurring and fulfilling obligations as a means of extending their personal power. Medea frankly tells Nérine that she intends to obtain Aegeus' protection by using her magic powers to liberate the king from prison and enlist him in her cause: "Voy-tu qu'en l'ouvrant je m'ouvre une retraite,/ Et que brisant ses fers, cette obligation/ Engage sa couronne à ma protection?" (Do you not see that in opening [the prison door], I open a retreat for myself, and that, in breaking his chains, I oblige his royal crown to protect me?, 1054-56). After being delivered from prison, Aegeus suffers a great burden of indebtedness. Far from revealing any inconsistency in proposing marriage to Medea, he shows appropriate conformity to a system of values according to which it would seem churlish not to offer one's life to the person who has just saved it.

The king's speech to Medea after she secures his release reeks almost painfully with the sense of gratitude and obligation:

Quoy, madame, faut-il que mon peu de puissance
Estouffe les devoirs de ma reconnoissance?
Mon sceptre ne peut-il estre employé pour vous?
Et vous seray-je ingrat autant que vostre espoux?

(Indeed, Madam, can my lack of power suffocate my dutiful gratitude? May my scepter be of no use to you? Am I to be as thankless to you as your husband?) (1265-68)

Beyond the obvious signs of obligation in such words as *devoir* and *reconnaissance,* the question of whether the king will be allowed to employ his scepter in Medea's service suggests various anxieties. The key terms for an understanding of these lines are the *peu de puissance* of the first line and the *ingrat* of the last. Aegeus' eagerness to acquit himself of his debt to Medea is really a fear of powerlessness. Ingratitude is to be deplored as a defenseless state, and conversely, the ability to engage others in obligations of gratitude indicates strength. So after accepting the invitation of asylum and the proposal of marriage that she has prompted Aegeus to offer, Medea tells him that she, in turn, would appreciate it if he would protect her servant: "Ayez soin de Nerine, et songez seulement/ Qu'en elle vous pouvez m'obliger puissamment" (Take care of Nérine, and just remember that through her you can oblige me powerfully, 1307-08). The ability to "oblige powerfully" is, indeed, so crucial to the action of the drama that the grim signal of the children's impending destruction is precisely their identification by both parents as "little ingrates" (1565, 1572).

Between Jason's farewell to the dying Creusa and his final confrontation with Medea, he delivers a monologue that reveals a dreadful potential for violence against his sons. In that they have been instrumental in the accomplishment of their mother's revenge, and in any case, can only serve as reminders of his own past love for the woman, the little boys are handy targets for their angry father: "Instruments des fureurs d'une mere insensée/ Indignes rejettons de mon amour passée" (instruments of your insane mother's fury, unworthy offshoots of my past love, 1561-62). This exclamation of rage bears comparison with Nérine's prior expression of sympathy for Creusa: "malheureux instrument du malheur qui nous presse" (Unhappy instrument of the misfortune closing in on us, 701), but the differences between the two passages are as striking as the similarities. Both Nérine and Jason perceive the child as being the tool of adult machinations, but Jason is somewhat less compassionate than his wife's servant, the bond of blood serving to augment rather than to mitigate his fury. He reviles the children as "unworthy offspring" (*indignes rejettons*), being especially piqued because these little "offshoots" of the paternal trunk reflect poorly on himself. He goes on to resolve that the "little ingrates" must be killed in order to punish their mother: "C'est vous petits ingrats que malgré la nature/ Il me faut immoler" (It is you, little ingrates, that, in spite of the bond of blood, I must sacrifice, 1565-66). This declaration that he must act "in spite of the bonds of blood" (*malgré la nature*) contrasts ironically with the textual evidence that his anger is fueled precisely by his narcissistic insistence on those very bonds. In any event, Jason's murderous revulsion against the children is directly proportional to the piety of his previous pronouncements of paternal devotion. Although, in a belated instant of clarity, he questions his shameful project, wondering aloud: "Toutefois qu'ont-ils fait qu'obeir à leur mere?" (But what have they done except obey their mother?, 1569), it is already too late. Jason's identification of his sons as *petits ingrats* is immediately seconded by Medea, who boasts that she has already enacted his revenge for him: "Leve les yeux perfide, et recognoy ce bras/ Qui t'a desja vangé de ces petits ingrats" (Lift up your eyes, you traitor and recognize this arm, which has already taken vengeance on the little ingrates for you, 1571-72).

Whereas Jason is troubled by the question of the children's innocence, Medea's ultimate satisfaction inheres in a sense of having redeemed her own lost innocence: "Mes desirs sont contents, mon pere et mon pays/ Je ne me repends plus de vous avoir trahis" (My desire is satisfied, my father and my country, I no longer repent of having betrayed you, 1607-08). In that she seems to regard the murder of the children as a matter of filial obligation, Medea resembles her Euripidean prototype; in that the word "innocence" is banished from her speech by the end of the play, she resembles her own beloved antagonist. The absence of the word from the final utterances of both characters is noteworthy because the concept is a recurring concern in this text, especially in Medea's speech. She has argued that she should pass for innocent in Corinth, though condemned elsewhere (484), and insisted that only a husband's support is required in order to prove a wife's innocence (876), begging Jason to salvage his innocence by being faithful in love (904). The irony, of course, is that all of these formulations tend to emphasize the relative, conditional quality of the term in such a way as to corrupt its basic meaning. The best example of this manipulative usage is Creon's command to Medea that she should render Jason innocent by absenting herself from the premises: "Rends-luy son innocence en t'esloignant d'icy" (Give him back his innocence by getting far away from here, 463). In fact, it is only Creusa who uses the word in a reliable way, entering on stage with the reference to the *tendre innocence* of Jason's children and asserting her own innocence with her dying words, in a pathetic appeal to her father: "Où fuyez-vous de moy cher autheur de mes jours?/ Fuyez-vous l'innocente, et malheureuse source/ D'où prennent tant de maux leur effroyable course?" (Whither are you fleeing dear author of my days? Fleeing the innocent and unhappy source from which so many troubles began their dreadful course?, 1396-98). Nothing in the text seems to contradict Creusa's estimation of herself as the "innocent and unhappy source" of the tragic action, and the epithet "innocent" forms one more verbal link between her and those other innocent and unhappy sources of misery, the children of Jason and Medea.

The "innocence" of the childlike character who is also a thoroughly sensual and appetitive creature is essential to an understanding of Corneille's text. Although there is no reason to assume the incompatibility of innocence and sensuality, or for that matter, the equivalence of desire and guilt, modern critics have sometimes taken Freud's observations on infantile sexuality as license to do so. Thus Greenberg assures his readers that his own insistence on "the child as victim" is not meant "to imply that these victims are necessarily innocent" because "at the bottom of all extreme longing for, identification with the other, is also the desire to be, to incorporate—that is, to kill—that other" (163). Even allowing for the fact that these remarks occur in a discussion of Racine, not Corneille, it seems reasonable to suggest that the values the critic assigns to the words "innocent" and "guilty" are rather different from those likely to have been operative in an age when "guilty" children were still liable to be burned at the stake. With respect to this practice, Michelet stresses the utility of the doctrine of original sin by quoting the Roman theologian, Spina: "Why does God permit the death of the innocent? He does so justly. For if they do not die by reason of the sins they have committed, yet they are guilty of death by reason of original sin" (xiii). In view of such pieties, Alice Miller criticizes the modern assumption that "Freud offended society by depriving people of the illusion of the innocent child." She contends that "a child's innocence is real, not an illusion," and furthermore, that "the reality of this innocence has practically never been accepted" (*Thou Shalt Not* 154). Her comments on the venerability of theoretical structures for inculpating the child underscore the originality and humanity of Corneille's insistence on the innocence of his murdered children.

Although the subversive import of this drama is evident in that the only major characters whom nobody ever accuses of being innocent are Creon and Aegeus, it is entirely in keeping with Corneille's fundamentally conservative orientation that an ultimately blameless child of his creation is, nevertheless, capable of ruinous mischief. In the world of this play, innocence alone is not enough to secure salvation. Only those who manage to insert themselves into the network of obligations and loyalties inherent in the quasi-feudal vision of social order at the heart of the action can survive and prevail. For all its sensual affirmation and witty iconoclasm, *Médée* is very much the product of an age in which the confrontation between rapid social change and conservative institutions resulted more notably in reaction than in reform. In this drama, the kings whose domination the unruly pretenders threaten are, by and large, no better than their challengers. A scion of corrupt royalty herself, Medea may suffer the lot of the dispossessed and exploited, but her ascendance through collusion with Aegeus and her rise to power over the bodies of her children evoke the disquieting specter of a land whose near future lies in a bloody alliance with absolutism.

In the end, Corneille's symbols are not quite as unambiguous as their political implications might suggest. Writing at a moment when a strengthened monarchy was widely regarded as the best response to the fear of social chaos, the playwright presented a world torn apart by petty betrayals and grasping factions. He also conveyed the glaring contradictions and the warring imperatives of the age in strikingly vivid and complex characterizations. Creusa is not only the spoiled daughter of privilege, but also an exploited and badly treated child. Aegeus is not only a lawless abductor but a wronged and vulnerable old man. The knight errant of the piece is the voice of wisdom, while the oppressed servant embodies the threat of treachery and disorder. Finally, Medea's victory over Jason is no exuberant triumph of brute force, but a demonstration of the superiority of art over military power: "Et que peut contre moy ta debile vaillance?/ Mon art faisoit ta force, et tes exploits guerriers/ Tiennent de mon secours ce qu'ils ont de lauriers" (And what harm can your weak valor do to me? My art gave you strength, and your warring exploits owe to my assistance the laurels that they hold, 1590-92). Corneille's drama expresses not only the worst fears of his contemporaries, but also their best hope. Neither his compassion for the victims of corrupt authority nor his skeptical view of the rise of absolutism diminishes the vigor with which he ultimately affirms the principles of order and creativity that herald the great age of French dramatic poetry.

5

Grillparzer and the Cycle of Abuse

Grillparzer's *Medea* dramatizes the connections between child abuse, sexual trauma, psychological dissociation, and political persecution that are implicit in the ancient and early modern treatments of the motif. First presented in Vienna in 1821, *Medea* is the third play in a trilogy named *Das goldene Vliess (The Golden Fleece)*, which embraces both epic and tragic elements of the ancient cycle of storiesabout Jason, Medea, and the Argonauts. Focusing on an anxious protagonist whose opponents proceed with all the delicacy of anti-Semitic witchhunters, and depicting a relentless concatenation of events in which the present moment is always hostage to a brutal past, the tragedy seems peculiarly relevant to twentieth-century experience. It also reflects the sensibility of a man of letters familiar with the works of Aeschylus, Euripides, Seneca, Apollonius, Calderone, Corneille, Racine, Shakespeare, Schiller, and Goethe, as well as the special concerns of a Viennese who lived from 1791 to 1872, during a notably troubled period in Austrian history. In *Das goldene Vliess*, Grillparzer combines grandeur of poetic vision with minute psychological observation, and his achievement seems all the more remarkable in view of the relative obscurity to which his work has been consigned for most of this century.

Though little known to modern English-speaking audiences, Grillparzer was famous during his lifetime, the entry which Lord Byron made in his diary on January 21, 1821 being a good indication of contemporary enthusiasm for the dramatist:

Midnight. read the Italian translation by Guido Sorelli of the German Grillparzer—a devil of a name, to be sure, for posterity, but they must learn to pronounce it. With all the allowance for *translation* . . . and above all, an *Italian* translation . . . the tragedy of Sappho is superb and sublime! There is no denying it. The man has done a great thing in writing that play. (Burkhard 5)

Byron's admiration was shared by George Meredith, who called Grillparzer "a poet of great genius" (Burkhard 9). In the twentieth century, positive appreciations of his work have been articulated by Samuel Solomon, for whom *Medea* "is perhaps the greatest drama in the German language" (*Plays on Classic Themes* 139) and George Steiner, who regards the poet as a "playwright of the first rank" (*The Death of Tragedy* 228-29). In the opinion of Hugo von Hofmannsthal, Grillparzer was "Austria's national poet, a spiritual link between the old Austria of Maria Theresa and the new Austria" of Hugo's own generation (Thompson 127). Critical emphasis on the peculiarly Austrian quality of Grillparzer's writing is consistent with the testimony of the author, who said that, "if you look at the country around you from the heights of the Kahlenberg, you will understand what I have written and what I am" (Pollak 33-34).

Though national consciousness is most evident in those works based on historical subjects, such as *König Ottokar's Glück und Ende,* and *Ein Bruderzwist in Habsburg*, it is also perceptible in *Das goldene Vliess*, the very title of which recalls the late medieval Order of the Knights of the Golden Fleece, the chivalric order of the House of Habsburg (Wandruska 95). Like the title of the entire work, the ruined towers and fortresses of the second play in the trilogy, *Die Argonauten* (*The Argonauts*), seem replete with nostalgia for a lost age of glory when the Habsburgs ruled as Holy Roman Emperors over vast areas of Europe, including Austria, Spain, the Low Countries, Hungary, parts of modern France, Germany, Italy, Poland and the Czech and Slovak Republics. The contemporary quality of Grillparzer's theater is not only evident in the propensity of certain characters to talk like reactionary despots, enlightened reformers, and Napoleonic heroes, but also in a generally gloomy perspective that reflects the discouraged mood of a crumbling Empire. Regularly at war with the French during the poet's formative years, Austria was defeated twice during the Revolutionary Wars (1797 and 1801) and twice during the Napoleonic Wars (1805 and 1809), enduring a process of slow decline throughout his lifetime. Witnessing the final dissolution of the Holy Roman Empire (1806), the establishment of the reactionary Holy Alliance at the Congress of Vienna (1815), the Revolution of 1848, and the wretched defeat of the Austrians by the Prussians in 1866, he spent all of his middle adult years under the oppressive regime of Clemens von Metternich, who imparted his name to the age (Pollak 33-34). The melancholy outlook of Austria during the early part of the nineteenth century was, moreover, a reflection of the generally subdued mood that reigned throughout Europe.

The ideals of emancipation and reform having suffered a beating in the course of various inglorious campaigns, the pessimism of the age was directly proportional to the optimism of the one preceding it. Thus Condorcet's theory of the inevitability of human progress (1794) was countered by Malthus' grim calculation of the insufficiency of arithmetically increasing food supply to sustain geometrically increasing populations (1798), and the expansive spirit of the Enlightenment, which Kant defined as man's liberation from his "self-caused immaturity" (132-39), gave way to Schopenhauer's vision of human beings as "children in a theatre before the curtain is raised, sitting there in high spirits and eagerly waiting for the play to begin," blissfully oblivious of their own resemblance to "innocent prisoners, condemned, not to death, but to life" ("On the Sufferings of the World," *The Essential Schopenhauer* 86). The pessimism of the philosopher who wondered if the human race would continue to exist at all if children were brought into the world by an act of pure reason made a profound impression on Grillparzer, who may have read *Die Welt als Wille und Vorstellung* (*The World as Will and Representation*) as early as 1819 (Thompson 145), and refers repeatedly to its author (*S.W.* 1.583: 3.231; 3.1159).

Anachronistic political institutions and somber philosophical currents notwithstanding, Grillparzer's Vienna was the cultural nucleus of the German-speaking world, and his social contacts included some of the great artists and musicians of the day, most notably Schubert, who set several of his poems to music, and Beethoven, with whom he hoped to collaborate on an opera. When Beethoven died, Grillparzer wrote his funeral oration. Although he was acquainted with such literary figures as Tieck, Hegel, and Goethe, he experienced singular discomfort in the company of those he admired, and is said to have burst into tears upon being introduced to Goethe. Having read *Tasso* and *Faust* with great enthusiasm, he nevertheless declined an invitation to spend an evening in private conversation with the great poet, feeling overwhelmed by the prospect "of being alone with Goethe for a whole evening" (Yates, *Grillparzer* 11-15). The failure of self-confidence which prompted an aspiring man of letters to decline an invitation from Goethe seems all the more noteworthy when the author in question is one who wrote a dramatic work which focuses as unrelentingly on psychological nuance as does *Das goldene Vliess*.

Grillparzer expressed interest in the Medea motif at the very beginning of his career, in 1817, the year in which he achieved his first theatrical success with *Die Ahnfrau* (*The Ancestress*). After reading Schlegel's lectures on dramatic art, he observed that he would like to write a tragedy based on the myth of Medea in which he would "motivate Medea's hatred against her children on their attachment to their kinder father" (Solomon, *Plays on Classic Themes* 137). During the winter of 1817-18, he also had occasion to attend several modern dramatizations of the myth—a drama by Gotter and the opera by Cherubini. Whatever the contributions of Schlegel, Gotter, and Cherubini to the genesis of *Das goldene Vliess,* the likelihood that they were tangential to the fundamental sources of Grillparzer's fascination with the myth is suggested by the evidence that his interest in the theme of destructive parenting preceded his speculation on

Medea's motivation and outlasted by many years the period from 1817 to 1820 during which he wrote his trilogy. *Die Ahnfrau,* which was essentially complete by September 1816, though not performed until the following January, is a play about the ghost of a woman who is doomed to haunt her family until all her descendants are dead. In "Das Kloster bei Sendomir," a short story published in 1827, a woman forced to choose between her own life and that of her child agrees to sacrifice the child. Finally, in the posthumously performed historical tragedy, *Ein Bruderzwist in Habsburg (Family Strife in Habsburg),* which Hugo von Hofmannsthal regarded as "the most significant historical an political tragedy written in the German language" (Thompson 109), the Emperor Rudolf condemns his own son to bleed to death. Even more suggestive than the author's persistent reversion to the theme of violence by parents against children is his anxiety about the self-revelatory quality of his enterprise. In this connection, the difference between critical and authorial misgivings about his first theatrical production is instructive.

Although *Die Ahnfrau* was a great popular success, it was criticized as a specimen of the "fate tragedy," a genre condemned as being fatalistic and incredible (Yates, *Grillparzer* 50). Whereas critics attacked the play on account of its form, Grillparzer himself seems to have been most uncomfortable with the revealing content of the work, lamenting that "there is something within me which says it is just as indecent to show one's inner self naked as one's outer self" (Yates, *Grillparzer* 6). Nor was this the only occasion when he chastised himself on this account. While writing *Das goldene Vliess,* he reproached himself for cold-heartedly exploiting the affections of Charlotte von Paumgartten in order to make psychological observations on which to draw his trilogy (Yates, *Grillparzer* 7). In a fragmentary dialogue called the "poète sifflé," written in 1829, a character named Adèle accuses dramatists of laying bare their inmost selves (Yates, *Grillparzer* 17-18). The author's chronic anxiety concerning the relationship between experience and creativity underscores the critical difficulty of assessing the importance of autobiographical elements in Grillparzer's imaginative works.

Without speculating excessively on the nature of the inner life that Grillparzer felt he was exposing in plays and stories depicting the faults of the parents and the fate of their progeny, we may well ask whether it is more important to know that the author had read Schlegel and visited the theater in 1817 than to know that, in the same year, his younger brother Adolph committed suicide by drowning (Yates, *Grillparzer* 6), or that, two years later, his work on the second part of the trilogy was interrupted by his own discovery of his mother's lifeless body in the bedroom where she had hanged herself (Hof and Cermak 15). If the circumstances of the latter event did not in themselves call to mind the Sophoclean tragedy on which Freud based his theory of the Oedipus Complex, Grillparzer's reflections on the matter might do so: "What I felt," he wrote, "can only be imagined by one who knew the almost idyllic nature of our common life. After she had no longer any resources of her own, I provided for all the necessities of our home, and thus I was to her both son and husband" (Pollak 76). The likelihood that Grillparzer's work on the trilogy served something of a cathartic function is suggested, moreover, by his description of the intensity with which he applied himself to the project in the fall and winter of 1818. He recalled in later years that he had never worked on anything with so much enjoyment (Yates, *Grillparzer* 7). Significantly enough, the climactic actions of both the first and the second plays in *Das goldene Vliess* involve the deaths of relatively blameless young men, Phrixus, murdered by the Colchian royal family, and Absyrtus, drowned in a suicidally heroic gesture. Insistence on this element, which does not occur in earlier dramatizations of the myth and seems, in fact, notably consistent with the spirit of Goethe's *Werther*, is a salient example of the way in which diffuse cultural currents and profound personal preoccupations tend to converge in Grillparzer's work. In short, his writing is no exception to the rule that the relationship between autobiographical projection and artistic creation is rarely simple.

Far from being faithful renderings of real people known to their author, Grillparzer's characters are elaborately constructed composite figures, and the writer's seemingly candid comments on the sources of his inspiration can be subtly misleading. His very emphasis on the importance of the affair with Charlotte as a model of the relationship between Jason and Medea may conceal more than it reveals if we consider that Grillparzer's Medea is just as much the badly treated daughter of Aeëtes and the wretched mother of her own children as she is the wife of Jason in this play. Whereas Charlotte was a newly married bride when Grillparzer became involved with her, Medea is the central figure in a merciless presentation of the parent/child relationship, and her portrait might be assumed to include details drawn from more than one model. Although Grillparzer stressed the connection between his personal experience and his female characters, the psychological acuity of his dramatic portraits is also apparent in such male characters as Jason, a figure inviting oedipal exegesis, who seeks in Medea both erotic fulfillment and maternal support. To be sure, the hero's dependence on a woman combining the qualities of both mother and lover is inherent in the ancient myth, which is replete with elements analogous to the myth of Oedipus. Like the ill-fated king of Thebes, Jason was abandoned as an infant because of oracular predictions, condemned as an adult to wander in exile, and suffered various trials as a consequence of his father's misadventures. Since the philandering propensities that distinguish the Euripidean Jason from the Sophoclean Oedipus also constitute an essential similarity between Grillparzer and his male protagonist, the possibility of an autobiographical interest in the theme of seduction is worth considering.

A man who enjoyed the company of women and created a number of sympathetic female characters, Grillparzer was nevertheless convinced that domestic entanglements were inimical to the creative enterprise and refused ever to marry. Deferring his initiation into the rites of love until he met Charlotte when he was twenty-eight, and tending to lose interest in any woman who had granted him her sexual favors, he was attracted in his middle years to very young women like Marie von Smolenitz and Heloise Hoechner, who were half his age. Though his habit of reproaching himself for using love affairs as "psychological experiments" suggests an exacting conscience and compassionate inclinations, the subtleties of his female characterizations seem nonetheless to be a benefit which he derived from dealings with the opposite sex. Tending to regard himself as the ultimate victim of a "professional" obligation to forego the comforts of a wife and family, he routinely sacrificed the women who loved him, along with himself, on the altar of Art. This was never more conspicuously the case than in his dealings with Katharina Fröhlich, who remained his devoted fiancée for over half a century though he never married her (Thompson 24-26; Hof and Cermak 48-68). While it is worth noting, at this point, that the theme of seduction is psychoanalytically linked to the theme of the threatening mother (Miller, *Thou Shalt Not* 80), Grillparzer's troubles with women may hardly be regarded as a personal peculiarity.

Even if the nature of his dealings with women suggests that Grillparzer was no gift to good housekeeping, it does not distinguish him from contemporary cultural ideals. Mozart's most famous operas celebrate the exploits of such legendary rakes as Don Giovanni and Count Almaviva (*Le nozze di Figaro*), while the quintessential hero of the age is Goethe's Faust, who manages to indulge all of his extravagant passions without ever having to pay the devil his due. The fate of Faust's child by Gretchen is, indeed, virtually the same as that of Medea's sons, and Schopenhauer's claim that "every man needs many women" (*Essential* 111) would seem to concede the inevitability of the problem. The autobiographical dimensions of such texts as *Faust* and *Das goldene Vliess* may seem rather beside the point in view of Oscar Werner's emphasis on the role of the unmarried mother in European culture during this period. Grillparzer's own awareness of the social implications of his drama is evident in a passage from *Der arme Spielmann* (*The Poor Fiddler*), a story published in 1847 in which he observes that "Juliet, Dido or Medea exist in embryo within every young servant girl who, half against her will, follows her insistent lover out of the dancing crowd" (*S.W.* 3.148).

A tale of seduction and betrayal in which parents mistreat children who either die young or live to abuse their own offspring, Grillparzer's trilogy might pass for an illustration of the psychological dynamics that Freud stressed in "The Aetiology of Hysteria" *(S.E.* 3:191-221), the paper articulating the controversial "seduction theory." Although the abuse that Medea endures at the hands of Aeëtes is physical and psychological rather than overtly sexual, the entire trilogy is pervaded by sexual suggestion, and the spectacular initial encounter between Jason and Medea in *Die Argonauten* constitutes a brilliant observation of the psychological continuity between child abuse and sexual abuse. Freud's exclusive insistence on sexual trauma in his early essay has, in any case, been criticized by Miller, who suggests substituting the term "trauma theory" for "seduction theory," arguing that "non-sexual traumas" as well as sexual ones may cause neuroses *(Thou Shalt Not* 41). However sensible her terminology may be for the practice of psychoanalysis, it tends to obscure the essential importance of the theme of seduction in nineteenth-century thought. Schopenhauer's conception of man as the plaything of a capricious Nature who seduces him through the lure of sexual pleasure into the onerous task of perpetuating the race is perhaps the best example of the cosmic implications of the theme: "Nature . . . the inner being of which is the will-to-live itself, with all her force impels both man and animal to propagate. After this, she has attained her end with the individual and is quite indifferent to its destruction" *(World as Will* 1.329-30). For all its brilliance, there is a disconcerting quality in this statement which is directly related to the gendered quality of its vision. Casting Mother Nature in the part of the wanton trifler and mankind in that of the foolish young thing, this articulation of philosophical pessimism constitutes a projection onto the "female" cosmic order of the flagrant exploitation that men of rank and privilege regularly practiced on lower-class girls and women. By positing the paradigm of sexual abuse as inherent in the order of the universe and displacing responsibility from patriarchal institutions onto a maternal "Nature," Schopenhauer exalts the terms of "seduction" and "abandonment" to the level of global metaphors for the human condition and finally concludes that the only hope of evading Mother Nature's nefarious ulterior motive resides in the denial of the treacherous will-to-live.

The philosophical precept that "deliverance from life and suffering cannot even be imagined without complete denial of the will" (Schopenhauer, *World as Will* 397) is curiously analogous to contemporary prescriptions for educating children by breaking their will at an early age. Believing that children are inclined by nature to every kind of wickedness, eighteenth- and nineteenth-century pedagogues recommended draconian measures for training small children in the "art of self-denial" (Miller, *For Your Own Good* 28), and the social consequences of their influential theories are underscored by Alice Miller, who demonstrates the link between the inculcation of cruelty in the nineteenth century and the psychology of fascism in the twentieth century. Articulating a theory of what she calls "poisonous pedagogy," she traces the continuity between the unrelenting brutality endured by Hitler as a child and the violent regime which "der Führer" eventually imposed on all of his subjects. She also argues that Hitler's assumption of the role of tyrannical patriarch virtually assured him the loyalty of a generation of Germans and Austrians who had been raised according to the pedagogical principle of breaking the child's will. As evidence of her thesis, she offers a close examination of widely read pedagogical treatises that give detailed instructions for breaking the will of a small child before he or she reaches the age of "consciousness."

Typical of the texts cited by Miller is an excerpt from an essay published by J. Sulzer in 1748. Observing that "it is quite natural for the child's soul to want to have a will of its own," the author earnestly proceeds to present remedies for this problem, warning parents that "things that are not done correctly in the first two years will be difficult to rectify thereafter." Recommending corporal punishment of infants and toddlers, Sulzer informs his readers that "one of the advantages of these early years is that then force and compulsion can be used." The reason why it is advisable to impose on the smallest child treatment that one would hesitate to inflict on an older one is that little children are less likely to remember what is done to them, tending to forget everything that happened to them in early childhood: "If their wills can be broken at this time, they will never remember afterwards that they had a will, and for this very reason the severity that is required will not have any serious consequences" (*For Your Own Good* xvii-xix). Sobering as this recommendation of punishment for babies may seem, it is by no means an idiosyncracy of the particular writer, who merely espouses views that were widely held by his contemporaries. Most notable in the above passage is the assertion that children do not remember their earliest experiences. Indeed the resistance of Freud's peers to his observation, in 1896, that "hysterical symptoms are derivatives of memories which are operating unconsciously" (Masson 280) seems especially significant in the context of such assumptions. In fact, the enormous emphasis that nineteenth-century thinkers such as Schopenhauer, Nietzsche, and Freud placed on the operation of the irrational, unconscious will was directly proportional to the strength of the belief among eighteenth- and nineteenth-century parents and educators that the youngest children could be beaten without traumatic consequences because they would forget everything that had been done to them.

Miller's articulation of the dynamics of what she calls "poisonous pedagogy" seems relevant to *Das goldene Vliess,* not only because certain characters, such as Medea, Phrixus and Absyrtus, are presented as the objects of parental abuse, their tragedies having the general quality of educational disasters, but because the peculiar receptivity to violent passions and anxious suffering manifested by such characters does not distinguish them from their peers. Jason, for example, may sometimes play the part of the petty despot, but he also displays the scars of the walking wounded. His propensity for invoking Plato's myth of the twin souls when embarking on an amatory campaign (*Argonauten* 1208-15; *Medea* 835) suggests the importance of Slater's comment on the famous passage in the *Symposium* where Aristophanes describes the origin of erotic yearning. Noting that the speaker's description of the behavior of the beings who long for reunion with those from whom they have been sundered "sounds very much like a modern clinical report of the apathy of mother-separated children," Slater observes that the "previous state" for which the lovers yearn seems to be the "mother-child dyadic" (112-13). His thesis is pertinent to Grillparzer's text because of the ancient sources of the plot and also because Grillparzer's Jason bemoans the cruelty of his fate in the manner of a Romantic hero.

The character of Jason is illuminated by Alan Pasco's speculation on a possible link between the dynamics of maternal deprivation and the phenomenal popularity of the melancholy outcast in the literature of the last century. Observing that readers who responded with enthusiasm to the essentially aristocratic lament of Chateaubriand's René were, for the most part, members of a middle class for which the future held "virtually unlimited possibility," Pasco remarks that the wonder is not that writers created so many versions of the Romantic hero, but that "so many people were willing to read the resulting litanies of despair." What the consumers and producers of Romantic literature often shared with its heroic and not-so-heroic protagonists were the scars of a wretched childhood scenario that might include the loss of a mother in childbirth, the dependence on a harried wet-nurse for nurturing, separation from a genuinely loving caretaker at an early age, or subjection to the rule of cruel guardians. Citing the cases of Heathcliff, René and Werther as examples of the hero as motherless "orphan" who bears an emotional resemblance to hospitalized children who become "tense, negative, restless and withdrawn," Pasco suggests that the condition known to twentieth-century health professionals as "maternal deprivation" may well have been epidemic in an age when women regularly died in childbirth, when there was no safe substitute for mother's milk, when competent wet-nurses were in short supply, and when infant care was largely the province of ignorant, impoverished women likely to be distracted by many cares. His speculation on the attraction that the melancholy hero who is isolated, misunderstood, moody, and starved for love exercised on nineteenth-century readers and theater-goers suggests that thousands of "hero-worshippers" may have seen in the Romantic hero a poetic projection of their own chronic longing for parental love.

The intuition of a connection between maternal deprivation and literary characterization seems relevant, not only to Grillparzer's melancholy Jason, but also to his Medea, who first appears as a motherless girl and whose emotional development is traced over a considerable period. Though this kind of continuity is only provided in the case of a single individual, it lends enormous credibility to her portrait and also illuminates other characters who resemble her in various ways. The importance of the hypothesis of faulty nurturing does not inhere in the specific effects of particular abuses, but rather in the fact that certain patterns of cruelty and bereavement are part of the field in which Grillparzer operates, and his gloomy drama reflects that field. Although Miller insists on the general significance of her theory, asserting that "all pedagogy is pervaded by the precepts of 'poisonous pedagogy' " (*For Your Own Good* 96), the fact that her sources are, for the most part, German texts makes her work seem especially pertinent to the explication of a nineteenth-century drama written in German. The paradoxical conviction that children have to be bullied into being good is, after all, the domestic equivalent of the concept of Enlightened Despotism that characterized Austrian public life during the Age of Reason. In a discussion of the Emperor Joseph II, Robert A. Kann observes that "the idea of imposing the rule of reason by force . . . is in itself irrational and this is indeed the tragic breach and contradiction in the Josephine system" (144).

Kann's analysis of the irrational aspects of the Enlightenment illuminates the context of a play in which the male protagonist is not only a legendary seducer and fashionable opportunist, but also an individual member of a dominant group for which Medea represents the peculiarly abhorrent Other. Though the procedure of scapegoating and the operation of prejudice are inherent in the ancient texts, the contempt and repugnance that Grillparzer's Medea inspires in the Greeks are of a special order not explainable as a faithful rendering of ancient antagonisms. Medea's exoticism, her sensuality, the oriental fashion of her dress, her reputation for deceit, her legendary knowledge of mysterious arts, her glorious past, and her wretched present—in short, every aspect of the characterization— lends an unmistakable cultural specificity to her Otherness. Though she is never labeled as such, she bears a notable resemblance to the contemporary stereotype of the Jew, concerning which Sander Gilman observes that the "essential Other for German-speaking lands is the Jew" (227). Whereas anti-Semitic beliefs and practices were challenged by the liberal ideals of the Enlightenment, and Austrian Jews were emancipated by the Edict of Tolerance in 1781, the assumption of Jewish inferiority persisted in discussions of the "Jewish question" during which debaters attributed the shortcomings of the Jews to environmental factors and speculated on the hypothetical conditions that might contribute to the "betterment of the Jews" (Katz 58, 69). Progress in the cause of integration did not dislodge the legendary figure of the sinister Jew from the popular imagination, and when the Napoleonic debacle put factions favoring social reform on the defensive, the forces of reaction flourished. In the summer of 1819, a number of cities in German-speaking lands were racked by the worst anti-Semitic riots in living memory (Gilman 163-64).

It is reasonable to assume that the "Jewish question" may have been a matter of some interest to Grillparzer when he sat down to write his *Medea* in November 1819, and the issue was, in any case, not a matter of fleeting concern for him. On two occasions, he wrote dramas in which Jews were central characters—*Esther* (1840), a fragmentary work based on the biblical story, and *Die Jüdin von Toledo* (*The Jewess of Toledo*, 1851). In these plays, as in *Das goldene Vliess*, the dynamics of communal persecution overlap the theme of generational conflict. The latter concern manifests itself, in all three works, in problematic relationships between young women and their paternal guardians. In that her father's avarice contributes to her downfall, Rachel, the female protagonist of *Die Jüdin von Toledo*, resembles both Medea and her Greek rival, Creusa. The paternal role in *Esther*, played by the heroine's scholarly uncle, Mordecai, is a saintly fellow by comparison with either Aeëtes or Rachel's father, Isaac, yet Mordecai is not above sacrificing his niece for a worthy cause. The argument that Medea is Rachel's spiritual sister need depend, in any case, neither on the contemporary context nor on structural parallels.

In visual details and interpersonal exchanges, the drama of Medea evokes the uneasy opposition between Gentiles and Jews in early nineteenth-century Austria. Recalling descriptions of the unassimilated Jew as "conspicuous by his strange raiment" (Katz 180), Medea appears in *Die Argonauten* wearing a dark red dress and black veil embroidered with mysterious golden symbols, and her unusual apparel becomes a conspicuous source of embarrassment to Jason after the couple arrives in Greece. More important than such particulars is the general way in which the disastrous sojourn in Corinth assumes the sordid quality of a witch hunt. If Grillparzer had set out to construct a drama depicting an anxious Jew surrounded by arrogant anti-Semites and patronizing liberals, he could hardly have improved on his mythological scenario. Presenting brutal interactions in which the psychology of individuals is enmeshed with complicated social, political, and economic forces, he emphasizes the public effects of private abuses. The characteristic cycle of self-regenerating abuse which pervades the entire trilogy is concisely and brilliantly articulated. In Medea's observation that "Denn wenn das Unglück dem Verbrechen folgt,/ Folgt öfter das Verbrechen noch dem Unglück" (For if misfortune sometimes follows crime, more often still does crime follow misfortune, *Medea* 1796-97).

Well-suited to the thematic project of tracing the sins of the fathers as they descend "upon the children unto the third and fourth generation" (Exodus 34.7), the form of the trilogy is essential to Grillparzer's treatment of the myth of Medea, and the author acknowledges the Aeschylean dimensions of his enterprise with repeated allusions to the *Oresteia*. Although considerations of space do not allow extensive analysis of the first two parts of *Das goldene Vliess* in the present essay, an analysis of *Medea* that did not refer to *Der Gastfreund* (*The Guest*) or *Die Argonauten* (*The Argonauts*) would make about as much sense as an exegesis of the *Eumenides* that dispensed with the rest of the *Oresteia*. Since the psychological immediacy and credibility of Grillparzer's *Medea* derive to some extent from the fact that it is the concluding work in a trilogy, I will underscore a few essential elements in the two plays that precede it in the tragic sequence.

Set in a Colchian landscape dominated by a giant statue of a god named Peronto, *Der Gastfreund* is a one-act play that opens on a scene in which the young Medea presides over a band of girls who have been out hunting. The first line of the play, announcing the death of a hunted creature that is about to be offered to a goddess named Darimba, recalls the tone of Schopenhauer's morose observation that "we are all like lambs in a field disporting themselves under the eye of the butcher, who chooses out first one and then another for his prey" (*Essential* 86). Medea's cheerful response to the news of the kill is replete with dramatic irony because the central action of *Der Gastfreund,* in which Medea's father Aeëtes kills the stranger Phrixus, is analogous to the predatory coup presented in the opening scene of the play. This event sets the tone, moreover, for all that will happen in the entire trilogy. Since the deaths of Absyrtus at the end of *Die Argonauten* and of Medea's children at the end of *Medea* are the culminating disasters in a series of tragic developments, the crime committed in *Der Gastfreund* confers on the climactic events of the second and third plays in the trilogy the appearance of a harvest, the seeds of violence sown by the irresponsible patriarch in *Der Gastfreund* having borne fruits to be culled by a later generation. Thus Phrixus' curse on the house of Aeëtes is as crucial to *Das goldene Vliess* as the curse of the charioteer, Myrtilus, on the descendants of Pelops is to the *Oresteia*. Not only presenting the initial atrocity from which every subsequent calamity ensues, *Der Gastfreund* also articulates the pattern for various abusive relationships in the entire work.

Beginning with a scene in which Medea, in the manner of Artemis, browbeats one of her followers for breaking a vow of chastity, and proceeding with a hostile confrontation between Aeëtes and his daughter, Grillparzer prepares the audience for Medea's eventual humiliation and revenge with an early demonstration of her capacity to play the roles of both *bourreau* and *victime*. When she reproaches her father for mistreating her in various ways, mentioning both psychological and physical abuse (121-27), the king responds by telling her to forget the past, assuring her that she deserved her punishment (128-29). His position amounts to an invocation of the abusive formula that serves as the title of Alice Miller's study—"this is for your own good." While the admonition to forget past grievances may appear to be an ironic comment on the pedagogical premise that children do not remember what is done to them in their early years, the interaction between father and daughter very evidently conforms to the paradigm of poisonous pedagogy in that it enacts a war of wills between unevenly matched parties. When Aeëtes tries to enlist his daughter's help in an ill-advised plan to despoil and murder Phrixus, the girl refuses to cooperate until threatened with abandonment, at which point she reluctantly complies with his wishes. Aeëtes finally succeeds in carrying out the noxious project which will eventually result in the destruction of both his children, and the play concludes with Medea succumbing to a hallucinatory trance in which she sees a vision of the Furies and utters prophecies of doom. Insistently focusing on sacrificial ceremonies recalling the origins of tragedy and the importance of hospitality, *Der Gastfreund* assumes a metapoetic quality by revealing a flaw in the assumption of cosmic order implied by classical aesthetics. Whereas ancient poetry was described by Schlegel as a "harmonious promulgation of the permanently established legislation of a world submitted to a beautiful order and reflecting in itself the eternal images of things" (342), Grillparzer's drama suggests that neither the sense of "beautiful order," nor the permanence of "established legislation," nor the "eternal images of things" can very well survive the spectacle of innocence slaughtered in the name of divine right by an avaricious criminal.

Although *Die Argonauten,* like *Der Gastfreund,* is set in Colchis, it unfolds against a radically altered landscape. Both dramas take place in a wilderness of rocks and trees, in view of the sea, but the first one begins, like the ancient tragic festivals, at dawn, before an altar, under the gaze of inscrutable gods, while the second begins at night, by the faint glow of a lamp positioned in the upper story of a half-ruined tower, with no gods in sight. While the chronological measure of time lapsed between the events of *Der Gastfreund* and those of *Die Argonauten* must be relatively short, the atmosphere of the one is as different from that of the other as Classical tragedy is different from Romantic drama. In keeping with Schlegel's observation that "the Romantic delights in dissimilar mixtures" (342), the scenes of *Die Argonauten* shift from night to day, from stormy to calm, from domestic squabbling to military deliberation. Though the vestiges of a Colchian pantheon survive in occasional references to such invented gods as Peronto and Heimdar, a kind of Colchian Hades, religion seems to have undergone a domesticating and trivializing process in the interval between *Der Gastfreund* and *Die Argonauten.* A communal, festive outdoor activity in the former play, it is a shadowy, sequestered, private concern in the latter. The chorus, in the form of Medea's band of followers, has disappeared, and Medea herself appears in the exotic robes of a sorceress, muttering incantations in the dark to a small-scale idol at a shadowy indoor altar. In the absence of any conspicuous divine presence, without the enthusiastic ministrations of a worshipping throng, religion seems germane to superstition, and Medea herself is as much a solitary eccentric as a sacred priestess.

The pattern established in *Der Gastfreund,* according to which Aeëtes tries to impose his will on Medea, who objects, complains, struggles, and then, faced with the scourge of paternal rejection, caves in, is repeatedly enacted in *Die Argonauten.* Although the basic situation is varied in the opening scene of the play by the fact that Aeëtes picks on his son Absyrtus instead of his daughter, the king's tendency to make unreasonable demands on his children, to project his own responsibilities on them, to force them into a nurturing role, to reproach them endlessly, and to make a general nuisance of himself remains the same. Evidently less skeptical and rebellious than his sister, Absyrtus shares with her the habit of supporting and assisting an irascible parent who, in this scene, responds to his son's steadfast devotion by calling him names, telling him to shut up, and finally, threatening to kill him: "Soll ich dich töten, Schwatzender Tor?" (Do I have to kill you, you chattering fool?, 46). Like Phrixus before him, Absyrtus is a good scout who plays his part without complaining, and actually seems to share his father's enthusiasm for making war on the newly arrived Argonauts. It is in order to enlist her support in the campaign against these foreign visitors that Aeëtes and Absyrtus are looking for Medea.

Though Medea has avoided her father since the murder of Phrixus, and initially refuses to help him in his current war, sensibly advising that he negotiate a settlement, she proves no more immune than ever to parental persuasion. Aeëtes has, in any case, refined his technique. Whereas, in *Der Gastfreund,* he merely threatens to abandon Medea, in *Die Argonauten* he responds to her resistance with a kind of negative psychology. Pretending indifference to his daughter, he beckons to his son, whom he favors with glowing approval: "Komm, mein Sohn, mein einzig Kind" (Come, my son, my only child, 209). That this remark is intended for Medea's benefit seems clear enough in view of the way Aeëtes has treated his "only son" in the preceding scene, and his creative manipulation of sibling rivalry is particularly notable in connection with a mythical character who is supposed by legend to have murdered her brother and is, in all accounts, notoriously vulnerable to the passion of jealousy. The ploy works like a charm. Medea immediately waffles, agreeing to help her father in his latest campaign and reaping the reward of a warm embrace. Thus Aeëtes plays the role of the seducer with his daughter, using his power over her and her need for affection as tools for compelling her cooperation in actions that her conscience cannot possibly condone.

The pattern of parental rejection followed by remorseful compliance of the rejected child that Aeëtes initiates in *Der Gastfreund* and refines in *Die Argonauten* becomes the essential model of Medea's dealings with other people until the very end of the trilogy. Presenting himself as Aeëtes' antagonist, Jason inherits the mantle of the abuser. When he penetrates into Medea's darkened chamber and wounds her with his sword before he ever gets a good look at her, he instantly wins her heart. Though he is both a bungler and a brute, managing to get himself into trouble at every turn, Medea finds herself irresistibly drawn to him and repeatedly saves his life. Torn between her loyalty to her father and her longing for the seductive Greek, she finally forsakes her old tormenter to follow the new one, who treats her with increasingly apparent cruelty as he becomes more and more certain of his power over her. The affinity between the old regime and the new one is immediately clear in the episode of the dragon's cavern, in which Jason persuades Medea against her better judgment and strong objections to brave the terrifying darkness and retrieve the golden fleece. The sexual symbolism of the scene has been emphasized by T. C. Dunham. Also essential is the fact that from the moment she meets Jason, Medea is once again in the position of complying with the violent desire of a tyrant who holds her in thrall. Thus, the turbulent first encounter of these notorious lovers constitutes a brilliant observation of the essential link between child abuse and sexual abuse.

The similarity between Aeëtes and Jason is painfully apparent in the interaction between Medea's lover and her brother. When Absyrtus and his followers intercept Jason and Medea on their way back to the ship with the fleece, the Argonaut takes the boy hostage and, in a manner worthy of Aeëtes, makes a tiresome display of commanding obedience. The project of breaking Absyrtus' will backfires when the prisoner, hellbent on glory, leaps to his death, shouting bravely to his father: "Ich komme Vater!/ Frei bis zum Tod!" (I am coming, Father! Free unto death!, 1751-52). The boy's insistence on freedom is excruciatingly ironic because his death is a masterpiece of overdetermination, seeming to fulfill both the ominous curse uttered by the dying Phrixus, and also the casual death threat spoken by Aeëtes in the opening scene of *Die Argonauten*. Since, however, the current catastrophe is most immediately a direct result of reckless arrogance on Jason's part, his heated denial of responsibility is inevitably ironic. Quick to condemn Aeëtes as the murderer of his son (1762), Jason foolishly insists on the king's responsibility for sins of omission that are ultimately comparable to those by which he himself will later destroy his own sons. Thus, as *Die Argonauten* ends, Phrixus' curse has already claimed the life of one of Aeëtes' children and the other one stands beside Jason on the deck of the Argo, anxiously hoping for the best as the ship heads out to sea. In that she has defied the constraints of an insufferable domination, she acts as if in accord with the cry of liberty on her dying brother's lips, and yet the Romantic rebellion of all the young characters in *Die Argonauten* recalls nothing so surely as Spinoza's observation, fondly quoted by

Schopenhauer, that "if a stone projected through the air had consciousness, it would imagine it was flying of its own free will" (*World as Will* 126).

If the end of *Die Argonauten* leaves Medea charting a course toward ruin, the opening scene of *Medea* finds her busily engaged in damage control. Standing on the beach at Corinth in the early morning, she directs the labors of a slave who dutifully digs the pit where the fabulous tokens of her former life, including the golden fleece, are to be buried. Medea's description of this undertaking leaves little doubt as to its meaning: "Die Zeit der Nacht, der Zauber ist vorbei/ Und was geschieht, ob Schlimmes oder Gutes,/ Es muss geschehn am offnen Strahl des Lichts" (The time of darkness and magic is past, and whatever happens, whether bad or good, must happen in the open light of day, 4-6). In burying the fleece, along with other emblems of her pagan strength, Medea espouses the values of the Enlightenment, renouncing the culture of her own people as belonging to a dark age of sentimentality, superstition, and sorcery. Despite her positive conviction, the nature of her activity provides an ambiguous spectacle, partly because the burial of tokens was often associated with witchcraft (Robbins 77), and also because the act of burial described as an affirmation of reason depends on a literal "repression" of past experience, and thus it constitutes a denial of continuity between past, present, and future. The irony inherent in the assumption that the reign of rationality may be founded on an initial act of denial is abundantly evident in the exchange between Medea and her servant, Gora, which begins when the latter enters and sees her mistress at work.

Surprised to see Medea burying the tokens of her former glory, Gora questions the wisdom of discarding objects that have protected their owner well. Medea dismisses this suggestion: "Der Schutz mir gab?/ Weil mehr nicht Schutz er gibt, als er mir gab,/ Vergrab ich sie. Ich bin geschützt genug" (That gave me protection? Since it no longer gives such protection as it once gave me, I am burying it. I am protected enough, 24-26).Seizing on the word *Schutz* (protection), she repeats the noun form twice, echoing it again in the past participle *geschützt*, from the verb *schützen*. Her insistence on the idea of "protection" lends a certain anxious quality to Medea's confident projections, also recalling the "törichter Schütze" (foolish marksman) who figures prominently in a parable told by Medea to her father in *Die Argonauten*. An omen of doom, the "törichter Schütze" shoots an arrow into the void only to discover that he has shot his own son (*Argonauten* 106-12). Unwittingly identifying her present "protector" with the foolish marksman/protector in her past, the speaker's insistence on the term *schützen* undermines the optimistic assumptions on. which her speech is based and also calls attention to the fundamental insecurity which inspires it. Gora, in turn, casts a shadow over Medea's urgent activity by reminding her of the inauspicious indications she pretends to ignore. Lamenting the fate that condemns a princess to such drudgery, she implies that Medea's marriage is a kind of servitude, and dismisses her "protector" as a traitor. In an ironic concession to Medea's insistence on a rosy reading of the future, Gora fairly hoots: "Vielleicht geschieht es!" (It may be so!, 56). Her sarcasm suggests that Medea's optimism depends on the unlikely eventuality that things will happen in the future as they have not happened in the past.

The exchange between mistress and maid reveals the full extent of Medea's disorientation. Unable to obtain sympathy even from her own servant, she endures Gora's scolding as if the woman were a surrogate for the punitive parent who is absent. When Gora concludes her exposition of Medea's many faults with the observation that the tokens of a deed may be buried, but not the deed itself (109-10), the terms of her warning recall the dilemma of Werner's infanticidal unmarried mothers, for whom the source of shame was an erotic deed, the token of which was a child. In emphasizing the futility of "concealment," Gora establishes a parallel between Medea's burial of the past and the unmarried girl's concealment of pregnancy. Since denial of pregnancy was regularly the prelude to killing a newborn child, the analogy has the effect of implying that the project of burial is an ominous development for Medea's children. The adamant tone of Gora's speech, consistent with a social order that often exacted a draconian toll on young women and their progeny, provokes Medea to insist ever more emphatically on the value of the present moment: "Der Augenblick,/ Wenn er die Wiege einer Zukunft ist,/ Warum nicht auch das Grab einer Vergangenheit?" (If the present moment may be the cradle of the future, why not also the grave of the past? 114-16). Considering that children are the essential link between past pleasures and present sorrows, any radical disjunction between past and present is, in itself, inauspicious with regard to their survival, and the exaltation of the fleeting present to the level of absolute value is inherently problematic.

Banal as rhetorical expansions on the joys of the present moment may be in the mouths of gallant adventurers, they are inconsistent with the parental role. Jason himself, in wooing Medea, expressed a longing to be transported to a star "Wo ohne Ursach, was geschieht, und ohne Folge" (Where whatever happens is without cause or consequence, *Argonauten* 1183). Whereas the seductive quality of such effusions depends precisely on the denial of consequences, the survival of those beings engendered in moments of passion depends on the willingness of some adult to mortgage the forseeable future. In the case of a father inclined to proceed from one delight to another, the requirement of a committed hand to rock the cradle nevertheless remains in force, the children of such a father often depending on the willingness of some "heroine" to become a part of the hero's past. To the degree that the "heroine" is expected to be the "fall guy" in the

Romantic scenario, Medea's exaltation of the present moment is as unlucky for her children as the affirmation of militarism by the ancient Medea is for hers (Euripides, *Medea* 250-51), because unrelieved hedonism is, like unrelenting militarism, incompatible with a nurturing role. In affirming the irresponsibility of the seducer, Medea reveals the extent of Jason's dominion over her, declaring her bondage to him by extolling his philosophy of life.

Here, as in *Die Argonauten,* the irrationality of Medea's plan does not prevent her from articulating the dimensions of her predicament with great acuity. Far from disputing Gora's claim that she was mistaken in the past and is miserable now, Medea simply concedes the point (117), proceeding to describe the plan to bury the past as a manipulative ploy for binding Jason to herself:

Die Macht, die meine Mutter mir vererbte,
Die Wissenschaft geheimnisvoller Kräfte,
Der Nacht, die sie gebar, gab ich sie wieder
Und schwach, ein schutzlos, hilfbedürftig Weib
Werf ich mich in des Gatten offne Arme

(The power that my mother bequeathed to me, the wisdom full of secret strength, I return to the night which gave it life, and weak, an unprotected wife in need of help, I throw myself into my husband's open arms.) (130-34)

In rejecting a maternal inheritance identified with the past, the night, and the exercise of magic powers, Medea cultivates a childlike, dependent sense of herself as weak and needing help. Her description of herself as *schutzlos* is revelatory.

Although the practical difficulties of Medea's situation are considerable, her insistence on the necessity of "protection" suggests that the project of casting Jason in the role of "protector" is a passive-aggressive strategy for securing his affection, and her cultivation of personal weakness suggests the operation of something resembling the "desperation anxieties" that Slater describes as typical of people who have endured maternal deprivation (115). If Jason hated Medea in the past, it was because she was a Colchian sorceress. When she becomes a model wife, he will love her: "Er hat die Kolcherin gescheut, die Gattin/ Wird er empfangen, wies dem Gatten ziemt" (He hated the Colchian but will receive the wife as it befits a husband, 135-36). Her use of the word *empfangen,* which may mean *conceive* as well as *receive,* contributes to the impression that she seeks in Jason a womblike, parental function of protection and provision to which she ascribes the power of fostering a new identity for herself. The limitations of this naive plan are underscored by Gora's generally skeptical and unsympathetic reception. In fact, the confrontation between Medea and Gora that introduces this tragedy constitutes a dialogue between the self as potential child-murderer, and a curmudgeonly interlocutor who performs the castigating function of an abusive superego. If Gora is the mildly sadistic conveyor of painful advice that Medea does not want to hear, Jason is the Other in terms of whom she defines herself, and for whose sake she eagerly relinquishes a large measure of personal integrity.

Although his exotic adventures, his disappointment in love, his fate as exile, and his self-indulgent eloquence lend Jason the aspect of a Romantic hero, there is an admixture of bourgeois propriety in his character that makes him seem rather like a parc ly of fashionable ideals. Interrupting the exchange between Medea and Gora, he immediately becomes the central focus of attention, and Medea's problems are conspicuously eclipsed by his. Talking to a servant about an anticipated audience with the king, Jason hardly notices Medea, who only succeeds in getting his attention by expressing sympathy for him (157-58). Her plan to gain the equivalent of parental protection from her man is thus ironically juxtaposed with the image of the nurturing support she seems obliged to provide for him. When, in the tone of a sympathetic mother, she notes that he has spent a restless night, pacing to and fro in the dark, he declares that he loves the dark and hates the light, neatly counterpointing Medea's recently stated enthusiasm for the daylight. Having effectively distinguished himself from the hordes of laboring philistines who are obliged to rest at night and toil by day, Jason proceeds to take his wife to task for the nonconformist fashion of her dress.

Frankly irritated by the visible signs of her exotic past, he begs her to set aside her Colchian costume and wear the garments of a Greek woman. In that this change is suggested as a denial of the past, it accords well enough with Medea's own plans: "Sei eine Griechin du in Griechenland./ Wozu Erinnrung suchen des Vergangnen?" (Be a Greek woman now that you are in Greece. Why seek remembrance of things past? 190-91). Compliantly removing her veil, Medea gives it to Gora, who grumbles unhappily, to the evident displeasure of the master. A sordid row between Gora and Jason is only prevented by the hasty departure of the women, in whose absence Jason throws himself on the grass and beats his breast, exclaiming melodramatically: "Zerspreng dein Haus und mach dir brechend Luft" (Leap out of your house [my heart] and, breaking, get some air, 203). Having scolded his wife in the manner of a proprietary husband, he proceeds to display the ailment described by Chateaubriand as "le vague des passions," the peculiar affliction of those who suffer from "a full heart, in an empty world" (62).

Though Jason's state of emotional excitement hardly distinguishes him from the woman he evidently despises, his view of the past differs notably from hers. While Medea wants to forget everything that happened before she met him, he seems most anxious to forget everything that happened after he met her. Yet the admonitory question, "Wozu Erinnrung suchen des Vergangnen?"

does not prevent the fellow who utters it from wallowing in memories of his own youthful days in Corinth. Lying on the grassy bank where he collapses the moment he is alone, Jason salutes the towers of the city that was the cradle of his golden youth (206). His use of the word *Wiege* (*cradle*), recalling Medea's vision of the present moment as the cradle of a happy future (116), celebrates the memory of a happy past unencumbered by responsibilities. When, toward the end of the act, Creon shows up, demanding an account of Jason's foreign wanderings, the "hero" offers up a tale of woe amounting to a prolonged lament for his lost youth. Exhibiting that sense of having been "cheated by history" which, for Lloyd Bishop, is the essence of the ailment known as *le mal du siècle* (Bishop 24), Jason is unmistakably a child of the Romantic Age, although his readiness to distinguish between his own past and that of his erstwhile partner in crime makes him seem rather less than heroic.

Far from being an utter villain, Jason displays a certain awareness of Medea's predicament (219-20), loyally begging the king's indulgence for her as well as for himself (552), yet he paves the way for Creon's eventual decree of banishment with the casual admission that his wife is an encumbrance the unburdening of which would grant him a new lease on life (553). Dutifully insisting on his family obligations—"Doch muss ich schützen was sich mir vertraut" (So must I protect that which entrusts itself to me, 554)—he presents himself as the passive object of responsibilities that have sought him out. His impatience with the role of protector is painfully obvious and his devotion to his wife and children is conspicuously unenthusiastic. In fact, Jason wastes little time in articulating the technical proviso whereby Medea may be destroyed with impunity. Responding to the king's anxiety about allowing Medea to remain in Corinth, Jason generously concedes the royal right to annihilate his entire family if his wife should cause any trouble: "Wenn sie nicht ruhig ist, so treib sie aus,/ Verjag sie, töte sie und mich—uns alle" (If she is not peaceful, drive her out, hunt her, kill her, and me too—all of us, 558-59). He also suggests that a sojourn in Greece should have the salutory effect of humanizing his barbarian wife: "Doch bis dahin gönn ihr noch den Versuch,/ Ob sies vermag, zu weilen unter Menschen" (But until then grant her the opportunity to see to dwell among human beings, 558-61). The implied distinction between human beings and Medea's kind is a breach in the facade of decency through which vile thoughts peep out.

The essentially racist suggestion that Medea is a member of a subhuman group encourages Creon in his barely concealed desire to send Medea packing. The king's hostility is evident in his admission that Medea's knowledge of magic arts frightens him and his warning that "the power to harm often engenders the desire to do so" (556) seems particularly ironic, issuing as it does from the most powerful person in sight. Though Jason's distinction between Medea and

Menschen is especially ominous in such company, it is consistent with his habitual pronouncements regarding his nearest and dearest. In admonishing Medea to renounce her native constume, he calls her kinsmen "monsters": "In Kolchis sind wir nicht, in Griechenland,/ Nicht unter Ungeheuern, unter Menschen!" (We are not in Colchis, but in Greece, not among monsters but among men, 182-83). When his sons, upon first appearing in Act One, fail to show proper respect for their father, he moans ruefully that he has bound himself to a band of savages: "Von trotzgen Wilden Vater und Gemahl!" ([I am] the husband and father of savages! 214). In an inspired variation on the traditional scenario in which Medea reproaches Jason for the hardships she has endured on his account, Grillparzer's Jason reminds Medea of the trouble to which his association with her exposes him:

Hast du vergessen, wies daheim erging,
In meiner Väter Land, bei meinem Ohm,
Als ich zuerst von Kolchis dich gebracht?
Vergessen jenen Hohn, mit dem der Grieche
Herab auf die Barbarin sieht, auf—dich?"

(Have you forgotten how it went at home, in my fatherland, at my uncle's, when I first brought you back from Colchis? Have you forgotten the scorn with which the Greek looks down on the barbarians, that is, on you?) (251-55).

Oblivious to the fact that he is not the only person on the scene who can never go home again, Jason seems to blame Medea, not only for the loss of his "fatherland," but also for the bigotry of his countrymen. His reproach is a remarkable demonstration of the general psychology of scapegoating.

Finding himself ambiguously balanced between the positions of citizen and refugee, Jason is in the process of consolidating his identity as an insider by projecting the role of outsider onto Medea. Having been given asylum at Creon's court in his youth, he is encouraged to assume the role of prodigal son when reunited with his former benefactor. That the welcome does not extend to his foreign wife is quite evident when Creusa questions him about his marriage to the barbarian: "In Kolchis liessen sie dich Greuel üben,/ Zuletzt verbanden sie als Gattin dir/ Ein grässlich Weib, giftmischend, vatermördrisch" (They said in Colchis you had done dreadful things and finally joined yourself in marriage with a monstrous, poison-mixing, father-murdering wife, 329-31). In a case of literal prejudgment, Creusa has made up her mind about Medea without ever meeting her. The words *Greuel* and *grässlich,* applied to the realm of the foreign, participate in the logic of Jason's distinction between monsters and men, and the adjective *giftmischend* accords equally well with ancient legends about the Colchian sorceress and traditional libels against witches and Jews (Robbins 398; Gilman 74). The epithet *vatermördrisch,* meaning *father-murdering* and, by implication, *patricidal, regicidal,* probably refers to the antirevolutionary political context, in which subversive suggestions were likely to be dismissed as emanations of a "Jewish-French conspiracy" (Gilman 64). Even as he conflates the concept of the barbarian with various contemporary stereotypes, Grillparzer insists on the irrationality of the "Greek" antipathy toward the outsider.

Gora describes the horror the Colchians inspire in the Greeks as a phenomenon that precedes and transcends all rational causes— "Ein Greuel ist die Kolcherin dem Volke" (To these people, the Colchian is a dreadful thing, 72), and the dramatic proof of her claim is apparent in the shrinking dread with which Creusa recoils from Medea's extended hand when the two are introduced. This rebuff prompts Medea to exclaim: "O weich nicht aus! Die hand verpestet nicht!" (Oh do not withdraw! This hand is not infected! 376). Falling indiscriminately on Jason's notorious wife and on her old servant, the Greek disdain for the barbarian offends Gora as well as her mistress (65), so that the trust between Medea and her servant, essentially that of loyalty between women in the Euripidean text, becomes one of misery shared by members of an alien minority in Grillparzer's play. Whereas Euripides' protagonist tells the Nurse, "if you are a woman and well disposed to your mistress, say nothing of my plan" (822-23), Grillparzer's Medea appeals to Gora with a statement of ethnic solidarity: "Du bist ein Kolcher und ich kenne dich" (You are a Colchian and I know you, 41) .

The psychological consistency of Grillparzer's Medea is most notable in her own acceptance of the negative Greek estimation of her people. Although Creon and Creusa revile her to her face, and the princess volunteers to take care of Jason's children as if their own mother were not present (349), Medea passively accepts the inevitability of their contempt, ruefully admitting that she herself would once have shuddered at the thought of a wretch like her present self: "Es war'ne Zeit, da hätt ich selbst geschaudert,/ Hätt ich ein Wesen mir gedacht, gleich mir!" (There was a time when I myself would have shuddered if I had imagined a being such as I, 397-98). Thus Grillparzer's barbarian sorceress not only has the aspect of the unassimilated Eastern Jew, she also resembles the self-hating Jews described by Gilman as accepting "the mirage of themselves generated by their reference group—that group in society which they see as defining them" (2). To a remarkable degree, Grillparzer's depiction of Medea's misadventure in Corinth conforms to this model. Just like the objects of anti-Semitic discourse who comply with negative assessments of themselves, earnestly embracing programs of "self-improvement" in the belief that mollification of the contemptuous majority will eventually lead to assimilation, Medea gladly gives up her native dress and customs in the hope of acquiring her husband's approval. Acting as if she could hear a voice within calling, "Become like us—abandon your difference and you may be one of us," she persists in a project of self-abnegation throughout Act Two, becoming ever more miserably degraded as she encounters what Gilman calls the "hidden qualifier of the internalized reference group, the conservative curse," that says, in effect, that "the more you are like me, the more I know the true value of my power, which you wish to share, and the more I am aware that you are but a shoddy counterfeit, an outsider" (2). With the failure of the liberal program Medea embraces in the first two acts of the play, there is an eruption, in Act Three, of violent antagonism between parties loyal to her and those allied with Jason. These hostilities provoke painful internal conflict in the protagonist, setting the stage for a spectacular eruption of the passions that were banished in the initial scene of the play.

In the period extending from the end of Act One throughout most of Act Two, Medea dedicates herself to the project of "self-improvement," a task in which Creusa serves as mentor. In that it is a teacher-student arrangement, the relationship between the two young women takes its place in the series of "pedagogical" fiascos that punctuate the steady progress toward catastrophe throughout the trilogy. Upon accepting Creusa's authority, Medea promises obedience and pleads for patience: "Ich will ja gerne tun, was ihr mir sagt,/ Nur sagt mir, was ich tun soll, statt zu zürnen" (I will gladly do what you tell me, only tell me what I should do, instead of getting angry, 406-07). Like the defensive gesture of a child accustomed to capricious violence, this pathetic request hints at the history of abuse that inclines the refugee to admire and idolize her royal host: "Du bist, ich sehs, von sittig mildem Wesen,/ So sicher deiner selbst und eins mit dir" (You are, I see, of a mild, modest nature, so self-confident and at one with yourself, 408-09). Since Creusa's initial treatment of Medea casts some doubt on the assumption of her mildness and modesty, Medea's perception of the princess as one who is "self-confident and at one with herself" may seem to be a function of the speaker's own sense of alienation. Assuring Creusa, in the manner of an earnest child, that she will be studious and good (411), Medea displays a dedication to the project of self-improvement that recalls the imploring stance of Jason when he courted her (*Argonauten* 1208-15). Both the passionate lover and the erstwhile object of his ardor share the quality of one who stares hungrily into the eyes of another as if hypnotized by an imagined promise of emotional sustenance.

In that Medea's situation as she stares into Creusa's eyes is equivalent to that of Phrixus gazing hopefully at Medea in *Der Gastfreund* (243-53), she has good reason to be apprehensive. The decision to entrust her fate to the princess seems particularly dubious, not only because it is an exact repetition of Phrixus' fatal error, but because of the evident hostility of the Corinthian royal family toward herself. Thus as Medea enrolls in Creusa's "school" she resembles the sufferer of traumatic disorders who "escapes from her situation not by action in the real world but rather by altering her state of consciousness." With respect to the process of "constriction or numbing" in which a person who is completely powerless "may go into a state of surrender," or "a state of detached calm, in which terror, rage and pain dissolve," Judith Herman notes the similarity between certain "detached states of consciousness" and "hypnotic trance states." Her observation that "traumatic events may serve as powerful activators of the capacity for trance" (42-43), seems particularly relevant to the world of Medea, in which Jason, haunted by unspecified horrors (765-71), is also mesmerized by a dream of love (835), while Medea reverts to trance-like states at the end of Act One (408-09), in the middle of Act Two (925-26), and in the climactic scene of Act Four (2073-99). If her inclination to abandon herself to the ministrations of a potential rival such as Creusa seems unwise, it is nonetheless credible, occurring as it does in a universe where every individual displays a heightened sensibility to interpersonal irritations and suggestions. This aspect of Grillparzer's characterization is peculiarly evident in the music lesson Creusa gives Medea in Act Two.

Although Grillparzer initially intended to contrast the nobility of his Greeks with the barbarism of his Colchians, planning to endow Creusa, in particular, with "a purity that is almost divine" and "the naivete that derives from purity" (Roe 86), the effect of the completed drama is rather more complicated than the schematic opposition sketched in his notes would lead us to expect. In fact, there is little in his presentation of Creusa to contradict Medea's eventual conclusion that her rival is a self-righteous, self-serving hypocrite. Though Creusa makes a conspicuous show of "educating" the barbarian, her understanding of the culture she purports to disseminate is singularly shallow, and her capacity to provide support and sympathy for her understudy is compromised by her evident attraction toward Jason. Most significantly, Creusa is as adept as Aeëtes in the use of punitive techniques for manipulating and controlling her student. That the association between the two women is doomed to deteriorate into an exercise in "poisonous pedagogy" is evident in that our first glimpse of Medea under Creusa's tutelage reveals a frustrated student berating her own fingers for their clumsiness: "Dass ich die strafen könnte, diese Finger, strafen!" (If only I could punish these fingers, punish them!, 589).

Dressed in Greek apparel, Medea is the very image of the outsider responding to the "liberal promise of assimilation." She laments the fact that her training in the martial arts has ill prepared her for the refinements of musical expression: "Nur an den Wurfspiess ist die Hand gewöhnt/ Und an des Weidwerks ernstlich rauh Geschäft" (This hand is only accustomed to the spear and the rough, arduous business of the hunt, 585-86). Juxtaposing the image of her vigorous former self with her wretchedly subdued present state, this complaint suggests an ironic contrast between the "barbarian" princess and the "civilized" apprentice musician. The use of the word *gewöhnt*, from *gewöhnen*, meaning *to accustom, to habituate, to familiarize*, stresses the importance of education in producing the observable distinction between the categories of "barbaric" and "civilized," Medea's deficiency in music being relative to her former proficiency in other arts. The fact that Creusa, the refined Corinthian, is an accomplished musician, while Medea, the awkward immigrant, is a devotee of the "business of the hunt," adds a certain cultural specificity to the scene. Even if Schopenhauer had not declared that "music is the highest grade of the will's objectivation" (*World as Will* 259), the extraordinary brilliance of musical culture in Grillparzer's Vienna would suggest the special significance of the theme of music. By endowing the Greek princess with lyrical competence, the author claims for her a quality of aesthetic sensibility that is a particular source of pride for German-speaking people. Conversely, his Medea, who describes herself as being more accustomed to the "business of the hunt" than to the ardors of the lyre, condemns herself to the rank of philistine as much by the admission of musical illiteracy as by the evocation of her savage past. In fact, Medea's use of the word *Geschäft*, which is the normal German word for *business*, evokes a world of commerce and monetary exchange which is as inconsistent with Medea's royal past as with her studious present. The word is, however, inseparable from the traditional stereotype of the Jew. Thus, the phrase "Weidwerks ernstlich rauh Geschäft" alludes to a hierarchy of cultural concerns in which the "savage," like the Jew, occupies a lower rank, and the artist, the musician, or the poet is exalted. Regardless of the degree to which the word *Geschäft* contributes to the sense of an affinity between the Colchian and the Jew, the music lesson underscores a peculiarly Austro-Germanic conception of the dichotomy between the "civilized" and the "barbaric."

Since Medea's "otherness" does not become a problem until she finds herself on alien territory, her eventual excesses seem to derive less from individual peculiarities than from intercultural frustrations. The very omission of the ethnic label at which the author strongly hints may constitute a disavowal of the libel that might inhere in the identification of the infanticidal mother as a Jew. Finally, the sympathetic treatment and autobiographical importance of his characters suggest that Grillparzer's examination of the dynamics of stereotyping is rather an examination of cultural factors that involve and disturb the author than a facile participation in popular projections. Although a play about an "oriental" heroine who resorts to crime when she is tormented by a community of smug bigots may seem to be as burdened by anti-Semitic assumptions as a play about a money-lender who demands a pound of flesh from an insolvent debtor, Grillparzer's drama, like Shakespeare's, tends ultimately to transcend the defamatory structures implicit in his text, and his appreciation of the continuity between accepted abuses and ostracized excesses is remarkable.

The spectacle of Medea reviling her fingers is emblematic of the psychodynamic pattern of the entire drama. Presenting the character as she carries out her father's punitive curse and her husband's domineering purpose, it reveals her need to project her pain onto a "member" of her own body, which she regards as both attached to and separate from herself. An important link between the habit of abuse inculcated in the past and the eruption of violence hovering in the future, the act of self-chastisement is also consistent with basic assumptions implicit in the present enterprise. In teaching Medea a song that Jason liked to sing when he was a boy, Creusa invites her student to celebrate an ideal that has already caused her considerable grief. In fact, the lyrics of the song constitute a prayer that the gods may anoint the head of the hero and arch his chest so that he may triumph over men and also over pretty girls (607-10). When Medea comments that the favors requested in the song have already been granted to Jason, Creusa is momentarily stumped, conceding that she never stopped to think about the song, having sung it simply because she had heard it sung. Thus the noble rescuer of the benighted savage reveals herself to be the intellectually passive purveyor of a culture she does not really understand. Not only uncritical of the foolish text she has chosen to teach, Creusa is notably intolerant of her student's critical observations.

When Medea is encouraged to explicate her controversial comment, she offers an irreverent acount of Jason's adventures in Colchis, describing the "hero" as one who stalked his human prey with merciless tenacity, luring his victim into a cruelly destructive trap (625-26). This suggestion that life with the hero is not such as to valorize the semi-mystical assumptions inherent in Jason's favorite song does not please Creusa, who scolds her charge for speaking badly of her husband. Pushed into a defensive position, Medea claims that Creusa does not know Jason very well. She complains that he is egotistical, opportunistic and irresponsible (630-33), chafing particularly at his penchant for making a virtue of his faults: "Er tut nur recht, doch recht ist, was er will" (He only does right because whatever he wants is right, 637). Resonating with the resentment of one whose will has been systematically frustrated, Medea's speech depicts Jason as combining the worst faults of the pseudo-Napoleonic adventurer and the Nazis of a later age who would insist that "might makes right." Her irreverent portrait of the local hero tests the limits of Creusa's patience, not only because the princess has a soft spot in her heart for Jason but because the condemnation of force implicit in Medea's diatribe strikes at Creon as well as Jason, hitting at the heart of a patriarchal order which has, on the whole, treated Creusa rather well. When Medea concludes her indictment with the rude admission that she sometimes wishes Jason were dead (639-40), her candor earns her the equivalent of a swift rap on the knuckles from her "gentle teacher."

As if Medea's expression of hatred provided retroactive justification for Creusa's initial revulsion toward the foreigner, the princess abandons her facade of benevolence, channeling her evident anger into a vehement expression of offended morality. Confronted with Creusa's indignant declaration that she would never, even on pain of death, presume to hate the man who was the father of her children, Medea objects that such debasement is more easily promised than accomplished. This defense provides Creusa with a golden opportunity to thumb her nose in the name of Christian forbearance: "Es wär wohl minder süss, übt' es sich leichter" (It would be less sweet if it were more easily put into practice, 649). Condemning Medea for being hard-hearted (654-55), and demonstrating her own charitable nature by wishing Medea good luck in her future plans for self-improvement, Creusa turns her back and begins to walk away. Rather than consider herself well rid of such an insufferably patronizing taskmaster, Medea responds with fear: "Du zürnst?" (You are angry?, 656), thus recalling the weary "statt zu zürnen" with which she first requested Creusa's help. Although the fact that the threat of abandonment elicits this particular response in the "student" may come as no surprise to observers of Medea's dealings with her father in *Der Gastfreund* and Jason in *Die Argonauten,* the readiness with which Creusa resorts to punitive manipulation casts the ostensibly gentle princess in an ambiguous light.

Frightened by the prospect of being deserted and eager to placate her angry mistress, Medea renews her promise to be dutiful and meek, resigning herself to the restricted role of handmaid: "Wie eine Magd will ich dir dienend folgen,/ Will weben an dem Webstuhl, früh zur Hand" (I want to follow you as a serving maid, weave at the loom with a ready hand, 691-92). Anticipating a life of household drudgery, she envisions herself toiling at the loom, a spiritual sister of Goethe's Gretchen spinning at the wheel. Her meditation on this dreary prospect is interrupted by the arrival of Jason, whose appearance at just this moment dramatizes the difficulty of Medea's position. Hardly bothering to greet his wife, he responds with obvious boredom when Creusa declares that she has befriended the newcomer, and bristles with sarcasm when Medea tells him she is learning to play the lyre and sing. Speaking in the tone of a stingy parent who has been asked to pay for the instruction of a child he regards as a lost cause, he mutters, "Viel Glück zu dem Versuch!" (Lots of luck with that project! 706). Notably indifferent to the education of a woman on whose progress he has staked the survival of his entire family, Jason is evidently bored stiff with his protegée, and only grants her his attention long enough to ask when she last checked up on the children. Despite protestations by both women to the effect that the children are playing safely nearby, he dispatches his wife on an errand so as to indulge his barely concealed desire to be alone with Creusa.

Grillparzer's depiction of the interaction between Jason and Medea in this scene is a good example of the feminist sensibility which Yates discerns in Grillparzer's work (*Viennese Popular Theater* 93-107). Once alone with Creusa, the hero may expand as eloquently as he pleases on the cruelty of his destiny, ornamenting his delivery with the most romantic flourishes imaginable, but the audience will not soon forget the spectacle of the aging adolescent treating his wife like an unpaid babysitter as he turns to unload the fullness of his heart into another woman's lap. A stark dramatization of the way in which traditional marital arrangements may turn a woman's children into instruments for controlling her, the playwright's technique in this scene is an inspired contribution to the project of demythologizing the glamorous hero. Though Jason seems to dominate the triangular relationship between himself and the two women, Creusa's discreet acquiescence in the unstated plan to evict the female outsider is crucial to the dramatic development. Tiresomely loquacious as Jason is about his unhappiness in marriage and his hostility toward his wife, Creusa's response to his long-winded complaint is markedly different from her reaction to Medea's grievance. Offended and indignant when the wife criticized her husband, she listens attentively with many a consoling sigh to Jason's prolonged lament, cheerfully embracing the considerable challenge of comforting the weary hero.

Because the complaint that Creusa finds so poignant is already well known to the audience, the exchange between the princess and her admirer is replete with dramatic irony. Here, as in Act One, his wife's departure is the signal for Jason to breathe a heavy sigh of relief, demonstrating the physical constriction he experiences in her presence (716). As in Act One, the speaker revels in remembrance of past glories and lamentations on present hardships. Elaborating on the theme of burial that Medea introduced in the opening scene of the play, he describes the present as a seed that must be buried so that the future may be born, clearly regretting the passage of a time when he could enjoy the present moment in the manner of one who basks in the shade of fruit trees, enjoying the abundance of nature (780-83). Jason's evident desire to "dig up" the past contrasts inauspiciously with Medea's determination to "bury" it, and every aspect of his litany has been introduced in Act One, including the metaphor of burial, the concept of antagonism between the past and the present, and the glorification of the past at the expense of the present. Repeating for Creusa's benefit the list of disappointments he confided to Creon at the end of Act One (493-97), the hero embellishes his account with colorful details that have the effect of nearly doubling the length of the tale (795-816). In fact, Jason resembles an actor on a cosmopolitan stage expanding on a routine that has found favor in the provinces. This impression is only strengthened when he extols the rarefied quality of the youthful experiences and shared memories that bind him to Creusa in a presumably unique intimacy: "Wie wir ein Herz und eine Seele waren" (How we were one heart and one soul, 835). Although the invocation of the Platonic concept of twin souls that served our hero well in his ardent courtship of Medea (*Argonauten* 1208-15) is an exquisite bit of irony, it is also entirely consistent with the peculiar psychology of the character.

For all his dreary repetitions and dubious intensities, Jason seems utterly sincere. A problematic and persuasive liar who believes his own fabrications, he is more compulsive than deliberate in his approach to desired objects. If this is not the first time the audience has heard him complaining of his misfortunes and declaring his undying devotion to an appealing soul mate, nor for that matter, the first time he stands, full of hope, before a beautiful woman in whom he perceives the magical promise of consolation and fulfillment, the language of love that he is ever ready to produce does not fail, in the case of Creusa, any more than it did with Medea, to provoke the desired effect. Demonstrating with her intermittent answers that she is quite prepared to play the role of indulgent maternal angel in Jason's life, Creusa waits until he stops to catch his breath, then interjects: "Was sorgst du denn? es ist für dich gesorgt" (Why are you so full of care? all that is taken care of for you, 787). Her eagerness to welcome the world-weary adventurer as if he were a homeless child is crucial for our understanding of the hero.

As tedious as Jason's stylized longing for love might seem to anyone who did not covet his attention, it would be banal enough in a neglected child. Even his gasping for breath whenever Medea leaves is consistent with the observed symptoms of emotionally deprived children (Blakeslee). The passivity noted by Bishop and Pasco as typical of the Romantic "malady" is especially evident in Jason's confession that he cannot understand how a nice guy like himself could have gotten into such a sticky situation:

Ich habe nichts getan was schlimm an sich,
Doch viel gevollt, gemöcht, gewünscht, getrachtet;
Still zugesehen, wenn es andre taten.
Hier Übles nicht gewollt, doch zugegriffen
Und nicht bedacht, dass Übel sich erzeuge.
Und jetzt steh ich vom Unheilsmeer umbrandet
Und kann nicht sagen: ich habs nicht getan!

(I have done nothing that was bad in itself, but have wanted, wished, desired, endeavored; quietly looked on as another did so. I have desired no evil, yet here seized hold without thinking that evil thus might be engendered, and now I stand, a sea of trouble surging round me, and cannot say I did not do it.) (765-71)

The insistent repetition of the word *nicht,* suggesting that negativity is as essential to Grillparzer's Jason as to his Euripidean prototype, also constitutes an essential link between tragic character and the "tense, negative, passive, withdrawn" children of Pasco's argument.

Like a defensive child, Jason begins by denying that he has done anything wrong. Freely confessing the desire that led to the events that caused his present trouble, he disconnects desire from responsibility by describing himself as one who only watched while another did wrong. The intensity of his emotion, unexplained by any visible cause, suggests that he is haunted by intrusive memories of events he does not care to mention. Although subsequent developments imply that Jason is probably troubled by recollections of the death of Peleas, viewers of the entire trilogy may consider that unexplained emotional intensity is a constant in Jason's character, which precedes his arrival in Corinth and is also reflected in the aspect of other characters, especially Phrixus and Medea. In the present case, Jason's use of the verb *erzeuge* (*to engender*) with the object *Übel* (evil) is ominously consistent with his and Medea's tendency to deplore the events that resulted in the births of the children. Even more suggestive is the use of the word *zugegriffen,* from *zugreifen* (*to take hold*). Evoking the grabbing action of a hungry child at the breast, the word is more than a little suggestive of Jason's habitual approach to women. In admitting that he cannot say he did not do the deed that haunts him, Jason denies his own denial in a seeming concession to the conspicuous appearance of wrong-doing that surrounds him, yet the constant punctuation of his speech with negations gives ample indication of his longing to deny personal responsibility for his present predicament. Thus Jason basically describes his life as something that has happened to him rather than something he has muddled up.

The premise that Jason's life is beyond his control implies the corollary thesis that he is the plaything of some higher power, and his dealings with Medea suggest that he has managed to promote her to the rank of "higher power." The awe in which he holds her is only partly obscured by the habit of disparaging her which he displays conspicuously in Act Two when Medea returns from the bogus errand on which he has sent her. Like a child engrossed in play, he persists in his egotistical ruminations, without acknowledging Medea's presence. In a pathetic attempt to attract his attention, his wife picks up the lyre and announces that she has learned to sing a song. Her imploring refrain—"Jason, ich weiss ein Lied!" (Jason, I know a song), is repeated three times (863, 874, 877) without effect, and it is finally only at Creusa's insistence that Jason interrupts his speech in order to answer his wife. Employing the contemptuous tone of a humorless adult with a troublesome child, he insists that he is in no mood for foolish things (896), snarling: "Was also willst du denn?" (So what do you want? 889). In view of the foolishness in which he has just been indulging himself, his attitude borders on the ludicrous. That Jason's intolerance for "silly games" is quite as variable as Creusa's disapproval of married grumblers becomes clear when, a minute after refusing to hear Medea, he turns to Creusa and asks her to sing for him (920). In the face of such stunning hostility, Medea tries to sing but fails, dropping the lyre, bursting into tears, and thereby giving Jason's claim that she is incapable of learning the quality of a self-fulfilling prophecy. When his blatant cruelty has the unintended effect of offending Creusa, he defends himself by assuring her that, appearances notwithstanding, Medea is the real aggressor in this scenario. Though he berates her as if she were a naughty child, Jason actually fears Medea as if she were a threatening parent.

For Jason, the memory of Medea as a formidable bulwark against impending danger has established her identity as a woman endowed with just those qualities of invulnerability and omnipotence that small children attribute to their mothers. Countering Creusa's expression of sympathy for Medea (908) with a patronizing rebuke, he proceeds to describe the notorious descent into the dragon's cave, recalling: "Wie sie sich mit dem Wurm zur Wette bäumte,/ Voll Gift der Zunge Doppelpfeile schoss,/ Und Hass und Tod aus Flammenaugen blinkte" (How she reared up equal to the serpent, shot out her double-darted tongue full of poison and glowered hatred and death from her blazing eyes, 914-16). Assuring Creusa that if she had seen Medea in the lair of the dragon, her heart would be steeled against the tears of the Colchian (917), Jason relies on a fanciful report of superhuman power in order to relegate his nemesis to the status of contemptible creature. Describing her with terms such as *bäumte,* which normally refers to the action of an animal rearing up on its hind legs, and *Zunge Doppelpfeile,* which evokes the forked tongue of a snake, he dehumanizes his human subject. The curiously sexual implication of the serpent "rearing up" to face the dreadful darkness of the cave underscores the admixture of erotic anxiety in Jason's loathing for his erstwhile lover. Just as the verbal portrait of Medea with "hatred and death" gleaming in her flaming eyes reflects Jason's own violent aggressions, so the image of Medea rising up and entering the mysterious cavern reflects the phallic preoccupations of a speaker for whom Medea's debasement is essential to the project of winning Creusa's favor. Presuming to instruct the princess on the demonic invulnerability of the pathetic human being in front of her eyes, Jason derives a myth of menacing power from a single demonstration of strength. Thus the hero may seem to anticipate the logic of twentieth-century fanatics who would invoke the myth of an international conspiracy of Jewish bankers in order to rationalize the murder of workers, peasants, paupers, housewives, and children. Quite as remarkable as Jason's imputation of monstrosity to Medea is the fact that the author does not offer the option of dismissing the speaker as a monster.

Since irrational intensity is apparent in everything he says, Jason seems ultimately quite as pathetic as his antagonist, with a character as dynamic and coherent as hers. Far from being a distinctive feature of his portrait, Jason's forlorn desperation establishes the essential bond between him and the women who succumb to his dubious charm. At this point, it is worth noting that Pasco's theory of maternal deprivation illuminates both the male and the female characters in Grillparzer's *Medea*. Since the thesis of the "unrocked cradle" emphasizes the psychology of the male protagonist, its utility as a tool for elucidating Jason's peculiar negativity, passivity and narcissism seems obvious, though the assumption that the character's disagreeable qualities derive from a history of grief still leaves us with the thorny question of why anybody but a hopeless masochist would sign up for a lifetime dedicated to the thankless task of consoling such a whiner. The critical problem, after all, is not why Jason has had a change of heart, loyalty never having ranked as his great strength anyway, but why are his female admirers falling all over each other in their eagerness to compete for the privilege of nurturing him. This seemingly inexplicable conundrum becomes more tractable if we consider that the women are acting out of a sense of longing and despair comparable to Jason's own. When, for example, our hero reproaches Creusa for wasting sympathy on Medea, he speaks in the tone of a patronizing adult to a child: "Kind, du verstehst uns beide nicht" (Child, you do not understand the two of us, 909). Calling his current soulmate a child, just as, at an analogous moment in *Die Argonauten,* he addressed Medea as if she were a child in need of instruction (1269), Jason reveals the domineering essence of his erotic project. Although his evident intention of transferring the status of special protegée from Medea to Creusa seems tiresome at best, Jason's admirers are undaunted in their rush to secure the doubtful advantage of his protection. Encouraged by women as starved for love as he is, Jason proceeds from conquest to conquest in a pattern suggesting that both the male victor and the female vanquished are acting in accordance with cultural prescriptions for dealing with chronic emotional hunger. Whereas the male who longs for love seeks an indulgent female upon whom to attach himself and exercise his power, the female practices a childlike compliance with male desire as a strategy for gaining attention and approval. The remarkable acuity with which Grillparzer observes this ritual is also evident in his presentation of the maternal role as a double bind that traps the individual between her finite nature and the infinite demands the child-hero makes upon her.

Though Jason is not a child, he is not too grown up to react with infantile resentment to the image of the imposing nurturer that he is constantly imposing on Medea. When, provoked beyond all endurance, Medea scuffles with her antagonists, accidentally breaks the lyre, and then, in shock, withdraws into a trance-like state, her misery only provokes Jason to further cruelty. While Medea stands staring off into space in the manner of the traumatized individuals described by Herman as escaping into "a state of detached calm in which terror, rage, and pain dissolve" (42), Jason regards her detachment as a sign of haughty arrogance: "Ha, was ist das? —Was stehst du siegend da?" (What is this? Why are you standing there in triumph? 926). The question suggests that Jason's blindness to Medea's present plight is a persistent function of the fact that she has snatched him so many times from the jaws of death. Though apparently alive and well at the Corinthian court, Jason has never left the dreaded cave. His imputation of disdainful pride to Medea is especially ironic because it comes at a moment when she is thoroughly bruised and humiliated. Her determination to study music symbolizes a dedication to the project of "learning to live among human beings," and the breaking of the lyre is an indication of her failure to achieve the full measure of "civilized" humanity. Since Jason has staked Medea's right to live on her ability to accomplish this task, and also, since her violent gesture may be interpreted as a repudiation of the program of self-improvement generally regarded as her only hope, the broken lyre legitimizes Jason's wish to be rid of her. Having proved herself to be an unreconstructed barbarian, she may henceforth be persecuted without restraint. In the concluding scene of Act Two, the procedures of pedagogical domination and psychological abuse begun in the music lesson and continued in the marital dispute culminate in the isolation of the alien within a solidly hostile camp where every member seems eager to comply with the communal project of expelling the foreign body.

The social implications of the quarrel between Jason and Medea are thrown into sharp relief by the arrival of the king and his entourage, the latter including a herald who accuses Jason and Medea of murdering Peleas and stealing the golden fleece. The notorious couple is exiled from Jason's native land. In response to this proclamation, Creon grants Jason absolution and refuge, banishes Medea from Corinth, and announces his intention to give Creusa in marriage to Jason. Thus, by the end of Act Two, Medea finds herself surrounded by openly declared enemies. Although her expulsion from the city by a band of privileged insiders is a traditional element of the plot, Grillparzer dramatizes the confrontation between individual and group that is implicit in his ancient sources. Depicting various characters who behave badly while deferring to the generally shared enthusiasm for ostracizing the foreigner, the playwright illustrates Freud's observation that "in a group, the individual is brought under conditions which allow him to throw off the repressions of his unconscious instinctual impulses." The fact that Creon is the one who throws the first stone is consistent with the Freudian assertion that "it is impossible to grasp the nature of a group if the leader is disregarded" (*S.E.* 18:74, 119). Calling Medea "something the wilderness vomited up" (1030), and reviling her as a kind of "infection" (1036), the king leads the way for Jason, who calls her a curse (*Fluch*, 1047) and an evil-doer (*Frevlerin*, 1054).

The epithet *Frevlerin*, derived from *Frevel*, meaning outrage, crime or sacrilege, is typical of the verbal hostilities between Medea and the Greeks in that it contains an encoded reference to negative cultural stereotypes. Having the connotation of *one who commits sacrilege*, *Frevlerin* shares with the various imputations of dirtying, poisoning, cursing, defiling, stealing, and murdering, which are hurled against Medea, the peculiar resonance of anti-Semitic discourse. The racist quality of prevailing opinion is evident in Jason's observation that Medea should go back to the bloody tribe where she belongs (1052), and the damaged sense of self occurring in members of an oppressed minority is apparent in Medea's despairing compliance with her tormentors. Accepting the accusation that she is an evil-doer (1063), she adds her voice to the chorus of her enemies, seemingly convulsed in a paroxysm of self-hatred: "Denn ich bin ein entsetzlich, greulich Wesen,/ Mir selbst ein Abgrund und ein Schreckensbild" (So I am a dreadful, destestable being, an abyss and an image of horror, even to myself, 1067-68). In that the word *Schrecken*, meaning horror, was the normal word for witchcraft in Germany (Robbins 222), it lends a particularly self-inculpating quality to Medea's speech. Not only sanctioning the general perception of herself as a malefactor and a witch, Medea speaks the language of the stingy Jew. When confronted with testimony that she was seen leaving the house of Peleas bearing the golden fleece, she whimpers that it was her payment: "Es war mein Lohn" (It was my payment, 984), resorting, as it were, to Shylock's argument.

Whereas, in ancient treatments of the myth, Medea's murder of Peleas is a given of the plot, Grillparzer explores the question of whether she is "guilty" or "innocent" in such a way as to emphasize the socially constructed quality of all such verdicts. Though the abjectly defensive position of the accused may have the subliminal effect of evoking the stereotype of the Jew, condemning Medea as guilty by a process of spurious analogy, the text suggests that she is actually innocent of the only specific crime with which she is charged. Insisting that she never did the deed (1038), Medea gives an entirely credible account of the death of Peleas in Act Three (1442-64), and her guilty appearance in Act Two seems to be rather a function of her emotional response to attack than a matter of actual guilt or innocence. Evidently more disturbed by the capricious favoritism of Creon's procedure than by the essential falsity of the charge against her, Medea asks: "Doch wie hab ich gefrevelt und für wen?" (But how have I done evil and for whom? 1064). To the degree that the present crisis resembles the situation in her youth when Aeëtes tormented her by flaunting his preference for Absyrtus, Medea's response to Creon's antipathy conforms to an established pattern. The complaint of unfairness is, however, an ineffectual defense that seems to concede the crucial issue. The link between Medea's present anxiety and her past experience is apparent in her musing on the recollected scene of Peleas' death: "Mich schaudert, denk ich an des alten Mannes Wut" (I shudder to think of the old man's rage, 984). Evidently immobilized by terror, she acts as if the ranks of her accusers were swollen with the phantoms of more than one angry old man. In her vulnerability to paternal intimidation, she demonstrates a receptivity to intrusive memories that is typical of clinically disturbed individuals for whom "the traumatic moment becomes encoded in an abnormal form of memory, which breaks spontaneously into consciousness" (Herman 37).

A response to trauma that is diametrically opposed to the constrictive effect of hypnotic anesthesia, intrusion, or the compulsive reliving of traumatic events, may alternate with defensive states of detachment in the survivors of abuse. It is particularly interesting to consider the curious inconsistencies of Grillparzer's characters in view of Herman's observation that "the dialectic of opposing psychological states is perhaps the most characteristic feature of post-traumatic syndromes" (47). Like Medea, Jason occasionally seems haunted and immobilized by past events, and yet, within moments of complaining to Creusa that he stands in a sea of surging troubles, unable to disassociate himself from what has happened (771), he resolutely denies all knowledge of wrongdoing, denouncing the herald as a liar: "Du lügst, nicht weiss ich um des Königs Sterben" (You lie. I know nothing of the king's death, 950). Thus, the hostage to a dreadful past benefits by an attack of fortuitous amnesia. In a rather more complicated instance of vacillation between troubled receptivity to intrusive memories and constricted consciousness of impending danger, Medea proceeds from her shuddering recollection of "the old man's rage" to an account of Jason's role in Peleas' death that implies the operation of hypnotic suggestion.

Recalling the day when the old king's daughters implored her to help their ailing father, Medea describes Jason as entering her room and peering insistently into her eyes as if to establish contact between his own unspoken desire and a corresponding impulse in herself: "Als säh ein Vorsatz, scheu in dir verborgen,/ Nach seinesgleichen aus in meiner Brust" (As if some purpose timidly hidden in yourself sought out its likeness in my breast, 1088-89). Though this intimation of hypnotic compulsion may be morally irrelevant, it is consistent with what the audience knows about the urgently seductive hero of *Die Argonauten* and the reluctantly compliant object of his passion. Claiming that Jason stared into her eyes while lamenting that the daughters of Peleas did not ask him for help so that he could prepare them a "healing" potion that would solve his own problems once and for all (1090-93), Medea suggests a comparison between Jason and Shakespeare's Richard the Second, who accomplished an assassination with the phrase "Have I no friend will rid me of this living fear?" (*Richard the Second* 5.4.2). Consistent with evidence linking a "capacity for trance" and "chronic autohypnotic states" with the experience of trauma (Herman 43; Shengold 98), the image of Jason holding Medea in thrall with a compelling gaze falls into the series of pseudo-hypnotic tableaux appearing at regular intervals in *Das goldene Vliess*. From Phrixus' encounter with Medea in *Der Gastfreund* (242-52), through the scene in Act Three of *Die Argonauten* when Jason and Medea stare longingly into each others' eyes (1172-1270), and the scene in Act One of *Medea* when the protagonist entrusts her fate to Creusa, the compelling or compulsive quality of a speaker transfixed in the stare of an exalted other recurs with notable regularity. The theme of hypnosis is particularly relevant to the psychological dynamics of Act Two in *Medea,* not only because of Medea's problematic description of past events, but because of the special importance of hypnosis for an understanding of certain kinds of interpersonal dynamics, a phenomenon well noted by Freud, who observed that the states of being in love and participating in groups are, like hypnosis, conditions in which "the object has been put in the place of the ego ideal" (*S.E.* 18:116).

As much inspired by Creon's moral leadership as he is displeased by Medea's testimony, Jason shakes off the mood of self-doubt that has plagued him since his arrival in Corinth, and registers an energetic complaint. Without bothering to refute Medea's claim, he nevertheless protests: "Machst mir zu Wesen meiner Träume Schatten,/ Hältst mir mein Ich vor in des deinen Spiegel/ Und rufst meine Gedanken wider mich?" (Must you give substance to the shadow of my dreams? Do you hold me up before the mirror of yourself, and call my own thoughts up against me? 1096-98). Implicitly accepting the idea that Medea was the mirror of his soul who enacted his desires, he vehemently denies responsibility for her actions, insisting on the technical difficulty of holding a person accountable for his thoughts: "Nichts weiss ich, nichts von deinen Tun und Treiben" (I know nothing, nothing at all about your goings on, 1099). Denying that he ever loved her, he declares the bond between them sundered, and joins the crowd in cursing her: "Und fluche dir, wie alle Welt dir flucht" (And I curse you as all the world curses you, 1104). Thus in the course of the act, Jason seems to be transformed from a parody of the Romantic hero into a devotee of the principle that "might makes right." Having projected the features of an abusive parent onto his chosen victim, he stubbornly insists on his ignorance of criminal acts about which he must have been aware. The insistence on domination, as conspicuous in this scene as the general reliance on defensive mechanisms of denial and projection, underscores the affinity between Grillparzer's characters and various other witch-hunters, ethnic cleansers, and builders of character. Finally, the quasi-parental assertion that Medea has brought her punishment on herself, articulated by Aeëtes in *Der Gastfreund* (128-29), and Jason in *Die Argonauten* (450-51), is reinvoked by Jason in the present crisis when Medea reproaches him for breaking his vows: "Selbst hast du das Versprechen dir verwirkt,/ Ich gebe hin dich deine Vaters Fluch" (You yourself have undone that promise for yourself; I give you over to your father's curse, 1108-09). As significant as the self-exculpating function of the abusive formula is the fact that it takes the form of an appeal to paternal authority.

The tendency of Grillparzer's characters to echo the opinions of the powerful gives them all a peculiarly spineless quality. None of the principal players in *Das goldene Vliess* ever demonstrates anything remotely resembling the courage of his or her convictions, and by the end of the second act of *Medea,* personal integrity is so conspicuous by its absence as to suggest that the pedagogical structures implicit in the language and the action of the first two plays had finally produced a community of wimps. Neither Medea's self-hatred nor Jason's brutality nor Creusa's piety is a departure from the communal consensus tending to affirm Creon's evident desire to be rid of the foreigner. Though the king behaves in an apparently arbitrary manner, his despotic demeanor does not conceal his essential cowardice, and the worst that can be said of him is that he is about as capricious and incompetent as Aeëtes. Having demonstrated the disastrous effects of exalting a bungling patriarch to the status of "ego ideal" in the first two parts of his trilogy, Grillparzer depicts in *Medea* a world in which all of the young adults seem terminally afflicted by moral cowardice. As if the proclamation of banishment served as a triggering mechanism for the release of general hostility that has been clumsily concealed until this time, the arrival of the herald provides the entire community with an excuse to denounce Medea. The energy with which various individuals revile her and the horror with which she recoils from their scorn suggest that, for every member of the group, the collectivity is endowed with the nurturing quality of a surrogate mother, functioning in accordance with Alice Miller's observation that "a group may provide a feeling of maternal warmth." The noteworthy tyranny of the group itself is comprehensible in terms of Miller's corollary perception that "when a group takes over this ersatz [maternal] role, although it gives the illusion of being an ideal mother, it mercilessly requires the same adaptation to its demands that the real mother once did" (*Thou Shalt Not* 84-85).

In the world of *Medea,* every character acts as if survival itself depended on obtaining or preserving the quasi-parental protection that Medea seeks in Jason; the curse that falls on her head is, conversely, the dreadful realization of the worst fears of an entire community in which every individual aspires to the reward of the "good child" and cringes at the fate of the "bad child." That Creon himself seems governed by an irrational insistence on security becomes evident in Act Three, when he praises Jason as a charismatic and indomitable military leader (1360-63). Even at the end of Act Two, however, when Medea exits menacing vengeance, Creon's instant promise of punishment suggests that he is no more independent of external incentives and threats than any other character in the play. Though the separation of the cursed/cursing from the protected/ protecting seems virtually complete when Creon turns from growling at Medea to calm his apprehensive daughter—"Du zittre nicht, wir schützen dich vor ihr" (Don't you quake, we'll protect you from her, 1151)—the royal reassurance recalls with savage irony the toll that Medea has to pay for depending on the "protection" of a strong man. In Grillparzer's drama, the promise of protection is regularly the first step on the road to catastrophe.

The task of reconciling Grillparzer's stated intention of motivating "Medea's hatred against her children on their attachment to their kinder father" with a dramatic text in which paternal ineptitude seems to be a universal impediment to human happiness poses an interesting critical problem. Although the playwright's enormous sympathy for Medea suggests that the process of mourning for his mother, intervening between the diary entry on *Medea* in 1817 and the completion of the trilogy in 1820, may have had a mellowing effect on his conception of the child-murdering mother, the degree to which the female protagonist actually does conform to the author's earliest noted thoughts on her character is particularly evident by the end of Act Three, when the children forsake Medea and cling to her rival. That the author manages to focus rather mercilessly on the mother's hostility toward her children without forfeiting sympathy for the character is a noteworthy achievement. His success depends partly on the cumulative effect of various frustrations that tend to mitigate Medea's culpability. Deprived of the staunch allies available to her ancient and early modern prototypes, she lacks the sympathy of the chorus and the help of an Athenian king. She also has to do without the consolation she might expect from the only other Colchian in town.

That Gora is no peacemaker is no news to anyone familiar with the first two plays in the trilogy. Even when her speech is patterned on ancient set pieces, such as the catalogue of disasters that befell Jason' s fellow Argonauts (1242-59), which recalls the third choral ode of Seneca' s tragedy (*Medea* 505-669), there is a peculiar bellicosity in everything she says. Whereas the Euripidean servant is clairvoyant in her anticipation of arrogant folly, the Senecan *nutrix* preaches philosophical restraint, and Corneille's Nérine displays a certain courtly discretion, Gora is an instigator. The tales she tells of Hercules burning to death in a poisoned garment sent by his jealous wife, and of Althaea killing her son to avenge her brother, are so close in spirit to the crimes that Medea actually does commit that the teller seems inextricably implicated in the mischief of the listener. If for no other reason, Gora is discredited by the fact that she has an ax to grind. Having been humiliated by Jason, whom she resents as the destroyer of her "child" (1297), she seems to welcome Creon's decree of exile as a positive development that will have the salubrious effect of forcing Medea to be her ally in the war against Jason. Thus, when Medea exits hastily upon the arrival of Jason and Creon, Gora exchanges hostile barbs with the men, remarking venomously that if Medea were more like herself they would not dare to treat her so. She also utters an ominous prediction that Medea will soon learn the error of her ways (1313-14). In setting herself up as a model for Medea, whose apprenticeship in revenge she presumes to direct, Gora proves herself to be the equal in folly of her royal adversary.

Creon's propensity for meddling is noted by Medea, who refers to the king as a "bitter enemy" who is leading Jason astray (1299). Though Medea can hardly be expected to have an unbiased view of Creon, her judgment is valorized by the exchange between Jason and Creon that follows the dialogue between Medea and Gora at the beginning of Act Three. The men are no sooner alone than Creon reaffirms his insistence on expelling the Colchians from Corinth (1321-22), and Jason bows to the king's stated wish with dutiful compliance. When the hero assumes his usual self-pitying stance, complaining that Medea will soon be free, like a healthy "filly," to scamper off without restraint, while he must bear the tiresome yoke of inactivity at court (1329-34), the king offers consolation, comparing Jason to a bow that springs back gingerly when it is freed from the hand that bends it (1335-39). The implication of the conceit, that Medea has been a trial and a burden to Jason, seems ironic enough in view of Medea's habit of rescuing Jason from danger, but the royal interpretation of events is welcome enough to Jason. Indeed, Creon's reassurance that Jason will grow strong when Medea is out of the way (1339) echoes Jason's own previous complaint to the king (553). To the extent that Creon takes his cues from Jason, the question of who is misleading whom seems legitimate, and yet Creon's particular contribution to impending disaster is essential.

Older and more powerful than Jason, Creon embraces the role of chief guru with great relish, responding to Jason's tiresome lament with a self-serving program of instruction. Distinguishing between the crimes of a man and the errors of a boy, he asserts that the former must be punished while the latter may be corrected (1345-46). There is, of course, no suggestion in Creon's pedagogical philosophy, that young women as well as young men may make mistakes. His plan to make Jason better (*bessermachen*) bears a curious resemblance, however, to the project of improving Medea's character that was undertaken by Creusa in Act Two, and continued by Gora in Act Three. Thus, in the manner of a benign teacher, Creon presents his view that Jason's break with Medea is a kind of sacrifice through which the hero may absolve himself from guilt for youthful errors and once again proceed as a powerful military leader: "Und stromweis wird die Jugend Griechenlands/ Um dich scharen gegen jedermann" (And like a torrent, the youth of Greece will gather round you against everybody, 1360-61). The speaker's gratuitous belligerence, apparent in the phrase *gegen jedermann*, underscores the spurious quality of Creon's campaign against Medea. That the royal personage is also motivated by greed is evident in his insistence on Jason's stature as the "mighty hero of the fleece" (1363). The very mention of the coveted prize is enough to halt the flow of Creon's pompous exposition on Jason's brilliant future. In his eagerness to ascertain the whereabouts of the fleece, he breaks off and asks: "Du hast es doch?" (You do have it don't you? 1364). Thus, like every other character who endeavors to instruct another in this play, Creon is the creature of his own passions, who presumes, nevertheless, to dispense rational wisdom to the unenlightened.

While Jason and Creon are busy goading each other on in acquisitive fantasies that all depend on the expulsion of the foreigners, Medea shows up and asks to speak to Jason. Although Creon advises his protégé against talking to the troublemaker, Jason grants Medea's request with an inherently unpersuasive declaration that he is not afraid of her (1393-94). No slave, moreover, to the hobgoblin of consistency, he insists on rigorous rationality in the presence of the woman about whom he habitually complains with great intensity. Confronted with a direct attack that includes sarcastic terms of admiration as well as various overt insults, Jason repeats his standard claim that Medea has brought her punishment on herself (1432). He insists on arguments with a curiously legalistic flavor: a majority has condemned Medea (1411), and, in any case, a person cannot be held responsible for his thoughts (1441). Reasoning as though Medea's detractors had been a lawfully constituted jury, and their antagonism the equivalent of an official verdict, he manifests the serene confidence of one who has been absolved of personal obligation by the decision of an omnipotent judge. Whereas his insistence on the logical claims of justice contrasts ironically with his own constant clamoring for special consideration, the juxtaposition of the emotionally extravagant persona Jason presents to Creon and Creusa with the model of calm restraint which he displays in Medea's company has the effect of exposing the dynamic irrationality inherent in the ideal of enlightened decorum. Grillparzer's version of the confrontation between the offensive rationalist and the offended "Fury" is particularly interesting in its formal aspect.

The hostile exchange between Jason and Medea that is a structural component of the ancient antecedents of this tragedy gains a good deal of dramatic immediacy from the simple fact that the form of the trilogy frees the author from the need to encumber his dialogue with expository material. Although the meeting with Jason is traditionally an opportunity for Medea to recite the litany of his obligations and mistakes, Grillparzer's heroine dispenses with the particular details of a history that is as well known to Jason as to herself, uttering a comparatively terse statement (1414-21) full of sarcasm, blame, and invective. In reproaching him, she speaks like an angry wife and not a prosecuting attorney or a classical heroine. The purpose of the traditional tirade, which makes Jason look shabby by contrasting his past promises with his present betrayal, is accomplished by dramatic technique rather than narrative exposition. Relying on the fact that spectators of the trilogy are as familiar with Jason's past as Medea is, Grillparzer proceeds, with great economy, to depict the controlled violence of abbreviated exchanges in which staccato fragments of speech are replete with passion and significance. Rather than respond to Medea's accusation with a long-winded defense, Jason puts an end to her complaint with a curt but effective threat: "Du schmähest. Das zu hören ziemt mir nicht./ Du weisst nun, was zu tun, und so leb wohl!" (You are insulting. It doesn't suit me to listen to this. You know what to do now, so fare well, 1422-23). These words, containing an echo of the line with which Creusa dismissed Medea in Act Two (656), have an instant effect on Medea, who backs down, begging Jason to stay: "Noch weiss ichs nicht, drum bleibe, bis ichs weiss./ Bleib! Ruhig will ich sein. Ruhig wie du" (I know nothing yet, so stay until I know. Stay! I'll be calm. Calm like you, 1424-25). Confronted with Jason's resignation from his instructional mission, Medea tries to renew her "studies" by pleading her own ignorance, deferring to his superior control, and promising to be quiet, in the manner of an earnest child. More eloquent than any account of past wrongs is this condensed reenactment of the situation in which Jason, like Aeëtes and Creusa before him, manipulates Medea's fear of abandonment. Thus, with the genius of a very great dramatist, Grillparzer deploys the sparest elements of dialogue to depict the abuses of the past in an excruciating present moment.

The only exception to the rule that the characters in this scene tend to communicate in short, quick snatches of intensely poignant speech is the occasion on which there is real information to be conveyed. This occurs when Medea describes the death of Peleas, the details of which are evidently unknown to Jason as well as the audience. Reminding her partner that it was at his request that she agreed to help the daughters of Peleas, Medea declares that she bled the old man, dressed his wounds, and left him in better condition than when she found him. When she went back to the palace to collect the fleece that had been promised to her, she found the patient raging in an apparent delirium as he bled to death from a fatal hemorrhage. Differing markedly from the ancient legends according to which Medea tricked the daughters of Peleas into dismembering their aged father, this story is an intriguing construction of an ordinary situation in which a mortal woman might be branded as a witch. Deconstructing a fabulous myth, Grillparzer suggests that the death of Peleas resulted from routine medical care rather than from anything so nefarious as witchcraft or treachery. To the degree that she contributed to Peleas' demise, Medea may have done so through ineptitude rather than malice. A skeptical allusion to the technique of blood-letting, which was still practiced in Grillparzer's day (Bariéty and Coury 18), her story also reflects the low esteem in which female healers were increasingly held as the practice of medicine became more prestigious and profitable in the nineteenth century (Ehrenreich and English 3-20). Containing *in nucleo* all the elements requisite for a witchcraft trial, Medea's account illuminates the abusive quality of projections of female omnipotence and also underscores the problem of disseminated responsibility. In that Peleas' death seems to have resulted from the combined errors, desires, and mischief of many people, none of whom actually committed murder, it raises the question of moral responsibility for communal events.

Credibly suggesting that, in a legal sense, Medea is as innocent of murder as her interlocutor, this speech (1443-64) inevitably disturbs Jason's calm equilibrium. Confronting him with the contradiction between the general assumption of her guilt and the strong probability of her innocence, Medea challenges Jason to examine his conscience. Since his enthusiasm for justice never depended on questions of innocence or guilt in the first place, her hope of winning his support is doomed from the start. Clearly implicated in the circumstances of Peleas' death, Jason can hardly advocate Medea's cause without inculpating himself, and he is disinclined to consider the degree to which he himself may have contributed to a development that has been defined as regicide. Thus, Medea no sooner finishes her tale than Jason turns on her with horror and denounces her as a witch (1465-66). The vehemence of his reaction is most remarkable in that he does not criticize her testimony on rational grounds. In fact, he concedes that Medea may indeed be innocent, but claims the point to be irrelevant because no one else was present when Peleas died and nobody will believe Medea's story (1509-10). His animated reaction to her claim of innocence has the appearance of deriving from the self-loathing which he suffers in recognizing the image of himself that emerges from her narrative. The essentially narcissistic quality of the bond between Jason and Medea is, indeed, most evident in the tendency of each character to reflect in words and actions the moral irresponsibility of the other. Both of them complain of being overwhelmed by circumstances beyond their control. Just as Medea defends herself against the charge of murder by claiming that Jason put her up to mischief, so Jason parries Medea's most grievous accusations by insisting that he acted out of compulsion: "Gezwungen nur" (Only under compulsion, 1561). Finally, Grillparzer's Jason shares with his Medea a curious concern for the approbation of other people. So it is that, having agreed to talk to her because he does not want her to think him a coward, he agrees to "give" her one of the children so that she will not think he is unfair (1597-98).

The bewildering quality of Jason's sudden announcement regarding the fate of the children is apparent in the explanation he gives to Creon when the king rejoins him toward the end of the act: "Sie soll nicht sagen, dass ich allzu hart/ Drum hab ich eins der Kinder ihr gewährt,/ In Leid un Not der Mutter lieber Trost" (She shall not say that I am too harsh, thus have I left one of the children, to be a comfort to his mother in her sorrow and need, 1617-19). Aside from the surprising concern for Medea's good opinion, and the essential arrogance of the assumption that the children are a kind of paternal property that may be granted to their mother on a whim, Jason's speech is remarkable for its tendency to suggest disturbing questions. If he is really convinced that Medea is a barbarian, a criminal, and a witch, why does he willingly offer to leave one of his sons with her? And if he believes that his own lot is more wretched than hers, why does he worry about her sorrow and need? The plan to placate the "monster" with a living child issues most apparently from Jason's bad faith. No less remarkable than his decision to relinquish a son in order to assuage his conscience is Creon's compliance with the project. Instantly affirming Jason's wish, the king confers the royal seal of approval on the foolish plan: "So ists, so wills der Vater" (So it is, so their father wishes, 1627). In keeping with the paternalistic essence of his character, Creon demonstrates more concern for the rights of the father than for the welfare of the child.

As Act Three draws to a close, Medea endures her ultimate humiliation. Her children appear, escorted by Creusa, who piously observes that her own kind speech has won their hearts, unaccustomed as they were to gentle treatment (1624-25). This suggestion that Medea is a bad mother seems vindicated when the boys remain by Creusa's side while their mother calls to them with outstretched arms. As it becomes clear that the children are not about to rush to her embrace, Medea accuses Creusa of restraining them, calling them names and reviling them for resembling their father (1667-68, 1684). Finally, her anger erupts in a violent question: "Wer gibt mir einen Dolch?/ Einen Dolch für mich und sie?" (Who will give me a dagger? A dagger for them and for me?, 1697-98). Medea' s misery seems vaguely reassuring to the rest of the assembled company. Creusa comments drily that she is not holding on to the children, and Jason repeats his untiring refrain—Medea has brought her punishment on herself (1699-1700). Seemingly inspired by the mother's negative example, Creon strikes an unwonted tone of pious magnanimity, urging his daughter to protect the children from their mother's wrath: "Führ sie ins Haus zurück,/ Nicht hassen sollen sie, die sie gebar" (Take them back into the house, they ought not to hate her who gave birth to them, 1704-05).

Although the children's defection may seem to be a crucial indictment of Medea's character, the ambiguities inherent in the event are worth noting. In the first place, the attentive spectator will have observed that Jason, as well as Medea, has been rejected by his sons (Act One 211-13). Secondly, Creusa's claim to have won the children's hearts through her gentle speech (*Mein mildes Wort*, 1624) suggests an interesting analogy between the princess and her prince charming, the word *mild* being associated with Jason, whom Medea has taunted with the sarcastic epithet *milder* no less than three times in the dialogue immediately preceding the arrival of the royal family on the scene (1416, 1418, 1421). Since the act of persuading through language is virtually indistinguishable from the technique of seduction, in which Jason is the demonstrated expert, Creusa's efficacious use of sweet talk might earn her the appellation that Gora confers on Jason and Medea repeats several times: "Den glattzüngigen Heuchler" (the slippery-tongued dissembler, 1208, 1209, 1213). That the mellifluous, caressing use of the tongue is a skill which Jason shares with Creusa is noted in Act Two by Medea, who scowls at the princess: "Du auch hier? weisse, silberhelle Schlange?/ O zische nicht mehr, züngle nicht so lieblich" (You here too? white, silverbright snake? O hiss no more, do not tongue-stroke [us] so lovingly, 1115-16). In fact, Jason and Creusa may seem to be the inheritors of a verbal tradition initiated by Aeëtes, whom Medea accuses of cajoling with "flattering words" (*Schmeichelworten, Gastfreund* 126). To the possible defense of Creusa, that she does not seem to tell deliberate untruths, one might easily respond that Aeëtes and Jason also seem unaware of their duplicity. Yet all of these characters are implicated by their peculiar use of language in the communal deceptions which pave the way to disaster. In the world of this play, the erosion of trust is inseparable from the abuse of language.

Whereas the breach of trust that is an essential thematic element in virtually all dramatic treatments of this myth depends primarily on the crucial fact of Jason's broken vows, Grillparzer augments the culpability of his adventuring hero by emphasizing Medea's basic decency and depicting her contribution to the deaths of Absyrtus and Peleas as unintentional. In absolving her of crimes attributed to her by legend, the poet puts Jason in the position of betraying a relatively blameless ally. When his Medea reproaches Jason, in the manner of the Euripidean prototype, for exposing their sons to the fate of stepchildren (1584, 1788-92), her complaint is credible precisely because Jason's royal benefactor is an incompetent fool whose commitment to the well-being of the children seems doubtful. The suggestion that the children are likely to be mistreated by their chosen guardians is consistent with the pattern of the entire work, in which paternal figures regularly betray those whom they have promised to protect, and youthful protagonists invariably misjudge the character of their protectors. If Medea's sons trust Jason and

Creusa more than they trust their mother, they may be following in the footsteps of Phrixus and Absyrtus, who trusted Aeëtes, or of Medea and Creusa, who set their hopes on Jason. Thus the children's rejection of their mother should be regarded as a barometer of communal malaise rather than an indictment of individual character. That anybody would choose to live with people who behave as badly in public as Creon, Creusa, and Jason ought not to be construed as a good sign. In the atmosphere of impending doom in which Act Three ends, the defection of the children is emblematic of the ominous liability of all human bonds. The blind faith which Aeëtes demanded from his children is a thing of the past. The rational structures which Medea embraced upon arriving in Corinth have failed. The character who has been identified since the opening scene of *Der Gastfreund* as the subjective center of this world lies in a state of total physical collapse.

Still prostrate in front of Creon's palace at the beginning of Act Four, Medea seems to have reached the nadir of misery. Standing nearby, Gora watches her agitated compatriot relive the moment when the children fled from her to Creusa. Uttering fragmented exclamations and loudly lamenting her losses, Medea winces at the thought of her enemies' smug laughter and articulates a suicidal wish that casts her father in the role of mercy killer: "Ich wollt, mein Vater hätte mich getötet/ Da ich noch klein war" (I wish my father had killed me when I was still little, 1799-1800). Considering the degree to which Aeëtes' relationship with his children conformed to the model of *bourreau/victime*, with the father playing the role of torturer/executioner and the children dutifully offering themselves up as compliant sacrifices, Medea's longing for the deceased *bourreau* as for an irretrievable deliverer is an ominous development. To make matters worse, the agent of her continuing chastisement is close at hand. Giving free rein to her talent for verbal abuse, Gora commands her mistress to quit moaning and pull herself together: "Steh auf! Was hilft Weinen? Steh auf!" (Stand up! What good does crying do? Stand up! 1730). Without the least hint of sympathy or comfort, Gora prods and scolds, complaining predictably enough that Medea has brought her troubles on herself, and being sure to add a reminder that if Medea had listened to Gora they would both still be safe at home in Colchis (1727-28). Having poured salt in the wound, she proceeds to rub it in by observing that, in any case, the children are only treating their mother as she treated her own father (1749). Though it was none other than Gora herself who presented the story of Althea and Meleager to Medea as a didactic tale, the old woman recoils with horror when her understudy turns her anger on the children (1784). Staring in total incomprehension when Medea asks her the name of that Greek woman who avenged her blood with her own blood, Gora insists that she cannot imagine what Medea has in mind. No more ready than Jason to recognize the fruits of her malice, Gora is arguably just as prodigal as he in sowing seeds of mischief.

Apart from the question of Gora's contribution to the general gloom, Medea's thinking on certain matters seems to have changed considerably between the third and fourth acts. Categorically opposed to the logic of punishment that Gora championed in Act One, Medea offered eloquent opposition to Creon's punitive policy in Act Three: "In dem du Frevel strafst, verübst du sie" (Wherein you punish wickedness, do you commit it, 1616). Yet in Act Four, she declares a burning desire to punish the children: "So will ich sie treffen, wie die Götter mich!/ Ungestraft sei kein Frevel auf der Erde" (So will I strike them as the gods struck me! Let no wickedness go unpunished on the earth, 1750-51). Grillparzer's insistence on the acquired quality of Medea's enthusiasm for revenge is emphasized in the character's observation: "Man hat mich bös genannt, ich war es nicht!/ Allein ich fühle dass mans werden kann" (They called me bad when I was not, only I'm beginning to feel that one might become so, 1849). In fact, the affirmation of punishment as policy provides a way out of the psychological impasse in which Medea now finds herself. Having been browbeaten by Gora for trying to please Jason, and reviled by Jason for maintaining contact with Gora, she endorses the precepts of all her spiteful mentors in espousing a policy of revenge. Medea now regrets that her capacity for inflicting harm is no longer equal to her malevolent desire because she relinquished her destructive talents when she buried her mother's gifts in Act One. While she is still whimpering impotently about the vengeance she would wreak if only she had the implements of her old arts, the sudden arrival of Creon puts her in the position of a person in a domestic quarrel who puts her hand into a drawer and finds a loaded gun.

Finding Medea in a wretched state of debasement, and leaving her exuberantly in command of herself, Creon unwittingly empowers her by indulging his own acquisitive appetite. In his eagerness to get his hands on the golden fleece, he has ordered his servants to dig up Medea's treasure, and now he angrily confronts her with it. Although he insists on appropriating the coveted prize, Creon allows Medea to keep the chest and its contents, a concession with which she is evidently pleased. Disarming the king with a display of renewed poise, Medea assures him that he will receive his just reward now that she is beginning to recover her old self (1952-53). The ironic implication of her cordial remark is lost on Creon, who is lulled by her apparent compliance into granting her a farewell interview with her sons. Since she has not asked to see the children, having added nothing to the death threat that was her last public statement regarding them, Creon's offer seems neither rational nor shrewd. Having deprived Medea of all he really wants from her, he makes a show of rewarding her for her good behavior, quite as if she were a child recovering her composure after a temper tantrum. By restoring her supernatural paraphernalia to

Medea, Creon enables her to embark on a dreadful course of action, and his visit marks the essential turning point in the tide of tragic action. Although classical and neoclassical versions of the drama posit a sequential order of events in which Medea's enemies exploit her, humiliate her, and then fall into the trap that she sets for them, Grillparzer's drama presents the dispossession and empowerment of the protagonist as simultaneous, indeed, as identical developments, both implicit in the single transaction whereby Creon deprives Medea of the golden fleece, leaving her with her box of magic tricks intact. An innovation of considerable originality and imagination, the device of the treasure chest deserves close scrutiny.

The "multiple weight of meaning" in the coffer that is both an "embodiment of the irrational" and a representation of "the Colchian past" has been noted by T. C. Dunham (79), and the symbol of the magic chest, inevitably recalling the myth of Pandora, is as essential to Grillparzer's *Medea* as the story of Phaethon to Seneca's text or the tale of Tereus and Procne to Corneille's. Since the burial of the coffer accomplished in the first moments of Grillparzer's *Medea* was defined as an end of magic, superstition, and witchcraft, heralding the dawn of a rational and liberal age, the recovery of the treasure, signaling a reversion to barbarism, may seem comparable in its ominous implications to the ancient myth attributing the misery of humankind to one woman's foolishness. The fascination that this story exercised on the contemporary imagination may be judged by the fact that Voltaire and Wieland both presented dramatic versions of it in the eighteenth century, and Goethe himself wrote a fragmentary play named *Pandora* in the winter of 1807-08, that was finally published in 1850 (Lichtenberger i-ix). Although Grillparzer, like the ancient Greeks, posits catastrophe as something issuing from a receptacle possessed by a woman, he alters the misogynist premises of the legendary tale. Whereas Pandora is entrusted by male deities with a casket belonging to them and evidently violates their trust by opening the lid and looking inside, Grillparzer's Medea is both the rightful owner of the chest and the one who judiciously refrains from opening it. The noxious contents of the coffer are only brought to light by the intervention of the greedy king. Thus Grillparzer derives a drama exposing the arrogance of male privilege from the elements of a myth underscoring the danger of female curiosity. The sexual implications of the "box" and the "fleece" it contains are essential to the meaning of his text.

Whereas the male characters in *Das goldene Vliess* are fascinated by the magical properties of the fleece as if it were endowed with something as essential as the lure of phallic potency, the female characters are relatively indifferent to its charm. Medea tries to dissuade Jason from risking his life for it, and she readily relinquishes it to Creon. The "box" that she inherited from her mother and gladly trades for personal security, although abandoned like a piece of rubbish by Creon, is Medea's essential source of power. Though the king fails to appreciate its value, and Jason seems oblivious to its existence, the miraculous revitalization that Medea experiences upon recovering it suggests a symbolic association between the treasure chest and personal resources that are sexual in origin. That Creon's appropriation of the fleece and his casual abandonment of its container should have such a singularly liberating effect on Medea underscores the inhibiting and crippling quality of the protection Medea sought in Jason. In this, the symbol of the coffer is consistent with the general tone of a drama that depicts the prescribed role of the "good wife" as a constraint rather than a benefit. Though Grillparzer's manipulation of traditional symbols is interesting from a feminist point of view, his use of the mythical coffer is most remarkable as a dramatization of the process that Freud called "the return of the repressed in dehumanized form."

Whereas the burial of the chest represents a denial of infantile energy and irrationality, its exhumation is tantamount to a resurgence of the exuberantly pugnacious qualities that Medea exercised at home in Colchis. The ominous hint of exultant self-recovery that appears during Creon's visit (1952-53) is repeated immediately upon his departure: "Doch Dank euch! Dank! Ihr gabt mir auch mich selbst" (Oh thank you! Thanks! You give me back myself, 1977). A change in Medea's dealings with Gora is discernible as soon as the king leaves. Though the nurse has dominated and disparaged her mistress throughout most of the play, Medea now assumes an imperious stance, requiring total submission from her servant. From this point until the end of the scene, she speaks to Gora almost entirely in the imperative, ordering her to open up the casket (1978), to serve as emissary to the royal family (1996), and give the princess the gifts which Medea has prepared for her (1998-99). When Gora inadvertently shakes a vessel containing precious salves, allowing a tongue of flame to leap out from under the lid, Medea growls: "Sagt ich dir nicht, du sollst nicht schütteln! (Didn't I tell you not to shake it? 2003). Like a stern disciplinarian reproving a naughty child, Medea demands absolute obedience, resuming the abusive tone she used with Peritta in *Der Gastfreund*. Thus the return of the repressed which is activated by the excavation of the chest allows Medea to revert from the role of one who obeys orders to that of one who must be obeyed. Inauspiciously enough, it is at precisely the moment when the repressed is identified as a license to abuse the weak that a slave woman arrives, escorting Medea's children.

The interaction between Medea and her sons is a remarkable dramatization of the simmering mutual resentment characteristic of parents and children locked into the dynamics of abuse. Once alone with the children, Medea beckons them to come to her but they shrink back in fear, their apprehension evidently proportional to their mother's increasing impatience. Cowering in the manner of a child afraid of being hit, the smaller boy declares that he is frightened and seeks reassurance that Medea will not strike him: "Tust du mir nichts?" (You won't do anything to me?, 2047). Medea responds by inculpating the child: "Glaubst? hättest dus verdient?" (Do you think so? Have you deserved to be? 2047). Mustering his small store of courage, the boy blurts out a bitter accusation: "Einst warfst mich auf den Boden, weil dem Vater/ Ich ähnlich bin, allein er liebt mich drum" (Once you threw me on the floor because I am like my father, only he loves me for it, 2048-49). He concludes his grievance by declaring that he will stay with his father and the nice lady (2050). Visibly disturbed, Medea grumbles about the child's resemblance to Jason and admonishes herself to be calm. When the children complain that they are sleepy, her displeasure issues in an ominous prediction that they will soon have their fill of sleep (2055). Ominously unattractive as it is, the portrait of Medea at home with her children is too well contextualized to constitute a simple indictment of individual character.

As their visit with their mother begins, the little boys are in exactly the same position that Medea herself has occupied throughout most of the trilogy. Caught between the conflicting claims of their father and their mother, they are in a double bind comparable to the predicament of Medea, caught between Jason's exhortations and Gora's admonitions. Similarly, when Medea inculpates her son as a means of defending herself against his implied accusation of abuse, she automatically reacts to him as Aeëtes, Jason, and Gora have continually responded to her. The pain that the children inadvertently cause their mother by comparing her to the "nice lady" seems all the more crucial in view of Aeëtes' technique of tormenting Medea by calling Absyrtus his "only child." Unwitting tools in a deadly game, the children are encouraged to abandon a mother for whom the very idea of abandonment has become a rarified form of agony. Nor does Grillparzer allow the audience to forget that Medea is taking the blame for some things that are clearly not her fault. When her sons complain that she is going to put them back on the ship where they used to get seasick all the time, they seem to be operating on the assumption that all the unhappiness they have ever endured is their mother's fault. Thus, the author seems to debunk the myth of maternal omnipotence even as he unmasks the sordid figure of the abusive parent.

The strength of Medea's affectionate sympathy for her sons is paradoxically evident in her last meeting with them. Watching them walk off in search of a resting place, she observes the solicitude with which the older child takes care of his little brother. Lending him his own jacket and putting his arm around him, the big boy leads the little one off to a spot where they can both lie down (2058-62). Like the Medea of Euripides, Grillparzer's protagonist seems incapable of looking at her children without sensing the folly of her dreadful plan.

Though her dealings with the children are corrupted by the habit of punitive violence, her indulgent impulses are evident in the pleasure she takes in watching them comfort each other, and the rift between mother and children is more complicated than it seems at first glance. Because the capacity to defy is an important indication of budding autonomy, the very defection of the children from their mother's side may seem a tribute to her, as does their evident ability to nurture one another. This indirect and ambiguous affirmation of the bond between Medea and her children underscores the essential fidelity of Grillparzer's characterization to the Euripidean model.

Like her Euripidean prototype, Grillparzer's Medea falters in her resolution to kill the children and only manages to talk herself into the deed by listening to the promptings of an internal voice that is all but stifled by the children's presence. As they lie down to rest, leaving their mother to reflect that she would give anything to be able to sleep as they do, she falls into a reverie on the distance between the blameless child she once was and the ruined creature she is now. In a monologue that seems to be a conversation between herself and a part of herself split off from the rest, she manifests the clinical detachment of one who feels "as though she is observing from outside her body, or as though the whole experience is a bad dream from which she will shortly awaken" (Herman 43). Lamenting that the story of her life seems alien to her, as if it were the narration of a stranger, she muses over scenes from her childhood, recalling happy days in Colchis when, untroubled by her present woes, she basked in the pleasures of her brother's companionship and her father's approval. The rosy glow that colors her retrospective account of girlhood in Colchis (2073-98) is inevitably ironic to an audience that has witnessed the turbulent drama of Medea's youth and adolescence. In fact, her lyrical reverie tends to whitewash all the principal players in the first two parts of the trilogy. Describing her former self as being pure, gentle, and as blameless as a child at her mother's breast, she recalls the altruistic sentiment that once united her brother and herself in helping a poor farmer whose crops had been destroyed by her father's royal huntsmen. The idyllic scene is completed by the arrival of the king, a benevolent patriarch who reaches out lovingly to his children, blessing them and calling them his life and joy. Although these hallucinated figures from her past offer consolation to Medea in her present misery, they contrast markedly with the surly crew the audience has seen in action. The pure and blameless girl Medea imagines herself to have been was a royal hunter with a haughty disposition; the brother whom she imagines as a spiritual twin was a reckless warrior. As for Aeëtes—the cruel, stupid tyrant of *Der Gastfreund* and *Die Argonauten* is hardly recognizable in the kindly monarch here remembered. Though Medea must certainly have been, at some point, as innocent as a baby at the breast, her idealized reconstruction of a past in which barbarism and cruelty are denied suggests that her perspective is colored by the effects of mourning. In any case, the constricted world of fantasy is soon disturbed by the intrusion of traumatic memories.

Speaking with increasing agitation, Medea accommodates the recollected image of her father by succumbing to an orgy of self-recrimination. Since Aeëtes was a gentle, provident fellow, her own deviation from the path he prescribed for her must necessarily have been inspired by wickedness and treachery: "Liebt seine gute Tochter! Gut? Ha gut!/ 's ist Lüge! sie wird dich verraten Greis!/ Hat dich verraten" (He loves his good daughter! Good? Ha, good! What lies! she will betray you, gray head, has betrayed you, 2098-2100). In a frenzied tone, she repeats the substance of her father's curse, a curse with which the tyrant from her past flagellates her visibly writhing present self. In her monologue, the angry voice that the Euripidean heroine addresses as her *thumos* is clearly identified as that of a paternal figure well known to the audience. Assuming the language of this vindictive parent, Medea enunciates the sentence of exile according to which she will have "no friend, no home, nowhere to lay her head" (2104-05). The concern for a place to lay her head is one that Medea shares with Jason, who uses virtually the same words in Act Three, when he excuses his plan to marry Creusa on the grounds that he needs a place where he can lay his head to rest (1552). Though Medea and Jason both act as if they were motherless children, her case differs from his in that she is the object rather than the agent of paternal punishment, and, furthermore, her punishment includes the death threat that her own voice now intones with ominous foreboding: "Wird dich verlassen, verstossen,/ Töten dich" (He will abandon you, cast you off, kill you, 2108-09). As if oblivious to the fact that the prophecy of doom is emanating from her own voice—as if, indeed, the vindictive, menacing spirit were looming over and closing in on her, Medea recoils in horror, calling out a terrified warning to her children. Waking them, she urges them to put their arms around her, revealing the childish need for comfort that is inherent in her ostensibly protective maternal impulse. The brilliance of Grillparzer's psychological portrait is nowhere more apparent than in the image of the desperate mother seeking refuge from the ghost of an angry parent in the arms of a sleepy child.

In dramatizing Medea's accessibility to the internalized demands of an abusive parent and the plight of her own children at the mercy of an inconsolable mother, Grillparzer anticipates Alice Miller's observation, with respect to the general compliance of Hitler's subjects, that "the men and women who carried out the 'final solution' did not let their feelings stand in their way for the simple reason that they had been raised from infancy not to have any feelings of their own but to experience their parents' wishes as their own" (*For Your Own Good* 81). Just as Aeëtes depended on his children for various kinds of support, so Medea turns to her own sons in her hour of terrible need. In keeping with the clinical observation that even a very young child can learn to play a nurturing role for a needy parent, Medea's sons actually seem to have a calming effect on their mother, whose anxiety subsides while she is holding them in her arms. Temporarily comforted, Medea sends the children back to their resting place, marveling at their capacity for blissful oblivion and wondering how they can sleep so peacefully while she is watching over them. Her ominous observation that they have never been in the hands of a worse enemy (2121-22) signals the end of a brief respite from intrusive memories.

Despite their evident ability to defuse the violent purpose that intermittently possesses Medea, the children seem to subject her to a burdensome restriction that is at odds with the prevailing current of her regressive passions. Just as Jason, experiencing Medea's presence as a hindrance to his personal desires, repeatedly exults in her departure (203, 716), so Medea now senses the nearness of her sons as a mixed blessing and sighs with relief when they leave her: "So sind sie fort! Nun ist mir wieder wohl" (So they are gone. Now I feel better again!, 2125). While her estrangement from the Greeks has the revitalizing effect of eliminating a major source of internal conflict, it also subjects Medea to the self-flagellating parental introjection that is part and parcel of her Colchian inheritance. In the ensuing crisis, the diverse components of her personality struggle for control of her. After the departure of the children, she remains calm for the length of time it takes to ask a series of nagging questions: What difference does it make if the children are with her? Must she not, in any case, endure the pain of exile? How can she leave her sons in the hands of her enemies? Is Jason any less a traitor? Is Creusa any less his bride? The line of inquiry that begins as a skeptical examination of the project of revenge soon deteriorates into a desperate lament for losses suffered as Medea imagines herself in the role of a forlorn child, bereft of family, all alone in an empty desert, dragging herself along on bloody feet (2131-35). Her divagation on the miseries of exile is abruptly interrupted as she stumbles onto a practical question of some urgency: Where will she go? This troubling thought is immediately followed by the traditional clincher: her enemies will laugh at her (2137). From this point on, the increasingly erratic measure of Medea's speech betrays the reappearance of an encroaching fury that gradually reclaims her. Reverting from the tone of bewildered child to that of vindictive parent, Medea continues to articulate her despair in interrogative structures: "Duldest du das?/ Ists nicht schon zu spät?" (Are you going to put up with that? Is it not already too late?, 2140-41). Ambiguous in content as well as in form, the words "Zu spät zum Verzeihn" (Too late to forgive, 2142) may express either the child's concession of defeat or the despot's cry of victory. In articulating the foreclosure of forgiveness, Medea seems to find a formal version of the psychic unity she so much admires in Creusa.

Though the angry patriarch is invisible, his urgent presence is audible in the hurried rhythm of Medea's speech as she anticipates the cries from the palace announcing the arrival of the poisoned gifts and heralding the advent of angry Corinthians determined to avenge the death of their princess: "Sie kommen, sie töten mich!/ Schonen auch der Kleinen nicht" (They are coming; they kill me and do not even spare the little ones!, 2147-48). In the virtual absence of a personal taskmaster, Medea attributes the murderous imperative to the operation of inevitable external exigencies. Thus, when she actually does hear the sound of tumult coming from the direction of the palace, she is persuaded that it is indeed too late to forgive:

Horch! jetzt rief's!—Helle zuckt empor!
Es ist geschehn!
Kein Rücktritt mehr!
Ganz sei es vollbracht! Fort!

(Hark! A cry! Light is flashing upwards! It has happened! No more going back! May it all come to pass! On with it.) (2149-52)

Apparently convinced that the murder of the children at the hands of the Corinthians can only be prevented by anticipatory violence, Medea goes off on her deadly errand in the manner of one who submits obediently to the dictates of an implacable destiny. Emerging shortly thereafter with a dagger in her left hand, she stands erect, holding up her right hand in an imposing gesture of command rather like the one that would be adopted by the National Socialists of the twentieth century as the notorious "Heil Hitler" salute. The clamor of her own inner voices having been drowned in blood, she stares straight ahead, the image of controlled self-possession, utterly still and silent as the Fourth Act comes to a close.

Dispensing with Medea's notorious escape in the dragon chariot and presenting Creon as unscathed by the general conflagration that kills Creusa, Grillparzer's final act is most interesting in that its structure reflects the generational conflict implicit in Medea's tragic monologue. Divided into two scenes, one devoted to the authoritarian progenitors of catastrophe and the other to their forlorn protégés, the fifth act begins with an acrimonious debate between Gora and Creon and ends with a final confrontation between Medea and Jason. Embodying an older generation of male and female representatives of Greek and Colchian factions, the king and the nurse engage in dialogue that is remarkable in depicting the highest and lowest ranking principal players as the participants in a sordid argument somewhat resembling a marital quarrel. Although Creon manages to have the last word, the class barrier separating the Corinthian monarch from the Colchian servant is blurred in a vituperative exchange that suggests that the self-appointed purveyors of moral instruction are quite unprepared to accept responsibility for their mistakes, each of them displaying great eagerness to project all of the blame onto the other party. Whereas Gora's *Schadenfreude* comes perilously close to rejoicing in murders having the commendable effect of humbling the opposition, the king abuses Gora physically in an attempt to make her confess Medea's whereabouts. Using a technique favored by child abusers because it leaves no external marks on the body, although it may cause internal injuries and bleeding in a small child, the royal personage grabs Gora and shakes her violently, threatening to shake the answer out of her along with her soul if she will not tell him what he wants to know (2223-25). With the arrival of Jason on the scene, Creon adds betrayal to the list of his offenses, dismissing his erstwhile "savior" as a source of "pollution" and abandoning him to his fate. Shortly thereafter, Creon exits wearily, declaring piously that there is work to be done (2281). Thus, the august paterfamilias last appears as an incompetent and oblivious fool who cannot wait until the ashes on his daughter's funeral pyre are cool before getting on with business as usual.

The exchange between Gora and Creon gives closure to the Corinthian disaster that is the focus of *Medea,* and the confrontation between Jason and Medea, set in a remote wilderness, brings the entire trilogy to a close. In this scene, Medea insists that she is a victim of a higher power, assuring Jason: "Ich bin ein Opfer/ Für eines andern Hand als für die deine!" (I am an offering for another hand than yours, 2307-08), so that the character who first appears in *Der Gastfreund* as a hunter exulting in her catch seems finally to have been caught by events, her last dialogue with Jason echoing ironically with the statement by her girlhood companions that "Das Opfer blutet" (The victim is bleeding). Though Jason's meeting with Medea concludes the epic adventure begun in Colchis, the substance of the final exchange between the two remains faithful to the tragic tradition in that the stricken parents insist on berating each other for their mutual losses even when there no longer seems to be any point in doing so. In this version of the hostile encounter, however, Medea displays a notably nontraditional sobriety and gravity. Whereas in treatments by Euripides, Seneca and Corneille the mythical virago exults with demonical energy as she rides off in her superhuman conveyance, Grillparzer's Medea exits a wiser and calmer woman than she has ever been. Thoroughly resigned to a wretched fate, she is far removed from the zealous hunter of *Der Gastfreund,* the impetuous lover of *Die Argonauten,* and the hopeful wife on whom the curtain rises at the beginning of *Medea,* as if, somehow, the murder of the children had purged her of all her exuberant passions. Badly scourged by events, she nevertheless goes from the position of dominated to dominating in dealing with her nemesis, and it is the measure of Jason's debasement that he must submit to instruction from a criminal wife. The radical change in Jason's fortunes is visibly manifest in this final scene, which finds the hero dragging himself along on the ground, hailing a peasant from whom he begs the most basic necessities.

Prostrate though he is, Jason has yet to comprehend the enormity of the blow that fate has dealt him, and his pompous speech contrasts ironically with his humble posture as he presents himself to the peasant: "Ich bin der Jason!/ Des Wunder-Vliesses Held! Ein Fürst! Ein König!/ Der Argonauten Führer, Jason ich" (I am Jason, the hero of the wonderful fleece, a prince, a king, the leader of the Argonauts, I Jason! 2293-95). The hero's persistent egotism is immediately apparent in that this statement begins and ends with the word *ich* and contains three separate utterances of his own name. Jason's presumption is countered by a recalcitrant interlocutor who bars his door against the suppliant and, following Creon's example, reviles him as a source of pollution (2296-97). Thus, the character who accused Medea of being a wicked, evil thing now endures the fate to which he abandoned her, even as the entire concept of pollution is discredited by the gratuitous and arbitrary basis of the accusation. Whereas the attribution of uncleanliness is dismissed as superstition, the humiliation of the conquering hero is emphatically accomplished. Not only is Jason physically prostrate throughout the entire last scene, he is literally stifled, being condemned from the moment Medea appears to listen while she speaks.

Grillparzer's sympathy for his criminal heroine is particularly evident in a final scene wherein she articulates, with a dignity contrasting markedly with Jason's maudlin whining, the philosophical principles on which the entire dramatic structure depends. In a speech reeking with pessimism, she responds to Jason's denunciation of her crime by reminding him that there are worse things than death, parrying his reproach with an accusation notable for its Stoic resonance: "Hättst du das Leben höher nicht geachtet,/ Als es zu achten ist, uns war nun anders" (If you had not regarded life as higher than it should be regarded, things would now be different for us, 2314-15). Whereas the Senecan quality of the admonition against overvaluing life is unmistakable, Medea seems to echo the Schopenhauerian description of children "condemned, not to death, but to life" (*Essential* 86) when she says: "Nicht traur ich, dass die Kinder nicht mehr sind. Ich traure, dass sie waren und dass wir sind" (I do not weep that the children are no more; I weep that they were and that we are, 2324-25). Though the pessimistic view she expresses accords well enough with the wretched state in which Medea and Jason find themselves at this point, it is arguably a culmination of the generally gloomy mood of Grillparzer's text rather than a specific response to the deaths of the children.

Presenting the essential fact of misery as essentially unchanged from the beginning of his trilogy to the end, Grillparzer departs significantly from the classical model in which one of the major characters always prospers at the expense of the other, Jason thriving while Medea languishes and vice versa. Whereas in earlier versions of the drama both characters are liable to a variety of particular hardships, such as loss of appetite, loss of reputation, loss of security, loss of love, and loss of progeny, Grillparzer's tragic conception posits life itself as the essential affliction. The classical categories of good and bad fortune do not really apply, and the ancient reversal of roles, though still in operation, acquires the quality of choreography. Thus, in Act One of *Medea,* Jason holds forth expansively while Medea defers to him meekly, but by the end of Act Five, Medea is as long-winded as Jason was in Act One while the formerly loquacious Jason is condemned to be seen and not heard. In the glow of royal favor, Jason insists that his suffering is worse than Medea's (1328), while the ultimately triumphant Medea hastens to assure Jason that her sorrow is worse than his (2345-47). The end of the tragedy finds Jason prostrate and physically distressed. A grown man crying for a drink of water, he seems to have reverted to the condition of the deprived child that was implicit all along in his constant search for affection.

Whereas Jason characteristically assumes the stance of a love-starved child and Medea that of an abused child, they are both broken in spirit by the course of disaster. Not only cut off from all affiliation and protection, Jason loses the power to control his own body, being prevented by physical debility rather than by divine intervention from avenging the deaths of his sons. Although he tries to attack Medea the moment he sees her, his limbs will not do his bidding: "O weh mir! Meine Glieder/ Versagen mir den Dienst!—Gebrochen!—Hin!" (Oh woe! My limbs refuse to serve me! Broken! Away! 2305-06). Aside from the suggestion of sexual impotence in this failure to "get satisfaction," Jason's use of the word *Gebrochen* is essential in that it underscores the pedagogical assumptions implicit in the language of the text. As if in some cosmic exercise of the wisdom according to which a child's character may be improved by breaking his or her will, Jason and Medea are both "broken" creatures who no longer expect to avoid the blows of fate and submit miserably to their punishment like naughty children caught in mischief. Neither one of them is any longer inclined to entertain the dream of happiness. The possibility of such a dream is emphatically dismissed by Medea: "Der Traum is aus, allein die Nacht noch nicht" (The dream is over but the night not yet, 2369). Thus the spirited girl who defied Aeëtes and the rebellious couple who evaded the reach of the tyrant are finally chastened by the inexorable discipline of events. Speaking for Jason as well as herself in a singularly mournful farewell, Medea also seems to voice the disappointment of an entire generation that witnessed the failure of revolution and the obstruction of reform.

Resonating not only with the pessimism of contemporary philosophical articulations but also with the grandeur of immortal poetry, Medea's speech plumbs the depths of cosmic despair: "Was ist der Erde Glück?—Ein Schatten!/ Was ist der Erde Ruhm?—Ein Traum!" (What is earthly happiness—a shadow! What is earthly glory—a dream!, 2366-67). Although her insistence on the ephemeral and inconsequential quality of human life echoes Euripides (*Medea* 1108), Seneca (*Troades* 372-408), Calderon (*La vida es sueno*), Shakespeare (*Macbeth* 5.5.23-28) and Goethe (*Werther* 13), transcending the sphere of personal delusion to cast a shadow on every familial and social ideal, Grillparzer's text ultimately subverts the peculiar perspective of his characters. Presenting a protagonist condemned to live in a world devoid of apparent divinity or meaning who nevertheless regards herself as a victim of destiny, Grillparzer questions the Schopenhauerian structure of his drama as surely as the Euripidean model deconstructs the tenets of Platonic idealism. Going beyond Medea's skeptical regard for values of the remote and recent past, the corrosove irony of Grillparzer's text also questions the reactionary rhetoric of the present moment. Medea's articulation of cosmic despair is so inconsistent with the petty machinations that have ground her down, and her troubles are so much a function of communal folly that, in the end, she seems never more clearly the product of poisonous pedagogy than when she intones the wisdom of the ages.

6

Medea in the
Twentieth Century

Although the proliferation of literary Medeas in our own age reflects the filicidal proclivities of a world described by Victor Perrera as waging "an undeclared war against its children" (25), the critical project of evaluating twentieth-century Medeas as a group is complicated by the variety of thematic concerns manifested in particular versions of the myth. Duarte Mimoso-Ruiz documents the existence of nearly a hundred treatments of the motif in this century alone, including works by German, French, English, American, Italian, Austrian, Danish, Brazilian, Russian, Swedish, Portuguese and Czech artists (209-18), and the focus of particular versions varies enormously. Whether the overt textual emphasis is on sexual ambiguity, physical abuse, sadomasochistic perversion, racial bigotry, capitalistic exploitation, or the apocalyptic vision, the theme of hostility to children remains an essential component of virtually all modern treatments of the ancient myth. For us, as for the ancient Greeks, the image of child-murder persists, both as a generic symbol of chronic disaster and as a sordid fact of life. I will argue that the number and variety of twentieth-century Medeas suggests a dynamic link between the general theme of child-murder and the specific concerns of particular texts.

The peculiar connection between ancient form and twentieth-century nightmares was eerily anticipated by Friedrich Nietzsche, whose essay, *The Birth of Tragedy*, heralds "the dawn of a new tragic age" (120-21) and whose character, Zarathustra, predicts that "henceforth children's laughter will well forth from all coffins" (*The Portable Nietzsche* 248). Probably the single most important discussion of tragic art written in modern times, *The Birth of Tragedy* posits tragic art as the issue of domestic agony, conceived in the stormy marriage of Dionysus and Apollo (19). Praising tragedy as an emanation of "the genius of the universe expressing its pain" (40) and the ancient Greeks as a people for whom "the highest pathos was but a form of aesthetic play" (134), Nietzsche marvels at the human progenitors of tragic perfection: "what suffering must this race have endured in order to achieve such beauty!" (146). Although the general tone of his meditation on tragedy, not to mention the intriguing resonance of his references to the gods as "frequenters of cruel spectacles" (*The Genealogy of Morals* 201), and to human beings as suffering on the "rack of sadistic conscience" (*Genealogy* 278), would seem to suggest the peculiar relevance of Nietzschean philosophy to the exegesis of dramatic Medeas, *The Birth of Tragedy* is an essay that vehemently reviles the author of the single most celebrated version of the ancient myth. Guilty by association with Socrates, that "daemon" and "monstrosity," Euripides is also culpable in his own right, "a bourgeois mediocrity" who dabbled in "inartistic naturalism," and created "heroes who have only counterfeit passions and speak in counterfeit speeches" (69-106). Charged with nothing less than the murder of myth itself, the "overweening Euripides" is unambiguously condemned, and the ire of the self-appointed magistrate is not mitigated by the fact that Euripides was already a well worn target in Nietzsche's day: "And though by way of punishment, Euripides has been turned into a dragon by all later critics, who can really regard this as adequate compensation?" (77). This entertaining diatribe, reflecting in its prosecutory structure the obsession with punishment implicit in the entire argument, presents an interesting problem for the present discussion: how to reconcile the enormous influence of Nietzsche's essay on tragedy with the persistence of modern writers in recreating the Euripidean drama of Medea. The question seems most relevant to the exegesis of certain decidedly Nietzschean conceptions of the myth.

The coy fin-de-siecle *Médée* presented by Catulle Mendès in Paris in 1898, with Sarah Bernhardt in the title role, is characterized by sexual predation, emotional extravagance, and flowery decor. In this play, Jason not only denies his love for Creusa, but also promises to sneak away from his young bride on their wedding night in order to be with Medea. Boasting that a virile fellow like himself, having known the love of a real woman like Medea, can hardly be tempted by the insipid charms of a child, he describes Creusa as a sweet young morsel who might appeal to an old man interested in "the innocent charms of incest" (109). Although he manages to disarm his angry wife by exciting her desire, he fails to keep the unlikely rendezvous he has arranged, and his frustrated nemesis kills the children in a spontaneous fit of rage. Whereas the emphasis on incestuous innuendo and seething sexuality in this play invite Freudian analysis, the insistence on explosive passion recalls Nietzsche's observation on the irrational nature of punishment in ages past when "culprits were not punished because they were felt to be responsible for their crimes; not, that is, on the assumption that only the guilty were to be punished; rather they were punished as parents still punish their children, out of rage at some damage suffered" (*Genealogy* 195). In this passage, the implied concept of progress is dismissed as irrelevant to the treatment of children by parents, an enterprise in which punitive impulse is presumed to prevail without modification. The image of childhood dominated by the winds of parental passion is essential for an understanding of Mendès' abrupt dénouement, the stark violence of which seems all the more shocking in the absence of the agonizing self-doubt endured by the ancient protagonist. An essentially modern feature of Mendès' scenario, the apparently unpremeditated outburst of blind fury is consistent with Nietzsche's view of the antithesis between thought and action: "Understanding kills action, for in order to act, we require the veil of illusion" (*Birth of Tragedy* 51).

The "veil of illusion" that hovers discreetly between understanding and action in Mendès' drama assumes central importance in the *Medea* by Thomas Sturge Moore. Published in 1920, in a volume called *Tragic Mothers* that also includes works entitled *Meleager* and *Niobe,* Moore's *Medea* presents a figure called the Curtain Bearer who, in the company of two Curtain Folders, performs the choral function of commenting on the action. True to their names, these characters spend much of their time on stage carrying, folding, and unfolding a curtain that recalls Nietzsche's description of tragedy as an emanation of "the desire to tear asunder the veil of Maya" (*Birth of Tragedy* 27). This reference to the Hindu concept of a godlike power to produce illusions, notable in its conflation of occidental and oriental concerns, is particularly relevant to Moore's *Medea,* a play written in the manner of the Japanese Noh drama. The author credited his friend, W. B. Yeats, with the idea of trying his hand at "this new form of drama" (Moore 3.34). In fact, Moore's *Medea* is one of many treatments of the myth that combine occidental and oriental elements, comparatively recent examples of such syntheses including the *Médée* presented by Philippe Franchini and Junji Fuseya in Paris in 1984, and the production of Euripides' *Medea* by the Japanese Toho Company at the New York Shakespeare Festival in 1986. The Medea motif may seem particularly compatible with the Noh tradition if we consider that there is a subgenre of the Noh called "madwoman pieces" (*Kyojomono*) and that both the Noh theater and ancient tragedy use traditional subject matter, masks, male performers, and choruses (*Noh Drama* 145). In Moore's *Medea*, the character who functions as the tormented exponent of "the desire to tear the veil asunder" is the filicidal mother herself. First appearing some time after the murder of her children, Medea is a devotee of Artemis and she has killed the children in order to destroy the "visible signs of her broken vow of chastity." A woman for whom the very fact of bearing children is a peculiarly problematic circumstance, Medea is the soul of remorse when she first appears in the company of a nymph named Proto to whom she confides her great longing for her sons. A short while later, upon hearing ghostly voices she recognizes as those of her deceased sons, Medea decides to bring the children back to life by means of her supernatural powers. When the phantom children learn of her conspicuously benevolent intention, they cry out in horror and pain at the prospect of being restored to life, and Medea is finally persuaded to abandon her hope of reviving them. The drama thus constitutes a playful illustration of the Schopenhauerian theme expressed by Grillparzer's Medea, that the dead are better off than the living (*Medea* 2324-25); the protagonist recalls the ancient tale, fondly cited by Nietzsche, of Silenus, who responded to the question of human possibility by stating: "What would be best for you is quite beyond your reach: not to have been born, not to be, to be nothing. But the second best is to die soon" (*Birth of Tragedy* 29).

Despite the austere philosophical underpinnings of this little play, there is a noteworthy vitality in the psychological conception of Moore's characters. Medea's repentance for her crimes is presented as stemming from a basically selfish motive: she wants to bring her sons back to life so that she can confess her crime to them and so obtain their forgiveness. As for the ghostly offspring themselves, they bear more than a little resemblance to flesh-and-blood children who tolerate the well-meaning attentions of tiresome grown-ups as best they can, though they would rather romp and play with their peers. The boys are more interested in their mother's bow and arrows than they are in her words of wisdom; they respond to her insistence on communicating with them as if she were begging them to eat their broccoli. Depicting the children as blithely cheerful mischief-makers and their mother as a deluded claimant for their affection, Moore posits the act of giving life to another as a basically selfish undertaking of dubious benefit to the recipient. In the last analysis, the drama is a well-observed and good-humored vignette demonstrating the psychology of parents and children in a manner quite consistent with Freud's remarks on the essential narcissism of most parents (*S.E.* 17:91). Like Nietzsche's observation that "parents turn children into something similar to themselves—they call that 'education' " (*Beyond Good and Evil* 107), Freud's perception of the egotistical nature of parental enterprise may seem prophetic with respect to Miller's theory of poisonous pedagogy. The impact of specifically Freudian theory on twentieth-century conceptions of tragic myth is nowhere more apparent than in the version of Medea presented by the German poet Hans Henny Jahnn (1894-1959).

Little known to English-speaking readers, Jahnn was considered by Walter Muschg to be "one of the creators of modern German literature" (Jordan 12), and his *Medea* (1926) is a remarkable articulation of starkly modern themes implicit in the Euripidean model. Presenting the violent relationship between a predatory pedophile and an African woman whose tragedy is, at least in part, the effect of racism, Jahnn's *Medea* flirts with the issues of interracial strife and sexual abuse of children while focusing insistently on such Freudian themes as oedipal rivalry, sexual ambiguity, and biology as destiny. In this play, the sons of Jason and Medea are adolescent boys, the elder of which is, like his father, infatuated by Creon's daughter. Thus the same erotic prize is sought by both father and son, and Jason's eventual betrothal to Creusa is a betrayal of both wife and son. With regard to the title role in this version of the myth, Mimoso-Ruiz observes that Medea becomes a "deviant avatar of Jocasta" (205), and the text is characterized by a pervasive sense of physical compulsion. Having saved Jason by means of her magic arts from the normal effects of the aging process, Medea has, for some unexplained reason, neglected to secure any such advantage for herself and therefore, in her middle age, must contend with Jason's constant whining about the relentless needs of his youthful body (Jahnn 54). Whereas Medea's contribution to the problem seems, like the love potion in *Tristan and Isolt* (Loomis and Loomis, 88-232), an obvious device for explaining what would have happened anyway, Jason's loss of interest in Medea is presented as a result of biological imperatives. While her husband pursues a teen-aged girl, Medea mourns for the loss of her youth and beauty, suffering so apparently from sexual frustration that the drama assumes the quality of a fatal confrontation between unrestrained male libido and raging female hormones.

Not content to evoke the Freudian themes of oedipal rivalry and biology as destiny, Jahnn also expands on the implications of sexual ambiguity which are inherent in his ancient sources. Pervaded by suggestions of homosexual intrigue and desire, Jahnn's *Medea* is a play in which the most noteworthy expressions of affection occur between male characters. There is a peculiarly tormented and sensual quality in the verbal interaction between the two brothers, and Jason himself is not insensitive to the charm of attractive males in his vicinity, observing that "Medea's house is full of good-looking men but not good-looking women" (Jahnn 17). Medea's ultimate violence is not only as spontaneous and explosive as that of Mendès' heroine, but is also a direct reaction to the expression of homoerotic affection between her sons. Upon walking into a bedroom, she finds the boys locked in a mutual embrace and stabs them to death. Although the belief that men are peculiarly inclined to philandering indulgences, like the assumption that women are especially disposed to fits of punitive violence, is entirely consistent with the theme of biology as destiny, the action of the play undermines the sexist implications of the text by suggesting that pernicious misogyny and defensive male bonding derive from the same socially constructed familial constellation that generates murderous rage toward children.

The bonded male couple is a recurring configuration in Jahnn's work (Jordan 17) and is also inherent in the mythical material from which the tragedy of Medea derives. In Apollonius'

Argonautica, Hercules is so bereaved when his male lover drowns in the Spring of Pegae that he abandons the expedition (1.1207-1357). The conspicuous role of homosexuality in ancient Greek culture prompts Slater to observe that "pederasty was far from being a trivial byproduct of Greek society; it became an almost vital institution, diluting the mother-son pathology, counteracting the rivalry between father and son, and providing a substitute father-son bond" (59). Although his argument that the "male child was at one and the same time a scapegoat for and an antidote to the penis-envy of the mother" (30-31) clearly refers to the context of Euripidean drama, it is also relevant to the Freudian dynamics of Jahnn's *Medea,* which presents maternal violence and male homosexuality as virtually inseparable phenomena. A possible link between homosexuality and certain patterns of parenting has also been suggested by Dorothy Bloch, who presents case histories of children for whom the fantasy that they belonged to the opposite sex functioned as a defense against violence (50-60). In a study entitled "The Jocasta Complex: Mothering and Genius," Matthew Besdine traces both homosexuality and genius to a type of family "whose core is dominated by the affect-hungry mother and by the absent, inept, distant, or aloof father" (259-77, 574-600). The very title of Besdine's essay might suggest the probability of homosexual import in a text wherein the myths of Medea and Jocasta are as deliberately conflated as in Jahnn's *Medea.* Yet the familial dynamic Besdine describes is the essential pattern of virtually all tragic Medeas, most of which focus, at least ostensibly, on heterosexual relations. In the last analysis, the brutal and sensational quality of Jahnn's *Medea* has little to do with the benign bonding between the sons, or, for that matter, with anything remotely resembling consensual adult homosexuality. The disquieting effect of the action inheres rather in its insistence on the unrestrained extravagance of sexual perversion in the adult characters.

Louise Kaplan's definition of a perversion as a "psychological strategy" demanding a "performance," the enactment of which "is designed to help the person survive, moreover to survive with a sense of triumph over the traumas of his or her childhood" (10) is probably relevant to the tragedy of Medea in all its forms. The fabulous golden objects—the fleece, the gown and the headband—like the treasure chest in Grillparzer's *Medea,* are magical emblems replete with fetishistic implications. The sexual sadism that Kaplan posits as inherent in the physical abuse of children (26) is spectacularly visible in the Senecan version of the tragedy, and the perverse potential of disciplinary ideologies, linked by Kaplan with the peculiarly modern family wherein "the abuse of children [is] justified in the name of advancing human progress" (427) is abundantly visible in the texts of both Corneille and Grillparzer. But the sadistic compulsion of the mother who kills her sons out of homophobic rage, like the pedophilic perversity of the father who is attracted to children of both

sexes, is mercilessly illuminated in Jahnn's *Medea,* a text that seems
lucidly comprehensible in terms of Kaplan's assertion that the
pedophile is not so much attracted "toward children" as he is "drawn
away from the adult female body" (437). In his loathing for Medea,
Jason seems analogous to the heterosexual Humbert Humbert, who
marries the mother of the twelve-year-old girl he desires. Once
married to Charlotte, Humbert endures the "heavy hips, round knees,
ripe bust, the coarse pink of her neck . . . and all the rest of that sorry
and dull thing: a handsome woman" (Nabokov 68). Psychoanalytic
emphasis on the connection between misogyny and pedophilia is
particularly interesting with regard to the fact that the figure of Medea
has been conflated, not only with that of Jocasta, but also with that of
Lolita.

     Robert Duncan's *Medea at Kolchis, the Maiden Head,*
presented at Berkeley in 1965, ten years after the publication of
Nabokov's *Lolita,* transposes the turbulent romance of the ancient
Argonautica epics to a twentieth-century university town. Consistent
with the culture of the sixties, the essential dramatic tension of this
play inheres in the antagonism between upstart adolescents and an
older generation represented by a garrulous old housekeeper and her
employer, Arthur, a curmudgeonly poet who plays a role roughly
analogous to that of the ancient Aeëtes. Arthur's pubescent daughter, a
girl between twelve and sixteen years of age, is named, improbably
enough, Medea. The younger generation also includes an aspiring
young poet named Jason, who arrives as the play begins, seeking a
mentor in the aging bard. The narcissistic encounter between the older
and the younger personae of the poet are short-circuited by the
intervention of the girl, who falls passionately in love with Jason.
When she steals the trophy symbolizing her father's poetic prowess,
Arthur has a heart attack and Jason elopes with the tempting child who
offers to fulfill all of his most urgent desires and ambitions. This
quintessentially "revolutionary" scenario, presented at the midpoint of
a decade notorious for youthful rebellion, in a town that witnessed its
share of militant demonstrations, may seem far enough removed from
the claustrophobic volatilities of Jahnn's tragedy, yet Duncan's Medea
resembles the adolescent sons of Jahnn's tragedy in the conspicuous
precocity of her sexual appetite.

     The particular refinement of sexual abuse by which the adult
male is encouraged to regard the immature object of his desire as
inviting an erotic embrace has been explored by Florence Rush, who
cites the film *Lolita* as a typical example of works in which "pubescent
girls" are positioned so that "corruption emanates directly from
themselves rather than [from] an invading spirit." Rush notes that
interest in the "sexy little girl" was particularly evident in the
mannequins of the 1960s, when "small, childish and infantile was
beautiful" and women who shopped in elegant shops "could hardly
find costumes long enough to cover their private parts" (126-29). To

the degree that Duncan's *Medea,* in whom "the girl's obsessive passion [prefigures] the woman's wrathful jealousy" (Duncan 43) seems to participate in the stereotype of the "inherently evil female child" (Rush 132), the character reflects abusive contemporary stereotypes that Rush places under the rubric of "the eroticization of the child." Her argument, suggesting that the derivation of an ideal of "platonic love" from such a text as the *Symposium* entails a large measure of denial, is consistent with Slater's observation that "Greek homosexuality had . . . a decidedly nonreciprocal quality, consisting of an older lover who pursued, protected, and gave, and a younger love-object who received, begged, and simply existed as a beautiful object" (58). Whereas Slater's observation is ostensibly concerned with homosexuality, his remarks on the nonreciprocal quality of sexual relations between adults and children may apply to heterosexual as well as homosexual relations between adults and children. The twentieth-century conception of the Argonautica romance as an encounter between a sexually aggressive girl-child and a hesitant, faltering young man reflects a perverse strategy for exonerating the adult participant in an essentially abusive relationship.

An interesting perspective on the sexy children, wicked women, and narcissistic men presented in the plays by Jahnn and Duncan is provided by Pier Paolo Pasolini's film *Medea,* released in 1969, with Maria Callas in the starring role. Like Duncan's play, Pasolini's film deals with elements of the Argonautica myth, tracing the adventures of Jason and Medea from the first encounter in Colchis to the notorious disaster in Corinth. Also like Duncan, Pasolini uses the myth of Medea as a vehicle for articulating antipatriarchal passions, his "tragic martyrs" having been described by Naomi Greene as "rebels against the social order" (165). While the play enacted in Berkeley presents the spectacle of an adolescent couple striking down the scion of adult authority, the cinematic version of the same events focuses relentlessly on violence against the young. There is a prolonged and astonishing enactment of ritual human sacrifice in the film that might serve to illustrate a passage from *The Golden Bough* (Frazier 503-05). Against an exquisite Mediterranean landscape, an attractive young fellow is led by his companions to an altar where, with all due ceremony, he is tied to a cross and hacked into little pieces. This scene, admired by Massimo Canevacci as a "masterpiece of visual anthropology" (Greene 127), is described by Greene as a "symbol for the entire film" (149). Mimoso-Ruiz praises Pasolini for his inspired deployment of sacred and ritual elements, describing *Medea* as a work "in which traditional psychology does not exist, and in which objects and gestures bear great importance . . . in describing the behavior of primitive beings" (70). Though Pasolini's depiction of human sacrifice may have the salutory effect of counterbalancing sentimental notions about the nature of characters associated with ancient fertility rituals, it also contributes to a problematic dehumanization of the female protagonist.

Since Pasolini credited Euripides as the inspiration for his screenplay (Snyder 194), the decidedly anti-Euripidean quality of the dichotomy between the "civilized" and the "primitive" in this film is worth noting. Although the Argonauts are presented, appropriately enough, as a bunch of coarse marauders, they constitute only a small part of the Greek enterprise in this work. Much more essential to the director's vision is the bond between the child, Jason, and the kindly Centaur who raises him. Comparable to the relationship between Jahnn's brothers and Duncan's poets, the intimacy between Jason and his teacher is the most important alliance between any two characters in this film. The philosophical dialogue between older and younger males is presented as a model of civilized human discourse, complementing the overtly heterosexual plot with a discreetly homosexual commentary. Greene's assertion that homosexual passion lurks "like a film beneath a film" (163) in this *Medea* is particularly interesting with respect to the voice-over dialogue between mentor and protégé that interprets the action. Certain long sequences, especially those occurring in Colchis, are presented as the fulfillment of ritual events by mute participants. Whereas the Greeks engage in verbal intercourse, the Colchians enact their savage rituals in a wild and wordless landscape. Architectural structures also serve to delineate the gap between the "civilized" Greeks and the "primitive" Colchians. The latter seem to live in huts and caves, while the Corinthians inhabit elegant stone buildings. There is clearly no room in Pasolini's conception of the gulf between the rational, progressive Greeks and the religious, womb-bound Colchians, for the fabulous ancient palace of Aeëtes, or for the fact that Euripides presents Colchian and Greek characters as equally articulate, comparably cultured, and equivalently socialized. The irony of ancient tragedy would seem to be a casualty of the transition from stage to film.

The assertion that "traditional psychology does not exist" in Pasolini's *Medea* is essentially problematic. To be sure, the figure of Medea is irremediably flattened out by the omission or abridgment of such elements as the sympathetic prologue by the Nurse, all references to broken vows, Medea's address to the Corinthian women, and the celebrated scene in which the mother endures her agony of indecision. With all due respect to the fact that film is a visual medium, a Medea deprived of speech is a Medea deprived of character. Although Pasolini's savage priestess is by no means speechless, she lacks the characteristic eloquence of the Euripidean model, and the dissociation between human speech and tragic action in this film leaves the plot teetering on the brink of incoherence. It is ultimately incredible that, in a community where public life is defined by such fierce rites as Pasolini envisages, the inexorable demands of group belief would allow the kind of autonomy that the director attributes to his Medea. With regard to this problem, Stephen Snyder observes that "every one is, in a sense, the sacrificial victim in the rite of spring, for the prevailing constraint upon motion is indeed a constraint upon individuation and personal identity" (97). All the more reason to be amazed when, almost immediately after the above-mentioned "rite of spring," Medea slinks off with an evidently untroubled countenance, capriciously steals the golden fleece from its sanctuary, and hands it over to Jason. Though it is evidently Jason's arrival that inspires Medea to defy the limits of tradition, Pasolini's depiction of the radical split between the culture of Colchis and that of Greece does not contribute to the credibility of the event, and the portrayal of Medea as an isolated loner who acts independently of any social order lends her qualities of invulnerability and omnipotence that are entirely consistent with the project of demonizing the character.

Pasolini's *Medea* is a misogynistic projection of infantile hostility operating in a world where men are sociable and attractive celebrants of life while women are negative, withholding harpies, unless they happen to be virginal princesses. In this film, Jason is, for the most part, a flirtatious and fun-loving fellow who, after arriving in Greece, is captured by the camera at a distance, reveling among graceful dancers. Medea, on the other hand, broods silently and alone, the image of the witch, glowering maliciously and menacingly into the camera at close range. Pasolini's perspective on his characters corresponds curiously enough to that of a child growing up in the kind of family described by Matthew Besdine: the father is seen from a comfortable distance, in the midst of various associates, and the mother appears up close, in all the intensity of a suffocating intimacy. Thus, cinematic technique defines the general outlook of the entire work, in which Centaur, man, and boy emerge as idealized human figures while woman remains the earth-bound enemy. To say that there is "no traditional psychology" at work in the distribution of these roles would seem to beg the question; it is tantamount to suggesting that misogyny is the natural order of things. There is, on the contrary, a readily discernible psychology in this work and it is indistinguishable from the one which Rheingold presents in his meditation on the "miasmal malignity" and "subtle sadism" of women (132). In fact, there has probably never been a more serenely and complacently malevolent Medea than Pasolini's savage virago. Before killing the children, she bathes them with the utmost maternal solicitude, and when one of them resists her, she coaxes him with honeyed words. Then, without discernible hesitation or doubt, she dries them off, dresses them for bed, rocks them lovingly in her arms and kills them in their sleep. Focusing on a figure of blood-curdling cruelty and treachery, Pasolini's film is, like Jahnn's tragedy, a text that underscores the dynamic link between the sadistic mother and defensive male bonding.

Whereas the essentializing implications inherent in the opposition of male "civilization" and female "barbarism" are tiresome, the directorial insistence on feminine cruelty is nevertheless relevant to the role that patriarchal systems have always reserved for some women. Beginning and ending with brutal mutilations of young male bodies, Pasolini's film inevitably recalls Kaplan's emphasis on the sexual sadism implicit in physical abuse, as well as Greven's observation that "sadomasochism among adults often involves the repetition and reenactment of childhood experiences" (180). In view of the conspicuous role of the Church in Italian public life, Pasolini's explicit insistence on the link between religious ritual and female violence has, moreover, the iconoclastic effect of depicting Medea as an inversion of the blessed Mary. In positing the destroying woman as the essential core of a disintegrating social order, Pasolini anticipates the scathing satire of the parodic *Medea* presented by the Ridiculous Theatrical Company in New York in 1987.

The script for the Ridiculous *Medea* was written in 1984 by Charles Ludlam, the founder of the company, but was not performed until three years later, about six months after the author died of AIDS. *Medea* was, in fact, the company's first official production after Ludlam's death. Famous for playing the female lead in his irreverent versions of such classics as *Camille* and *Salammbô*, Ludlam recoiled from playing the part of Medea because the "notion of killing his own children was too disturbing" (802). The author's evident misgivings with regard to the project of exploiting the tragedy of child-murder for comic effect are paradoxically commensurate with his intuitive grasp of the comic potential inherent in the theme of hostility to children. In fact, his Medea enters snarling, "I hate you children," and exits boasting that she has killed the children because she hated Jason more than she loved her sons (812). The comic quality of this tragic horror depends partly on the incongruously ultra-colloquial speech of the Ridiculous players. Confronted with Jason's spurious self-defense, Medea exclaims: "This is the pits!" Yet the peculiar tone of the work is most conspicuous in borrowings from Euripides that derive special significance from the Ridiculous context, as when the essentially sacrilegious complaint of the ancient Jason, that "there should have been some other way for mortals to beget children, and there should not have been a female kind" (573-74) becomes, in the Ridiculous version, an aggressively profane version of the company's most characteristic joke: "Oh God, if only men could find another way to beget children, they could do away with women altogether" (806). Like any inspired conception of classical myth, Ludlam's *Medea* tends to expose layers of meaning that are latent in the ancient model.

Whereas the Euripidean tragedy might serve to illuminate Kaplan's claim that "normalized gender stereotypes are the crucibles of perversion" (14), the Ridiculous *Medea* affirms the subversive assertion by Valerie Solanas, that "the only honest males are transvestites and drag queens" (Kaplan 357). The deliberate deconstruction of traditional gender roles is immediately apparent in the transvestite casting: in the 1987 production, Black-Eyed Susan and Everett Quinton alternated in the roles of Medea and the Nurse, so that each female role was played by a man in drag every other night. Though the degree to which this technique is "nontraditional" may be questionable in view of the theatrical conventions of ancient Athens, where all female roles were played by male actors, the distance between the reverent context of ancient tragedy and the iconoclastic enthusiasm of the Ridiculous Company is nevertheless an essential source of parodic ambiguity. In Ludlam's version, Jason's breathtaking hostility toward Medea is comic precisely because it is undisguised and exuberant rather than furtive and hypocritical. While the macho denial of the Euripidean Jason barely conceals the diffuse desire simmering beneath his cover of smug propriety, the unapologetic spite of the Ridiculous Jason gleefully celebrates the erotic origin of aggression. Finally, the contradiction between overt piety and covert perversity in the ancient drama tends, in the gay parody, to be abolished by a procedure that collapses the distinctions between public and private, pious and perverse, male and female. The significance of Ludlam's text is ultimately inseparable from the troubled context in which the play was first performed.

Six years into a dreadful epidemic that struck the male homosexual community with disproportionate severity, Ludlam's death confronted his many admirers with a grim reminder of an essential public issue. In this work, the sense of looming catastrophe is only thinly veiled by the cloak of black humor. The logic of scapegoating, inherent in the ancient tragedy, is peculiarly relevant to the modern health crisis, in which the difficulty of implementing an effective campaign of education and prevention is augmented by the public perception of disease as a scourge of minorities such as homosexuals and drug abusers. The way in which homophobia and denial have contributed to an inherently formidable organizational problem is a matter of record (Perrow and Guillén 1-44). Thus, in October 1986, at a time when the epidemic had already claimed the lives of thousands of people, six hundred of whom were children, an initiative urging sex education for school children inspired virulent indignation in parents who evidently preferred that young people should die rather than be tainted by the iniquity of sexual activity. The figure of Phyllis Schlafly, fuming that "the American people will not put up with teaching safe sodomy in the classroom" (Weintraub) lends a disconcerting topicality to the ancient virago who appears in the Ridiculous satire, and the suggestion by certain fundamentalists that AIDS is a scourge by which God punishes the sinful represents the dismal emergence in public affairs of the punitive logic of child abuse. By exaggerating the demonic aspect of the parental avenger and presenting a drama in which the strategic murder of children makes about as much sense as the irrational response to the AIDS epidemic, Ludlam ridicules the obscene claim that human suffering is the effect of cosmic wrath.

Although the subversive implications of the Ridiculous *Medea* may be somewhat illuminated by reference to disquieting aspects of the contemporary context, they actually extend beyond the bounds of particular civic issues. As a drama in which the only event recognizable as perverse or unnatural is the self-righteous revenge of a controlling parent whose gender is ultimately both ambiguous and irrelevant, the satire deconstructs the conservative assumptions inherent in such dualistic oppositions as perverse/normal and natural/unnatural. For all its provocative masquerade and kinky innuendo, the Ridiculous *Medea* is most distinguished from works by Jahnn, Duncan, and Pasolini in that it contains no suggestion of sexual intercourse between adults and children, thus implying that the free expression of sexuality among responsible adults is the best safeguard against the perversion of relationships between adults and children. Louise Kaplan's patently Freudian assertion that "all children are little perverts" (220) reveals, moreover, the psychoanalytic basis of the link between homophobia and hostility to children that is inherent in the Ridiculous text. In decrying homosexuals, the persecutor projects onto a human scapegoat qualities which are intolerable precisely because they have been aggressively routed out of his or her childish self. Thus, homophobia derives from the fundamental process by which the anger engendered in the punished child "is transformed with time into a more or less conscious hatred directed against the self or substitute persons" (Greven 126). The dynamics of scapegoating in versions of *Medea* by Jahnn, Duncan, Pasolini, and Ludlam are related to the specific antagonisms generated by the coercive construction of gender-role identity in the bosom of the modern bourgeois family. Though the distance between the peculiarly Freudian emphasis of the earliest of these works and the scathing social commentary implicit in the last may seem enormous, the basic concerns which they all share tend to valorize Nietzsche's observation that "madness is rare in individuals—but in groups, parties, nations and ages it is the rule" (*Beyond Good and Evil* 90). The Ridiculous *Medea* is a salient example of the continuing relevance of the ancient logic of the scapegoat to the social sickness of the twentieth century.

Homophobia and racism, which both contributed to the spread of AIDS in the 1980s (Perrow and Guillén 1-9), are thematically linked in Jahnn's *Medea,* in which the African protagonist who is ostracized because of her race and gender vents her rage on offspring whose racial and sexual identity is ambiguous. In the decade following Jahnn's presentation of this portentous tragedy, a period characterized by global economic crisis, a flourishing Ku Klux Klan in the United States, and the ascent to power of notorious bigots in European nations, the theme of child-murder was linked to that of racism in several transpositions of ancient myth to modern context. In France, Henri-René Lenormand presented a play called *Asie* (*Asia*) (1931), in which an Indo-Chinese princess married to a French adventurer kills her sons when their father abandons her for the blond daughter of a colonial official. In the United States, Countee Cullen, the "poet laureate" of the Harlem Renaissance, published a "translation" of the Euripidean tragedy in which an African woman is betrayed by a white man (1935), and Maxwell Anderson wrote *The Wingless Victory* (1936), a drama in which the daughters of a Malaysian princess and a New England sea captain are persecuted by their father's countrymen and finally killed by their desperate mother. Though the theme of the interracial marriage, essential to Grillparzer's tragedy, is implicit in the ancient opposition between Greek and barbarian, literary insistence on the noxious effects of racism was particularly conspicuous in literary versions of Medea produced in the decade preceding the Holocaust.

A dramatist who enjoyed remarkable success in France during the period between the two world wars, Henri-René Lenormand (1882-1951) set his version of the myth of Medea in the context of growing antagonism between French colonizers and their Indochinese subjects. Presenting the encounter between an enterprising Frenchman and the daughter of the King of the Sibangs, a people compared by Robert Emmett Jones with those portrayed by Malraux in *Les Conquérants* (*The Conquerors*), *Asie* is notable for the sensitivity of its characterizations. Both the princess Katha Naham Moun, and Aimée de Listrac, her rival for the affections of the wheeler-dealer, De Mezzana, are dynamic and sympathetic female characters; the sons of De Mezzana and the princess act like real children and not miniature adults. Their particular dilemma is immediately apparent in that each of them has two names; Vincent and Julien in polite society, they are called Apait and Saida by their mother. The psychological acuity of the work is apparent in the conflicting loyalties of the doomed children, whose characteristic squabbling reflects the continual quarreling between their parents. Vincent tends to defend his father, while Julien regularly takes his mother's side (Lenormand 53, 135). The racist implications of the recurring domestic disputes are apparent in De Mezzana's frank determination to make "white boys" out of these "two little lost monkeys whimpering on the edge of the forest" (41). The representative quality of De Mezzana's racism is, moreover, underscored by reception accorded to the little boys when they arrive in France. Accompanied by Aimée on a visit to their new school, the children are mocked by the science teacher, who entertains the other members of the class with snide remarks about "exotic fauna" (*la faune exotique*). Thus encouraged, the white children snicker with amusement, casting sidelong glances at their guests while the "poisonous pedagogue" takes vicarious pleasure in the cruelties he inspires (73). In short, the brutality of the colonial order is so vividly depicted in this play that the mother's fierce resolve to save her sons from becoming "the lackeys of monsters" seems entirely credible, effectively preparing the way for her decision to kill them. After poisoning her children, she leaps to her death from a great height.

It is quite possible that *Asie* was known to Cullen, who earned his living as a French teacher and spent a good deal of time in France between 1926 and 1938 (Perry 8-14). Although the idea of an interracial Medea may have been suggested by Lenormand's play, it was nevertheless consistent with contemporary American interest in the themes of mixed marriage and racial injustice, Langston Hughes' *Mulatto* having proved to be a great success on Broadway in the 1935-36 season. While Cullen's *Medea* is essentially faithful to the spirit of the Euripidean tragedy, his departures from the ancient model are worth noting. He reduces the size of the chorus to only a couple of women, omits Medea's speech to the Corinthian women, and eliminates literary allusions likely to be unfamiliar to the modern American audience. Except for the choral interludes, set to music by Virgil Thomson, Cullen's *Medea* is, like Lenormand's, written in prose. Though information about early productions of the work is scarce, the publication of the text provoked reactions ranging from racist condescension to liberal enthusiasm. In the *New York Times*, Peter Monro Jack called the work "an interesting experiment in reducing a Greek tragedy to the content and colloquialism of a folk tale with characteristic Negro sentiment and rhythm," while Philip Blair Rice observed, in *The Nation,* that "Mr. Cullen has rendered Euripides' best known tragedy into living and utterable English. If there is to be a popular revival of interest in the Greek drama, it appears that this is more likely to originate in Harlem than in the universities." More recently, in an anthology of African American writers, Richard Barksdale and Keneth Kinnamon dismiss the play as a portrait of a "great woman whose story has nothing to do with race or social doctrine" (529). Though a full account of the fluctuations in Cullen's critical stock is beyond the scope of this essay, the reception of his *Medea* is generally consistent with Shucard's observation that contemporary critics "were too gentle with Cullen for non-poetic reasons" and "Afro-American critics of the 1960s . . . [were] too harsh with him" (26).

In retrospect, it seems fair to suggest that the importance of Cullen's *Medea* lies neither in the likelihood of its generating a surge of enthusiasm for classical drama nor in the extraordinary quality of its portraiture, but in the achievement of a complex and significant cultural synthesis. No mere tribute to the art of Euripides, the text is an expression of fundamental autobiographical and social concerns. Himself an abandoned child who was initially raised by a woman who was probably his grandmother and later adopted by the Reverend Frederick Asbury Cullen, the poet probably found in Euripides' forlorn protagonist an objective correlative for peculiarly personal experiences and anxieties. Medea may represent Cullen's own abandoned mother, the son she deserted when his father disappeared, or the troubled adult inheritor of a childhood haunted by experiences of desertion and abandonment. Reputed to have been more interested in the company of men than of women (Lewis 76-77), Cullen may have identified with Medea as the spurned object of a male lover. His interest in the myth was no casual matter; in addition to the text published in 1935, he also wrote a prologue dealing with the young lovers in Colchis and an epilogue set in Athens at the court of Aegeus twenty years after the murders in Corinth (*My Soul's High Song* 570-601). These additions underscore the theme of filicide in several ways. To begin with, the appearance of Absyrtus as a boy of ten or twelve in the prologue lends a chilling quality to Medea's allusion, in the epilogue, to her brother's death and dismemberment (600). In the epilogue, Cullen also presents an invented character named Pandion, Medea's son and Aegeus' heir. On the eve of assuming power in Athens, Pandion is suddenly killed by an old sailor who turns out to be Jason, determined to avenge the murder of his sons. His project backfires when Medea reveals that Pandion was really Jason's son and not Aegeus'. Finally, the roles of Absyrtus and Pandion in the expanded version of the play, which Cullen called *Byword for Evil* (Early 76), emphasize the central importance of murderous hostility toward children. The peculiar significance of Cullen's drama inheres, however, in the interracial structure of his plot.

The critical inclination to dismiss this play as irrelevant to African American concerns is inconsistent with Cullen's conspicuous involvement in contemporary social issues (Lumpkin 114), not to mention the evidence of his entire literary oeuvre. The themes treated in *Medea* are those that interested him throughout his life. In poems such as "Heritage," "Atlantic City Waiter," and "Pagan Prayer," he expressed the sense of alienation characteristic of the exile and the malaise of the displaced "pagan" in a smugly "civilized" society (Baker 32). In "The Ballad of the Brown Girl, an Old Ballad Retold," he depicted the tragic marriage of an African princess and a white aristocrat from Kentucky. The interracial *Medea* is, indeed, such a logical development in Cullen's career that it is tempting to regard the critical neglect of the text as being somehow related to the problem posed by the Euripidean denouement. The very wording of Barksdale and Kinnamon's judgment that Medea "has nothing to do either with race or sccial doctrine" recalls Page's insistence that "the act of infanticide is entirely outside our experience, we . . . know nothing of it."

The social significance of Cullen's *Medea* is evident not only in the broad outlines of the confrontation between his white adventurer and his bereaved African, but also in the details of his text, a single example of which may serve to demonstrate the point. When, in his final meeting with Medea, Jason curses his nemesis, he exclaims:

"Would that your mother's milk had been poison in your mouth and killed you at her breast!" (300). This retroactive curse, which is absent from the Euripidean text, recalls an episode from Harriet Beecher Stowe's *Uncle Tom's Cabin* in which the character Cassie, herself the daughter of a white master and a black slave, reacts to a history of betrayal and abuse by feeding laudanum to the child she has borne her current master. Holding the baby to her breast, she lulls it to sleep, once and for all. The reference to the doomed mulatto child is doubly relevant to the action of Cullen's tragedy, because it emphasizes both the plight of the abandoned woman and her child's vulnerability to abuse. Insisting poignantly on the nightmare of African American history, Cullen's *Medea* conflates the themes of filicide and racism in an indictment of peculiarly American traditions. Ultimately, the denial of social interest in the content of the play seems curiously inconsistent with the fact that the text was first published in a volume containing one of Cullen's angriest poems, "Scottsboro, Too, Is Worth Its Song."

The final poem in *Medea and Some Poems* is a bitter complaint about a generation of writers who, having made a cause celebre of Sacco and Vanzetti in the 1920s, remained comparatively quiet about the case of the Scottsboro boys in the 1930s. In "Not Sacco and Vanzetti" (*On These I Stand* 103), Cullen himself deplored the "legal infamy" that led to the execution, in 1927, of two Italian immigrants for murders they were accused of committing in 1920. Upton Sinclair's novel, *Boston* (1928), and Maxwell Anderson's play, *Winterset* (1935), reflect the widespread view that the case against the defendants had more to do with their radical politics and their ethnic origins than with the meager evidence against them. When, in 1931, an Alabama court indicted seven black men on charges of raping two white women, and all seven defendants were subsequently condemned to death, there was no such wave of indignation in the contemporary literary community, although African Americans had been systematically excluded from the jury that condemned the alleged offenders. Whether Maxwell Anderson's *The Wingless Victory,* produced at the Empire Theater in New York the year following the publication of Cullen's *Medea,* was a spontaneous reaction to current events or a belated response to the charge of apathy, the play focuses sharply on the issue of racial prejudice.

Anderson's transposition of the ancient myth of Medea to a modern setting unfolds in the town of Salem, Massachusetts, in the year 1800. Though the time frame of the action affords a certain amount of aesthetic distance, the choice of Massachusetts as the site of tragic conflict underscores the essential themes of bigotry and persecution: the drama occurs in the home of the notorious Salem witchcraft trials, in the same state, moreover, that had recently witnessed the "legal infamy" of the Sacco and Vanzetti executions. A reference to the Scottsboro case is implicit in the basic assumption on which *The Wingless Victory* is based—that the mere suggestion of sexual intercourse between blacks and whites is enough to destroy the facade of decency displayed by ordinary white Americans. The alterations Anderson makes in the traditional plot and his treatment of character tend, in general, to emphasize the communal responsibility for ultimate disaster.

Both Jason's liaison with the local princess and Medea's revenge against the royal family are eliminated from this version. Anderson's "Jason," the New England sea captain, Nathaniel McQueston, and his "Medea," the Malaysian Oparre, are destroyed by social pressures that seem to be as banal as they are irresistible. Though there is a hint of potential intimacy between Nathaniel and a neighbor who confesses that she had a crush on him before he set out for the South Seas, Nathaniel does not betray Oparre for another woman. Unfortunately, he does make the mistake of expecting her to live with his bigoted family, the members of which are frankly apalled by Nathaniel's dark-skinned wife. Both his mother and his brother, the minister Phineas McQueston, are persuaded by the rich cargo in the hull of the ship after which the play is named to "tolerate" Oparre and her children. Nathaniel himself not only puts up with the mean-spirited townspeople, but foolishly tries to win their acceptance by lending money to a number of his neighbors. When the news arrives that his wealth was obtained by shady dealings, the altruistic Puritans offer to strike up a deal: Nathaniel may remain in Salem with impunity if he will only agree to ship his wife and children out. Enraged by the hypocrisy and greed of Phineas, who insists that he is only interested in saving his brother's soul but stands to gain everything if Nathaniel leaves, Nathaniel gives in. Initially agreeing to send Oparre and the children away rather than let his brother "win," he later repents and decides to sacrifice everything for love. When he reaches Oparre on board the ship, however, she has already divided up the contents of a vial of poison among herself and the children. Nathaniel and Oparre reaffirm their love for each other while she lies dying in his arms. Thus, in Anderson's treatment of the myth, individual antagonists are ultimately absolved while the institutional bigotry of a quintessentially American community is condemned.

As the curtain rises on the first act, a pregnant maid, determined to protect her lover, is vilified by a group of sanctimonious church elders in a scenario that recalls the colonial New England context of Hawthorne's *Scarlet Letter*. When the girl complains that the town's severity to her will probably result in the death of her child, Phineas replies that he "can make no distinction between the sin and the fruits of the sin" (5). The theme of religion as a child-devouring monster is later articulated by Oparre herself, who accuses the Puritans of worshipping the "Moloch and Jahveh" of the Old Testament (109). In the final act, alone with her children and servant in the cabin of the ship, she foresees a wretched future for her outcast daughters, imagining that they will be shunned as "half-breeds" and doomed to spend their lives "in the brothels of the East" (118). At this point, the originality of Anderson's depiction of the abandoned children as girls is worth noting. This strategic revision, evidently designed to augment the credibility to Oparre's decision to kill her daughters, is based on the dubious assumption that death is preferable to prostitution. It is also an important departure from a sexist tradition lamenting the loss of male children in a world where "excess female mortality" is a perennial fact of life. In any case, Anderson's treatment of the ancient myth begins and ends with reminders of the ways in which patriarchal hierarchies engender the exploitation and abuse of women and children.

Although *The Wingless Victory* had a respectable run of 110 performances, and Katharine Cornell was acclaimed in the role of Oparre, the play was not blessed with critical favor. Consideration of the relationship between dramatic text and social context was conspicuously absent from the contemporary review by Brooks Atkinson, who described the play as a "melodrama in verse" when it opened. The tendency of academic critics to echo his negative precedent is evident in essays by Alfred S. Shivers, who dismisses the work with the observation that "the third act is, of course, sheer melodrama" (105) and Mabel Driscoll Bailey, who regrets that the play's "unity of tone is damaged by a greater emphasis on race tensions than the romance requires" (142). Atkinson's comment that "to the Salem pietist, a Malay princess is black flesh and an offense to heaven" suggests, moreover, that the critical establishment that consigned Anderson's play to the dust heap was part of the problem that the writer set out to attack. In fact, Atkinson describes the theme of the play as "religious bigotry," and the forces that destroy Oparre and her children as "villainy" or the "finger of fate," treading lightly over the problem of racial bigotry despite the circumstance that the community depicted by Anderson is one in which a man asks his brother: "How do you wipe the smell off when you wake up in the morning?" (33). Never mentioning such words as *racism* and *racist*, the critic merely deplores the cruelty of the townspeople toward the foreign woman as a kind of aesthetic excess presumably inseparable from the "melodramatic" quality of the work.

In retrospect, even certain positive comments about the play seem problematic. Mabel Driscoll Bailey's claim that "Oparre is magnificent" (143) notwithstanding, the character's inclination to turn the other cheek may seem excessive to a late twentieth-century reader. On the other hand, the assertion that Nathaniel is unworthy of tragic treatment because "he acquired his wealth by piracy" (Bailey 143) suggests a certain naïveté with regard to both the ancient antecedents and the modern analogues of Anderson's drama. Aside from the general difficulty of distinguishing the activities of Argonauts from those of pirates, the spiritual kinship between Nathaniel McQueston and the antiheroic protagonists of such novels as *An American Tragedy* and *The Great Gatsby* (both published in 1925) would probably have been quite apparent to Anderson's audience. In fact, Nathaniel, who is rather less offensive than the ancient Jason, and rather more sympathetic than either Clyde Griffiths or Jay Gatsby, is a character thoroughly in keeping with a tradition of American outlaws that goes back at least as far as the Boston Tea Party. The portrait of Nathaniel is, moreover, like that of Oparre, inseparable from the situation in which the character finds himself. Thus the cultural significance of such works as *The Wingless Victory* is lost in critical discussions focusing indefatigably on isolated aesthetic concerns. As for the particular charge that the third act is melodramatic, one might very well argue that the conclusion of this play is no more melodramatic than that of *Romeo and Juliet*, to which, in fact, it bears a certain structural resemblance.

Far from being an encumbrance to dramatic development, the insistence on racial conflict in the *Medeas* of the 1930s is a meaningful reflection of the affinity between ancient and modern ethnocentrisms, and it suggests that the drama of child murder is as inseparable from issues of the widest magnitude in the twentieth century as it was in the fifth century B.C.E. Coinciding not only with racial crisis in the United States but also with Mussolini's invasion of Ethiopia, a campaign heralding the global conflict of the 1940s and the eventual disintegration of vast colonial empires, the plays by Cullen and Anderson seem prophetic with respect to the civil rights movement of the 1960s just as Lenormand's *Asie* seems clairvoyant with regard to the French and American involvements in Indochina after World War II. The socially engaged *Medeas* of the 1930s, emphasizing the imperialistic antagonisms inherent in the ancient Greek tragedy, were neither the first nor the last versions of the myth to dramatize the violence of colonial regimes. In the turbulent 1960s, when over thirty African nations obtained their independence, the Finnish writer Willy Kyrklund depicted the conflict between an African woman and her white male nemesis in a play called *Medea fra Mbongo* (1967), and the American playwright, Jim Magnusen, wrote a similarly patterned drama entitled *African Medea* (1968). The filicidal plot as structuring device for presenting the conflict between masters and slaves is also essential in Toni Morrison's novel, *Beloved* (1987).

The resemblance between *Beloved* and *Medea* is noted by Stanley Crouch in an article entitled "Aunt Medea" which dismisses the book as a "black-faced holocaust novel" (202-09). While the analogy between Morrison's Sethe and the Euripidean Medea is important, as I have argued elsewhere (*Disorderly Eaters* 61-77), Crouch's essay is a curiously mean-spirited critique of a justly celebrated novel. Based on the actual experience of a nineteenth-century woman named Margaret Garner, Morrison's narrative explores the common ground between a brutal ancient myth and the historical milieu of laboring African Americans whose daily lives are devoted to the exhausting problem of keeping body and soul together in a world haunted by the twin specters of slavery and racism. Witches, ghosts, and dragons are just as much a part of the action at 124 Bluestone Road, Cincinnati, as they are in the tragic and epic structures of Euripides and Apollonius, and the character Sethe is not only a "Medea" by virtue of her defiant action; she is also accused of something like "hubris" by the women of Cincinnati (171), who perform a choral function comparable to that of the Corinthian women in the Euripidean play. A role approximating that of the Aeschylean Furies, who torment those who spill the blood of kin, is reserved for the title character, Beloved, the ghost of the baby Sethe kills when the slave-catchers close in on her. First appearing many years after the bloody event, Beloved returns to haunt a remorseful mother who is as vulnerable to self-punishment as the ancient protagonist recoiling with dread before her own *thumos*. Both a phantom of the past and a part of Sethe's own mind, Beloved is a wretched emanation of grief, the exorcism of which is the essential action of the novel.

The connection between mourning and infanticide is stressed by both Euripides and Morrison. Although Morrison's sequence of events, in which the killing is followed by years of festering misery, distinguishes *Beloved* from *Medea*, in which the mother's sense of loss precedes and precipitates the act of child-murder, the link between aggravated sorrow and eruptive violence is evident in both works. The psychological similarities between the novel and the play derive most apparently from the circumstance that they both share a basic structure that encompasses the act of infanticide, the relationship between mother and child, the critical involvement of a community of women, and curiously analogous casts of supporting characters. The roles of Baby Suggs and Stamp Paid resemble those of the ancient Nurse and Tutor; Paul D, the lover who competes with Sethe's children for the bounty of her love, recalls the ancient expectation of inevitable hostility between stepparents and stepchildren. At the end of the novel, the absurd arrival of Sethe's white male benefactor in a horse-drawn cart is structurally comparable to the appearance of the dragon chariot at the end of the tragedy. Although Sethe reacts violently against the "whiteman," managing, unlike Medea, to preserve both her humanity and her integrity, the possibility of appealing to prevailing patriarchal powers is a significant element in both the novel and the tragedy. The only essential character who seems to be absent from this thumbnail sketch of parallel elements in the two works is Jason.

In *Beloved*, the representative of established power who drives Sethe to the crime of infanticide is the arrogant foreman, called "schoolteacher." Without being quite as overtly wicked as Harriet Beecher Stowe's Simon Legree, the pedantic schoolteacher, who elevates racism to the level of moral philosophy, is all the more dangerous for being a respectable member of the southern community. His views on the differences between the "cannibal" customs of the "coloredpeople" and the "civilized" ways of the "whiteman" are not only an ironic counterpoint to the narrative depiction of a white society that regularly swallows poor blacks alive; schoolteacher's presumption is curiously equivalent to that of the ancient Jason, who justifies his most obnoxious offenses with references to the distinction between "barbarians" and "Greeks." For schoolteacher, the word *cannibal* functions like the ancient epithet *barbarian* as a declaration of cultural superiority that justifies every kind of abuse. In that his stupid cruelty costs the lives of her friends, her husband, and her children, schoolteacher is Sethe's personal nemesis; in that his arguments resemble those of common nineteenth-century apologists for slavery (Fitzhugh 84; Seabury 133), he is also the voice of a vicious social institution. As a vigorous disseminator of the doctrine of "scientific" racism, he also illustrates the dynamics of poisonous pedagogy that are conspicuous in versions of Medea by Corneille, Grillparzer, and Lenormand. In fact, Morrison confirms the link between institutional abuse of children and the persecution of minorities by choosing the name *schoolteacher* for her least sympathetic character. If the world of *Beloved* is predicated on the systematic corruption of young minds, its essential horror inheres in the routine destruction of young bodies.

The fact of having killed a child distinguishes Sethe from her peers no more than it separates Medea from the ordinary ancient family. Morrison's protagonist, who owes her very life to the circumstance that her mother chose "to keep her," may be said to share the lot of the ancient Greek child whose life literally depended on the outcome of the traditional ceremony in which a father signaled the decision either to raise the child or to expose it. Loath to nurture offspring conceived as a result of forced relations with white masters, Sethe's mother kept only one child, the one fathered by a black lover. In this, her parent resembles the woman, Ella, of whom we are told that "her puberty was spent in a house where she was shared by father and son, whom she called 'the lowest yet', " and that she "delivered, but would not nurse, a hairy white thing, fathered by the 'lowest yet', " which "lived five days never making a sound" (256-59). We are given to understand, moreover, that such accounts of slave women unwilling to raise up children for hated masters constitute only the tip of the iceberg. More horrible than any particular incident of child murder is the scrap of "red ribbon knotted around a curl of wet wooly hair, clinging to its bit of scalp" which Stamp Paid fishes out of the river in the course of an ordinary work day (180). A world where such things may be found in the water for the trouble of bending over is, by definition, a world where children can be killed with impunity.

The murder of children in *Beloved* is a function of the peculiar role of the exploited black woman. Valued as "property that reproduces itself without cost" (228), Morrison's Sethe resembles the ancient Medea in that her capacity to nurture and protect is prodigious. Arriving in Cincinnati with fresh wounds from a terrible beating, feet swollen and bleeding from an awful overland journey in the late days of pregnancy, ragged clothes, a hollow belly and the precious burden of an infant born on the way, Sethe joyfully resumes the task of nursing her babies, recalling later: "When I got there, I had milk enough for all" (198). Supporting herself and her daughter on her earnings as a cook, she welcomes Paul D and Beloved into her home and prepares a feast to celebrate the happiness they bring her: "There was no question but that she could do it. Just like the day she arrived at 124—sure enough, she had milk enough, she had milk enough for all" (100). The ghost of Sethe's dead baby is, indeed, the issue of an overwhelming grief commensurate with her mother's boundless love. When Denver remarks that the baby throws a powerful spell, Sethe replies, "No more powerful than the way I loved her" (4). In the light of Sethe's seemingly miraculous ability to feed her children in the absence of evident social support, the ancient assumption of the magical potential inherent in maternal love gains new meaning.

Though the term *magical* seems appropriate enough for describing the activities of "earth mothers" and "witches," many of the supernatural phenomena in Medea and Beloved are ultimately derived from economic exigencies. Whether the advantages of maternal providence are described as *magical,* or as *economical,* their utility for the purposes of men like Jason and schoolteacher is nevertheless undoubted, and the materialistic dimensions of the filicidal scenario are inescapable in *Beloved,* where the threat of starvation is a grinding fact of life, and slaves who live on a diet of bread, beans, hominy, and vegetables are beaten for stealing meat, and runaway slaves hide in caves and "fight owls for food" (66). Sethe spends her childhood in the care of a wet nurse who rarely has enough milk for her when she finishes nursing the "whitebabies." The personal outrage she suffers at the hands of the schoolteacher's nephews when they strip her, flog her, and hold her down so as to suck the milk from her swollen breasts is described, primarily, as an economic violation. In the wake of this "alimentary rape," Sethe resolves that "nobody will ever get [her] milk no more except [her] children" (200). The particular nature of this offense is crucial, not only because it dramatizes the role of the black woman as nurturing figure, but because it suggests the ubiquity of maternal deprivation in the slave-holding economy. Sethe's resolve to save her milk for her children seems, after all, no more remarkable than the fact that the nephews, having obtained absolute control over an attractive woman, manifest no more urgent desire than to gratify their own infantile oral cravings. For the slaves themselves, escape from the southern farm is tantamount to a reprieve from constant hunger, and the arrival in free territory is the occasion for feasting. In fact, the city of Cincinnati is the regular site of festivals in this book—the celebration given by Baby Suggs in honor of Sethe's escape, the carnival to which Paul D takes Sethe and Denver on the day that Beloved shows up, the feast which Sethe prepares for her family as a demonstration of her love for Paul D. Morrison's emphasis on "bread and butter" issues constitutes an important link between the world of *Beloved* and the context of ancient tragedy.

Celebrated during regular annual festivals in honor of the god Dionysus, ancient tragedy was predicated on the order of agricultural societies in which the ever-present threat of famine gives peculiar significance to intervals of ritual feasting. The alternation of festival and famine that is evident in the geographical and political context of *Beloved* is implicit in the performance of ancient tragedy. It is an opposition, moreover, which is pervasive in the structure of Morrison's novel. When, in the grip of overwhelming grief, Sethe wastes away to a shadow of her former self, while Beloved, the phantom child who feeds parasitically on her mother's substance, grows sleek and fat, the text seems to suggest, on the level of character, an analogy with the ancient concept of periodic feasting and fasting. Embodying the extremes of want and plenty, these figures may also call to mind the economic inequities that have survived the abolition of legal slavery by more than a century in this country. Though the distance between novelistic and dramatic treatments of child murder is considerable, it is by no means impassable, and the substantial affinity between Morrison's novel and Euripides' tragedy is arguably as remarkable as the historical and stylistic differences between the two works. While the Euripidean text may seem to reflect the structured order of the ruling masters, and Morrison's fiction to evoke the relaxed effusions of the liberated slaves, such distinctions are inherently problematic because the order of tragedy is not as controlled, and the freedom of narrative is not as extensive as one might imagine. Just as Euripides was criticized in antiquity for the "episodic" and "spectacular" quality of his drama, the nineteenth-century slave narratives on which Morrison's story depends were liable to be criticized as "improbable" and "inflammatory" by contemporary readers. The writers of these accounts were so anxious to avoid offending an essentially white middle-class reading public that they subjected themselves to a rigorous process of self-censorship concerning which Morrison observes that "over and over, the writers pull the narrative up short with a phrase such as 'But let us drop a veil over these proceedings too terrible to relate.' " Conversely, she describes her own job as one of ripping away "that veil drawn over 'proceedings too terrible to relate'"(*Inventing the Truth* 109-10). Thus, her conception of literary enterprise suggests an analogy between the role of the novelist and that of such tragic figures as Tiresias or Cassandra, as if the author's clairvoyance might enable the modern reader to obtain the kind of wisdom implied in the ancient maxim, "Know thyself."

The perception of the writer's role as analogous to that of the ancient seer is one Morrison shares with Robinson Jeffers (1887-1962), the author of the most successful twentieth-century production of a dramatic Medea. Fond of distinguishing himself from "religion-/ Vendors and political men" who "Pour from the barrel, new lies on the old, and are praised for kindly wisdom," Jeffers expressed a special affinity for the figure of Cassandra, doomed to "mumble in a corner a crust of truth, to men/ And gods disgusting" ("Cassandra," *S.P.* 78). Despite his sense of himself as a voice crying in the wilderness, the text of Jeffers' *Medea, Freely Adapted from the Medea of Euripides* (1946) and the Broadway production of the play (1947) were both greeted with extraordinary critical and popular acclaim. Hazel Hansen of the Department of Classics at Stanford praised the work extravagantly, assuring Jeffers that "Medea is a living breathing person, no longer the strange witch from the fringe of the Greek world. . . . We classicists will always be deeply indebted to you" (Bennett 195), and Brooks Atkinson extolled Judith Anderson for her performance in the title role, proclaiming that "she understands the character more thoroughly than Medea, Euripides, or the scholars, and it would be useless now for anyone else to attempt the part" (Review of *Medea*). After a full season in New York, the production opened the following September in San Francisco, eventually traveling all over the United States, to England, France, Italy, Germany, Denmark, Australia, Hawaii, and Czechoslovakia. The success of the drama had the effect of promoting book sales, so that *Medea* sold twice as many copies as any other book hitherto published by Jeffers. The many revivals of the work include a 1965 production starring Gloria Foster in New York, and a return to Broadway in 1982 with Zoë Caldwell in the title role and Judith Anderson as the Nurse. Video tapes of the Caldwell-Anderson production have been widely distributed. This reception lends Jeffers' *Medea* the aspect of an anomaly, considering that Euripides only obtained third prize for the original production of the play at the tragic festival in 431 B.C.E.

That Jeffers should achieve his greatest success in the most social of literary genres is remarkable because he was not, in any sense of the word, a thespian. Claiming to know "nothing about the theatre" (Bennett 224), Jeffers spent most of his adult life in the then remote village of Carmel, California, dedicating himself to a peculiar philosophy called "inhumanism," which celebrated the beauty of the natural world and decried the persistence of anthropocentric thinking among his fellows. Acclaimed as a genius in the 1920s, he was subject, in the 1930s and 1940s, to increasingly hostile attacks that were at least in part related to the eccentricity of his political views. Describing Jeffers as "an isolationist at a time when the war against fascism took on aspects of a holy crusade" (48), Alex Vardamis cites Ruth Lechlitner as an example of contemporary impatience with Jeffers' stance: "plain annihilation of humankind (followed by peace) will do

Mr. Jeffers nicely. Provided . . . that he can sit in his stone tower, surrounded by California scenery, while the whole disgusting business is going on, and dash off a last poem or two before peace gathers him to her bosom" (Zaller 46-47). Condemned as pessimistic and misanthropic in his lifetime, Jeffers has been defended by several critics in recent years. William Nolte argues that, in the light of subsequent developments, Jeffers' pessimism is no longer worthy of the name (*Rock and Hawk* 143), and Czeslaw Milosz recommends that "before condemning his misanthropy, one must recall that he was neglected by people who placed great value on meat, alcohol, comfortable houses, and luxurious cars, and only tolerated words as if they were harmless hobbies" (*Centennial Essays* 272). It is also worth noting that the radical decline in Jeffers' critical fortunes coincides with the publication of poetic texts focusing on the way in which revered social institutions tend to swallow children whole.

The image of Moloch, the ancient child-devouring deity linked with the Old Testament Jahveh in Anderson's *Wingless Victory* (109), is essential to Jeffers' *Dear Judas,* a volume in which the title poem presents Mary blaming herself for the death of her son:

The mothers, we do it:
Wolf-driven by love, or out of compliance, or fat convenience:
A child for Moloch. I am that woman: the giver of blood and milk to
    be sacrificed. (*Collected Poetry*, hereafter referred to as "*C.P.*" 1.42)

The initial publication of this work in 1929 was the occasion of the first in a series of hostile reviews by Yvor Winters, who generally regretted the "high pitch of emotion" in Jeffers' poetry, and declared that "Dear Judas," in particular, had "no quotable lines" (64-69). Another low point in the critical reception of Jeffers' work is marked by the publication of *Solstice* in 1935. This volume, in which the title poem is a disturbing transposition of the myth of Medea to a California setting, was the occasion for Lechlitner's above-quoted remarks, and was also criticized by Philip Blair Rice for expressing ideas resembling "good fascism" (Vardamis 48). The reaction to such works as *Dear Judas* and *Solstice* suggests the possibility that Jeffers' insistence on the relevance of the ancient theme of child-murder to modern religious and political concerns may have contributed to his waning favor among contemporary critics.

A prolific and erudite poet, Jeffers regularly dealt with the filicidal myths of antiquity. "The Humanist's Tragedy", first published in *Dear Judas*, is a poem inspired by the *Bacchae,* and *The Tower beyond Tragedy* (1925) is based on the *Oresteia.* Both *Cawdor* (1928) and *The Cretan Woman* (1954) are treatments of the myth of Hippolytus. Though Jeffers protested, in his youth, that he did not "care for Euripides . . . nor for any Greek drama" (Bennett 62), and even after writing his own *Medea* claimed that "the story of Medea is about a criminal adventurer and his gun moll: it is no more moral than the story of Frankie and Johnny; only more ferocious" (Bennett 205), the myth of Medea nevertheless proved singularly congenial as a vehicle for expressing passionately held convictions of his own. The Euripidean emphasis on war might, in itself, suggest an affinity between the ancient tragedian and a modern poet who was, all his life, emphatically opposed to American military policy. In fact, Jeffers regularly dealt with the Euripidean theme of war as a child-murdering enterprise. In "Contemplation of the Sword (April, 1938)," he refers to war as "the massacre, more or less intentional, of children and women" (*C.P.* 2.544), and in "Drunken Charlie," he wrote, "There are men plotting to kill/ A million boys for a dead dream" (*C.P.* 3.106). The chorus of his *Medea* describes war as a recurring crisis of patriarchal culture— "Women hate war but men will wage it again" (39) and anticipates the perennial renewal of catastrophe: "The nations remember old wrongs and destroy each other" (63). The particular relevance of such generalities to American society is implied in the speech of Medea, who describes the women of the chorus as having come "to peer at [her] sorrow." Observing that "nothing is ever private in a Greek city," she concedes that "whoever witholds anything/ Is thought sullen or proud . . . undemocratic/ I think you call it" (16-18). The similarity between the character who bristles irritably about the well-meaning intrusion of her neighbors, and the author, who could not endure the metropolitan bustle of mainstream America, is unmistakable. But *Medea* is not only a poem about war, or a complaint about the tyranny of the majority. It is a dramatization of parental revulsion in the face of the routine procedures that regularly turn ordinary children into producers, consumers, and defenders of American culture.

The question "what will become of our children?" is implied in this play by the protagonist herself: "But when misfortune comes it is bitter to have children, and watch their starlike/ Faces grow dim to endure it" (41-42). In this connection, it is worth noting that Jeffers was rather more explicit with regard to the various "fortunes" and "misfortunes" of American children in "Solstice." A treatment of the filicidal plot that is more thoroughly demythologized than the play, "Solstice" presents the quarrel between a wealthy rancher named Andrew Bothwell and his estranged wife, Madrone, both of whom want custody of their two sons. When the well-dressed Bothwell shows up at his wife's door with a buyer for the ranch and a court order requiring that she hand the boys over to him, Madrone asks Andrew what he plans to do for the children. She is told: "They'll live at home with me. They'll have pleasures and advantages you cannot possibly: radio, motion-pictures, books,/ The school, the church. And when they're old enough to go up to college" (*C.P.* 2.495). Madrone is so delighted at the prospect of all the good things in store for her children, that she kills them before Bothwell can take them anywhere.

Her reaction is not so much a calculated move to thwart her nemesis as an act impelled by her own horror at the living death Bothwell envisions for them. When it is too late, she regrets that she did not find a way to save her sons, mournfully reproaching herself:

> I was too senseless-confident
> Until the degradation had you in its hands, I did what a senseless
> Caged beast killing her cubs . . . Oh . . Oh . . Oh . . I beast
> I did it. (*C.P.* 2.510)

Madrone Bothwell's attitude toward "the degradation" is evidently equivalent to Jeffers' own.

In *Medea,* Jeffers conveys by means of symbols and gestures the contempt for "the degradation" that is explicit in Madrone Bothwell's speech. When her sons return from delivering the poisoned gifts to Creusa, they are described, in Jeffers' stage directions, as having their hands full of toys that have been given to them: "The elder boy carries a decorated bow and arrows; the younger boy has a doll, a brightly painted wooden warrior." The text also specifies that Medea, "gazing at the boys, retreats slowly backward from them" (64-65). The visual effect of the scene is to present Medea's movement away from her children as a specific reaction to the sight of the new toys. As if galvanized by an internal warning against "Greeks bearing gifts," Medea recoils from the material emblems of the dominant culture that is about to swallow up her children. For a sense of the specifically American implications of this scene, we may examine the connotations of such words as "toys" and "play" in Jeffers' own poetic vocabulary. For Jeffers, "toys" and "play" are the pernicious emblems of a frivolous "civilization" in which he considers himself as much an alien as the barbarian Medea in ancient Greece. In "The Trap," he wrote:

> I am not well civilized, really alien here: trust me not.
> I can understand the guns and the airplanes,
> The other conveniences leave me cold.
>
> "We must adjust our economies to the new abundance . . . "
> Of what? Toys: motors, music-boxes,
> Paper, fine clothes, leisure, diversion.
>
> I honestly believe (but really I am an alien here: trust me not)
> Blind war, compared to this kind of life,
> Has nobility, famine has dignity.
>
> Be happy, adjust your economies to the new abundance;
> One is neither saint nor devil, to wish
> The intolerable nobler alternative. (*C.P.* 2.415)

For Jeffers, the term *civilization* is inseparable from the idea of a bourgeois happiness that equates success with the accumulation of useless toys. The scathing irony inherent in the assertion that even the intolerable alternatives of war and famine would be better than these "conveniences" may be judged by what he said about one of these grim options. Regularly goaded to sarcasm by the news of war, he responded to the Spanish Civil War with a poem called "Sinverguenza," in which he refers to the "masters of powerful nations" as creatures snarling "like cur-dogs over a bone," and to the blood of the Spanish people as "The first drops of a forming rain-storm" (*C.P.* 2.548). When the rainstorm finally broke, he fairly seethed, declaring, in "The Bloody Sire": "It is not bad. Let them play./ Let the guns bark and the bombing plane/ Speak his prodigious blasphemies" (*S.P.* 76). In this scenario, "toys" are the stuff of a vile "economy of abundance" which regularly engenders war, the ultimate human "play." Thus, the mindless prosperity offered by the affluent society as an alternative to the wars and famines of the ages is a leering swindle.

Although there is no denying that speculations on the relative merits of famine generally emanate from the minds of those whose bellies are full, the concerns that are shared by the insistently detached Jeffers and the socially engaged Morrison are worth noting. Whereas Jeffers focuses on the moral corruption of the privileged and Morrison depicts the wretched privations of the dispossessed, the economic perversions of the affluent society are condemned as emphatically by the poet's haughty queen as by the novelist's earthy cook. If the specter of famine seemed remote to Jeffers' public at a moment when the United States was at the pinnacle of world power and reminders of the "poor little children in Europe" were especially useful for shaming well-fed children into finishing the food on their plates, the intervening decades have made images of starving children an ordinary fact of everyday existence. As the twentieth century draws to a close, the widening gulf between rich and poor Americans seems intractable, and Morrison's retroactive insistence, in such novels as *Sula, The Bluest Eye,* and *Beloved* on the ways in which the prosperity of the white middle class has always entailed the sacrifice of other people's children, is an essential corrective to the assumption of general prosperity inherent in Jeffers' *Medea.* Yet Jeffers' poetry functions, like Morrison's fiction, as a valorization of Marx's perception that "at the same pace that mankind masters nature, man seems to become enslaved to other men or to his own infamy" (338). The particular relevance of the infanticidal drama to the situation in which the citizens of the Western nations found themselves at mid-century is evident in that Jeffers' *Medea* was not the only treatment of the ancient myth to appear in the aftermath of World War II.

Written in the same year as Jeffers' tragedy, Anouilh's *Médée* is comparable to its American counterpart. Though both plays deemphasize the theme of interracial hostility that was so conspicuous in treatments of the myth dating from the twenties and thirties, and both react to the contemporary cultural context with a spasm of disgust for human folly and brutality, the American version was acclaimed far and wide, while the French one was never even staged until 1953, and seems to have pleased the critics little better than the public. Insisting on considerations of form and tone, on the offensive character of the protagonist, and on the dubious wisdom of imposing the "dreadful dénouement" on a modern audience (Thody 35; McIntyre 46-47; Ginestrier 87), the detractors of the play echo standard objections to the Euripidean model. Among the play's defenders, however, Philippe Jolivet observes that the antagonism between Anouilh's Jason and Medea corresponds to the dynamic conflict that animates most of the author's work (87), and Alba della Fazia suggests that Medea may be regarded as a "stock character" in Anouilh's oeuvre, since Antigone, Joan of Arc, and various other female characters "are all atavisms of Medea" (104). Della Fazia underscores the essential importance of filicidal passion in this play, noting that Medea's hostility toward her children is evident in her caustic speech as well as in her notorious deeds (32). The resemblance between *Medea* and *Antigone,* a play that was enormously successful when produced in 1944, suggests that the general lack of enthusiasm for *Medea* may be partly owing to the change in the public mood that occurred between the grueling 1940s and the prosperous 1950s.

A place where theft, lust, betrayal, and murder are routine banalities, the world of Anouilh's *Medea* is most vividly described in the monologue delivered by the protagonist just after she sends the children off to the palace carrying the fatal presents:

Et toi, nuit pesante, nuit bruissante de cris étouffés et de lutte, nuit grouillante du bond de toutes les bêtes qui se pourchassent, qui se prennent, qui se tuent, attends encore un peu s'il te plaît, ne passe pas trop vite. . . O bêtes innombrables autour de moi, travailleuses obscures de cette lande, innocences terribles, tueuses. . . C'est cela qu'ils appellent une nuit calme, les hommes, ce grouillement géant d'accouplements silencieux et de meurtres.

(And you, heavy night, noisy night full of cries and struggling, night swarming with the leaping of all the beasts which pursue, capture and kill each other, wait a bit, don't pass too quickly. . . O countless beasts all around me, nameless workers of this land, terrible murderous innocences. . . This is what they call a calm night, this giant swarming full of silent couplings and murders.) (393)

The sexuality and violence of this "giant swarming full of silent couplings and murders" is all the more insidious in that it occurs quietly in the dark. Medea leaves little doubt, furthermore, as to the kind of evil that might inspire her preoccupation with "nameless workers" and "terrible murderous innocences": "Cette lande touche à d'autres landes et ces landes à d'autres encore jusqu'à la limite de l'ombre, où des millions de bêtes pareilles se prennent et égorgent en même temps" (This land borders on other lands and those lands on still others up to the border of the dark, where millions of similar beasts capture and slaughter each other all at the same time, 393). The world of Stalin's purges and Hitler's final solution lies sleeping peacefully in the night that surrounds Medea, and her enemies are individuals who have made their peace with the quotidian horrors of that world. In fact, the caravan in which Medea immolates herself and her children bears a curious resemblance to the one that furnishes Brecht's Mother Courage with her ignominious livelihood, and the ultimate refusal of Anouilh's protagonist to climb onto her wagon and keep moving constitutes a rejection of the fate that Courage accepts, that of continuing with business as usual. Whereas Medea's monologue expresses the revulsion of an isolated individual confronted with unspeakable brutality, the dialogue between Medea and Jason echoes French public discourse of the late 1940s with its speculation on the possibility of affirming human values in the face of dehumanizing imperatives.

Like the debate between Antigone and Creon in *Antigone,* the opposition between Medea and Jason has been described as a sparring match between an unyielding idealist and a tempered realist (Thody 35; della Fazia 39), and Anouilh succeeds so well in giving his tragic heroines worthy antagonists that the question of which character is more sympathetic, or whose argument is more credible, has inspired some controversy. Harvey straddles the fence, observing that Jason "may seem something of a sophist after a bit of cheap happiness, or again he may seem like the first of Anouilh's heroes to have a grain of common sense" (122), while Thody, like McIntyre and Ginestrier, finds that Jason's "arguments are completely convincing, largely because Medea, unlike Antigone is totally unsympathetic from the start" (35). Steiner's discussion of the earlier play suggests, moreover, that Anouilh's Antigone is no more convincing than his Medea (*Antigones* 193). This verdict is problematic, to say the least. Although the communal tragedy consists, in the Sophoclean *Antigone* as well as in the Euripidean *Medea,* precisely in the fact that a representative of tyranny prevails, the question to ask is not "Who wins?" but "What does he or she win?" Anouilh's *Antigone* would not have had the long run that it had in occupied Paris if people of various political persuasions had not been able to see in Creon an ambiguous embodiment of fascist power. But in his *Medea,* written several years after the spectacularly successful *Antigone,* the collaboration of Creon and Jason has a rather less ambiguous quality than that, for instance, of Creon and Ismene in *Antigone.* When Medea rejects "le sale petit bonheur" (dirty little happiness) that Jason describes as "realism," she is espousing a political position that was rather less controversial in 1946 than it was in 1944.

In an article entitled "What Is a Collaborator?" ("Qu'est-ce qu'un collaborateur?"), written in 1945, Sartre argues that a certain brand of "realistic" discourse is irremediably tainted with bad faith, and that the allied victory should be regarded as confirming the failure of so-called "realistic politics." Urging the adoption of "politics based on principles" that will contribute to the elimination of the "species of pseudo-realists" who recently suffered such a conspicuous defeat, he praises the success of the partisan resistance as demonstrating "que le rôle de l'homme est de savoir dire *non* aux faits même lorsqu'il semble qu'on doive y soumettre" (that the role of man is to know how to say *no* to circumstances even when it seems that one must submit to them, 60-61). In that the contest between Jason and Medea assumes the form of a quarrel between one who says "yes" to a corrupt established order and one who says "no," Anouilh's text recalls Sartre's. Although the gender-specific quality of the term "man" might seem to invite a feminist interpretation of this repartée, Medea's use of the word "homme" is consistent with Sartre's, in which "man" also means "human being." Exceeding the limits of sexist resentment, her contempt extends to all of humankind, dismissing Jason in a blast of misanthropic fury that implies the identity of human creatures and the "countless beasts" of her own nightmare vision. In terms of Sartre's argument, Medea's rejection of current "circumstances" makes her the only "man" in sight.

The untenability of Jason's position may be inferred, not only from the fact that he says "yes," but also by the nature of what he affirms. Though Creon regularly embodies the "banality of evil" in dramatizations of the myth of Medea, Anouilh underscores the specifically infanticidal quality of the reigning monarch. For example, when Creon grants Medea's request for a temporary reprieve from banishment, he confesses that he feels guilty about all the children whose deaths he has already caused: "Je devrais repousser ta prière. . . Mais j'ai beaucoup tué, Médée, moi aussi. Et dans les villages conquis où j'entrais à la tête de mes soldats ivres, beaucoup d'enfants" (I should reject your plea. . . But I, too, have killed many, Medea. And in the conquered villages where I entered leading my drunken soldiers, many children, 374). In 1946, when the memory of several conquering armies was fresh in the minds of French theater-goers, the identification of Creon as a triumphant invader would have been unlikely to endear him to a Parisian audience. Although the possible reference to recent history is discreetly understated, the delineation of the child-murdering aspect of military enterprise is clear. Medea insists on this point when she responds to Creon's concession by calling the king an old lion who has lost his claws and is prevented from doing his "job" by the thought of all the little children he has killed. She dismisses his speech as a cheap ploy inconsistent with a career of slaughtering innocents, disparaging the king as "un si brave homme au fond, un incompris, mais qui a tout de même égorge son compte d'innocents quand il avait encore des dents et les membres solides" (such a good man after all, one who is misunderstood, but who has, all the same, slaughtered his share of innocents when he still had teeth and solid members, 374). In suggesting that Creon resorts to virtue because he is no longer equipped for vice, Medea recalls the speech of Nietzsche's Zarathustra, who laughs "at the weaklings who thought themselves good because they had no claws" (*Portable* 230). The reference to failing "members," insinuating that Creon is sexually impotent, is also in keeping with the Freudian tone of a text in which the protagonist describes herself as "amputated" when she learns of Jason's defection. In that the exchange between Medea and Creon leaves little doubt that the king is affably respectable wickedness personified, it tends to undermine the assumption that Jason's plan to ally himself with the old scoundrel is a morally ambiguous project.

Though Jason and Medea are toughened characters who have left a bloody trail of betrayals behind them, Jason's repudiation of his partner in crime seems particularly insidious because of the "fraternal" quality of the bond between the two. Medea refers to the fratricidal story of Cain and Abel in deploring Jason's treachery: "Race d'Abel, race des justes, race des riches, comme vous parlez tranquillement. C'est bon, n'est-ce pas, d'avoir le ciel pour soi et aussi les gendarmes" (Abel's race, race of the just, race of the rich, how placidly you speak. It's good, isn't it, to have heaven on your side, and also the police, 389). Nor is this the only example of Anouilh's insistence, in this text, on the theme of betrayed brotherhood. Jason himself remembers that the young Medea was, in former days, like a "little brother" to him: "Les as-tu oubliés ces jours où nous n'avons rien fait, rien pensé l'un sans l'autre? Deux complices devant la vie devenue dure, deux petits frères qui portaient leur sac côte à côte tout pareils" (Have you forgotten those days when we never did anything, never thought anything without each other? Two accomplices facing life when the going got rough, two little brothers just alike carrying their load side by side, 386). The passage is remarkable, not only in its persuasive evocation of the love Jason and Medea once shared, but in depicting the liberated, egalitarian nature of the bond between them. In abandoning Medea, Jason is not only sleazily self-indulgent, but also a traitor to the revolutionary principles of equality and fraternity.

If, in the twentieth century, the cry of "Liberté, Egalité, Fraternité" is the echo of a lost age, it is not one that can ever be forgotten by a people whose national anthem is "La Marseillaise." The value of remembering the past is, furthermore, an essential concern in this drama. A particularly interesting example of the emphasis on the theme of memory is, indeed, the suggestion that Medea's story may serve the useful purpose of terrifying little children. Creon is the first to make this point: "Ton histoire est venue jusqu'à moi. Tes crimes sont connus ici. Le soir . . . les femmes les racontent aux enfants pour leur faire peur" (Your history has come to my attention. Your crimes are known here. In the evening, women relate them to their children in order to frighten them, 368). This intriguing use of the word *histoire,* meaning both *story* and *history,* may suggest that all of history is, like the tales told to children, an instrument the strong use to bludgeon the weak. Medea herself seems to espouse this theory when she tells Creon: "Qu'il ne reste de Médée qu'une grande tâche noire sur cette herbe et un conte pour faire peur aux enfants de Corinthe le soir" (Let nothing remain of Medea but a big black spot on this lawn and a tale with which to frighten the children of Corinth in the evening, 371). Jason also seems to subscribe to this view of history when he comments that, henceforth, no mothers will name their little girls "Medea": "il n'y aura pas d'autres Médée, jamais, sur cette terre. Les mères n'appelleront jamais plus leurs filles de ce nom. Tu seras seule, jusqu'au bout des temps, comme en cette minute" (There will be no more Medeas, ever, on this earth. Nevermore will mothers give that name to their little girls. Until the end of time you will be alone, as you are this minute, 382). Breaking the frame, the playwright attributes to the character knowledge that he could not possibly possess, as if Anouilh, speaking through Jason, were to observe that "history" exonerates the movers and shakers who cause the deaths of the innocent, selecting for vilification only those who actually carry out the most conspicuous "executions." Whereas many boys are named "Jason," no girls are named "Medea." Thus "history" is a matter, not just of what is remembered, but also, of what is forgotten.

The antisocial quality of Jason's defection is evident in his own most abbreviated statement of desire: "Je veux l'oubli et la paix" (I want forgetfulness and peace, 379). In effect, his willingness to hold his nose while plugging into a criminal social system so as to secure his own peace and "happiness" tends to justify Medea's seemingly cantankerous complaint vis-à-vis Corinthian civic life: "Cela pue le bonheur" (It stinks of happiness, 357). The moment of truth, for Medea, comes when she realizes that her own sons will eventually assume their places as cogs in the detested machine. For this reason, she avoids their eyes, perceiving in them a kind of "trap": "Piège des yeux d'enfants, petites brutes, têtes d'hommes" (Trap of children's eyes, little animals, heads of men, 396). Like the Euripidean Medea, Anouilh's protagonist dreads looking into the eyes of her children, fearing that the sensual bond that ties her to them may prevent her from saying "no." But Medea's revulsion toward the cultural process that will turn her sons into seekers of happiness like their father is also comparable to the shrinking gesture with which Jeffers' protagonist recoils from her loot-laden children. In Anouilh's *Medea,* as in Jeffers', destructive rage is inseparable from the knowledge of what it means to bring up children in a complacent bourgeois order founded on an unstated principle of human sacrifice.

The implications of the fact that such writers as Jeffers and Anouilh should have written versions of the myth of Medea at virtually the same historical moment are worth noting. Although both texts reflect the influence of such figures as Nietzsche and Freud, they both share the quality of attempting to articulate a human response to the overwhelming inhumanity of current events, and they may be described as analogous products of a single cultural crisis. Anouilh may insist on the contemporary European concerns of collaboration and resistance, while Jeffers stresses the unholy alliance between the economics of abundance and the politics of empire, but these differences seem less striking in retrospect than certain salient similarities. Both writers deplore the peculiarly egocentric ideal of happiness fostered by consumer societies, and both express exasperation with "civilized" and "rational" discourse. In either case, the emotional intensity is directly proportional to the butchery and brutality that had recently been committed in the name of venerable ideals. In the last analysis, both Jeffers and Anouilh seem to have found, in independently realized conceptions of the defiant woman who refuses to offer milk and honey to Moloch, an emblem of resistance to the specter of mass conformity. These spectacular representations of revolt may seem, however, to be the last gasp of a dying cause. In the general prosperity and relative quiescence of the postwar years, Jason's longing for "l'oubli et la paix" would prove to be the wave of the future.

In the immediate aftermath of World War II, Anouilh envisioned Jason as picking up the pieces of his life and forgetting about the past. In contrast, the *Medea* presented by Matthias Braun at the Luisenburger Festspiele in 1958 urges the members of the audience to remember things they might prefer to forget. Written by a young German born in the year Hitler came to power (1933), the play is one of several treatments of ancient tragedies by the same author. The historical relevance of his focus is evident in that his versions of Aeschylus' *The Persians* and Euripides' *The Trojan Women* are, like their ancient models, plays about war that dramatize the sufferings of the vanquished. The banality of abusive power is, moreover, essential to Braun's *Medea,* in which corporal punishment is a salient component of social interaction: Creon threatens to hit Medea if she refuses to control herself (338), and the nurse observes that the Colchian woman regularly beats her own children (410). A menacing character, so persistently cranky and obnoxious that she even manages to alienate the traditionally loyal Nurse and Corinthian women, Braun's Medea recalls her Senecan antecedent, not only because of her bad temper, but also because of the generally gratuitous quality of her offenses. In this version, Jason seems to have contributed little to Medea's past mischief and is, at present, trying to muddle through as best he can. The project of abandoning Medea and marrying Creon's daughter seems to be a last desperate resort on his part. Although Braun's play participates in the logic of the scapegoat to such an extent that the central character seems like a creature offered up to the audience as an object of opprobrium, Karl Kerényi nevertheless describes the text as a "Germanification" of ancient tragedy which deliberately aims "to shake up the man in the street" ("Vorwort" 27-28).

Not only a malcontent and troublemaker, Medea is an abusive public figure whose petulance recalls the notorious Führer who reigned in Germany during Braun's childhood. In depicting Medea as a maniacal individual surrounded by passive burghers who allow her to wreak havoc in their midst, Braun attacks the mood of public complacency that prompted Alexander and Margarete Mitscherlich to observe that "Germans have shown a minimum of psychological interest in trying to find out why they became followers of a man who led them into the greatest material and moral catastrophe in their history" (9). The analogy between the German people under Hitler and the Corinthian women, whose failure to restrain Medea makes them responsible for her crimes, is crucial for an understanding of Braun's drama. When the children are killed and all the principal players depart, the chorus remains on stage. Rather than revile the outsider, the women castigate themselves:

Wir aber kehren zurück zu ihr
Die am Blut liegt, der Stadt
An das Sterbelager.
Aus unsere Mitte wuchs
Und von uns gelitten aber der Schaden

(But we turn back to it, the [place] steeped in blood, the city by the death camp. The harm grew in our midst, and was suffered by us.) (444)

The references to the place "steeped in blood," the "city by the death camp," and the "harm that grew in our midst and was suffered by us" leave little doubt regarding the contemporary implications of Braun's drama. The chorus reproaches itself for passive aquiescence in public evil: "Lange hätten wir ihn auf unseren Strassen sehn können/ Und hätten wissen müssen, das/ Ist nicht der Friede" (We could see it in our streets for a long time, and should have known that this was not peace). Mindless insistence on peace, which seems indistinguishable from the credo of "forgetfulness and peace" espoused by Anouilh's Jason, is retroactively condemned as a morally derelict denial of violence. Finally, the women of the chorus identify themselves with the nightmare of the past, and also with the members of the audience: "Nun sind wir vorbei, und anderes kommt./ Ihr die uns seht, wir waren euch gleich" (Now we are [of the] past; something else is beginning. You who behold us, we were once like you, 444). The identification of the mournful chorus with the quiescent spectators has the effect of deconstructing the dichotomy between the past and the present. Thus, the members of the audience, deprived of a sympathetic heroine, are nonetheless asked to see the relevance of her speech and action to their own lives.

In establishing the bond between the past and the present, Braun's drama recalls the Brechtian emphasis on the concept of the *Jetztzeit* (*the presence of the now*), a *nunc stans* in which time stands still, where past and future converge not harmoniously but explosively, in the present instant (Mitchell, xvii). In fact, a cursory consideration of the *Medeas* by Jahnn, Anouilh, and Braun has the effect of retroactively illuminating the Euripidean drama, which Aristotle regarded as inconsistent with ideal tragic form. Far from articulating a "cathartic" expurgation of "pity and fear," the Euripidean text anticipates the Senecan technique of depicting a world dominated by "negative examples," and does not allow for the possibility of an untroubled identification with any particular character. The drama of Medea has thus, arguably, always been "Brechtian" in its aesthetics. The frenzied *Medeas* produced by Seneca and Braun suggest, moreover, that the formal similarities between the two works derive from the fact that they are both reflections of extreme political tyranny rather than the working out of specific artistic strategies. Just as the Senecan *Medea* seems haunted by the ghosts of Caligula and Tiberius, so Braun's tragedy recalls little men who triggered storms of fire and blood by trying to revive "the grandeur that was Greece, the glory that was Rome."

The connection between the abuse of children and the corruption of politics that is overtly articulated in Braun's *Medea* is implicit in all twentieth-century treatments of the myth. Of particular interest with regard to the theme of hostility to children in modern versions of the myth is the fact that, in the United States, the general decline of confidence in public figures coincides with the appearance of dramatic treatments of the Medea motif in which cosmic issues are completely eclipsed by scenes of domestic violence. Thus in 1975, after a decade in which political assassinations, military defeats and government scandals dominated the news, Francine Ringold presented a drama in Wichita, Kansas, in which the confining interior of a middle-class home proves fatal to the offspring of a self-indulgent couple so involved with various toys and games that they have little time left for their children. Though the drama begins with the children alone on stage, bickering with each other and playing games to amuse themselves in their parents' absence, the dialogue between the children is soon interrupted by Jason, a handsome university professor who greets his progeny with charming affability and promptly tells them to make themselves scarce. Evidently intent on working out some abstract intellectual problem, the importance of which he asserts but does not explain, Jason gets down on the floor and starts playing with the "tinker toys." The subsequent arrival of Jason's wife, the elegant "Emz," signals the onset of a marital quarrel that recalls the refined cruelties of Albee's *Who's Afraid of Virginia*

Woolf? The violence of the "war" between the parents is eventually absorbed and internalized by the children, who decide, in a manner reminiscent of Hardy's *Jude the Obscure,* to do everybody a favor by "making themselves scarce" once and for all: they hang themselves. Thus, the process by which children are routinely encouraged to assume responsibility for the problems of their parents is incorporated into the very structure of this play, which posits a connecting link between parental hostility and juvenile suicide.

In that toys and games are essential elements of her text, and also in that the dénouement of her play depends on the reception by the children of a previously encoded message, Ringold's drama reflects the influence of the school of psychotherapy known as "transactional analysis." Significantly, the title of her play, *The Games People Play,* is the same as that of Eric Berne's best-selling book, published in 1964, although Ringold confesses that she only became aware of Berne's book after the initial performance of the play, when a member of the audience called it to her attention. That the case is one of cultural affinity rather than direct influence is suggested by the fact that the concept of "play" as an essential component of human affairs is not the unique invention of transactional analysis. Historian Johan Huizinga argued, in *Homo Ludens: A Study of the Play Element in Culture* (1944), that "play" is the ultimate human activity and all serious enterprise may be traced to it. The relevance of this thesis to the history of tragedy is particularly evident since the verb to play is the one we normally use to describe the activities of both actors and musicians, and dramatic works are called "plays." In that he rejects the adult tendency to regard work as serious business and play as juvenile foolishness, Huizinga may be considered a pioneer in deconstructing the antichild bias inherent in the context of tragedy. His perspective hardly seems radical if we consider, moreover, that the idea of "game-playing," so conspicuous in Jeffers' *Medea,* is implicit in the Euripidean text, in which Medea cautions Jason against "opposing foolish games with foolish games" (*Medea* 891). Yet Ringold's insistence on "game-playing" represents a noteworthy development in the process of demythologization that is discernible in post-Enlightenment *Medeas.* The spectacle of the father who chases his children away so as to have their toys to himself provides an irreverent counterpoint to the popular image of "the little boy who refuses to grow up," which is as fundamental to the myth of Jason and Medea as it is to the tale of Peter Pan and Wendy. Ringold's play is, moreover, not the only twentieth-century *Medea* that employs the idea of "game-playing" as a structural device.

Whereas *The Games People Play* dramatizes the plight of children who die because their parents insist on playing silly games, Rudi Gray's *Medea and the Doll,* presented in New York in 1984, is based on the assumption that a child's life may be saved if her mother can be persuaded to play therapeutic games. Like Peter Shaffer's

Equus (1973), *Medea and the Doll* presents the interaction between a psychiatrist and a disturbed patient. The "action" of the play, involving only the analyst, Winston, and a woman named Nilda, who has been referred to him because she beat her child with the cord of an iron, takes place entirely in the doctor's office. Depending on the transactional perception that "games are dramatic and require the players to assume roles of persecutor, rescuer and victim" (Goulding and Goulding 31), the drama entails several instances of strategic role-switching, the first of these occuring when, in the course of listening to the troubles of the poor single woman in front of him, Winston associates her story with a memory from his own past. The dialogue between doctor and patient comes to a temporary halt as Winston turns to the audience and reveals, in a prolonged aside, that in his college days, he once courted and won the favor of a pretty undergraduate whom he abandoned when she got pregnant. He now wonders aloud if that girl might not eventually have found herself in the same predicament as Nilda. Thus the role of the rescuer is fleetingly identified with that of a kind of persecutor, and the particular scenario being enacted assumes a certain general significance. With a sober sense of his own involvement in the misery of his bewildered patient, Winston returns to the present and produces a doll with which he invites Nilda to "play" a game. Whereas the mind of the seducer is explored in Winston's monologue, the dissociations of the battered child are dramatized in the scene wherein Nilda, hypnotized, plays the role of her own mother, and projects a lifetime of rage onto the doll, which is identified as her own "bad" self. By the end of the session, both the seducer and the seduced, the abuser and the abused, gain insight into the complexity of their habitual roles, parting on a mildly hopeful note. Thus in Gray's anti-tragic play, the activity of game-playing is not only a metaphor for adult irresponsibility, but also the agent of therapeutic change.

The distance between Gray's transactional drama and the aesthetics of ancient tragedy was stressed in a contemporary review by Stephen Holder who complained that the playwright's "laborious casebook study" scarcely tried to "transcend the clinical" and also, that the emotional liability of the doctor seemed "implausible." Not entirely negative in his assessment of the production, Holder praised Maria Ellis, who played the part of Nilda, for turning the character "into a complex and whole character—a little girl with a hard, brassy shell" who is "alternately saucy, petulant, tyrannical and seductive." It is tempting to observe that the critical perspective that approves the *seductive* quality of the abused female child while dismissing the confession of the exploitive adult male as "implausible" seems related to the "clinical" concerns that the critic finds so tiresome. In the last analysis, however, the judgment that *Medea and the Doll* is a disturbing play with a memorable female protagonist does very little to distinguish this text from the Euripidean model.

Though the structure of *Medea and the Doll* is nontraditional, the degree to which its psychological dynamics conform to those of the ancient Greek tragedy is noteworthy. For all of their banality, Gray's portraits of exploitive male and abusive female characters correspond well enough to the fundamentals of their traditional prototypes; the crucial concept of role reversal and the ultimate identity of persecutor and persecuted are also contained in the ancient text. Though Nilda is neither as magnificent nor as terrifying a character as Medea, her ordeal presents the audience, nonetheless, with the disturbing spectacle of the self being attacked by a part of the self, thus dramatizing the link between brutality endured in childhood and the kind of dissociative split that is so apparent in the agon of the ancient protagonist. In exploring the connection between Nilda's idealization of her cruel mother and her compulsion to mistreat her own child, Gray demonstrates the pedestrian origins of a fabulous myth. His play leaves little doubt, moreover, that the pathetic Nilda is much more frightening to her child than Medea is to any audience. The admittedly limited cultural impact of such experimental works as this one and the one by Ringold does not ultimately diminish their importance as evidence of the essential continuity between tragic pathos and clinical pathology.

Although the negative reception of Gray's *Medea* is consistent with a tradition of curmudgeonly carping that extends all the way back to Aristotle, the number of new treatments of the Medea motif to appear in the 1980s suggests that critical detractors have had little effect on the cultural enterprise of "playing" with the myth of child-murder. In addition to interpretations of the Euripidean text by Yukio Ninagawa and Alkis Papoutsis (1986), the 1980s witnessed revivals of operatic *Medeas* by Cherubini (1981-82), and Charpentier (1984), of the ballet by Martha Graham (1982), the play by Robinson Jeffers (1982), and a one-act "Medea" by Dario Fo and Franca Rame (1983), which was originally performed in Milan in 1977. Original treatments of the motif appearing in these years include the already-mentioned works by Franchini and Fuseya (1984), Gray (1984), and Ludlam (1987), as well as an opera by Robert Wilson with a score by Kevin Bryars (1984), a play entitled *Medea/Sacrament* by Elizabeth Fuller and Conrad Bishop (1983), and Heiner Müller's *Verkommenes Ufer Medeamaterial Landschaft mit Argonauten (Despoiled Shore Medeamaterial Landscape with Argonauts)*.

A "nihilistic optimist" whose work "presumes the catastrophes which mankind is working toward," Müller insists that "the theatre's contribution to [the prevention of those catastrophes] can only be their representation" (*Hamletmachine* 126). Acclaimed as the "inheritor of Brecht's mantle" (Weber, *The Battle* 7), he is the most frequently produced dramatist in modern Germany, and his treatment of Hamlet (*Hamletmachine*) was produced in New York in 1986 under the direction of Robert Wilson. Among his many plays are a number of versions of ancient themes, including *Herakles 5* (1966), *Philoktet* (1966), *Ödipus Tyrann* (1967), and several treatments of Medea—*Medeaspiel* (*Medeaplay* 1974) and *Verkommenes Ufer Medeamaterial Landschaft mit Argonauten* (1983). Like other writers who have dealt with the myth of Medea, Müller assumes the role of a latter-day Cassandra, predicting, for example, that a "reunified Germany will make life unpleasant for its neighbors" (*Interview*). The historical perspective of his *Verkommenes Ufer* is characteristically disquieting.

Set in a post-apocalyptic landscape, Müller's dramatization of the myth of Medea is divided into three parts, the first of which was written thirty years before the initial production of the completed work in Berlin in 1983 (*Hamletmachine* 124). The opening section, *Verkommenes Ufer*, takes place in the middle of a littered terrain in the suburbs of East Berlin, with its lakes, commuter trains, housing developments, and pollution. Although *Medeamaterial*, the central portion of the work, entails the onstage presence of three actors— Jason, Medea and the Nurse—the interaction among them is limited. Except for bits of dialogue at the beginning and end, *Medeamaterial* is a monologue by Medea. For Müller, who regards Jason's story as the quintessential "myth of colonization," Medea's extended speech functions as an empowerment of the colonized. The final sequence of the play, entitled *Landschaft mit Argonauten,* evokes an image of the earth in a "terminal state of pollution by technologies, art and war, ending with the extermination of the voyager who turns into a landscape, the landscape of his death" (*Hamletmachine* 124-25). The cosmic dimensions of ancient tragedy are implicit in this scene, about which the playwright observes, "as in every landscape, the I in this segment is collective" (*Hamletmachine* 126).

In *Medeamaterial*, Medea addresses her children with words which describe the immediate present while resonating with echoes of the past:

Wen liebt ihr mehr Den Hund oder die Hündin
Wenn ihr dem Vater schöne Augen macht
Und seiner neuen Hündin und dem König
Der Hunde in Korinth hier ihrem Vater
Vielleicht ist euer Platz an seinem Trog

(Who do you like better, the dog or the bitch, when you make nice eyes for your father and his new bitch and the king, the big dog here in Corinth, maybe your place is at his trough.) (Stücke 189)

Reminiscent of the contemptuous tone with which Jeffers' Medea reviles "the great dog of Corinth" and the "dog's daughter's husband" (27, 33), this passage articulates the despair of a woman who knows that she cannot possibly compete against the seductive blandishments of the opposition. In that she responds with rage to the perception that the children will inevitably love her affluent oppressors more than herself, Müller's protagonist falls squarely into a tradition of modern Medeas that includes works by Grillparzer, Jeffers, and Anouilh. Although such well-observed details as the question "who do you like better?" recalling banal irritations endured by children from all classes, display the author's psychological acuity, the reference to Creon's "trough" underscores the essential economic implications of his drama.

The image of animals feeding at troughs is a symbol of dehumanized consumption at least as old as Plato's *Republic,* in which Socrates compares those "who have no experience of wisdom and virtue and spend their whole time in feasting and self-indulgence" to cattle: "Bent over their tables, they feed like cattle with stooping heads and eyes fixed upon the ground; so they grow fat and breed, and in their greedy struggle kick and butt one another to death with horns and hoofs of steel" (312-13). Whereas Plato can hardly have suspected the degree to which this nightmare would be realized in the mass culture of late twentieth century industrial economies, Müller's *Verkommenes Ufer* is set amid the relentlessly regenerated wreckage of such a society, and his *Medeamaterial* is uttered by the human "refuse" of such a society. Medea knows that her children will be forced to choose between social value and physical appetite: "Seh ich nicht eure Auge glänzen/ Im Vorschein auf das Glück der satten Bäuche" (Don't I see your eyes gleaming in anticipation of the happiness of full bellies? 189). Creon's "trough" may symbolize the prosperity of the Federal Republic in particular, and Western Capitalism in general; the spectacle of the *Verkommenes Ufer* also represents the ecological "fall-out" of all industrial society, and it thus establishes a dynamic link between the greedy appetites of the "children" and wanton destruction of cosmic proportions.

In the opening lines of *Verkommenes Ufer,* the speaker describes particular items in the piles of garbage cluttering the waterfront—cookie boxes, cigarette wrappers, condoms, torn menstrual napkins, blood and feces—the sordid debris of a large modern city. Particularly gruesome is the allusion to "Abflussrohre/ Kinder ausstossend in Schüben gegen den Anmarsch der Würmer" (Wastepipes excreting children in batches against the advance of the worms, 185). The image of "wastepipes excreting children in batches" transposes the Freudian equation, "gold = feces = baby," from the realm of dreams into that of gross reality, insisting on the modern capacity for turning life into rubbish. By suggesting that the installation of indoor plumbing may facilitate disposal and concealment of the small corpses that have been the product of human folly at every stage of history, Müller exposes the ugly underbelly of "progress." His insistence on the squalid domestic aspects of the quarrel between Jason and Medea is always subordinate to his focus on the connection between private comforts and public calamities.

Expanding on the excremental implications of the reference to wasted children in *Verkommenes Ufer, Landschaft mit Argonauten* compares the medium of television to a special kind of indoor plumbing: "Der Bildschirm speit Welt in die Stube" (The picture screen vomits world into the living room, 192). The radical transformation in the nature of popular culture which is implicit in this image does little to mitigate the ancient blight of deferred infanticide: "Die Jugend von heuter Gespenster/ Der Toten des Krieges der morgen stattfinden wird" (The youth of today are the ghosts of the dead of the war that will take place tomorrow, 193). Finally, the perspective of the Landschaft is leering and macabre:

Meine Finger spielen in der Scheide
Nachts im Fenster zwischen Stadt und Landschaft
Sahn wir dem langsamen Sterben der Fliegen zu
So stand Nero über Rom im Hochgefühl

(My fingers playing in your vagina, at night we watched, through the window, between city and landscape, the prolonged dying of the flies; so stood Nero, exultant over Rome.) (193)

In this passage, the regenerative sexuality that is the central core of ancient sacrament is relegated to the background of a sordid vision of "the prolonged dying of the flies." The reference to Nero suggests that the withering insects may be pioneers on a path down which all of humanity is hastening, so that the figure of Nero, who supposedly fiddled while Rome burned, is analogous to that of the modern consumer, eagerly pursuing ever newer and "sexier" diversions while the planet becomes uninhabitable.

As if to confirm Müller's insistence on the connection between ancient tragedy and modern entertainment, Medea made a surprise appearance not too long ago in a situation comedy that "the picture screen vomited" into millions of American living rooms. In an episode of *Northern Exposure,* a television series chronicling the lives of people living in a fictional town called Cicely, Alaska, the character Shelly, pregnant with her first child, dreams that she wanders into a cosmic support group for mothers. There she meets Queen Victoria, Olympia (mother of Alexander the Great), Medea, and a young African American who introduces herself as Mother Nature. After listening to Olympia complain about how her son left home at the age of seventeen and never came back, Shelly turns to Medea and asks, with characteristic naïveté: "So Medea, what about your kids?" Bewildered by Medea's apparent uneasiness, Shelly turns to Mother Nature for an explanation, finally exclaiming, as the truth dawns on her: "You offed your kids!" In fact, Shelly's comic nightmare dramatizes terrors usually reserved for tragedy. That the theme of hostility toward children, embodied by Medea and articulated by the long-suffering Olympia, is the central focus of the entire episode becomes clear when, in the concluding moments of the show, the mutually antagonistic Joel and Maggie discover that they have something important in common: both of them hate babies. Maggie insists that she never wants to become a mother and Joel describes infants as "germs with footed pajamas." Although this revelation, signalling a temporary rapprochement between two characters locked in a melodramatic love-hate relationship, may indicate the degree to which popular perceptions of the war between the sexes have changed since ancient times, it is worth noting that the reconciliation between these comic adversaries is achieved by means of a polite separation between public and private problems.

In the never-never land of Cicely Alaska, there is little suggestion that the decision to forego parenthood might have anything to do with misgivings about bringing children into a world where the future is not what it used to be. But Derrida asserts that "the only 'subject' of all possible literature, of all possible criticism, its only ultimate and a-symbolic referent, unsymbolizable, even unsignifiable" is "that toward which nuclear discourse and the nuclear symbolic are still beckoning: the remainderless and a-symbolic destruction of literature" (28). Although this reference to the apocalypse insists on the obliteration of literary archives rather than on the loss of human life, it shares with various treatments of the myth of Medea a vision of the future destroyed by deranged adults. Jahnn and Pasolini may underscore the theme of sadomasochism; Lenormand, Cullen, and Anderson may focus on interracial hatred; Braun and Gray may explore the connection between domestic violence and public abuses; yet Greven argues that sadomasochism, hatred, and domestic violence, like the apocalyptic vision Müller imagines, may all be consequences of the culturally sanctioned abuse of children. Since "the painful punishment of children creates the nuclear core of rage, resentment, and aggression that fuels fantasies of the apocalyptic end of the world" (206), it constitutes the essential condition for ensuring that human society will be dominated and ruined by rapacious, destructive adults. It is precisely because the dreadful menace of the annihilating parent has always possessed the status of the "unassimilable wholly other" attributed by Derrida to the specter of nuclear holocaust, that the ancient figure of Medea seems, more than ever, a myth for our time.

Works Cited

Anderson, Maxwell. *The Wingless Victory*. Washington D.C.: Anderson House, 1936.

Anouilh, Jean. *Nouvelles pièces noires*. Paris: La Table ronde, 1958.

Apollonius Rhodius. *The Argonautica*. Trans. R. C. Seaton. Loeb Library. Cambridge, Mass.: Harvard University Press, 1961.

Aptekar, Herbert H. *Anjea: Infanticide, Abortion and Contraception in Savage Societies*. New York: Godwin, 1931.

Ardrey, Robert. *African Genesis: Personal Investigation into the Animal Origins and Nature of Man*. New York: Atheneum, 1961.

Arendt, Hannah. *Eichmann in Jerusalem: A Report on the Banality of Evil*. New York: Viking, 1965.

Ariès, Philippe. *Centuries of Childhood: A Social History of Family Life*. Trans. Robert Baldick. New York: Knopf, 1962.

———. *L'Enfant et la vie familiale sous l'ancien régime*. Paris: Editions du Seuil, 1973.

Aristophanes. *The Complete Plays of Aristophanes*. Ed. Moses Hadas. New York: Bantam, 1978.

Aristotle. *On Poetry and Style*. Trans. G.M.A. Grube. New York: Bobbs Merrill, 1958.

Arrowsmith, William. "Euripides' Theatre of Ideas." In Erich Segal, 1968, 13-33.

Atkinson, Brooks. "Review of *The Wingless Victory* by Anderson." *New York Times* 24 Dec. 1936, L20.

———. "Review of *Medea* by Jeffers." *New York Times* 21 October 1947, B27.

Bailey, Cyril. *Religion in Virgil*. Oxford: Clarendon Press, 1934.

Bailey, Mabel Driscoll. *Maxwell Anderson: Poet as Prophet*. New York: Abelard Schuman, 1957.

Bakan, David. *The Slaughter of the Innocents: A Study of the Battered Child Phenomenon*. San Francisco: Jossey-Bass, 1971.

Baker, Houston A., Jr. *A Many-Colored Coat of Dreams: The Poetry of Countee Cullen.* Detroit: Broadside Critics Series, 1974.

Balmary, Marie. *Psychoanalyzing Psychoanalysis: Freud and the Hidden Fault of the Father.* Trans. Ned Lukacher. Baltimore: Johns Hopkins University Press, 1982.

Bariéty, Maurice, and Charles Coury. *Histoire de la médecine.* Paris: Presses Universitaires de France, 1971.

Barksdale, Richard, and Keneth Kinnamon. *Black Writers of America: A Comprehensive Anthology.* New York: Macmillan, 1972.

Bender, Lauretta. "Psychiatric Mechanisms in Child Murders." *Journal of Nervous and Mental Diseases* 80 (1934): 32-47.

Bénichou, Paul. *Morales du Grand Siècle.* Paris: Gallimard, 1948.

Bennett, Melba Berry. *The Stone Mason of Tor House: The Life and Work of Robinson Jeffers.* USA: Ward Ritchie, 1966.

Berne, Eric. *The Games People Play.* New York: Grove, 1964.

Besdine, Matthew. "The Jocasta Complex: Mothering and Genius." *Psychoanalytic Review* 55 (1968): 259-77, 574-600.

Bettelheim, Bruno. *Freud and Man's Soul.* New York: Vintage, 1984.

Bishop, Lloyd. *The Romantic Hero and His Heirs in French Literature.* Berne:Peter Lang, 1984.

Bizet, Georges. *Carmen.* Libretto by H. Meilhac & L. Halévy. New York: Schirmer, 1959.

Blakeslee, Sandra. "New Research Links Depression with Asthma Deaths in Children." *New York Times* 30 May 1989, C3.

Bloch, Dorothy. *"So the Witch Won't Eat Me": Fantasy and the Child's Fear of Infanticide.* Boston: Houghton Mifflin, 1978.

Boccaccio, Giovanni. *Decameron.* A cura di Cesare Segre. Milano: Mursia, 1970.

Bongie, Elizabeth Bryson. "Heroic Elements in the *Medea* of Euripides." *TAPA* 107 (1977): 27-56.

Boswell, John. *The Kindness of Strangers: The Abandonment of Children in Western Europe from Late Antiquity to the Renaissance.* New York: Pantheon, 1988.

Bouthoul, Gaston. *L'Infanticide différé.* Paris: Hachette, 1970.

Braun, Matthias. *Medea.* In Kerényi, 1963, 393-444.

Brown, Norman O. *Life against Death: The Psychoanalytical Meaning of History.* Middletown, Conn.: Wesleyan University Press, 1977.

Browne, Malcolm. "Relics of Carthage Show Brutality amid the Good Life. *New York Times* 1 September 1987, C13.

Burkhard, Arthur. *Franz Grillparzer in England and America.* Vienna: Bergland Verlag, 1961.

Calderon de la Barca. *Obras completas.* Ed. Angel Valbuena Briones. 3 vols. Madrid: Aguilar, 1966.

Cameron, A. "The Exposure of Children and Greek Ethics." *Classical Review* 46 (1932): 105-14.

Chateaubriand, François René de. Préface d'*Atala*. 1805. *Atala René*. Préface par
    Pierre Reboul. Paris: Garnier, 1964.
Chaucer, Geoffrey. *The Works of Geoffrey Chaucer*. Ed. F.N. Robinson.
    Boston: Houghton Mifflin, 1961.
Cherubini, Luigi. *Medea: An Opera in Three Acts*. Text by Benoit Hoffman.
    Milan: Ricordi, 1958.
Coffin, Arthur B. *Robinson Jeffers: Poet of Inhumanism*. Madison: University
    of Wisconsin Press, 1941.
Conacher, D. J. *Euripidean Drama: Myth, Theme and Structure*. Toronto:
    University of Toronto Press, 1970.
Corneille, Pierre. *Médée*. Texte établi & présenté par André de Leyssac. Genève:
    Librairie Droz, 1978.
———. *Oeuvres Complètes*. Préface de Raymond Lebègue Présentation et notes
    de André Stegman. Paris: Editions du Seuil, 1963.
Corti, Lillian. "*Medea* and *Beloved*: Self-Definition and Abortive Nurturing in
    Literary Treatments of the Infanticidal Mother." In *Disorderly Eaters:
    Texts in Self-Empowerment*, Ed. Lilian R. Furst and Peter W. Graham,
    University Park: Pennsylvania State University Press, 1992.
Costa, C.D.N., ed. *Medea*. Seneca Lucius Annaeus. Oxford: Clarendon Press,
    1973.
Crouch, Stanley. "Aunt Medea." *Notes of a Hanging Judge: Essays and
    Reviews, 1979-89*. New York: Oxford, 1990.
Cullen, Countee. *On These I Stand: An Anthology of the Best Poems of
    Countee Cullen*. New York: Harper, 1927.
———. *The Medea and Some Poems*. New York: Harper, 1935.
———. *My Soul's High Song: The Collected Writings of Countee Cullen,
    Voice of the Harlem Renaissance*. Ed. Gerald Early. New York: Anchor,
    1991.
Daly, Martin, and Margo Wilson. "A Sociobiological Analysis of Human
    Infanticide." In Glenn Hausfater and Sarah Blaffer Hrdy 1984, 847-502.
Darwin, Charles. *The Origin of Species by Means of Natural Selection or the
    Preservation of Favored Races in the Struggle for Life and the Descent
    of Man and Selection in the Relation to Sex*. New York: Modern
    Library, 1936.
della Fazia, Alba. *Jean Anouilh*. New York: Twayne, 1969.
Derrida, Jacques. "No Apocalypse, Not Now (Full Speed Ahead, Seven Missiles,
    Seven Missives)." *Diacritics* 14 (Summer 1984).
Deutsch, Helene. *Psychology of Women*. 2 vols. New York: Grune & Stratton,
    1945.
Diodorus Siculus. *Bibliotheca historica*. Trans. C.H. Oldfather. Loeb Classical
    Library. Cambridge, Mass.: Harvard University Press, 1960.
Disend, Michael. "Have You Whipped Your Child Today?" *Penthouse*
    January 1982: 57-64, 182-87.
Doubrovsky, Serge. *Corneille et la dialectique du héros*. Paris: Gallimard, 1963.

Duby, Georges. *Medieval Marriage: Two Models from Twelfth Century France.* Trans. Elborg Forster. Baltimore: Johns Hopkins University Press, 1978.

Duff, J. Wight. *A Literary History of Rome in the Silver Age, from Tiberius to Hadrian.* New York: Barnes & Noble, 1964.

Duncan, Robert. *Medea at Kolchis: The Maiden Head.* Berkeley: Oyez-Berkeley, 1965.

Dunham, T.C. "Symbolism in Grillparzer's *Das goldene Vliess.*" *PMLA* 75 (1960): 75-82.

Early, Gerald. "Introduction." In Countee Cullen, 1991, 3-76.

Easterling, P.E. "The Infanticide in Euripides' *Medea.*" *Yale Classical Studies* 25 (1977): 177-91.

Ehrenreich, Barbara, and Deirdre English. *Witches, Midwives, and Nurses: A History of Women Healers.* New York: The Feminist Press, 1973.

Eliade, Mircea. *The Myth of the Eternal Return or, Cosmos and History.* Trans. Willard R. Trask. Bollingen Series 46. Princeton N. J.: Princeton University Press, 1974.

———. *Myths, Dreams and Mysteries: The Encounter between Contemporary Faiths and Archaic Realities.* Trans. Philip Mairet. London: Harvill, 1960.

Elliott, Alan, ed. *Medea.* Euripides. London: Oxford University Press, 1979.

Engels, Donald. "The Problem of Female Infanticide in the Greco-Roman World." *Classical Philology* 75 (1980): 112-20.

———. "The Use of Historical Demography in Ancient History." *Classical Quarterly* 34 (1984): 386-93.

Erikson, Erik. *Childhood and Society.* New York: Norton, 1963.

Euripides. *The Complete Greek Tragedies.* Ed. David Grene and Richard Lattimore. 5 vols. Chicago: University of Chicago Press, 1960.

———. Trans. Arthur S. Way. Loeb Classical Library. 4 vols. Cambridge, Mass.: Harvard University Press, 1966-71.

———. *Medea.* Ed. Alan Eliott. London: Oxford University Press 1979.

Farnell, Lewis Richard. *Greek Hero Cults and Ideas of Immortality.* The Gifford Lectures. Oxford: Clarendon Press, 1921.

Feder, Lillian. *Madness in Literature.* Princeton N. J.: Princeton University Press, 1980.

Federici, Carla. *Réalisme et dramaturgie; Etude de quatre écrivains: Garnier, Hardy, Rotrou, Corneille.* Paris: Nizet, 1974.

Ferenczi, Sandor. "The Unwelcome Child and His Death Instinct." *International Journal of Psychoanalysis* 10 (1929): 125-29.

Finley, Moses I. *Ancient Slavery and Modern Ideology.* New York: Penguin, 1983.

Fitzhugh, George. *Sociology for the South, or the Failure of Free Society.* New York: Burt Franklin, 1965.

Flynn, William R. "Frontier Justice: A Contribution to the Theory of Child Battery." *American Journal of Psychiatry* 127 (3) (September 1970): 375-79.

Foley, Helene. "Medea's Divided Self." *Classical Antiquity* 8 (1) (April 1989): 61-85.

Fontana, Vincent. "We're Losing the Battle." In Richard Gooding et. al., 1981, 4.

François, Carlo. *Raison et déraison dans le théâtre de Pierre Corneille.* York S. C.: French Literature Publications, 1979.

Frazer, James George. *The Golden Bough: A Study in Magic and Religion.* Abridged ed. New York: Macmillan, 1958.

Freud, Anna. *The Ego and the Mechanisms of Defense.* 5th ed. New York: International Universities, 1980.

Freud, Sigmund. *The Standard Edition of the Complete Psychological Works of Sigmund Freud.* Trans. from the German under the general editorship of James Strachey and Anna Freud. London: Hogarth, 1966-74.

Freund, Philip. *Myths of Creation.* London: W. H. Allen, 1964.

Fumaroli, Marc. "Melpomène au miroir: La Tragédie comme héroïne dans Médée et Phèdre." *Saggi e ricerche di letteratura francese* 19 (1980): 173-205.

Garden, Maurice. *Lyon et les Lyonnais au XVIIIᵉ siècle.* Paris: Les Belles Lettres, 1972.

Gay, Peter. *Freud, A Life for Our Time.* New York: Norton, 1988.

Gil, David. *Violence against Children: Physical Child Abuse in the United States.* Cambridge, Mass.: Harvard University Press, 1970.

Gilligan, Carol. *In a Different Voice: Psychological Theory and Women's Development.* Cambridge, Mass.: Harvard University Press, 1982.

Gilman, Sander. *Jewish Self-Hatred: Anti-Semitism and the Hidden Language of the Jews.* Baltimore: Johns Hopkins University Press, 1986.

Ginestrier, Paul. *Anouilh.* Paris: Editions Seghers, 1969.

Girard, René. *Violence and the Sacred.* Trans. Patrick Gregory. Baltimore: Johns Hopkins University Press, 1977.

Goethe, Wolfgang von. *Pandora.* Paris, Fernand Aubier, n.d.

Golden, Mark. "The Exposure of Girls at Athens." *Phoenix* 35 (1981): 316-31.

Gooding, Richard, Richard Johnson, and Cy Egin. "We're Losing the Battle." *New York Post* 5 October 1981, 4.

Goulding, Mary, and Robert I. Goulding. *Changing Lives through Redecision Therapy.* New York: Brunner-Mazel, 1979.

Greenberg, Mitchell. *Subjectivity and Subjugation in Seventeenth-Century Drama and Prose: The Family Romance of French Classicism.* New York: Cambridge University Press, 1992.

Greene, Naomi. *Pier Paolo Pasolini: Cinema as Heresy.* Princeton, N. J.: Princeton University Press, 1990.

Greer, Germaine. *Sex and Destiny: The Politics of Human Fertility.* New York: Harper & Row, 1984.

Greven, Philip. *Spare the Child: The Religious Roots of Punishment and the Psychological Impact of Physical Abuse.* New York: Knopf, 1990.

Grillparzer, Franz. *The Poor Fiddler.* Trans. Alexander and Elizabeth Henderson. New York: Ungar, 1967.

———. *Samtliche Werke Ausgewahlte Briefe, Gesprache, Berichte*. Ed. Peter Frank and Karl Pörnbacher. 4 vols. Darmstadt:Wissenschaftliche Buchgesellschaft, 1969.

Hadas, Moses. Introduction. *The Stoic Philosophy of Seneca: Essays and Letters*. New York: Norton, 1968.

Harris, Marvin. *Cannibals and Kings: The Origins of Cultures*. New York: Random House, 1977.

Harris, Marvin, and Eric B. Ross. *Death, Sex and Fertility: Population Regulation in Preindustrial and Developing Societies*. New York: Columbia University Press, 1987.

Harvey, John. *Anouilh, A Study in Theatrics*. New Haven, Conn.: Yale University Press, 1964.

Hausfater, Glenn, and Sarah Blaffer Hrdy. *Infanticide: Comparative and Evolutionary Perspectives*. New York: Aldine, 1984

Helfer, Ray. "The Responsibility and Role of the Physician." In Ray Helfer and C. Henry Kempe, 1968.

Helfer, Ray, and C. Henry Kempe, eds. *The Battered Child*. Chicago: University of Chicago Press, 1968.

Henry, Denis, and Elisabeth B. Walker Henry. *The Mask of Power: Seneca's Tragedies and Imperial Rome*. Chicago: Bolchazy & Carducci, 1985.

Herman, Judith Lewis. *Trauma and Recovery*. New York: Basic Books, 1992.

Hesiod. *Hesiod, the Homeric Hymns and Homerica*. Trans. Hugh G. Evelyn-White. Cambridge, Mass.: Harvard University Press, 1964.

Hof, Hans, and Ida Cermak. *Grillparzer: Versuch einer Pathographie*. Wien: Bergland Verlag, 1961.

Holder, Stephen. "Review of Medea and the Doll by Rudi Gray." *New York Times* 14 October 1984, sec. 1, 63.1.

Homer. *Iliad*. Ed. David B. Monro and Thomas W. Allen. Oxford: Clarendon, 1966.

Huizinga, Johan. *Homo Ludens: A Study of the Play Element in Culture*. Boston: Beacon, 1955.

Hunt, David. *Parents and Children in History: The Psychology of Family Life in Early Modern France*. New York: Basic Books 1970.

Jack, Peter Monro. Review of Medea and Some Poems, by Countee Cullen. *New York Times* 12 January 1936, sec. 6, 15.1.

Jahnn, Hans Henny. *Medea, Tragödie*. Mit einem Nachwort von Heinz Ludwig Arnold. Stuttgart: Philipp Reclam, 1963.

Janeway, Elizabeth. *Man's World, Woman's Place: A Study of Social Mythology*. New York: William Morrow, 1971.

Jeffers, Robinson. *Selected Poems*. New York: Vintage, 1965.

———. *Medea Freely Adapted from the Medea by Euripides*. New York: Samuel French, 1976.

———. *The Collected Poetry of Robinson Jeffers*. Ed. Tim Hunt. Stanford: Stanford University Press, 1989.

Johansson, Sheila Ryan. "Deferred Infanticide: Excess Female Mortality during Childhood." In Glenn Hausfater and Sarah Blaffer Hrdy, 1984, 463-85.

Johnson, Barbara. "Apostrophe, Animation and Abortion." *Diacritics* 16 (1) (Spring 1986): 32-39.

Johnson, Sarah Iles. "Introduction." *Medea: Essays on Medea in Myth, Literature, Philosophy and Art.* Ed. James J. Clauss and Sarah Iles Johnson. Princeton, N. J.: Princeton University Press, 1997.

Jolivet, Philipe. *Le Théâtre de Jean Anouilh.* Paris: Michel Brient et Cie, 1963.

Jones, John. *On Aristotle and Greek Tragedy.* New York: Oxford University Press, 1962.

Jones, Robert Emmet. *Henri-René Lenormand.* Boston: Twayne, 1984.

Jordan, Gerda. Introduction. *Thirteen Uncanny Stories by Hans Henny Jahnn.* Trans. Gerda Jordan. New York: Peter Lang, 1984.

Joyce, James. *Ulysses.* New York: Vintage, 1961.

Kann, Robert A. *A Study in Austrian Intellectual History from Late Baroque to Romanticism.* New York: Praeger, 1960.

Kant, Immanuel. *The Philosophy of Immanuel Kant: Moral and Political Writings.* Ed. Carl J. Friedrich. New York: Modern Library, n.d.

Kaplan, Louise. *Female Perversions: The Temptations of Emma Bovary.* New York: Doubleday, 1991.

Katz, Jacob. *Out of the Ghetto: The Social Background of Jewish Emancipation, 1770-1870.* New York: Schocken, 1978.

Kellum, Barbara. "Infanticide in England in the Later Middle Ages." *History of Childhood Quarterly: The Journal of Psychohistory* 1 (1974): 367-88.

Kempe, C. H., F. N. Silverman, B. F. Steele, W. Droegemueller, and H. K. Silver. "The Battered Child Syndrome." *JAMA* 181: 17-24.

Kerényi, Carl. *The Heroes of the Greeks.* Trans. H. J. Rose. New York: Grove, 1962.

———. "Vorwort" to *Medea: Euripides, Seneca, Corneille, Cherubini, Grillparzer, Jahnn, Anouilh, Jeffers, Braun.* Munich: Theater der Jahrhunderte, 1963.

Knox, Bernard. *Word and Action: Essays on the Ancient Theatre.* Baltimore: Johns Hopkins University Press, 1979.

Kohl, Marvin. *Infanticide and the Value of Life.* New York: Prometheus, 1978.

Kott, Jan. *The Eating of the Gods: An Interpretation of Greek Tragedy.* Trans. Boleslaw Taborski and J. Czerwinsky. New York: Random House, 1973.

Krüll, Marianne. *Freud and His Father.* Trans. Arnold Pomerans. New York: Norton, 1986.

Kyrklund, Willy. *Medea fra Mbongo.* Copenhagen: Forening for Boghaandvaerk, 1970.

Lachman, Charles. "The Reverend Shocker: Kids Get Religion on a 12-Volt Chair." *New York Post* 10 July 1981, 5.

Langer, William. "Checks on Population Growth: 1750-1850." *Scientific American* February 1972, 91-100.

———. "Infanticide: A Historical Survey." *History of Childhood Quarterly: The Journal of Psychohistory* 1 (1974): 353-65.

Lenormand, Henri-René. *Théâtre Complet.* Paris: Albin Michel, 1938, 7-147.

Levin, Ira. *Rosemary's Baby*. New York: Dell, 1967.

Levi-Strauss, David. "The Youngest Homeless: A Threnody for Street Kids." *The Nation* 1 June 1992: 752-54.

Lewis, David Levering. *When Harlem Was in Vogue*. New York: Knopf, 1981.

Lichtenberger, Henri. Introduction to *Pandora* by Goethe. Paris: Fernand Aubier, n.d., i-ix.

Loomis, Roger Sherman, and Laura Hibbard Loomis. *Medieval Romances*. New York: Modern Library, 1957.

Lorenz, Konrad. *On Aggression*. Trans. Marjorie Kerr Wilson. New York: Bantam, 1977.

Lucas, F.L. *Seneca and Elizabethan Tragedy*. New York: Haskell House, 1966.

Ludlam, Charles. *The Complete Plays*. New York: Harper & Row, 1989.

Lumpkin, Shirley. "Countee Cullen." *Dictionary of Literary Biography*. American Poets, 1880-1945. Detroit: Bruccoli Clark, 1986.

Magnusen, Jim. *African Medea*. 1968. New American Plays. Ed. William M. Hoffman. New York: Hill & Wang, 1971.

Malamud, Bernard. *The Fixer*. New York: Farrar, Straus & Giroux, 1966.

Mallinger, Léon. *Médée étude de littérature comparée*. 1897. Geneva: Slatkine Reprints, 1971.

Malthus, Thomas. *An Essay on the Principle of Population As It Effects the Future Improvement of Society with Remarks on the Speculations of Mr. Godwin, M. Condorcet, and Other Writers*. Ed. Antony Flew. New York: Penguin, 1982.

Márquez, Gabriel Garcia. "The Solitude of Latin America." *New York Times* 16 February 1983, E16.

Marthan, Joseph. *Le Vieillard amoureux dans l'oeuvre cornélienne*. Paris: Nizet, 1979.

Marting, Diane. "Patriarchy vs. Intrigue: The Function of Aegeus in Euripides' and Corneille's Medea Plays." *Papers in Romance* 2 (1) (July 1980): 121-26.

Marvick, Elizabeth Wirth. *Louis XIII: The Making of a King*. New Haven, Conn.: Yale University Press, 1986.

Marx, Karl. *Selected Writings*. Ed. David McLellan. New York: Oxford University Press, 1985.

Masson, Jeffrey Moussaieff. *The Assault on Truth: Freud's Suppression of the Seduction Theory*. New York: Penguin, 1985.

Mause, Lloyd de. "The Evolution of Childhood." *The History of Childhood: The Untold Story of Child Abuse*. New York: Peter Bedrick, 1988. 1-73.

McDermott, Emily A. *Euripides' Medea: The Incarnation of Disorder*. University Park: Pennsylvania State University Press, 1989.

McIntyre, H.G. *The Theatre of Jean Anouilh*. London: Harrap, 1981.

Mendès, Henri. *Médée, drame en trois actes, en vers*. Paris: Bibliothèque Charpentier, 1903.

Michelet. Jules. *Satanism and Witchcraft: The Classic Study of Medieval Superstition*. Trans. A. R. Allinson. New York: Carol Publishing Group, 1992.

Miller, Alice. *For Your Own Good: Hidden Cruelty and the Roots of Violence.* Trans. Hildegarde Hannum and Hunter Hannum. New York: Farrar, Straus & Giroux, 1984.

―――. *Thou Shalt Not Be Aware: Society's Betrayal of the Child.* New York: NAL, 1984.

Milosz, Czeslaw. "Robinson Jeffers." In Robert Zaller, 268-73.

Mimoso-Ruiz, Duarte. *Médée antique et moderne; aspects rituels et socio-politiques du mythe.* Strasbourg: Association des Publications Universitaires, 1982.

Mitchell, Stanley. Introduction to *Understanding Brecht,* by Walter Benjamin. London: Unwin, 1977.

Mitscherlich, Alexander, and Margarete Mitscherlich. *The Inability to Mourn: Principles of Collective Behavior.* New York: Grove, 1975.

Montague, Ashley, ed. *Man and Aggression.* New York: Oxford University Press, 1968.

Moore, Thomas Sturge. *Tragic Mothers.* London: Grant Richards, 1920.

Moore, Thomas, and William Butler Yeats. *Their Correspondence.* Ed. Ursula Bridge. London: Routledge & Kegan, 1953.

Morrison, Toni. *Sula.* New York: NAL, 1982.

―――. *Beloved.* New York: NAL, 1987.

―――. *Inventing the Truth: The Art and Craft of Memoir.* Ed. William Zinsser. Boston: Houghton Mifflin, 1987.

Mousnier, Roland. "The Permanent Crisis in French Society." *The Impact of Absolutism in France: National Experience under Richelieu, Mazarin, and Louis XIV.* Ed. Frank Church. New York: John Wiley, 1969.

Müller, Heiner. *Hamletmachine and Other Texts for the Stage.* Ed. Carl Weber. New York: PAJ, 1984.

―――. *Stücke.* Herausgegeben und mit einem Essay von Joachim. Fiebach Berlin: Henschelverlag Kunst und Gesellschaft, 1988.

―――. *The Battle: Plays, Prose, Poems.* Ed. and Trans. Karl Weber. New York: PAJ, 1989.

―――. Interview. "In Germany, a Warning from Heiner Müller." *New York Times* 8 July 1990, H5.7.

Muratore, M. J. *Cornelian Theater: The Metadramatic Dimension.* Birmingham, Ala.: Summa Publications, 1990.

Nabokov, Vladimir. *Lolita.* New York: Berkley Medallion, 1955.

Nadal, Octave. *Le Sentiment de l'amour dans l'oeuvre de Pierre Corneille.* Paris: Gallimard, 1948.

Nietzsche, Friedrich. *The Birth of Tragedy and The Genealogy of Morals.* Trans. Francis Golffing. Garden City: Doubleday, 1956.

―――. *The Portable Nietzsche.* Trans. and Ed. Walter Kaufman. New York: Penguin, 1982.

―――. *Beyond Good and Evil: Prelude to a Philosophy of the Future.* Trans. Walter Kaufmann. New York: Vintage, 1989.

Noh Drama: Ten Plays from the Japanese. Selected and translated by the special Noh committee, Japanese Classics Translation Committee, Nippon

Gakujutsu Shinkokai. 2nd printing. Rutland, Vermont: Charles E. Tuttle, 1961.

Nolte, William H. *Rock and Hawk: Robinson Jeffers and the Romantic Agony.* Athens: University of Georgia Press, 1978.

Noonan, John Thomas, Jr. *Contraception: A History of Its Treatment by the Catholic Theologians and Canonists.* Cambridge, Mass.: Harvard University Press, 1966.

Northern Exposure. CBS. KTVF Fairbanks. Written by Barbara Hall. Dir. Jim Charleston. Exec. Prod. Diane Frolov and Andrew Schneider. 3 January 1994.

Ovidius, Naso Publius. *Metamorphoses.* Trans. Frank Justus Miller. Loeb Classical Library. Cambridge, Mass.: Harvard University Press, 1951.

Page, Denys Lionel. Introduction. *Medea,* by Euripides. 1938. Oxford: Clarendon, 1955.

Paris, Matthieu. *La Grande Chronique de Matthieu Paris.* Trans. A. Huillard-Bréolles. Paris: Paulin, 1840.

Pasco, Allan H. "The Unrocked Cradle and the Birth of the Romantic Hero." MLA Convention. San Francisco, December, 1987.

Pasolini, Pier Paolo, Dir. *Medea.* With Maria Callas (Medea), Massimo Girotti (Creon), Giuseppe Gentili (Jason), and Laurent Terzieff (Centaur). San Marco Films. Rome, 1969.

Patterson, Cynthia. "'Not Worth the Rearing': The Causes of Infant Exposure in Ancient Greece." *TAPA* 115 (1985): 103-23.

Perrera, Victor. *Unfinished Conquest: The Guatemalan Tragedy.* Berkeley: University of California Press, 1993.

Perrow, Charles and Mauro F. Gullén. *The AIDS Disaster: The Failure of Organizations in New York and the Nation.* New Haven, Conn.: Yale University Press, 1990.

Perry, Margaret. *A Bio-Bibliography of Countee P. Cullen 1903-1946.* Westport, Conn.: Greenwood Press, 1971.

Piers, Maria. *Infanticide: Past and Present.* New York: Norton, 1978.

Plato. *The Republic.* Trans. Francis McDonald Cornford. New York: Oxford, 1968.

———. *The Last Days of Socrates: Euthyphro, The Apology, Crito, Phaedo.* Trans. Hugh Tredennick. New York: Penguin, 1969.

———. *The Symposium.* Trans. W. Hamilton. New York: Penguin, 1969.

Pollak, Gustav. *Franz Grillparzer and the Austrian Drama.* New York: Dodd Mead, 1907.

Pollitt, Katha. "Marooned on Gilligan's Island: Are Women Morally Superior to Men?" *The Nation* 255 (1992): 799-807.

Pomeroy, Sarah B. "Infanticide in Helenistic Greece." In *Images of Women in Antiquity.* Ed. Averil Cameron and Amelie Kuhrt. London: Croom Helm, 1983.

Pratt, Norman T. *Seneca's Drama.* Chapel Hill: University of North Carolina Press, 1983.

Pucci, Pietro. *The Violence of Pity in Euripides'* Medea. Ithaca, N. Y.: Cornell University Press, 1980.

Racine, Jean. *Théâtre Complet.* Texte établi par Mauricc Rat. Paris: Garnier, 1960.

Radbill, Samuel X. "Children in a World of Violence: A History of Child Abuse." In Ray Helfer and C. H. Kempe, 1968, 3-22.

Rado, Sandor. "An Anxious Mother: A Contribution to the Analysis of the Ego." *International Journal of Psychoanalysis* 9 (1928): 219-26.

Rameckers, Jan M. *Kindesmord in der Literatur der Sturm und Drang Periode: Ein Beitrag zur Kultur und Literatur Geschichte des 18 Jahrhunderts.* Rotterdam: Nijgh & Van Ditmar's Uitgevers-Maatschappij, 1927.

Reckford, Kenneth J. "Medea's First Exit." *TAPA* 99 (1968): 329-59.

Rheingold, Joseph C. *The Mother, Anxiety and Death: The Catastrophic Death Complex.* London: J. & H. Churchill, 1967.

Rice, Philip Blair. "Euripides in Harlem." *The Nation* 141 (1935): 336.

Ringold, Francine. *The Games People Play.* Unpublished play. Performed in Wichita, Kansas, 1975.

Robbins, Rossell Hope. *The Encyclopedia of Witchcraft and Demonology.* New York: Bonanza, 1981.

Roe, Ian F. *An Introduction to the Major Works of Franz Grillparzer, German Dramatist and Poet, 1791-1872.* Studies in German Language and Literature, Vol. 7. Lewiston, N. Y.: Edwin Mellen, 1991.

Romilly, Jacqueline de. *La Tragédie Grècque.* Ed. Robert Flacelière. Littératures Anciennes. Paris: Presses Universitaires de France, 1970.

Rosenmeyer, Thomas G. *Senecan Drama and Stoic Cosmology.* Berkeley: University of California, 1989.

Rush, Florence. *The Best Kept Secret: Sexual Abuse of Children.* New York: McGraw Hill, 1980.

Sale, William. *Sickness, Tragedy, and Divinity in the Medea, the Hippolytus and the Bacchae.* Melbourne, Australia: Aureal, 1977.

Samuels, Steven. "Charles Ludlam: A Brief Life." In Charles Ludlam, 1989, ix-xx.

Sartre, Jean-Paul. *Situations III.* Paris: Gallimard, 1949.

Schatzman, Morton. "Paranoia or Persecution: The Case of Schreber." *History of Childhood Quarterly: The Journal of Psychohistory* 1 (1974) 62-88.

Schlegel, Augustus William. *A Course of Lectures on Dramatic Art and Literature.* Trans. John Black. London: Henry G. Bohn, 1964.

Schlesinger, Eilhard. "On Euripides' *Medea.*" In Erich Segal, 1968, 71-89.

Schopenhauer, Arthur. *The Essential Schopenhauer.* London: Unwin, 1962.

———. *The World as Will and Representation.* Trans. E.F.J. Payne. 2 vols. New York: Dover, 1969.

Scrimshaw, Susan C. M. "Infanticide in Human Populations: Societal and Individual Concerns." In Glenn Hausfater and Sarah Blaffer Hrdy, 1984, 439-62.

Seabury, Samuel. *American Slavery Distinguished from the Slavery of English Theorists and Justified by the Law of Nature*. Miami: Mnemosyne, 1969.

Segal, Erich, ed. *Euripides: A Collection of Critical Essays*. Englewood Cliffs, N. J.: Prentice Hall, 1968.

Seneca, Lucius Annaeus. *Epistulae Morales*. Trans. Richard M. Gummere. 3 vols. Loeb Library. Cambridge, Mass.: Harvard University Press, 1967.

————. *Tragedies*. Trans. Frank Justus Miller. Loeb Library. Cambridge, Mass.: Harvard University Press, 1968.

————. *Moral Essays*. Trans. John W. Basore. 3 vols. Loeb Library. Cambridge, Mass.: Harvard University Press, 1970.

Seneca the Elder. *Declamations*. Trans. M. Winterbottom. 2 vols. Loeb Library. Cambridge, Mass.: Harvard University Press, 1974.

Shaffer, Peter. *Equus*. New York: Penguin, 1985.

Shahar, Shulamith. *Childhood in the Middle Ages*. Trans. Chaya Galai. New York: Routledge, 1990.

Shakespeare, William. *The Complete Works of William Shakespeare* Ed. Alfred Harbage. Baltimore: Penguin, 1975.

Shaw, George Bernard. *Androcles and the Lion, Overruled, Pygmalion*. New York: Dodd Mead, 1930.

Sheleff, Leon Shaskolsky. *Generations Apart: Adult Hostility to Youth*. New York: McGraw Hill, 1981.

Shengold, Leonard. *Soul Murder: The Effects of Childhood Abuse and Deprivation*. New Haven, Conn.: Yale University Press, 1989.

Shivers, Alfred S. *Maxwell Anderson*. Boston, Twayne, 1976.

Shorter, Edward. "Review of *Slaughter of the Innocents* by David Bakan." *History of Childhood Quarterly: The Journal of Psychohistory* 1 (1973), 178-80.

Shucard, Alan. "Countee Cullen." *Dictionary of Literary Biography*. Vol. 51. Detroit: Bruccoli Clark, 1987.

Simon, Bennett. *Tragic Drama and the Family: Psychoanalytic Studies from Aeschylus to Beckett*. New Haven, Conn.: Yale University Press, 1988.

Sinniger, William, and Arthur E. R. Boak. *A History of Rome to AD 565*. 6th ed. New York: MacMillan, 1977.

Skrine, Peter. *The Baroque: Literature and Culture in Seventeenth-Century Europe*. New York: Holmes & Meier, 1978.

Slater, Philip Elliot. *The Glory of Hera: Greek Mythology and the Greek Family*. Boston: Beacon Press, 1968.

Smith, Selwyn M. *The Battered Child Syndrome*. London: Butterworth, 1975.

Snyder, Stephen. *Pier Paolo Pasolini*. Boston: Twayne, 1980.

Solomon, Samuel, ed. and trans. *Grillparzer: Plays on Classic Themes*. New York: Random House, 1960.

————. *Pierre Corneille: Seven Plays*. New York: Random House, 1969.

Sprenger, Jacobus, and Heinrich Kramer. *Malleus Maleficarum*. Trans. Montague Summers. Bungay, Suffolk: John Rodker, 1928.

Sprengnether, Madelon. *The Spectral Mother: Freud, Feminism and Psychoanalysis*. Ithaca, N.Y.: Cornell University Press, 1990.

Stegman, André. "La Médée de Corneillc." In *Les Tragédies de Sénèque et le théâtre de la renaissance*. Ed. Jean Jacquot. Paris: Editions du centre nationale de la recherche scientifique, Royaumont, 1962, 113-26.

———. *L'Héroisme cornélien: genèse et signification*. Paris: Librairie Armand Colin, 1968.

Steele, Brandt F., and Carl B. Pollock. "A Psychiatric Study of Parents Who Abuse Infants and Small Children." *The Battered Child*. Ed. Ray E. Helfer & C. Henry Kempe. Chicago: University of Chicago Press, 1968.

Steiner, George. *The Death of Tragedy*. New York: Knopf, 1963.

———. *Antigones*. New York: Oxford, 1984.

Stern, Edward S. "The Medea Complex: The Mother's Homicidal Wishes to Her Child." *Journal of Mental Science* 94 (1948): 321-31.

Stowe, Harriet Beecher. *Uncle Tom's Cabin*. New York: Bantam, 1981.

Suetonius, Tranquillus. *The Lives of the Caesars*. Trans. J. C. Rolfe. 2 vols. Loeb Classical Library. Cambridge, Mass.: Harvard University Press, 1979.

Sumner, William Graham. *Folkways: A Study of the Sociological Importance of Usages, Manners, Customs, Mores and Morals*. Boston: Athenaeum, 1906.

Tacitus, Publius Cornelius. *The Annals*. Trans. John Jackson. 2 vols. Loeb Library. Cambridge: Harvard University Press, 1956.

Tapié, Victor. *France in the Age of Louis XIII and Richelieu*. Trans. D. McN. Lockie. New York: Praeger, 1975.

Thody, Philip. *Anouilh*. London: Oliver & Boyd, 1968.

Thompson, Bruce. *Franz Grillparzer*. Boston: Twayne, 1981.

Thucydides. *The Peloponnesian War*. Trans. Rex Warner. New York: Penguin, 1980.

Trexler, Richard. "Infanticide in Florence: New Sources and First Results." *History of Childhood Quarterly: The Journal of Psychohistory* 1 (1973): 98-116.

Tripp, Edward. *The Meridian Handbook of Classical Mythology*. New York: Signet, 1974.

Updike, John. *Rabbit, Run*. New York: Fawcett Crest, 1960.

———. *The Witches of Eastwick*. New York: Knopf, 1984.

Valerius Flaccus. *The Argonautica*. Ed. T. E. Page. Trans. J. H. Mozley. Loeb Library. Cambridge: Harvard University Press, 1963.

Van Hook, La Rue. "The Exposure of Infants at Athens." *American Philological Association Transactions and Proceedings* 51 (1921): 134-45.

Vardamis, Alex. "Robertson Jeffers: Poet of Controversy." In Robert Zaller, 1991, 44-67.

Vellacott, Philip. *Ironic Drama: A Study of Euripides' Method and Meaning*. London: Cambridge University Press, 1975.

Wandruska, Adam. *The House of Habsburg: Six Hundred Years of a European Dynasty.* Trans. Cathleen Epstein and Hans Epstein. Westport, Conn.: Greenwood Press, 1975.

Watling, E.F., ed. Introduction. *Seneca: Four Tragedies and Octavia.* New York: Penguin, 1966.

Weber, Beat. *Die Kindesmörderin im deutschen Schriftum von* 1770-95. Bonn: n.p., 1974.

Weber, Carl, ed. *Hamletmachine and Other Texts for the Stage,* by Heiner Müller. New York: PAJ, 1984.

———. *The Battle: Plays, Prose, Poems,* by Heiner Müller. New York: PAJ, 1989.

Webster, T. B. L. *The Tragedies.* Euripides. London: Methuen, 1967.

Weintraub, Bernard. *The York Times* 2 April 1987, A12.

Werner, Oscar Helmuth. *The Unmarried Mother in German Literature with Special Reference to the Period 1770-1800.* 1917. New York: AMS, 1966.

Wertham, Frederic. *The Show of Violence.* Garden City, N. Y.: Doubleday, 1949.

West, Rebecca. "Kafka and the Mystery of Bureaucracy." *Franz Kafka: A Collection of Criticism.* Ed. Leo Hamalian. New York: McGraw Hill, n.d.

Wiley, W. L. "Corneille's First Tragedy: *Médée* and the Baroque." *L'Esprit Créateur* 4 (1964): 135-48.

Williams, Glanville. "The Legal Evaluation of Infanticide." In Marvin Kohl, 1978, 115-27.

Williamson, Laila. "Infanticide: An Anthropological Analysis." In Marvin Kohl, 1978, 61-70.

Winters, Yvor. *Uncollected Essays and Reviews.* Ed. Francis Murphy. Chicago: The Swallow Press, 1973.

Wolff, Lawrence. *Postcards from the End of the World: Child Abuse in Freud's Vienna.* New York: Atheneum, 1988.

Yates, W. E. *Grillparzer: A Critical Introduction.* London: Cambridge University Press, 1972.

———. "Nestroy, Grillparzer and the Feminist Cause." In *Viennese Popular Theatre.* Exeter: n.p., 1985, 93-107.

Zaller, Robert, ed. *Centennial Plays for Robinson Jeffers.* Newark: University of Delaware Press, 1991.

Zilboorg, Gregory. "Sidelights on Parent-Child Antagonism." *American Journal of Orthopsychiatry* 2 (1932): 32-43.

Index

About the Author

LILLIAN CORTI is an Assistant Professor in the English Department at the University of Alaska, Fairbanks. She has taught Comparative, World, and Women's Literature at various institutions, including Brooklyn College, Queens College, the University of Tulsa, and Marien Ngouabi University in Brazaville, the Congo, where she was a Fulbright Visiting Professor.

ISBN 0-313-30536-6

90000>

9 780313 305368

HARDCOVER BAR CODE